A Grammar
for Biblical Hebrew

C. L. Seow

Abingdon Press
Nashville

A GRAMMAR FOR BIBLICAL HEBREW

Copyright © 1987 by Choon Leong Seow

Ninth Printing 1994

This book is printed on recycled acid-free paper.

Library of Congress Cataloging-in-Publication Data

SEOW, C. L. (CHOON LEONG)
A grammar for Biblical Hebrew / C. L. Seow.
p. cm.
English and Hebrew.
Includes indexes.
ISBN 0-687-15683-1 (alk. paper)
1. Hebrew language—Grammar. I. Title.
PJ4567.S424   1987   87-19386
492.4'82421—dc19

MANUFACTURED IN THE UNITED STATES OF AMERICA

CONTENTS

PREFACE

Biblical Hebrew is an endangered field in Christian theological education. Whereas it once was required that all ministerial candidates have competence in the language, most institutions involved in the training of ministers now offer Hebrew only as an elective, a luxury for the curious and a burden for the unfortunate. A few ecclesiastical bodies hang on to the requirements of a "working knowledge"—something tantamount to the ability to impress one's congregation with a few Hebrew words or, at best, the ability to represent the opinions of others. To be sure, the problem is not a willful disregard for the language of the Old Testament. Rather, students are often frustrated by the amount of time expected—given the present resources—to gain competence enough to work independently with the language. And most ministers simply cannot afford to spend more than a year in grammar study.

Yet, first-year Hebrew is usually taught with the expectation that the students will move into an intermediate course, followed by another at the advanced level. At the end of the introductory course, one can normally expect only to read simple Hebrew prose with confidence. Otherwise, facility in reading poetic and difficult prosaic texts is acquired "by experience"; lexical skills are gained by trial and error. Moreover, it is often necessary also to make the transition from the artificial sentences of the beginner's textbook to the actual text of the Bible—with all its apparent difficulties. Students are urged to continue their learning through directed reading of actual biblical texts. But only the most persistent students continue.

Given so many necessary courses in the diverse fields of theological education and the limited amount of time available to the student, it seems to me that a new introductory textbook should cover enough grammar and contain enough exercises in reading actual biblical texts to render further grammar courses unnecessary.

I am convinced that the essentials of Hebrew grammar can be taught in one course, but I will also insist that one must not understate what is essential for competent reading and exegesis. If most students will have only one year of the language, then that introductory course has to be comprehensive enough to equip them for the task and joy of reading the Hebrew Bible.

A feature of this grammar is the careful analysis of Hebrew forms (morphology). The major obstacle in learning Hebrew is in the morphology, not in the syntax. Beginning readers struggle with Hebrew precisely because they do not understand the forms enough to know how to use a lexicon effectively. Hence, there is the common notion that Hebrew is difficult because over half the forms are irregular or doubly irregular. But forms are difficult and have to be learned by rote only when one does not understand them. The detailed explanations, therefore, are provided to help one understand. The student should not be expected to reproduce the historical explanations given in this book. If the rules seem difficult at first, they will cease to be so in time. The principles are laid out in the early lessons, but they are repeated throughout the book. By repetition the student will become familiar with the rules. For this reason, I believe, the lessons will become easier and easier after the first third of the book, when the rules no longer seem mechanical.

In place of the traditional nomenclature for the verbs, I have adopted the sigla used by other Semitists. The sigla are descriptive of all the forms in each conjugation; the traditional names, insofar as they mirror only the third person masculine singular forms, merely provide labels under which the forms are subsumed. Moreover, the simplified system facilitates comparison of Hebrew with other Semitic languages, should one choose to do so at a later stage.

The emphasis from the beginning to the end of this book is on reading the Hebrew Bible. The examples in the lessons are taken directly from the Bible, as are the individual forms, phrases, sentences, and passages in the exercises. These are carefully chosen with the help of S. Mandelkern's *Veteris Testamenti Concordantiae*. Since the materials for translation are all taken from the Bible, one will become most familiar with the forms and constructions that occur most frequently there. Time is not unduly expended on exceptions, though the exceptions are usually provided in the grammar for future reference. The student is presented again and again with the biblical language in all its peculiarities. Hence, when one begins to work independently on the biblical text, one stands on familiar ground.

This book is designed for use in the classroom. It is not a self-teaching grammar, although those with a flair for languages may benefit from it even without the guidance of an instructor. In either case, the student who completes this book will (1) have read from every book of the Hebrew Bible, (2) know most Hebrew words that occur fifty times or more, and (3) be able to use a standard Hebrew-English lexicon to locate forms and their definitions. Indeed, students will begin to use the lexicon after the first four lessons and instructors should urge the students to practice using it throughout the course.

It should be noted that proper names are not given in the vocabulary, nor are they translated in the notes. This is deliberate, for in reading the Hebrew Bible, one simply will recognize the proper names from context and verify them in the dictionaries. A list of these names (with the normal spelling in the standard English translations) is provided, however.

This book is dedicated to the frustrated and eager students whom it has been my blessing to teach, and from whom I also have learned. I write to pass on the love and knowledge of Hebrew imparted to me by my professors, particularly Thomas O. Lambdin, whose influence on me is evident at every turn. I would like to thank professors James F. Armstrong and J. J. M. Roberts, my teachers and colleagues, for the willingness to use earlier versions of this grammar and for their encouragement and criticisms. I am also indebted to Dr. David Packard for access to the amazing Ibycus computer for word processing. My students Daniel and Katherine Schwan kindly read part of my manuscript and saved me from many errors. Michael Davis and Jerry Gorham also gave their time generously in helping me with the proofs. Above all, I must acknowledge my gratitude to Lai King, my companion for life, whose strength and resourcefulness have sustained me through the final stages in the preparation of this book.

C. L. SEOW
Princeton, 1986

A Glossary of Technical Terms

Afformative: A form coming after the main stem of a word.

Anaptyxis: An additional ("helping") vowel inserted between consonants to facilitate pronunciation.

Antecedent: The word or phrase to which a pronoun refers.

Aphaeresis: Absence or loss of a letter.

Doubling: Two consonants occurring consecutively in a word, without any vowel in between.

Gemination: Same as doubling.

Inflection: Change in form in a word to indicate number, gender, person, etc.

Intransitive Verb: A verb that does not take a direct object.

Masoretes: Jewish scholars who copied biblical texts and added diacritical markings to the consonantal texts.

Metathesis: Transposition of letters.

Predicate: A word or phrase that states something about the subject.

Preformative: A form coming before the main stem of a word.

Preterite: Simple past tense.

Proto-Hebrew: Hypothetical early stage of Hebrew.

Spirant: A consonant whose pronunciation is characterized by continuous friction.

Stative Verb: Verb that describes a state rather than an action (e.g., "be great", "be good").

Stop: A consonant whose pronunciation causes a temporary closing of the breath passage.

Syncopation: The shortening of a word by dropping an original vowel or syllable.

Transitive Verb: A verb that takes a direct object.

Unvoiced: Used to describe consonants whose pronunciation requires no exertion of the vocal chord.

Voiced: Used to describe consonants whose pronunciation causes the vocal chords to vibrate.

ABBREVIATIONS, SYMBOLS, AND SELECT BIBLIOGRAPHY

Abbreviations

abs.	absolute state
BDB	Brown, Driver, Briggs, *A Hebrew and English Lexicon of the OT*
Chron.	Chronicles
cp	common plural
cs	common singular
cs.	construct state
Dan.	Daniel
Deut.	Deuteronomy
Esth.	Esther
Exod.	Exodus
Ezek.	Ezekiel
fp, fp.	feminine plural
fs, fs.	feminine singular
Gen.	Genesis
GKC	Gesenius, Kautzsch, Cowley, *Hebrew Grammar*
Hab.	Habakkuk
Hagg.	Haggai
Hos.	Hosea
Isa.	Isaiah
Jer.	Jeremiah
Josh.	Joshua
Judg.	Judges
Kings	Kings
Lam.	Lamentations
Lev.	Leviticus
Mal.	Malachi
Mic.	Micah
mp, mp.	masculine plural
ms, ms.	masculine singular
MT	Masoretic text
Nah.	Nahum
Neh.	Nehemiah
Num.	Numbers
Obad.	Obadiah
pl.	plural
Prov.	Proverbs

Ps. Psalms
Qoh. Qohelet (Ecclesiastes)
Sam. Samuel
sg. singular
Song Canticles (Song of Songs)
v verse
Zech. Zechariah
Zeph. Zephaniah

Symbols

* a hypothetical form, not actually attested
\> developed to
\< developed from

Select Bibliography

Background
Harris, S. *Development of the Canaanite Dialects*. New Haven, 1939.
Kutscher, E. Y. *A History of the Hebrew Language*. Jerusalem, 1982.
Moscati, S. *An Introduction to the Comparative Grammar of the Semitic Languages*. Wiesbaden, 1964.

Grammars
Blau, J. *A Grammar of Biblical Hebrew*. Wiesbaden, 1976.
Gesenius, W., E. Kautzsch, and A. Cowley. *Hebrew Grammar*. Oxford, 1910.
Lambdin, T. O. *Introduction to Biblical Hebrew*. New York, 1971.

Lexica
Brown, F., S. R. Driver, and C. A. Briggs. *A Hebrew and English Lexicon of the Old Testament*. Oxford, 1907.
Holladay, W. *A Concise Hebrew and Aramaic Lexicon of the Old Testament*. Grand Rapids, 1971.
Köhler, L., and W. Baumgartner. *Lexicon in Veteris Testament Libros*. Leiden, 1953. Supplement, 1958.

Syntax
Davidson, A. B. *Hebrew Syntax*. 3d edition. Edinburgh, 1901.
Williams, R. *Hebrew Syntax*. 2d edition. Toronto, 1967.

LESSON I

1. Alphabet

The Hebrew alphabet consists of twenty-two signs. Each sign was originally pictographic and represents a consonant.[1] The first letter *'ālep̄* ("cattle"), for example, was pictographically represented and subsequently stylized, simplified, or otherwise modified:

Phoenician	Greek	Aramaic	Modern Cursive
𐤀	Ⱥ	A	✗	/c

The script used in most modern editions of the Hebrew Bible is related to the Aramaic "square script," which was used also at Qumran. This script is so named because most of the characters can be written within an imaginary square frame.

For economic and other reasons, modern journals and books which contain discussions of biblical Hebrew often use transcription instead of Hebrew characters. The use of transcription also facilitates diachronic (historical) and synchronic (comparative) study of the language. It is important, therefore that the student be familiar with a standard transcriptional system, although one should not become dependent upon mental or physical transcription for reading.

Hebrew is an ancient Semitic language. Thus it is not easy for the modern English speaker to reproduce, or even know, the exact sounds of the Hebrew phonemes. Nevertheless, we are able to reconstruct from tradition, and from transcriptions of Hebrew in other languages, the approximate pronunciation of each consonant.

The following is a table of the Hebrew alphabet:

[1] Actually each of the letters ו, ח, ע, צ, and שׁ represents more than one sound in an earlier stage of the language, but the details are beyond the scope of this grammar.

1

"The square Aramaic script"

Name	Sign		Transliteration	Approximate Pronunciation
	Medial	Final		
ā́lep̄	א		ʾ	a glottal stop
bêt	ב		b	b, as in "ban"
	ב		b̲	v, as in "van"
gîmel	ג		g	g, as in "god"
	ג		ḡ	g, as in "dog"
dā́let	ד		d	d, as in "day"
	ד		d̲	th, as in "they"
hē	ה		h	h, as in "hay"
wāw	ו		w	w, as in "way"
záyin	ז		z	z, as in "zion"
ḥēt	ח		ḥ	ch, as in "loch" _gutt. "ch"_
ṭēt	ט		ṭ	t, as in "bet"
yōd̲	י		y	y, as in "yet"
kap̄	כ		k	k, as in "king"
	כ	ך	k̲	ch, as in "Bach" _kum, "ch"_
lā́med̲	ל		l	l, as in "lake"
mêm	מ	ם	m	m, as in "mother"
nûn	נ	ן	n	n, as in "neck"
sā́mek̲	ס		s	s, as in "sack"
ʿáyin	ע		ʿ	a peculiar guttural
pe(h)	פ		p	p, as in "pat"
	פ	ף	p̄	f, as in "fat"
ṣād̲ē	צ	ץ	ṣ	ts, as in "bets" _kum_ Z
qôp̄	ק		q	q, as in "plaque"
rêš	ר		r	r, as in "rash" _throat r not rolled_
śîn	שׂ		ś	s, as in "seen"
šîn	שׁ		š	sh, as in "sheen" "sch"
tāw	ת		t	t, as in "tank"
	ת		t̲	th, as in "thank"

if lost consonant in a word

Notes:

i.   א is a glottal stop, a sound produced by momentary stoppage of breath in the throat. It is similar to the deliberate break one makes between two clear vowels, for example, "re'acquaint."

ii. The sound of ע is difficult to reproduce in English. Its approximate sound is like a voiced ה.

2. Writing

a. Besides the final forms ך, ן, ף, and ץ, only ק extends below the imaginary square which surrounds each letter in the square script. ל is the only character that extends above the imaginary square.

Compare the relative sizes and shapes of the consonants:

א ב ג ד ה ה ו ז ח ט י כ ך ל מ ם נ ן ס ע פ ף צ ץ ק ר ש שׂ ת

b. Hebrew is written from right to left, but in transcription one represents the characters from left to right:

מֶלֶךְ   *mlk̲*   אֱלֹהִים   *'lhym*
בִּקְעָה   *bq'h*   יִשְׂרָאֵל   *yśr'l*

c. When *kap̄, mêm, nûn, pe(h),* or *ṣādē* occurs at the end of a word, it always takes the final form (ך, ם, ן, ף, ץ); when it occurs independently, or at the beginning or the middle of a word, it takes the "medial" form (כּ, מ, נ, פ, צ). This distinction between "medial" and "final" forms, however, was not made until the third century B.C.E. This distinction is also not made in transcription:

כָּלֵךְ   *klk̲*   מַיִם   *mym*
נָתַן   *ntn*   צִיץ   *ṣyṣ*

3. Gutturals

The consonants א, ה, ח, and ע are called "gutturals" because they are generally pronounced from the back of the throat (Latin *guttur*). Gutturals tend to affect the quality of vowels after them because of their point of articulation. Thus, with the frequent exception of א, gutturals prefer "a" class vowels (see Lesson II.1, 9).

Moreover, gutturals, along with ר, cannot be doubled.

4. Bĕḡaḏ Kĕp̄aṯ

a. The consonants *bêṯ, gîmel, dálet, kap̄, pe(h)*, and *tāw*, known by the mnemonic *bĕḡaḏ kĕp̄aṯ*, may be stops or spirants. This distinction between stops and spirants is not made in unpointed texts; but in the Masoretic text, stops are indicated by a dot (called a *dāḡēš*) within the letter (see 5a below). In transcription, a spirant is marked by a line below it or, in the case of ‫ב‬ and ‫פ‬, by a line above it.

We may characterize the consonants as follows:

Stops		Spirants	
Voiced	Unvoiced	Voiced	Unvoiced
‫ב‬ b ‫ג‬ g ‫ד‬ d		‫ב‬ b̄ ‫ג‬ ḡ ‫ד‬ ḏ	
	‫כ‬ k ‫פ‬ p ‫ת‬ t		‫כ‬, ‫ך‬ k̄ ‫פ‬, ‫ף‬ p̄ ‫ת‬ ṯ

b. To distinguish the stops from the spirants, apply the following rules in sequence:

   i.   Stops may be doubled; spirants are never doubled.

   ii.   A *bĕḡaḏ kĕp̄aṯ* letter preceded by a vowel will be a spirant, unless it is doubled.

   iii.   A *bĕḡaḏ kĕp̄aṯ* letter preceded by a consonant will normally be a stop.

   iv.   A *bĕḡaḏ kĕp̄aṯ* letter in the initial position will always be a stop, unless the preceding word ends in a vowel.

   v.   A *bĕḡaḏ kĕp̄aṯ* letter in the final position will always be a spirant, unless it is doubled (which is rare).

Study the following examples, paying attention to the application of the rules above and the pronunciation of the *bĕḡaḏ kĕp̄aṯ* letters in each case:

example	rule	pronunciation
‫מכם‬ *mikkem*	i	mikkem
‫מלכים‬ *mĕlākîm*	ii	mla-cheem

מִשְׁכָּן	*miškān*	iii	mish-kan
כֹּהֵן	*kōhēn*	iv	ko-heyn
מֶלֶךְ	*mélek*	ii, v	mé-lech
קֶבֶר	*qéber*	ii	qé-vr
בַּעַל	*báʿal*	iv	bá-ʿal
בָּבֶל	*bābel*	iv, ii	ba-vel
זַרְעוֹ בוֹ	*zarʿô ḇô*	ii, iv	zar-ʿo vo
טוֹב	*ṭôḇ*	ii, v	tov

5. Dāḡēš

A *dāḡēš* is a dot put within a consonant:

a. To indicate that a *bĕḡaḏ kĕp̄aṯ* letter is a stop, not a spirant. A *dāḡēš* used in this manner is called a *dāḡēš lene* (a weak *dāḡēš*).

b. To indicate that a consonant is doubled (e.g., מ = *mm*, נ = *nn*, שׁ = *šš*). When a *dāḡēš* is so used, it is called a *dāḡēš forte* (a strong *dāḡēš*).

6. Dāḡēš in Bĕḡaḏ Kĕp̄aṯ Letters

Since *bĕḡaḏ kĕp̄aṯ* letters may be doubled when they are stops, a *dāḡēš* within such a consonant may be weak (indicating only a stop, but not doubling) or strong (indicating both a stop and doubling). One is usually able to determine the character of a *dāḡēš* in such situations by the position of the consonant within a word.

a. In an initial position, the *dāḡēš* always indicates a stop, not doubling.

b. In a medial position, the *dāḡēš* indicates only a stop if it is immediately preceded by a consonant; it indicates doubling if it is preceded by a short vowel (see II.1). Hebrew does not permit clusters of more than two consonants.

c. In the rare instance when it is in a final position, the *dāḡēš* will indicate doubling.

Exercise 1

A. Write the following in Hebrew:

1. *yśr'l*	3. *ṣlmwṯ*	5. *ṭwḇ*
2. *hlk*	4. *ywnṯn*	6. *hʿrym*

7. *gnb̠*	12. *b'r*	17. *knʿn*
8. *ṣyṣ*	13. *yʿwp̄p̄*	18. *qyryh*
9. *mlk̠*	14. *zrwʿ*	19. *kpym*
10. *ḥšk̠*	15. *sws*	20. *kmwhw*
11. *śrym*	16. *mʿṭ*	

B. Transcribe the following (Gen. 1:1–4):

בְּרֵאשִׁית בָּרָא אֱלֹהִים אֵת הַשָּׁמַיִם וְאֵת הָאָרֶץ: ² וְהָאָרֶץ הָיְתָה תֹהוּ וָבֹהוּ וְחֹשֶׁךְ עַל־ ³ פְּנֵי תְהוֹם וְרוּחַ אֱלֹהִים מְרַחֶפֶת עַל־פְּנֵי הַמָּיִם: וַיֹּאמֶר אֱלֹהִים יְהִי אוֹר וַיְהִי־אוֹר: וַיַּרְא אֱלֹהִים אֶת־הָאוֹר כִּי־טוֹב וַיַּבְדֵּל אֱלֹהִים בֵּין הָאוֹר וּבֵין הַחֹשֶׁךְ:

---

² The sign ׃ marks the end of a verse. See Appendix C.1.

³ The horizontal stroke, called a *maqqēp̄*, joins a word to what follows it. See Appendix C.3.

LESSON II

1. Simple Vowels

a. There are three classes of vowels in Hebrew: a, i, and u. In each class one finds vowels that are short and long. Short vowels are not marked in transcription; long vowels are marked by a horizontal stroke (*macron*) above the letter.

b. The following is a summary of the simple vowels in Hebrew. To indicate the relative position of the vowel points, we mark them with the letter בּ, but our concern at this point is with the vowels only.

Class	Sign	Trans.	Name	Approx. Pronunciation
a	בַ	a	*pátaḥ*	**a**, as in "am"
	בָ	ā	*qāmēṣ*	**a**, as in "father"
i	בֶ	e	*sĕḡōl*	**e**, as in "met"
	בֵ	ē	*ṣērê*	**e**, as in "they"
	בִ	i or ī	*ḥíreq*	**i**, as in "unique"
u	בָ	o	*qāmēṣ-ḥāṭûp̄*	**o**, as in "loft"
	בֻ	u or ū	*qibbûṣ*	**u**, as in "rule"
	בֹ	ō	*ḥṓlem*	**o**, as in "role"

Notes

i. The vowel points are usually placed under the consonant and pronounced after it: אָדָם *'āḏām*, מֶלֶךְ *mélek*.

ii. The *ḥṓlem* is always placed at the top left hand corner of the consonant it follows: הֹלֵךְ *hōlēk*, קָטֹן *qāṭōn*.

iii. The *ḥṓlem* may be confused with the supralinear dot of the letters שׁ and שׂ. A *ḥṓlem* after שׁ ordinarily coalesces with

7

the dot on the top left corner of that consonant and only one dot is written. In some editions of the Hebrew Bible, a *ḥólem* before שׁ may also coalesce with the dot that marks that consonant.

שֹׁפֵט	*šōpēṭ*	שֹׂנֵא	*śōnē'*
יֹשֵׁב	*yōšēḇ*	שֹׂבֵר	*śōḇēr*

iv. As indicated in the table above, *ḥíreq* and *qibbûṣ* may be short or long. The short vowel is far more common. For this reason, when the vowel is long, a vertical stroke called a *méteḡ* (bridle) is sometimes placed after the vowel to call attention to its length. When the vowel occurs in a clearly open syllable (see 7.d of this lesson), it is always long. If the vowel occurs in an accented syllable, it is always long, even if the syllable is closed. Thus, the student should assume that a *ḥíreq* or *qibbûṣ* is short, unless (α) there is *méteḡ*, (β) it is in an open syllable, or (γ) it is in an accented syllable.

v. For the distinction between *qāmēṣ* (ā) and *qāmēṣ ḥāṭûp̄* (o), see section 8 of this lesson.

vi. A vowel that follows a final *kap̄* or *nûn* will ordinarily appear to the left of that consonant: כָּמֹוֹךָ *kāmóḵā*, תָּבֹואֶן *tāḇô'nā*.

2. *Matres Lectionis*

a. In the earliest phase of the development of Hebrew, vowels were not indicated at all. Thus, for example, צדק could be vocalized and translated in numerous ways: *ṣāḏěqā* (she is righteous), *ṣāḏěqū* (they are righteous), *ṣidděqā* (she proved righteous), *ṣadděqô* (his being righteous), *ṣéḏeq* (righteousness), *ṣiḏqî* (my righteousness), *ṣiḏqō* (his righteousness), *ṣěḏāqā* (righteousness), *ṣaddîq* (righteous), etc. In the premonarchic period of Israel's history, all these words would have been written simply with the three consonants, *ṣdq*.

b. In the monarchic period, the alphabetic signs ה, י, and ו were introduced at the end of words to indicate final long vowels in the three vowel classes. The signs used in this way are not real consonants; they are merely markers indicating long vowels. Hence, they are called *matres lectionis* (mothers of reading).

The addition of these *matres* greatly reduces the options for translation. For example, if we consider again the forms of *ṣdq*, adding ה would limit the possibilities to words with final ā. Thus, צדקה may be either *ṣādĕqā* (she is righteous), *ṣiddĕqā* (she proved righteous), or *ṣĕdāqā* (righteousness).

    c. A third stage in the development of the spelling system came when *matres* were used, not only in final position, but also internally. For example, the presence of י in צדיק indicates that the word must be vocalized as *ṣaddīq* (righteous), and not something else. By the same token, the personal name *ṣādōq* (Zadok) is written in late spelling with an internal *mater* ו: צדוק.

    d. With the addition of the vowel points by the Masoretes, the text was further clarified. One no longer needs to choose from several possibilities. The letters צדקה may have been read in different ways, but once the vowel points are introduced, it becomes clear just which form is intended.

    e. *Matres* are usually marked in transcription by a circumflex accent (^) over the vowel. We will follow this convention, except that the ה *mater* (which, incidentally, occurs only as a final *mater*) will be indicated by the letter *h* in parentheses.

    f. The following is a summary of long vowels marked by *matres*. Once again, to show the relative position of the vowel points, we will mark them with the consonant כ but we are concerned here only with the vowels.

Class	י-mater	ו-mater	ה-mater
a			כָה ā(h)
i	כִי î כֵי ê כֵי ê		כֶה e(h) כֵה ē(h)
u		כּו ô כּו û	כֹה ō(h)

    g. Vowels with *matres* are known by both the names of the vowel and the *mater*. Thus, *ḥîreq yōḏ* (ִי), *ḥōlem wāw* (ֹו), and so forth. Only ו (û) has a distinctive name, *šûreq*.

    h. Since ה at the end of a word could be taken as a *mater* or an actual consonant, the final consonant ה is marked by a dot with it called a *mappîq*. Compare the following:

אִשָּׁה	*ʾiššā(h)* a woman	אִישָׁה	*ʾîšāh* her husband
סוּסָה	*sûsā(h)* a mare	סוּסָה	*sûsāh* her horse

Note also the distinction in transcription between the *mater* (*h* in parentheses) and the consonant *h* (not in parentheses).

3. Full Writing and Defective Writing

Many vowels are regularly written with *matres*. When a word is written with a *mater*, it is said to be "full"; when it is written without a *mater*, it is said to be "defective."

Full		**Defective**	
יָבוֹא	*yābô'*	יָבֹא	*yābō'*
יָשִׂים	*yāśîm*	יָשִׂם	*yāśīm*
יָקוּם	*yāqûm*	יָקֻם	*yāqūm*

When ָ is a defective writing for ִי, it is certainly long. Likewise, when ֻ is defective for וּ, it is long.

4. Simple *Šĕwā'*

The simple *šĕwā'* may be vocal or silent. Both are represented by the sign ְ placed under the consonant. The vocal *šĕwā'* is represented by *ĕ* in transcription; the silent *šĕwā'* is not transcribed.

a. The vocal *šĕwā'* is a half or reduced vowel, something like the first vowel in the English word "careen."

The ְ in a word is vocal (i.e., *ĕ*) when:

   i. It is at the beginning of a word:[1] בְּכֹר *bĕkōr*, יְדַבֵּר *yĕdabbēr*.
   ii. It is the second of two ְ in immediate succession: יִשְׁמְרוּ *yišmĕrû*, מִזְבְּחִי *mizbĕḥî*. But see b.i, below.
   iii. It comes immediately after a strong *dāḡēš*: דִּבְּרוּ *dibbĕrû*, יִפְּלוּ *yippĕlû*.
   iv. It comes immediately after a long vowel: יֵלְכוּ *yēlĕkû*, יִירְאוּ *yîrĕ'û*.

b. The silent *šĕwā'* has no phonetic value and is not represented in transcription.

The ְ in a word is silent when:

   i. It is at the end of a word, even if it is the second of two ְ in immediate succession: תֵּשְׁתְּ *tēšt*, אַתְּ *'att*, מֶלֶךְ *mélek*.

---

[1] But the ְ in שְׁתֵּי (two) is silent—that is, *štê*, not *šĕtê*.

Note: The final *šĕwā'* is actually rather exceptional. It appears only in words ending in the rare consonant cluster, with final *k*, or final *tt*.

ii. It is the first of two ֽ in immediate succession: יִשְׁמְרוּ *yišmĕrû*, מִזְבְּחִי *mizbĕḥî*.

iii. It comes immediately after a short unstressed vowel: וַיְהִי *wayhî*.[2]

iv. It comes immediately after a stressed vowel:[3] שֹׁבְנָה *šōbnā(h)*, לֵכְנָה *lēknā(h)*.

5. Composite Šĕwā's   *treat us vocalized*

a. There are three classes of "composite" *šĕwā*'s:

Sign	Translit.	Name	Pronunciation
ֲ	ă	*ḥāṭēp̄-páṯaḥ*	= *páṯaḥ*
ֱ	ĕ	*ḥāṭēp̄-sĕḡôl*	= *sĕḡôl*
ֳ	ŏ	*ḥāṭēp̄-qāmēṣ*	= *qāmēṣ-ḥāṭûp̄*

b. Gutturals never take the simple vocal *šĕwā'*. As a rule, they also prefer the *ḥāṭēp̄*s.[4]

6. Stress

a. The primary stress of an independent word usually falls on the ultima (last syllable). Less frequently it falls on the penultima (next to last syllable). In this book, words that are penultimately stressed will be marked by an acute accent (´) over the penultimate stress. Otherwise, one should assume that the stress falls on the ultima.

---

[2] There is one exception. Under the first of two identical consonants the ֽ is vocal: הַלְלוּ־יָהּ *halĕlû-yāh* (not *hallû-yāh*).

[3] But ֽ is vocal in הֲלְאָה *hālĕ'ā(h)* to there.

[4] Occasionally, a *ḥāṭēp̄-páṯaḥ* is found with a nonguttural consonant, usually to ensure that the *šĕwā'* is understood as vocal. For example, we get הֲלְלוּ instead of הַלְלוּ (cf. 4.b.iii in this lesson).

דָּבָר *dāḇār* (stress on ultima)

מֶלֶךְ *mélek* (stress on penultima)

b. The stressed syllable is said to be "tonic" (i.e., tone bearing); the syllable immediately before that is said to be "pretonic," and the syllable before the pretonic syllable is "propretonic."

7. Syllables

a. A syllable will always begin with one and only one consonant; it cannot begin with a vowel.[5]

b. A syllable will always have one and only one vowel, whether that vowel be short, long (with or without *mater*), or reduced (i.e., a *šĕwā'*).

c. A syllable may be stressed or unstressed.

d. A syllable may end with a consonant or a vowel. When it ends in a consonant, it is said to be "closed"; when it ends in a vowel, it is said to be "open." When a syllable ends in a consonant, that consonant is always marked by a silent *šĕwā'*, but the last consonant of a word is not so marked (thus, never דָּבָר or יֵשֵׁב).[6]

Study the following examples carefully, paying attention to the proper division of syllables:

דָּבָר	*dā/ḇār*	כְּרֻבִים	*kĕ/rū/ḇîm*
מְלָכִים	*mĕ/lā/ḵîm*	מֶרְחָק	*mer/ḥāq*
מִשְׁכָּן	*miš/kān*	נִסְעוּ	*nis/'û*
מִדְבָּר	*miḏ/bār*	יִפְּלוּ	*yip/pĕ/lû*
פִּיהוּ	*pi/hû*	יִשְׁקְלוּ	*yiš/qĕ/lû*
מְדַבֵּר	*mĕ/dab/bēr*	וַיְהִי	*way/hî*[7]

8. *Qāmēṣ Ḥāṭûp*

As we have learned, ָ may be either *qāmēṣ* (ā) or *qāmēṣ ḥāṭûp* (o). In a closed syllable, ָ will always be *o*; elsewhere it is always *ā*. In addition, a *méteḡ* (see Appendix C.4) may appear with ָ to indicate that it is *ā*, not *o*.

---

[5] The only apparent exception to this rule is the conjunction וּ (û), used in certain situations (see V.5.b, c).

[6] On the other hand, final ךְ always has the silent *šĕwā'*, for example, עִמָּךְ, מֶלֶךְ.

[7] A short, unstressed vowel in an open syllable is rare; conversely, a long, unstressed vowel is rarely in a closed syllable. Thus, וַיְהִי is to be pronounced as *wayhî*, not *wayĕhî*; חָכְמָה is either *ḥāḵĕmā(h)* or *ḥoḵmā(h)* but not *ḥāḵmā(h)*.

שָׁמְרָה *šomrā(h)* keep!   שָׁמְרָה *šāmĕrā(h)* she kept
חָכְמָה *ḥokmā(h)* wisdom   חָכְמָה *ḥākĕmā(h)* she is wise

9. Furtive *Pátaḥ*

Before the final gutturals ה, ח, and ע, an additional nonsyllabic *pátaḥ* appears under the guttural if the word does not already end in an "a-class" vowel. This glide element (it is *not* considered a vowel) is pronounced before the final guttural, though it is written under it. In transcription, this "furtive *pátaḥ*" is often indicated by a raised letter "a," but in this book we will indicate it by means of the letter "a" in parentheses *before* the guttural.

> גָּבוֹהַּ *gābô(a)h* tall
> רוּחַ *rû(a)ḥ* spirit, wind
> רֵעַ *rē(a)ʿ* friend

10. Quiescent *ʾĀlep̄*

Whenever א closes a syllable, it is not vocalized even though the Hebrew character is written in the text. The silent *šĕwāʾ* never appears under the א in such a case. In transcription we represent this quiescent א in parentheses: לֵאלֹהִים *lē(ʾ)lōhîm*, to God.

Vocabulary

Nouns:

אָדָם earthling, "Adam," people
אֲדָמָה earth, ground
אֹהֶל tent. *Verb:* אָהַל camp
אוֹר light
בְּרִית covenant, treaty. בְּרִית עוֹלָם covenant of perpetuity =
    perpetual covenant
גּוֹי nation
דָּבָר word, thing, affair, matter
זָהָב gold

חֹדֶשׁ   new moon, month. *Adjective:* חָדָשׁ new

כֹּהֵן   priest

כֶּסֶף   silver, money

מֶלֶךְ   king. *Verb:* מָלַךְ reign, rule ˊ

נָבִיא   prophet

עֶבֶד   servant, slave. *Verb:* עָבַד serve, work, till, worship

עוֹלָם   eternity

קֹדֶשׁ   holiness, holy place. *Adjective:* קָדוֹשׁ holy

קוֹל   voice, sound, thundering

שַׁעַר   gate

Exercise 2

A.   Write the following in Hebrew:

1. *ya'ăqōḇ*
2. *ḥokmā(h)*
3. *šēmôṯ*
4. *lēwî*
5. *gāḇô(a)h*

6. *rĕ'ūḇēn*
7. *wîhûḏā(h)*
8. *'ărôn*
9. *sûsô*
10. *śĕḏē(h)*

11. *wayhî*
12. *'iššā(h)*
13. *'îš*
14. *mal'āḵî*
15. *šōmē(a)'*

B.   Divide each of the above words into syllables.

C.   Transcribe and translate the following:

1. אֲדָמָה
2. חָדָשׁ
3. בְּרִית
4. עוֹלָם
5. שַׁעַר

6. כֶּסֶף
7. נָבִיא
8. כֹּהֵן
9. חֹדֶשׁ
10. קֹדֶשׁ

11. דָּבָר
12. קוֹל
13. זָהָב
14. גּוֹי
15. אוֹר

divide + decide if open or closed

LESSON III

1. Gender and Number

There are two genders (masculine and feminine) and three numbers (singular, dual, and plural) in Hebrew. Beyond the masculine singular (ms) form, the gender and number of each noun are marked by distinctive endings:

	Masculine	**Feminine**
Sg.	no ending	הָ or ת
Dual	יִם	יִם
Pl.	יִם	וֹת

a. Masculine singular (ms) nouns have no special endings.

סוּס   horse

מֶלֶךְ   king

יוֹם   day

b. Feminine singular (fs) nouns have either הָ or ת endings.

    i.   Feminine nouns with הָ ending are always stressed on the final syllable.

          סוּסָה   mare

          מַלְכָּה   queen

    ii. Feminine nouns with וֹת or יֹת endings are also stressed on the last syllable.

          בְּרִית   covenant

          מַלְכוּת   kingship, royalty, kingdom

    iii. Feminine nouns which are stressed on the penultima originally ended in consonant clusters. To avoid the consonant cluster, an anaptyctic ("helping") vowel is inserted between the last two consonants.

15

מִשְׁמֶרֶת* > מִשְׁמֶרֶת obligation
דַּעַת* > דַּעַת knowledge
קְטֹרֶת* > קְטֹרֶת incense

Some feminine nouns are not marked as feminine.

אֵם	mother	חֶרֶב	sword
אֶרֶץ	earth, land	יָד	hand
עִיר	city	עַיִן	eye
רוּחַ	wind, breath	רֶגֶל	foot

> *Notes:*
>
> α. Nouns that are neuter in English may be regarded as feminine in Hebrew (e.g., עִיר city, חֶרֶב sword).
> β. Nouns of the feminine sex are always feminine (e.g., אֵם mother).
> γ. Parts of the body that come in pairs are normally feminine (e.g., רֶגֶל foot, יָד hand).

c. Masculine plural (mp) nouns are normally marked by the ending יִם.

שִׁיר	song	שִׁירִים	songs
סוּם	horse	סוּסִים	horses

d. Feminine plural (fp) nouns are normally marked by the ending וֹת. For nouns ending in הָ, the וֹת ending is added in place of the הָ ending.

סוּסָה	mare	סוּסוֹת	mares
תּוֹרָה	law	תּוֹרוֹת	laws
מִשְׁמֶרֶת	obligation	מִשְׁמָרוֹת	obligations

It should be noted that feminine nouns which are unmarked for gender in fs. are usually marked for gender in the fp.

אֶרֶץ	land	אֲרָצוֹת	lands
חֶרֶב	sword	חֲרָבוֹת	swords

e. The dual in Hebrew is marked by the ending יִם, regardless of gender. The ending was originally *áym, but the diphthong *ay in Hebrew takes an anaptyctic vowel before the following consonant.

	Singular		**Dual**	
Masc.	יוֹם	a day	יוֹמַיִם	two days

Fem.   שָׁנָה a year   שְׁנָתַיִם two years

In Hebrew, the use of the dual is restricted mainly to:
 i. Nouns that come in natural pairs:

יָדַיִם two hands

רַגְלַיִם (two) feet

 ii. Certain expressions of time:

יוֹמַיִם two days

פַּעֲמַיִם twice

 iii. Measures of two:

שְׁנַיִם two

מָאתַיִם two hundred

A few nouns that have no apparent relation to the dual number are always marked as duals. This is true also of many geographical names.

מַיִם water

שָׁמַיִם heaven, sky

מִצְרַיִם Egypt

יְרוּשָׁלַם [1] Jerusalem

2. Cases of Nouns

Before the writing of the earliest biblical texts, cases were indicated by short vowels at the end of the nouns: *u* for the nominative case (indicating subject), *i* for the genitive case (often indicating possession), and *a* for the accusative (indicating object). Thus, we may reconstruct a paradigm for the singular noun in Proto-Hebrew as follows:

	Masculine		**Feminine**	
Nom.	*malku*	king (subject)	*malkatu*	queen (subject)
Gen.	*malki*	of a king	*malkati*	of a queen
Acc.	*malka*	king (object)	*malkata*	queen

By the end of the second millennium, short vowels were dropped. Consequently, there is no formal indication of cases in biblical Hebrew.

---

[1] This name is always spelled defectively—יְרוּשָׁלַם for יְרוּשָׁלַיִם. See appendix C.5.

The fs. noun, מַלְכָּה (*malkatu/i/a*) "queen," for instance, may be nominative, genitive, or accusative. One can only determine by context, and often by syntax, just which is the case.

3. Vowel Changes in Nouns with Endings

The addition of a feminine or plural ending may cause certain vowel reductions (i.e., reduction of full vowels to *šĕwā'*) or contractions due to shifts of stress from the old ending to the new ending. But (i) long vowels marked by *matres*, (ii) the long vowel *ō*, and (iii) closed syllables cannot be reduced.

Priority is placed first on the reduction of the propretonic (see II.6) vowel. If the propretonic vowel is reduced, no further reduction takes place; but if the propretonic vowel cannot be reduced, the pretonic vowel is reduced, if possible.

a. Vowel Reduction

The following rules should account for most of the vowel changes that take place. Apart from these, one should assume no vowel change when the ending is added.

i. In the propretonic open syllable, *ā* (◌ָ) reduces to *šĕwā'*.

נָבִיא	but	נְבִיאָה	prophetess
נָבִיא	but	נְבִיאִים	prophets
חָכָם	but	חֲכָמִים	wise men

ii. In the propretonic open syllable, *ē* (◌ֵ) reduces to *šĕwā'*.

לֵבָב	but	לְבָבוֹת	hearts
עֵנָב	but	עֲנָבִים	grapes

iii. If there is no reduction in the propretonic syllable, *ē* in a pretonic open syllable is reduced to *šĕwā'*.

שֹׁפֵט	but	שֹׁפְטִים	judges
מוֹעֵד	but	מוֹעֲדִים	assemblies

Note: *ā* in a pretonic position is not reduced:

מִשְׁפָּט	מִשְׁפָּטִים	judgments

b. Contraction

i. *áyi* contracts to *ê*:

זַיִת	but	זֵיתִים	olives
אַיִל	but	אֵילִים	rams

ii.   *áwe* contracts to *ô;*

מָוֶת but   מוֹתִים deaths

c. Nouns with Final הָ.

The הָ ending is removed before the mp., fs., or fp. endings are added.

חֹזֶה but   חֹזִים seers
רֵעֶה but   רֵעָה friend

Vocabulary

body parts in pairs = feminine

Nouns:

אֹזֶן	(du. אָזְנַיִם) ear *fem.*
אַיִל	ram
אֵל	god, God, (the god) El
אֱלֹהִים	God,[2] gods. As a proper name, or when referring to Israel's God, it is treated as singular. Elsewhere it should be translated as "gods." The singular אֱלוֹהַ is derived secondarily from אֱלֹהִים
אֵם	(fp. אִמּוֹת) mother
אֶרֶץ	(fs.) land, earth
דָּם	blood
דֶּרֶךְ	(ms. or fs.) way, road
חֶרֶב	(fs.) sword
יָד	hand, power
לֵב/לֵבָב	(ms., but mp. לְבָבוֹת) heart, mind
מַיִם	(always dual) water
מִשְׁפָּט	judgment, justice, right, custom. *Verb:* שָׁפַט judge
נֶפֶשׁ	(fs.) self, will
סוּס	horse
עַיִן	(fs.) eye, spring
פָּנִים	(always mp.) face, presence. *Verb:* פָּנָה face, turn
פַּעַם	step, occurrence

[2] The form of the noun is plural, but the referent is singular. This is sometimes called "plural of majesty."

רֶ֫גֶל foot

שָׁמַ֫יִם (always dual) heaven, sky

Exercise 3

A. Give the plural of the following:

1.	בָּמָה	11.	מִלְחָמָה	21.	כּוֹכָב
2.	שִׁיר	12.	חָכָם	22.	הֵיכָל
3.	אָדוֹן	13.	צְדָקָה	23.	בְּהֵמָה
4.	צַדִּיק	14.	דָּבָר	24.	לֵבָב
5.	יָד	15.	גִּבּוֹר	25.	מִשְׁפָּחָה
6.	אֵל	16.	מַלְאָךְ	26.	כֹּהֵן
7.	אַ֫יִל	17.	זָקֵן	27.	יְשׁוּעָה
8.	עוֹלָם	18.	מִנְחָה	28.	תּוֹרָה
9.	אַמָּה	19.	עוֹלָה	29.	עֵנָב
10.	מוֹעֵד	20.	חוֹמָה	30.	דָּם

B. Write the following in Hebrew:

1. face	5. prophets	9. water
2. (two) hands	6. heaven	10. (two) eyes
3. God	7. priests	11. judgments
4. (two) ears	8. mothers	12. ground

LESSON IV

1. Triliterality of Hebrew Words

The meaning of a Hebrew word is determined by its "root" (usually comprised of three "radicals," or root letters), and by its pattern (i.e., the combination of the radicals with various vowels and prefixes and suffixes, if any).

a. The Hebrew root defines a word inasmuch as it gives the basic semantic field within which words with that root fall. The basic nuances of a root are so important that some standard lexica list words according to their roots, rather than their final forms. In the lexicon edited by Brown, Driver, and Briggs (*BDB*), for example, the word מִשְׁכָּן is not listed under the letter מ but under the root שׁכן. The implication is that מִשְׁכָּן is semantically related to שׁכן (dwell). Indeed, any word with the radicals שׁכן will probably have something to do with dwelling at a place. In understanding the nuances of a word, it is often helpful to know all the words that are derived from or built on the same root.

b. To facilitate discussion of word patterns, it is customary to use a paradigmatic root *qtl*. The letter *q* stands for the first radical, *t* for the second radical, and *l* for the third. For example, the word מֹלֶךְ is said to be of the *qōṭēl* pattern, whereas נָבִיא is of the *qāṭîl* pattern, and מִדְבָּר is of the *miqṭāl* pattern. This system allows us to make generalizations about nuances suggested by certain word patterns. For instance, the *qaṭṭāl* pattern in nouns generally denotes professions (e.g., דַּיָּג fisherman, גַּנָּב thief, מַלָּח sailor), whereas the adjectival pattern *qiṭṭel* generally denotes bodily defects (e.g., עִוֵּר blind, אִלֵּם mute, פִּסֵּחַ lame).

c. For more general discussions of verb types, it is convenient to refer to the first radical as I, the second radical as II, and the third radical as III. For example, "I-*Nûn*" verbs are those whose first radical is נ (e.g., נָתַן give, נָפַל fall, נָטַע plant), and "III-א" verbs are those whose third radical is א (e.g., מָצָא find, מָלֵא fill, יָצָא go forth).

2. Weak Radicals

Word patterns can sometimes be problematic for the beginning student because certain "weak" radicals are more susceptible to change,

21

or are more likely to cause morphological changes than the "strong" ones. These "weak" radicals are not as intimidating, however, if one becomes aware of their idiosyncrasies.

a. *Gutturals*

   i. Since gutturals (and ר) cannot be doubled (I.3), when the normal word pattern calls for doubling at the position where the guttural or ר stands, we may get (α) compensatory lengthening of the vowel preceding the guttural, but the guttural is not doubled. When compensatory lengthening takes place, *a* (ַ) > *ā* (ָ), *i* (ִ) > *ē* (ֵ), and *u* (ֻ) > *ō* (ֹ).

     Not *פַּרֵשׁ but פָּרֵשׁ (*qaṭṭāl* pattern)
     Not *חִרֵשׁ but חֵרֵשׁ (*qiṭṭēl* pattern)
     Not *בֻּרַךְ but בֹּרַךְ (*quṭṭal* pattern)

     When nothing happens to the guttural or to the preceding vowel, we say that there is (β) virtual doubling of the guttural.

     אַחִים = '*aḥḥîm* [1]
     הַהֵיכָל = *haḥḥêkāl*

   ii. As we have previously learned (II.5), gutturals never take the simple vocal *šĕwā'*, and prefer the composite *šĕwā'*.

Strong Roots		**With Guttural**	
מְלָכִים	but	עֲבָדִים	(*qĕṭālîm* pattern)
יַשְׁמִיד	but	יַעֲמִיד	(*yaqṭîl* pattern)

   iii. Again, as we have learned (I.3; II.9), gutturals prefer "a-class" vowels. Thus,

Strong Roots		**With Guttural**	
מְדַבֵּר	but	מְשַׁלֵּחַ	(*mĕqaṭṭēl* pattern)
שְׁמֹר	but	שְׁלֹחַ	(*qĕṭōl* pattern)

b. *Nûn*

    As a rule, a *nûn* standing immediately before another consonant (i.e., without an intervening vowel) will get assimilated into that following radical. Examples:

---

[1] Since an unaccented short vowel in an open syllable is virtually impossible in Hebrew, this word cannot be '*a/hîm*.

מַנְתָּן* > מַתָּן *mattān* (*maqṭāl* pattern)

מַנְשָׂא* > מַשָּׂא *maśśā'* (*maqṭāl* pattern)

יִנְפֹּל* > יִפֹּל *yippōl* (*yiqṭōl* pattern)

If the radical that follows the *nûn* happens to be a guttural or ר, we will get compensatory lengthening or virtual doubling in accordance with 2.a.i, above.

מִנְאֶרֶץ* > מֵאֶרֶץ from a land (compensatory
                        lengthening)

מִנְרֹאשׁ* > מֵרֹאשׁ from a head (compensatory
                        lengthening)

מִנְחוּץ* > מְחוּץ outside (virtual doubling)

c. *Wāw and yōd*

  i. With very few exceptions,[2] original ו in initial position has become י (e.g., *וְלֹד>יָלַד, *וּשֵׁב>יָשַׁב). In the lexica, original I-*Wāw* roots are listed with true I-*Yōd* roots.

  ii. When ו is not in initial position, it remains unchanged. Thus, הִתְוַדַּע (from ידע, originally *וְדַע), יִוָּדַע, הִתְוַכַּח (from יכח, originally *וכח), and so on.[3] When *w* is preceded by an '*a*' vowel, we get a diphthong *aw. Stressed *aw takes an anaptyctic vowel and becomes *áwe*; but unstressed *aw contracts to *ô*:

        מָוֶת death   but   מוֹתִי my death

        אָוֶן trouble but   אוֹנָם their trouble

        תָּוֶךְ midst   but   תּוֹכִי my midst

    In each of these cases, the ו is not merely a *mater*; it is part of the root.

  iii. When *y* is preceded by an *a* vowel, we get a diphthong *ay. Stressed *ay takes an anaptyctic vowel and becomes *áyi*; unstressed *ay contracts to *ê*:

        בַּיִת house   but   בֵּיתִי my house

        עַיִן eye   but   עֵינִי my eye

        אַיִל ram   but   אֵילִים rams

---

[2] Notably the conjunction ו (and) and the noun וָו (nail).

[3] On the other hand, we have forms like מְיֻדָּע (see XXIII.1f) where ו has become י even though it is not in the initial position. But these are exceptional.

iv.   Nouns and verbs that originally ended in וֹ or י will normally appear with final ה. In the lexica, such roots are listed as III-ה, together with roots that are genuinely III-ה. For simplicity sake, we will call original III-ו/י roots III-ה (to be distinguished from original III-ה). III-ה nouns frequently end in הֶ (e.g., שָׂדֶה field, חֹזֶה seer). A few nouns retain the III-י (e.g., פְּרִי fruit, כְּלִי vessel).[4] A few monosyllabic nouns with ָ or ָ are also III-ה (אָב father, אָח brother, עֵץ tree).

3. Nouns with Prefixes

Many nouns are marked by prefixes that are not part of the root.
a. Nouns with מ prefix.
Nouns with מ prefixes were originally either of the *maqṭāl* or *maqṭēl* patterns. The former is a pattern denoting nouns of place; the latter is the pattern for nouns of instrument. Such patterns, however, are not limited to nouns of place and instrument.

i.   *maqṭāl*
The *maqṭāl* pattern is rarely preserved in strong roots, but it is evident in nouns with I-Guttural. It is also evident in nouns with I-*Nûn* (with assimilation of נ), I-*Wāw* (with contraction of **aw* > *ô*), and I-*Yōḏ* (with contraction of **ay* > *ê*). Examples:

Root	Noun	
לאך	מַלְאָךְ	messenger
אכל	מַאֲכָל	food
נתן	מַתָּן gift (מַנְתָּן*>מַתָּן)	
ישב	מוֹשָׁב residence (מוֹשַׁב*>מוֹשָׁב)	
ישר	מֵישָׁרִים level ways (מַישָׁרִים*>מֵישָׁרִים)	

Some feminine forms are also built on the *maqṭāl* pattern (e.g., מַחֲשֶׁבֶת thought, מַמְלָכָה kingdom).

ii.   *miqṭāl*
In biblical Hebrew, earlier *maqṭāl* usually dissimilates to *miqṭāl*.

מִשְׁכָּן tabernacle	>	מַשְׁכָּן*
מִדְבָּר desert	>	מַדְבָּר*

---

[4] The plural forms of such nouns usually retain the י as a consonant: גְּדִי goat—גְּדָיִים goats; אֲרִי lion—אֲרָיִים lions, etc. But the plural of כְּלִי is כֵּלִים, not *כְּלָיִים.

In a few instances, *maqṭāl* dissimilates to *meqṭāl* (מֶרְחָק distance; מֶרְכָּבָה chariot; מֶמְשָׁלָה government).

iii. *maqṭēl*

מַפְתֵּחַ   key

מוֹקֵשׁ   trap (מוֹקֵשׁ* <)

Feminine forms:

גלל   מְגִלָּה   scroll

סלל   מְסִלָּה   highway

iv. III-ה Nouns

In III-ה nouns, no distinction is made between *maqṭāl* and *maqṭēl*. Most nouns in this class simply end in הֶ if they are masculine, and הָ if they are feminine:

שתה   מִשְׁתֶּה   banquet

קנה   מִקְנָה   acquisition

v. II-*Wāw/Yōḏ*

For II-*Wāw/Yōḏ* nouns in this class, the prefix is always מָ.

קום   מָקוֹם   place

לון   מָלוֹן   lodge

When the feminine or plural ending is added, מָ > מְ in accordance with III.3.a.i.

מָרוֹם height but מְרוֹמִים heights

מָכוֹן abode but מְכוֹנָה abode

b. Nouns with ת Prefix.

נפח   תַּפּוּחַ apple (תַּנְפּוּחַ* < תַּפּוּחַ)

ישב   תּוֹשָׁב resident (תַּוְשָׁב* < תּוֹשָׁב)

ימן   תֵּימָן south (תַּיְמָן* < תֵּימָן)

Feminine Forms:

פאר   תִּפְאֶרֶת glory

קוה   תִּקְוָה hope

ירה   תּוֹרָה law

בנה   תַּבְנִית plan

בוא   תְּבוּאָה produce

הלל   תְּהִלָּה praise

c. Nouns with א Prefix.

צבע   אֶצְבַּע   finger

יתן   אֵיתָן   everflowing stream (אֵיתָן* > אֵיתָן)

[The student should now do exercise 4.A before proceeding to the next section of this Lesson.]

4. Geminate Nouns

Geminate nouns are those with identical second and third radicals (i.e., *qll*). Feminine and plural forms are easy to recognize, since gemination (doubling) is indicated by a *dāḡēš forte*. Biblical Hebrew, however, does not tolerate gemination at the end of a word. Consequently, the ms. of the monosyllabic geminate nouns will show only two radicals.[5]

   a. "a" type (*qall*)

	sg.		pl.
	עַם people		עַמִּים peoples
	אַמָּה cubit		אַמּוֹת cubits

   b. "i" type (*qill*)

	sg.		pl.
	חֵץ arrow		חִצִּים arrows
	פִּנָּה corner		פִּנּוֹת corners

   c. "u" type (*qull*)

---

[5] It is evident that gemination (doubling) is always lost at the end of a word (thus in the ms.). In all other forms, gemination is indicated by a *dāḡēš forte*. Moreover, original *i is lengthened to *ē*; original *u is lengthened to *ō*. Short *a* does not lengthen to *ā*, except in יָם (< *yamm). Thus

    *qall > *qal* (*'*amm* > '*am*)

    *qill > *qēl* (*ḥiṣṣ > *ḥēṣ*)

    *qull > *qōl* (*ḥuqq > *ḥōq*)

When gemination is expected in a guttural or ר, we get compensatory lengthening of *a* to *ā*.

שַׂר	(ruler)	but	שָׂרִים	(rulers)
הַר	(mountain)	but	הָרִים	(mountains)
פַּר	(bull)	but	פָּרָה	(cow)

Nouns that were originally *qanl, *qinl, and *qunl are absorbed into the *qall, *qill, *qull types by virtue of the assimilation of the *nûn*:

   '*anp* > '*app* > '*ap̄* (nose)

   '*inz* > '*izz* > '*ēz* (goat)

חֹק statute   חֻקִּים statutes
חֻקָּה statute   חֻקּוֹת statutes

5. Segolates

Segolates are nouns which were originally monosyllabic, with two *different* consonants at the end (i.e., *qaṭl, *qiṭl, *quṭl). Since Hebrew does not normally tolerate a consonant cluster at the end of a word, an anaptyctic vowel (usually a *sĕḡôl*) is inserted between the last two consonants. The resulting word appears to be disyllabic, though the penultimate stress suggests otherwise. Through a process of vowel harmony, we get nouns that are so dominated by *sĕḡôl* that the original distinction between *qaṭl, *qiṭl, and *quṭl is no longer made in the independent singular nouns. Regardless of the original vowel, these nouns generally appear as *qéṭel*, except that *quṭl nouns always appear as *qóṭel*, and many *qiṭl nouns will appear as *qéṭel*.[6]

Since gutturals generally prefer "a-class" vowels, the presence of a guttural may affect one or both *sĕḡôl* in a segolate noun (e.g., זֶרַע seed, רֹחַב breadth, נַעַר lad).

The plurals of segolates are all formed the same way. Depending on the gender of the noun, the plural will always have the pattern *qĕṭālîm* or *qĕṭālôt*:

a. *qaṭl*

מֶלֶךְ king   מְלָכִים kings
עֶבֶד servant   עֲבָדִים servants
נֶפֶשׁ self   נְפָשׁוֹת selves
אֶרֶץ land   אֲרָצוֹת lands

The student should remember that a root that appears to be geminate, but is not listed in the dictionaries as such, may only be secondarily geminate. One should conjecture that the second radical may, in fact, be a *nûn* that has been assimilated.

Finally, it should be noted that a few *qill nouns get assimilated into the *qall group in the singular, but not in other forms:

סַף (threshold)   סִפִּים (thresholds)
פַּת (morsel)   פִּתִּים (morsels)

[6] Despite the formal similarity of the segolates in the independent forms of the singular, one can generally tell what the original vowel of a segolate might have been. The clues are found in any corresponding feminine form, forms with pronominal suffixes (see XI.2.c), and/or in the pausal form (see Appendix C.2). For example, we would not know if *mélek* was originally *malk, *milk, or *mulk, if *mélek* were the only datum we had. But since we know (i) that "queen" is *malkā(h)*, (ii) that "my king" is *malkî*, and (iii) that *mélek* becomes *mālek* when in pause, we are safe to conclude that *mélek* was originally *malk.

b. *qiṭl*

קֶ֫בֶר	grave	קְבָרִים	graves
עֵ֫דֶר	herd	עֲדָרִים	herds

c. *quṭl*

בֹּ֫קֶר	morning	בְּקָרִים	mornings
חֹ֫דֶשׁ	new moon	חֳדָשִׁים	new moons
אֹ֫הֶל	tent	אֳהָלִים	tents

6. Irregular Plurals

Some plural nouns look substantially different from the singular. The following are some of the most important:

אָב	father	אָבוֹת	fathers
אָח	brother	אַחִים	brothers
אִישׁ	man	אֲנָשִׁים	men
אִשָּׁה	woman	נָשִׁים	women
בַּ֫יִת	house	בָּתִּים	houses
בֵּן	son	בָּנִים	sons
בַּת	daughter	בָּנוֹת	daughters
יוֹם	day	יָמִים	days
עִיר	city	עָרִים	cities
רֹאשׁ	head	רָאשִׁים	heads

For a fuller list of noun types, see Appendix A.

Vocabulary

Nouns:

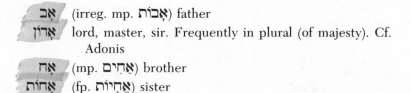

אָב (irreg. mp. אָבוֹת) father

אָדוֹן lord, master, sir. Frequently in plural (of majesty). Cf. Adonis

אָח (mp. אַחִים) brother

אָחוֹת (fp. אֲחָיוֹת) sister

אִישׁ (irreg. mp. אֲנָשִׁים) man, husband. אֲנָשִׁים is actually the
plural of אֱנוֹשׁ. The expected plural אִישִׁים is rare

אֱנוֹשׁ humanity, a human

אִשָּׁה (irreg. fp. נָשִׁים) woman, wife. Note the doubling of שׁ.
This suggests that the root is אנשׁ, with the assimilation of נ. Thus, אִשָּׁה is lexically related to אֱנוֹשׁ, not
אִישׁ

בַּיִת (irreg. mp. בָּתִּים) house

בֵּן (irreg. mp. בָּנִים) son. בֵּן is also used in general for an
individual or a singular number of a species. So "sons
of Israel" = Israelites, "sons of prophets" = members of
the prophetic guild, "son of a bow" = an arrow, etc.

בַּת (irreg. fp. בָּנוֹת) daughter.[7] Also used idiomatically, like
בֵּן, for individual of a group or species

הַר mountain

יוֹם (irreg. mp. יָמִים) day. *Adverb:* יוֹמָם daily

יָם (mp. יַמִּים) sea

כְּלִי (mp. כֵּלִים) vessel, instrument, weapon

מַלְאָךְ messenger, angel

מָקוֹם (mp. מְקוֹמוֹת) place

עִיר (irreg. fp. עָרִים) city

עַם (mp. עַמִּים, also irreg. עֲמָמִים) people

פְּרִי fruit

רֹאשׁ (irreg. mp. רָאשִׁים) head, top. רִאשׁוֹן the first, former.
רֵאשִׁית first, beginning

שַׂר commander, ruler, prince

---

[7] Actually *bat* is derived from original *bint (i.e., *bint > *bitt > *bat*). With suffixes we get
בִּתִּי my daughter, בִּתּוֹ his daughter, etc.

Exercise 4

A. Find the roots of the following with the help of a lexicon:

1.	תּוֹעֵבָה	21.	מְנוֹרָה
2.	מִבְצָר	22.	תְּחִלָּה
3.	מַצָּב	23.	מוֹקֵשׁ
4.	מַפֶּלֶת	24.	מִקְנָה
5.	מִזְמוֹר	25.	מַגֵּפָה
6.	אֵיתָנִים	26.	מאֹזְנַיִם
7.	מַחְסֶה	27.	עֲנִי
8.	מָלוֹן	28.	מוֹרֶה
9.	מָנוֹר	29.	מַבָּט
10.	תִּקְוָה	30.	כְּלִי
11.	מִשְׁתֶּה	31.	עַתָּה
12.	תְּנוּפָה	32.	מִבְטָח
13.	מִרְעֶה	33.	מַחֲשָׁבָה
14.	תּוֹצָאוֹת	34.	מוֹצָא
15.	מַעֲשִׂים	35.	מַסַּע
16.	נְבִיאָה	36.	אֶזְרָח
17.	מוֹלֶדֶת	37.	מַרְאֶה
18.	חֲצִי	38.	מִלְחָמָה
19.	מֵיתָר	39.	מִקְדָּשׁ
20.	תּוֹלְדוֹת	40.	מֶמְשָׁלָה

B. Give the plural of the following:

1.	מֶלֶךְ	11.	שַׂר	21.	הַר
2.	עֶבֶד	12.	בֵּן	22.	דֶּרֶךְ
3.	נַעַר	13.	בַּת	23.	אֹהֶל
4.	נֶפֶשׁ	14.	עַם	24.	פַּר
5.	אֶרֶץ	15.	עִיר	25.	אֵם
6.	עֵדֶר	16.	בַּיִת	26.	רֹאשׁ
7.	חֹדֶשׁ	17.	אִישׁ	27.	מַלְאָךְ
8.	חֹק	18.	אִשָּׁה	28.	אָדוֹן
9.	יוֹם	19.	אָב	29.	כְּלִי
10.	יָם	20.	אָח	30.	מָקוֹם

LESSON V

1. Definite Article

There is no indefinite article in Hebrew. Thus מֶלֶךְ means either "king" or "a king."

The definite article does not appear in independent form; it is always prefixed to the word that it defines.

a. The usual form of the definite article is הַ + a *dāḡēš forte* in the following consonant.

מֶלֶךְ a king   הַמֶּלֶךְ the king

דָּבָר a word   הַדָּבָר the word

b. Before א and ר it is always הָ (i.e., with compensatory lengthening).

אִישׁ a man   הָאִישׁ the man

רֹאשׁ a head   הָרֹאשׁ the head

c. Before ה and ח it is usually הַ with virtual doubling.

הֵיכָל a palace   הַהֵיכָל the palace

חֹדֶשׁ a new moon   הַחֹדֶשׁ the new moon

d. Before ע it is usually הָ; rarely הַ.

עִיר a city   הָעִיר the city

e. Before unaccented הָ and עָ, and accented or unaccented חָ, it is always הֶ with virtual doubling.

הָמוֹן an uproar   הֶהָמוֹן the uproar

עָוֺן an iniquity   הֶעָוֺן the iniquity

חָזוֹן a vision   הֶחָזוֹן the vision

f. A few words are vocalized differently when they take the definite article.

אֲרוֹן an ark   הָאָרוֹן the ark

אֶרֶץ a land   הָאָרֶץ the land

גַּן a garden   הַגָּן the garden

31

הַר a mountain   הָהָר the mountain

חַג a festival   הֶחָג the festival

פַּר a bull   הַפָּר the bull

עַם a people   הָעָם the people

[The student should now do Exercise 5.A before continuing with this Lesson.]

2. Prefixed Prepositions

The prepositions בְּ (in, by, with), כְּ (like, as, according to), and לְ (to, for) are prefixed to the word and clarify the spatial or temporal position of the word. In these abbreviated forms the preposition is always insepa-rable from the word, although in some poetic texts one finds the longer forms בְּמוֹ, כְּמוֹ, and לְמוֹ occurring independently.

a. Before a word without the definite article, the "inseparable" preposition is simply prefixed.

עִיר a city   בְּעִיר in a city

מֶלֶךְ a king   כְּמֶלֶךְ like a king

דָּוִד David   לְדָוִד to David

b. When it is prefixed to any word beginning with an initial *šĕwā'*, the following general rules of *šĕwā'* apply:

i. When two simple vocal *šĕwā'*s are brought together, the first becomes *i*, the second becomes silent.

     בְּ + גְּבוּל   >   בִּגְבוּל (*biḡbûl*) in a territory

     כְּ + מְלָכִים   >   כִּמְלָכִים (*kimlāḵîm*) in a kingdom

If, however, the second *šĕwā'* stands under a *yōḏ*, it is not preserved at all.

ii. When a simple vocal *šĕwā'* immediately precedes a com-posite *šĕwā'*, the former assumes the corresponding short vowel of the latter.

     בְּ + חֲלוֹם   >   בַּחֲלוֹם (*baḥălôm*) in a dream

     בְּ + אֱמֶת   >   בֶּאֱמֶת (*be'ĕmet*) in truth

     בְּ + אֲהָלִים   >   בָּאֳהָלִים (*bo'ŏhālîm*) in tents

Before אֱלֹהִים, however, we get בֵּ, כֵּ, לֵ with the quiescence of א (see II.10).

     בְּ + אֱלֹהִים   >   בֵּאלֹהִים with God

c. When it is added to a noun with the definite article, the הִ of the definite article disappears, the preposition assumes the vowel of the definite article, and any doubling of the following radical is preserved.

לְ + הַמֶּלֶךְ	>	לַמֶּלֶךְ	for the king
לְ + הָאִישׁ	>	לָאִישׁ	for the man
בְּ + הֶהָרִים	>	בֶּהָרִים	in the mountains
בְּ + הָאָרֶץ	>	בָּאָרֶץ	in the land

d. Before a stressed syllable the preposition לְ frequently takes the long vowel ָ.

לָנֶצַח to eternity

לָבֶטַח securely

3. Other Forms of Prepositions

a. Some prepositions stand independently; e.g., אַחַר (after, behind) לִפְנֵי (before), תַּחַת (under, instead of), נֶגֶד (opposite, in front of).

אַחַר הַמַּבּוּל after the flood

אַחַר הַצֹּאן behind the flock

לִפְנֵי הָאָרוֹן before the ark

תַּחַת הָעֵץ under the tree

תַּחַת דָּוִד instead of David

נֶגֶד הָעָם in front of the people

b. Some prepositions are linked to the following word by means of a *maqqēp*;[1] e.g., אֶל־ (to, unto), עַל־ (on, upon, concerning, beside), עַד־ (as far as, until).

אֶל־הָעִיר to the city

עַל־הָאָרוֹן upon the ark

עַד־הַנָּהָר as far as the river

4. The Preposition מִן־

The preposition מִן־ (from, away from, because of) never occurs independently.

---

[1] See Appendix C.3.

a. It may be linked to the following by a *maqqēp̄*.

מִן־הָאָרֶץ from the land

מִן־הָעִיר from the city

This form of the preposition is common for nouns with the definite article, but it is exceedingly rare otherwise.

b. It may be treated as a prefixed preposition in the following ways:

i. The נ is assimilated (absorbed) before a strong radical *no 3 labials/nasals in a row*

מִנְמֶלֶךְ* > מִמֶּלֶךְ from a king

מִנְשָׁמַיִם* > מִשָּׁמַיִם from heaven

ii. Before gutturals and ר it is usually מֵ (with compensatory lengthening) and, rarely, מֶ (with virtual doubling).

מִנְעִיר* > מֵעִיר from a city

מִנְהַר* > מֵהַר from a mountain

This rule also applies when מִן is prefixed to a noun with the definite article.

מִנְהָאָרֶץ* > מֵהָאָרֶץ from the land

מִנְהֶעָרִים* > מֵהֶעָרִים from the cities

iii. With nouns beginning with יְ we get the contraction of מִי > מִיְ.

מִיהוּדָה > מִיהוּדָה* > מִנְיְהוּדָה*

5. Form of the Conjunction וְ.

The conjunction ו (and, but) is treated as an inseparable particle. It is vocalized as follows:

a. Before most consonants it is וְ.

דָּבָר a word וְדָבָר and a word

עֶבֶד a servant וְעֶבֶד and a servant

הָעֶבֶד the servant וְהָעֶבֶד and the servant

b. Before the labials ב, מ, and פ it is וּ.

בַּיִת a house וּבַיִת and a house

מֶלֶךְ a king וּמֶלֶךְ and a king

פְּרִי a fruit וּפְרִי and a fruit

c. Before any strong consonant with a vocal *šĕwā'* it is וּ.

דְּבָרִים words   וּדְבָרִים and words

d. With words beginning with יְ we get the contraction of וִי > וְיִ > וִיְ.

יְהוּדָה Judah   וִיהוּדָה and Judah

e. Before a composite *šĕwā'* it takes the corresponding short vowel of the composite *šĕwā'*.

חֲמוֹר an ass   וַחֲמוֹר and an ass

אֱמֶת truth   וֶאֱמֶת and truth

חֳלִי sickness   וָחֳלִי and sickness

f. Before אֱלֹהִים it is וֵ with the quiescence of א.

אֱלֹהִים God   וֵאלֹהִים and God

g. Before a stressed syllable it is frequently וָ.

רַע evil   וָרַע and evil

6. Loss of Gemination

The consonants ו, י, ל, מ, נ, and ק, and any of the *s*-consonants (ס, צ, שׂ, and שׁ) frequently lose the *dāḡēš forte* when followed by a *šĕwā'*.

הַמְרַגְּלִים*   >   הַמְרַגְּלִים the spies

הַיְאֹר*   >   הַיְאֹר the Nile[2]

7. Final Remarks on the Use of the Definite Article

a. In poetic texts, the definite article is not needed to express definiteness.

b. The definite article may have a demonstrative force, particularly with time words.

הַיּוֹם *this* day = today

הַשָּׁנָה *this* year

הַפַּעַם *this* time

---

[2] This general rule applies in other situations as well and, as we shall see later, familiarity with it will save the student untold anguish in finding roots for certain words.

c. The definite article may be used with a vocative force.

הַמֶּלֶךְ   O King!

הַכֹּהֵן   O Priest!

Vocabulary

Prepositions:[3]

אַחֲרֵי/אַחַר	after, behind. *Adverb:* אַחֲרֵי כֵן/אַחַר כֵּן afterward
אֶל־	unto, into to(ward)
בְּ	in, with, by, among, through, as (in the essence of)
בֵּין	between. Note the idiom: ... וּבֵין ... בֵּין and, less frequently, ... לְבֵין ... בֵּין between ... and ...
כְּ	like, as, about, according to. Note the idiom: כְּ ... X, כְּ Y, X and Y alike
לְ	to, for, in regard to, in reference to
לִפְנֵי	before, *to the face of*
מִן	from
נֶגֶד	in front of
עַד־	as far as, until
עַל־	upon, on, over, concerning, beside. It should be noted that אֶל־ and עַל־ are frequently confused
תַּחַת	under, beneath, instead of

Note: Sometimes two prepositions may be combined for emphasis. This is particularly frequent with the preposition מִן. Example: מִתַּחַת under, מֵעַל above, etc.

Nouns:

אָרוֹן	ark (of covenant)
הֵיכָל	palace, temple
חַטָּאת	sin, sin offering. *Adjective:* חָטָא sinful. *Verb:* חָטָא sin

---

[3] Prepositions tend to have a wide range of meaning. For more details, see GKC para 119, and the lexica.

חַיִל   strength, valor, power

חֹשֶׁךְ   darkness

יהוה   YHWH (the name of Israel's God). Not pronounced
by pious Jews and, hence, not precisely vocalized.
In the Hebrew Bible, the vowels of אֲדֹנָי "my Lord"
are superimposed on the "Tetragrammaton" (thus,
יְהֹוָה or יְהוָה). When the consonantal text has
אדני יהוה "my lord YHWH," the text is pointed
with the vowels for אֲדֹנָי אֱלֹהִים "my lord, God"
(i.e., אֲדֹנָי יְהוִֹה)

לַיְלָה   (irreg. ms.; mp. לֵילוֹת) night

עָוֹן   guilt

Exercise 5

A. Write the following in Hebrew:

1. the people	11. the mountains
2. the princes	12. the sin
3. the cities	13. the new moon
4. the man	14. the men
5. the land	15. the lands
6. the palace	16. an ark
7. the guilt	17. the ark
8. the women	18. the sword
9. the mountain	19. the kings
10. the prophets	20. the seas

B. Write the following in Hebrew:

1. among kings	6. with the sword
2. for the servant	7. with swords
3. from the land	8. from the head
4. in the palace	9. among prophets
5. with a sword	10. like the prophets

11. the man and the woman
12. from city to city
13. among the men
14. in the mountains
15. and in the cities
16. for God
17. women and men
18. from heaven to earth
19. from Judah (יְהוּדָה)
20. fathers and sons

C. Translate the following into English:

1. תַּחַת דָּוִד
2. כֶּסֶף וְזָהָב
3. לִפְנֵי הָאָרוֹן
4. שָׂרִים וַעֲבָדִים
5. אֶל־פְּנֵי הָאָדֹן יְהוָה
6. בֵּין מַיִם לָמָיִם
7. נֶגֶד הָהָר
8. לִפְנֵי מֹשֶׁה וְלִפְנֵי אַהֲרֹן
9. מִיּוֹם עַד־לַיְלָה
10. בַּחַגִּים וּבֶחֳדָשִׁים וּבַשַּׁבָּתוֹת⁴

11. לִיהוּדָה
12. בֵּין אֱלֹהִים וּבֵין נֶפֶשׁ
13. פָּנִים אֶל־פָּנִים
14. כָּעָם כַּכֹּהֵן
15. אַחַר הַמֶּלֶךְ
16. אַחַר הַחֹשֶׁךְ
17. הַמַּיִם מִתַּחַת הַשָּׁמַיִם
18. מִלִּפְנֵי הַכֹּהֲנִים
19. הַמַּיִם בַּיַּמִּים
20. יָד תַּחַת יָד רֶגֶל תַּחַת רֶגֶל

---

⁴ חַג festival

LESSON VI

1. Inflection of the Adjective

The inflectional categories and endings of the adjective are similar to those of the noun (see Lesson III), except that the dual adjective is not attested.

The inflection of טוֹב (good) is as follows:

ms	טוֹב	mp	טוֹבִים
fs	טוֹבָה	fp	טוֹבוֹת

The following are the most common types of adjectives:

a. *qāṭôl* type (e.g., גָּדוֹל great)

ms	גָּדוֹל	mp	גְּדוֹלִים
fs	גְּדוֹלָה	fp	גְּדוֹלוֹת

b. *qāṭēl* type (e.g., כָּבֵד heavy)

ms	כָּבֵד	mp	כְּבֵדִים
fs	כְּבֵדָה	fp	כְּבֵדוֹת

c. *qāṭāl* type (e.g., יָשָׁר straight)

ms	יָשָׁר	mp	יְשָׁרִים
fs	יְשָׁרָה	fp	יְשָׁרוֹת

d. *qall* type (e.g., רַב many, much)

ms	רַב	mp	רַבִּים
fs	רַבָּה	fp	רַבּוֹת

Adjectives of this type behave like the *qall* nouns (see IV.4.a). Thus, when a guttural is the geminate radical, we get compensatory lengthening of the first vowel in the forms with endings; רַע evil:

39

ms	רַע	mp	רָעִים
fs	רָעָה	fp	רָעוֹת

e. III-ה *type* (e.g., קָשֶׁה difficult)

ms	קָשֶׁה	mp	קָשִׁים
fs	קָשָׁה	fp	קָשׁוֹת

2. Uses of the Adjective *check examples*

a. The attributive adjective qualifies the noun in such a way that it forms a phrase with the noun. When an adjective is used in this way, it agrees in gender, number, and definiteness with the noun it modifies, regardless of the form of the noun. It also comes after the noun, not before it, as is the case in English ("the *good* man").

Study the following examples of the attributive adjective, paying close attention to (i) the agreement of gender, number, and definiteness in each case, and (ii) the word order:

אִישׁ טוֹב a good man

הָאִישׁ הַטּוֹב the good man

אֲנָשִׁים טוֹבִים good men

הָאֲנָשִׁים הַטּוֹבִים the good men

אִשָּׁה טוֹבָה a good woman

הָאִשָּׁה הַטּוֹבָה the good woman

נָשִׁים טוֹבוֹת good women (not נָשִׁים טוֹבִים)

הַנָּשִׁים הַטּוֹבוֹת the good women (not הַנָּשִׁים הַטּוֹבִים)

b. The predicative adjective does not form a phrase with the noun. Rather, it functions as a predicate that describes the state of the subject (the noun). When so used, the adjective agrees with the noun in gender and number, but it never takes the definite article. It also tends to come before the noun, although it may also follow the noun.

Study the following examples carefully, and note that in every case the definite article is not used with the adjective, although the noun may be definite.

טוֹב הָאִישׁ the man is good

הָאִישׁ טוֹב the man is good

טוֹבִים הָאֲנָשִׁים   the men are good

הָאֲנָשִׁים טוֹבִים   the men are good

טוֹבָה הָאִשָּׁה   the woman is good

הָאִשָּׁה טוֹבָה   the woman is good

טוֹבוֹת הַנָּשִׁים   the women are good (not טוֹבִים הַנָּשִׁים)

הַנָּשִׁים טוֹבוֹת   the women are good

Since the predicate adjective does not take the definite article, there may be some ambiguity when it is used with indefinite nouns. Thus, אֲנָשִׁים טוֹבִים may mean either "good men" or "men are good." The precise meaning must be determined from context. In a case like טוֹבִים אֲנָשִׁים, however, it is clear that the adjective is a predicate, since the attributive adjective normally stands after the noun.

c. The adjective in Hebrew may be used as a substantive. This use is particularly frequent when the adjective has the definite article.

הַזָּקֵן   the old man, elder

הַקָּדוֹשׁ   the holy one

הָרַע   the evil, the evil one

3. Comparative

There is no independent word in Hebrew for the English word "than." Instead, comparison is expressed by the adjective—less commonly by a verb—plus the preposition מִן placed before the noun that is surpassed.

גָּדוֹל יְהוָה מִכָּל־הָאֱלֹהִים   YHWH is *greater than* all the gods (Exod. 18:11)

גָּבוֹהַּ מִכָּל־הָעָם   *taller than* all the people (1 Sam. 9:2)

חָכָם אַתָּה מִדָּנִיֵּאל   you are *wiser than* Daniel (Ezek. 28:3)

4. Simple Nominal Sentence

A simple nominal sentence in Hebrew consists of a subject and a predicate standing in juxtaposition, with the emphatic element normally in first position. The tense of the sentence must be inferred from the context. When the context is not provided, one simply assumes that the present tense is intended.

יְהוָה מֶלֶךְ   *YHWH* (is) king (Ps. 10:16)

עִמָּנוּ אֵל   God (is) *with us* (Isa. 8:10)

בַּשָּׁמַיִם כִּסְאוֹ   *In heaven* (is) his throne (Ps. 11:4)

5. Nouns in Apposition

A noun is sometimes clarified by another noun in apposition.

הַנָּהָר פְּרָת   the river, Euphrates = the Euphrates
river (1 Chron. 5:9)

הַנַּעַר הַנָּבִיא   the lad, the prophet = the prophetic lad
(2 Kings 9:4)

נַעֲרָה בְתוּלָה   a lass, a virgin = a virgin lass
(1 Kings 1:2)

Vocabulary

Adjectives:

אַחֵר	(fs. אַחֶרֶת) another, other
גָּדוֹל	great, big, large
זָקֵן	old
חָזָק	strong, powerful
חַי	alive, living. Substantive in both genders, "living thing, animal." חַיִּים "life" (as in לְחַיִּים "to life")
חָכָם	wise. *Noun:* חָכְמָה wisdom
טוֹב	good, beautiful
יָפֶה	handsome, beautiful
יָקָר	precious, valuable, rare
יָשָׁר	straight, just
כָּבֵד	heavy, severe, important. *Noun:* כָּבוֹד glory, honor
צַדִּיק	righteous. *Nouns:* צֶדֶק, צְדָקָה rightness, righteousness
קָטֹן	(also קָטָן, קְטַנָּה, קְטַנִּים) small, insignificant
רַב	many, much, abundant, mighty. *Noun:* רֹב abundance
רַע	bad, evil, ugly
רָשָׁע	wicked, criminal

Nouns:

אֶבֶן	(fs.; fp. אֲבָנִים) stone

חֶסֶד faithfulness, loyalty, devotion (cf. Hasidim)

מְאֹד might, power. Most frequently used as adverb
occurring after adjectives, e.g., טוֹב מְאֹד very good

מִלְחָמָה battle

רוּחַ (fs.) spirit, wind, breath

Adverb:

לֹא no, not

Exercise 6

A. Translate the following into Hebrew:

1. a righteous man
2. a holy nation
3. great is the day
4. the living
5. great wisdom
6. a very wise man
7. YHWH is holy
8. the matter was good
9. the great city
10. God is in the land
11. a great devotion
12. many days
13. what's just and good[1]
14. a wise woman
15. in a holy place
16. a new king
17. the wicked thing
18. the righteous man
19. precious stones
20. a small city

B. Translate the following into English:

1. לְאִישׁ אַחֵר
2. אֶל חַי
3. רוּחַ־רָעָה
4. טוֹב מִבָּנִים וּמִבָּנוֹת
5. בֵּין טוֹב וּבֵין רַע
6. יְהוָה עַל־מַיִם רַבִּים
7. כַּצַּדִּיק כָּרָשָׁע

---

[1] That is, "the just and the good."

8.   הַשָּׁמַיִם הַחֲדָשִׁים וְהָאָרֶץ הַחֲדָשָׁה

9.   עַם רַב

10.   לֵאלֹהִים אֲחֵרִים

11.   צַדִּיק יְהוָה

12.   הָאֲנָשִׁים הָרְשָׁעִים

13.   טוֹב וְיָשָׁר יְהוָה

14.   עַל־אֲרָצוֹת רַבּוֹת וְעַל־מַמְלָכוֹת [2] גְּדוֹלוֹת

15.   בְּעַם כָּבֵד וּבְיָד חֲזָקָה

16.   הַטּוֹבוֹת טוֹבוֹת מְאֹד וְהָרָעוֹת רָעוֹת מְאֹד

[2] מַמְלָכָה kingdom

LESSON VII

1. Verbal Patterns

The verbal patterns (*binyānîm*) are named after their respective third masculine singular (3 ms) forms,[1] for it is in these forms that the differences between the various paradigms are most evident. The basic *binyān*—including the verbal patterns *qāṭal*, *qāṭēl*, and *qāṭōl*—is traditionally called *qal* ("light, easy"), even though we get this *qal* pattern only in stative verbs with geminate roots. Other *binyānîm* receive their names from the 3ms Perfect forms of a paradigmatic root פעל. Hence we have the designations *nip̄ʿal* (for the *niqṭal* pattern), *piʿēl* (for *qiṭṭēl*), *puʿal* (for *quṭṭal*), *hip̄ʿîl* (for *hiqṭîl*), *hop̄ʿal* (for *hoqṭal*), *hitpaʿēl* (for *hitqaṭṭēl*) and so forth.

In view of the irregularities that accompany the II-Guttural roots, and because of the awkwardness of classifying all the basic patterns as *qal*, we will adopt the sigla used by scholars in the study of Semitic verbal patterns. The basic *binyān* is called G (for German *Grundstamm*, "basic stem") other sigla indicate the prefixes, infixes, or doubling of the respective verbal patterns. Passive *binyānîm* are designated by the letter *p*.

The following are the seven main *binyānîm* in Hebrew:

Siglum	Pattern	Characteristic(s)	Traditional Name
G	qāṭal		Qal = light
	qāṭēl		
	qāṭōl		
N	niqṭal	prefixed **n**	Nip̄ʿal
D	qiṭṭēl	doubling of second radical	Piʿēl
Dp	quṭṭal	doubling of second radical	Puʿal
H	hiqṭîl	prefixed **h**	Hip̄ʿîl
Hp	hoqṭal	prefixed **h**	Hop̄ʿal
HtD	hitqaṭṭēl	prefixed **h**, infixed **t**, doubling of second radical	Hitpaʿēl

---

[1] The meanings and inflections of the various *binyānîm* will be considered in later lessons. For now, the student may wish to turn to the synopsis of the *binyānîm* for the strong verb in Appendix B. Note the verbal patterns and categories.

2. Forms of the G Active Participle

a. The Basic Forms.

The participle is inflected like the adjective; but the fs ending of the participle is ordinarily הַ֒, not ה‎ָ. The alternate fs form קְטֵלָה is uncommon.

ms	קֹטֵל	mp	קֹטְלִים
fs	קֹטֶלֶת	fp	קֹטְלוֹת

kill

The G active participle of verbs with strong radicals, I-Guttural, I-*Nûn*, I-*Yōd*, and Geminate roots are all inflected normally.

b. II-Guttural Verbs.

Since gutturals do not take the simple vocal *šĕwā'* (II.5), the composite *šĕwā'* is found wherever one would expect a vocal *šĕwā'*. For example, שאל "ask":

ms	שֹׁאֵל	mp	שֹׁאֲלִים
fs	שֹׁאֶלֶת	fp	שֹׁאֲלוֹת

ask

c. III-ה, ח, ע Verbs.

As we have previously learned, final ה, ח, and ע tend to add the *furtive pátaḥ,* and prefer a-class vowels (II.9). Therefore, the forms of the G active participle of שמע "hear" are as follows:

ms	שֹׁמֵעַ	mp	שֹׁמְעִים
fs	שֹׁמַעַת	fp	שֹׁמְעוֹת

hear

d. III-א Verbs.

Since א tends to be quiescent whenever it closes a syllable (II.10), the fs. participle of such verbs are vocalized slightly differently from the ordinary form. For example, מצא "find":

ms	מֹצֵא	mp	מֹצְאִים
fs	מֹצֵאת	fp	מֹצְאוֹת

find

e. III-ה Verbs.

III-ה verbs (not to be confused with III-ה) have endings like nouns and adjectives of such roots. For example, גלה "uncover":

ms	גֹּלֶה	mp	גֹּלִים
fs	גֹּלָה	fp	גֹּלוֹת

Although uncommon, an alternate fs form like בֹּכִיָּה is attested.

f. II-*Wāw/Yōḏ* Verbs.

Verbs with ו or י as the second radical normally preserve only the first and last consonants in the G active participle. No distinction is made between II-*Wāw* and II-*Yōḏ*. For example, קוּם "arise":

ms	קָם	mp	קָמִים
fs	קָמָה	fp	קָמוֹת

Synopsis of Forms of the G Active Participle				
Root	ms	mp	fs	fp
קטל	קֹטֵל	קֹטְלִים	קֹטֶלֶת	קֹטְלוֹת
שאל	שֹׁאֵל	שֹׁאֲלִים	שֹׁאֶלֶת	שֹׁאֲלוֹת
שמע	שֹׁמֵעַ	שֹׁמְעִים	שֹׁמַעַת	שֹׁמְעוֹת
מצא	מֹצֵא	מֹצְאִים	מֹצֵאת	מֹצְאוֹת
גלה	גֹּלֶה	גֹּלִים	גֹּלָה	גֹּלוֹת
קום	קָם	קָמִים	קָמָה	קָמוֹת

[Do Exercise 7.A before continuing with the lesson. If you miss more than 5 forms, you should review the above two sections before proceeding.]

3. Uses of the Participle

a. The participle, being a verbal adjective, retains some of the properties of the verb. It suggests *continuous* occurrence of an activity or a mode of being.

יֹשֵׁב עַל־כִּסֵּא רָם וְנִשָּׂא	*sitting* upon a throne (*being*) *high* and lifted up (Isa. 6:1)
מַלְאֲכֵי אֱלֹהִים עֹלִים וְיֹרְדִים	angels of God *ascending* and *descending* (Gen. 28:12)

A verbal tense is not indicated in the Hebrew participle; it must be inferred from context. Context will determine if a participle refers to occurrences in the past, present, or immediate future.

   i.   Present

דּוֹר הֹלֵךְ וְדוֹר בָּא וְהָאָרֶץ לְעוֹלָם עֹמָדֶת

      A generation *comes* and a generation *goes*, but the earth *stands* forever (Qoh. 1:4)

   ii.   Past

יְהוָה קֹרֵא לַנַּעַר

      YHWH *was calling* the boy (1 Sam. 3:8)

וְרִבְקָה אֹהֶבֶת אֶת־יַעֲקֹב

      but Rebecca *loved* Jacob (Gen. 25:28)

   iii.   Imminent Future

      The participle, particularly when it is preceded by הִנֵּה (VIII.5), may indicate imminent action. Hence it is often rendered "about to (do something)."

שָׂרָה אִשְׁתְּךָ יֹלֶדֶת לְךָ בֵּן

      Sarah your wife is *about to bear* for you a son (Gen. 17:19)

הִנֵּה הָעַלְמָה הָרָה וְיֹלֶדֶת בֵּן

      the young woman is pregnant and *about to bear* a son (Isa. 7:14)

  b. The participle may be used as an attributive or a predicative adjective.

   i.   When it is used like an attributive adjective, the participle agrees in number, gender, and definiteness with, and comes *after*, the noun it modifies:

הָאִישׁ הָעֹמֵד	the standing man
הָאִשָּׁה הָעֹמֶדֶת	the standing woman
הָאֲנָשִׁים הָעֹמְדִים	the standing men
הַנָּשִׁים הָעֹמְדוֹת	the standing women

In the phrase הָאִישׁ הָעֹמֵד, the action word הָעֹמֵד, "standing," specifies and describes the noun הָאִישׁ. It is not just any man of whom the phrase speaks, but "the man, the one standing." Thus הָעֹמֵד functions like an attributive adjective. The expression "the man, the standing one" may be compared with the adjectival phrase הָאִישׁ הַטּוֹב "the man, the good one" (or "the standing man" // "the good man"). In idiomatic English, one would translate the participle in this case with the relative pronoun "who." The tense is not specified in Hebrew, so the Hebrew הָאִישׁ הָעֹמֵד could mean "the man who stands," "the man who stood," and so forth.

Consider the translation of the participle in the following examples:

בָּרוּךְ הַבָּא בְּשֵׁם יְהוָה

blessed is *the one who comes* in the name of YHWH
  (Ps. 118:26)

הָאֲנָשִׁים הָעֹלִים מִמִּצְרַיִם

the men *who went up* from Egypt (Num. 32:11)

The participle could be indefinite if the noun is indefinite.

כְּאֵשׁ אֹכֶלֶת

like a *consuming* fire (Exod. 24:17)

ii. When the participle is used as a predicative adjective, it comes after the noun and agrees with the noun in gender and number, but it never takes the definite article:

הָאִישׁ עֹמֵד	the man is standing
הָאִשָּׁה עֹמֶדֶת	the woman is standing
הָאֲנָשִׁים עֹמְדִים	the men are standing
הַנָּשִׁים עֹמְדוֹת	the women are standing

If the noun is indefinite, the participle could be attributive or predicative; the proper translation will depend on the context.

c. Like the adjective, the participle may be used as a substantive.

יֹשֵׁב	dwelling, one who dwells	= dweller, inhabitant
שֹׁמֵר	keeping, one who keeps	= keeper
אֹהֵב	loving, one who loves	= lover

d. In many instances, the participle is used in such a way that some indefinite subject has to be supplied.

אֵלַי קֹרֵא מִשֵּׂעִיר   unto me (someone) *calls* from Seir
        (Isa. 21:11)

Vocabulary

Verbs:

אָהַב	love. *Noun:* אַהֲבָה love
אָכַל	eat, consume, devour. *Nouns:* אֹכֶל, אָכְלָה food
אָמַר	say
בּוֹא	come, enter
בָּנָה	build (*cf.* בִּנְיָן structure, building)
גָּלָה	remove, uncover, reveal, go into exile
הָלַךְ	walk, go
יָדַע	know. *Noun:* דַּעַת knowledge
יָלַד	bear, beget. *Noun:* יֶלֶד boy, child
יָצָא	go out, go forth
יָרַד	go down, descend
יָשַׁב	dwell, sit, remain
מָצָא	find
נָתַן	give, deliver, set, permit
עָבַר	cross over, pass over, transgress. עבר בְּ X pass through X
עָלָה	go up, ascend. *Noun:* עֹלָה burnt offering
עָמַד	stand
עָשָׂה	make, do. *Noun:* מַעֲשֶׂה deed
קוּם	arise, stand up
קָרָא	call, proclaim. קרא לְ X call/summon X
שָׁאַל	ask, inquire
שָׁמַע	hear, listen, obey

Exercise 7

A. Give the gender, number, and verbal root of the following participles. If you do not know the meaning of the verb, look it up in a lexicon.

1.	עֹשֶׂה	4.	שֹׁמֵעַ	7.	שָׁמָה
2.	אֹמְרִים	5.	בָּא	8.	יֹדַעַת
3.	עֹלִים	6.	עֹמֶדֶת	9.	אֹכֶלֶת

10. מֹצְאִים	17. נֹתְנִים	24. יֹרְדִים
11. קְרָאת	18. קָמָה	25. שָׁמַעַת
12. סֹבֵב	19. הֹלְכוֹת	26. בָּאִים
13. בֹּכִיָּה	20. עֹשִׂים	27. עֹבְרִים
14. יֹצֵאת	21. רֹאֶה	28. שָׁב
15. יָרֵעַ	22. יֹלֶדֶת	29. בָּאוֹת
16. צָם	23. בֹּנִים	30. גֹּלֶה

B. Write the following in Hebrew:

1. the people who dwell in the land
2. he who comes
3. inhabitants (who are) in the land
4. YHWH was passing by
5. God knows
6. the men were saying to YHWH
7. the ones who went down to (אֶל־) the sea
8. the people who asked
9. other cows[2] were going up
10. a heart that listens
11. and Athaliah[3] was reigning over the land
12. many people were going from the road
13. evil[4] is going forth from nation to nation
14. a voice cries out in the wilderness[5]
15. a hearing ear and a seeing eye

[2] פָּרוֹת cows
[3] עֲתַלְיָה Athaliah
[4] רָעָה evil
[5] מִדְבָּר wilderness

LESSON VIII

memorize!

1. Independent Personal Pronoun

Independent Personal Pronoun					
3 ms	הוּא	he, it	3 mp	הֵם / הֵמָּה	they
3 fs	הִיא	she, it	3 fp	הֵנָּה	they
2 ms	אַתְּ / אַתָּה	you	2 mp	אַתֶּם	you *or mixed group*
2 fs	אַתְּ	you	2 fp	אַתֵּן / אַתֵּנָה	you
1 cs	אֲנִי / אָנֹכִי	I	1 cp	אֲנַחְנוּ	we

a. Forms

i. The 3 fs form is normally written as הוּא in the Penta-teuch—i.e., it is pronounced as *hî'*, even though the con-sonants suggest *hû'*.

ii. The doubling of the *t* in the second person forms suggests the assimilation of the *nûn:*

2 ms   *אַנְתָּ > אַתָּ or אַתָּה

2 fs   *אַנְתְּ > אַתְּ

2 mp   *אַנְתֶּם > אַתֶּם

2 fp   *אַנְתֵּן > אַתֵּן

iii. An archaic form אַתִּי is attested for the 2 fs.

iv. Several forms are vocalized and/or accented differently when they are in pause.[1]

b. Usage

The independent personal pronouns are mainly used as subjects of sentences, particularly when attention is called to the subject.

אֲנִי יְהוָה   *I am* YHWH (Exod. 6:2)

= emphasis

[1] See Appendix C.2.

אַתָּה הָאִישׁ   *You are* the man (2 Sam. 12:7)

מֵחָרָן אֲנַחְנוּ   *We are* from Haran (Gen. 29:4)

2. Marker of Definite Accusative

Frequently in Hebrew prose, and far less commonly in poetry, an untranslatable particle אֵת / אֶת־ is used to mark the definite accusative (i.e., the direct object of the verb). A noun is said to be definite when it is a proper name, a noun with a definite article, or a noun with a pronominal suffix.

The marker of definite accusative must immediately precede the noun and ordinarily comes after the verb and subject. If there are several direct definite objects, the marker is repeated before each one.

בָּרָא אֱלֹהִים אֵת הַשָּׁמַיִם
וְאֵת הָאָרֶץ   God created *the heaven* and *the earth* (Gen. 1:1)

וְכָל־הָעָם רֹאִים אֶת־הַקּוֹלֹת   and all the people perceived *the thunderings* (Exod. 20:18)

If an indirect object (marked by לְ) is involved, the marker of definite accusative normally comes after the indirect object.

יְהוָה אֱלֹהֶיךָ נֹתֵן לְךָ אֶת־
הָאָרֶץ הַטּוֹבָה   YHWH your God is giving to you *the good land* (Deut. 9:6)

The indefinite direct object is not marked.

הוּא יָלְדָה בֵן   she bore *a son* (Gen. 19:38)

3. Pronominal Accusative

When the direct object of a verb is a pronoun, that pronoun is indicated by the accusative marker with a pronominal suffix. The objective pronouns are as follows:

3 ms	אֹתוֹ	him, it	3 mp	אֶתְהֶם / אֹתָם	them
3 fs	אֹתָהּ	her, it	3 fp	אֶתְהֶן / אֹתָן	them
2 ms	אֹתְךָ	you	2 mp	אֶתְכֶם	you
2 fs	אֹתָךְ	you	2 fp	–not attested–	you
1 cs	אֹתִי	me	1 cp	אֹתָנוּ	us

The objective pronoun ordinarily follows the verb, but it may precede the verb for emphasis or to express contrast.

אֹתְךָ רָאִיתִי צַדִּיק   *you* I have seen righteous (Gen. 7:1)

וְהָרְגוּ אֹתִי וְאֹתָךְ יְחַיּוּ   they will kill *me*, but *you* they will keep alive (Gen. 12:12)

4. Prepositions with Pronominal Suffixes

a. Inseparable prepositions בְּ and לְ:

3 ms	לוֹ	to him	בּוֹ	in him
3 fs	לָהּ	to her	בָּהּ	in her
2 ms	לְךָ / לְכָה	to you	בְּךָ / בְּכָה	in you
2 fs	לָךְ	to you	בָּךְ	in you
1 cs	לִי	to me	בִּי	in me
3 mp	לָהֶם [2]	to them	בָּהֶם / בָּם	in them
3 fp	לָהֶן	to them	בָּהֶן	in them
2 mp	לָכֶם	to you	בָּכֶם	in you
2 fp	לָכֶן	to you	בָּכֶן	in you
1 cp	לָנוּ	to us	בָּנוּ	in us

The preposition בֵּין also takes the pronominal suffixes like בְּ and כְּ, except that the anomalous 1 cp form בֵּינוֹתֵנוּ "between us" occurs along with בֵּינֵינוּ, and בֵּינוֹתָם "between them" occurs with the regular form, בֵּינֵיהֶם.

b. Prepositions עִם and אֵת:[3]

---

[2] Frequently in poetic texts we get לָמוֹ instead of לָהֶם.

[3] The prepositions עִם / עִם־ and אֵת / אֵת־, both meaning "with," may be used with or without pronominal suffix. Both prepositions are of geminate roots and may be compared with nouns of the *qill* type (IV.4.b), except that we have עִם instead of *עֵם, as one would expect. Thus, even though the preposition אֵת / אֵת־ without the suffix looks identical to the marker of definite accusative, it is historically of different origin and vocalization. The student should compare the suffixal forms of the preposition אֵת with the suffixal forms of the accusative marker.

3 ms	אִתּוֹ	with him	עִמּוֹ	with him
3 fs	אִתָּהּ	with her	עִמָּהּ	with her
2 ms	אִתְּךָ	with you	עִמְּךָ	with you
2 fs	–not attested–		עִמָּךְ	with you
1 cs	אִתִּי	with me	עִמִּי / עִמָּדִי	with me
3 mp	אִתָּם	with them	עִמָּם / עִמָּהֶם	with them
3 fp	–not attested–		–not attested–	
2 mp	אִתְּכֶם	with you	עִמָּכֶם	with you
2 fp	–not attested–		–not attested–	
1 cp	אִתָּנוּ	with us	עִמָּנוּ	with us

c. Prepositions כְּ and מִן:[4]

3 ms	כָּמוֹהוּ	like him	מִמֶּנּוּ	from him
3 fs	כָּמוֹהָ	like her	מִמֶּנָּה	from her
2 ms	כָּמוֹךָ	like you	מִמְּךָ	from you
2 fs	כָּמוֹךְ	like you	מִמֵּךְ	from you
1 cs	כָּמוֹנִי	like me	מִמֶּנִּי	from me
3 mp	כָּהֶם	like them	מֵהֶם	from them
3 fp	כָּהֵן / כָּהֵנָּה	like them	מֵהֶן / מֵהֵנָּה	from them
2 mp	כָּכֶם	like you	מִכֶּם	from you
2 fp	כָּכֵן	like you	מִכֵּן	from you
1 cp	כָּמוֹנוּ	like us	מִמֶּנּוּ	from us

d. Prepositions אֶל־, עַל־, and others

The prepositions אֶל־ (to), עַל־ (upon), אַחֲרֵי (after), לִפְנֵי (before),

---

[4] The כְּמוֹ־ base is obviously related to the archaic and poetic form of the preposition (V.2), but the reduplication of מִן is anomalous. In any case, the suffixes of both prepositions are the same. It should be noted that the 3 ms מִמֶּנּוּ is derived from original *מִמֶּנְהוּ, and 3 fs מִמֶּנָּה is derived from *מִמֶּנְהָ. Thus, the preposition מִן has two forms with identical suffixes (3 ms and 1 cp). Both forms were originally distinguished:

3 ms *מִמֶּנְהוּ > מִמֶּנּוּ

1 cp *מִמֶּנְנוּ > מִמֶּנּוּ

תַּחַת (under), עַד־ (until), and סָבִיב (around) take the pronominal suffixes as follows:

3 ms	אֵלָיו	to him	עָלָיו	upon him / it
3 fs	אֵלֶיהָ	to her	עָלֶיהָ	upon her / it
2 ms	אֵלֶיךָ	to you	עָלֶיךָ	upon you
2 fs	אֵלַיִךְ	to you	עָלַיִךְ	upon you
1 cs	אֵלַי	to me	עָלַי	upon me
3 mp	אֲלֵיהֶם	to them	עֲלֵיהֶם	upon them
3 fp	אֲלֵיהֶן	to them	עֲלֵיהֶן	upon them
2 mp	אֲלֵיכֶם	to you	עֲלֵיכֶם	upon you
2 fs	–not attested–		–not attested–	
1 cp	אֵלֵינוּ	to us	עָלֵינוּ	upon us

5. הִנֵּה = *behold, listen* (= *yo', what's up!*)

a. The word הִנֵּה, also spelled הֵן / הֶן־, may take the pronominal suffixes as follows:

3 ms	הִנּוֹ	3 mp	הִנָּם
3 fs	–not attested–	3 fp	–not attested–
2 ms	הִנְּךָ	2 mp	הִנְּכֶם
2 fs	הִנֵּךְ / הִנָּךְ	2 fp	–not attested–
1 cs	הִנֶּנִּי / הִנְנִי	1 cp	הִנֶּנּוּ / הִנְנוּ

The forms 1 cs הִנְנִי and 1 cp הִנְנוּ are derived from הִנֶּנִּי and הִנֶּנּוּ respectively—that is, with the loss of gemination in accordance with V.6.

b. This word is usually placed at the beginning of a quote to emphasize the presence of a person or persons, or the immediacy and reality of an event. In many cases, it is used with a participle to indicate an event in the near future (see VII.3.a.iii). There is no equivalent of this word in English, although it is frequently, and rather inadequately, translated as "Behold!" The proper translation of the word depends upon the context in which it is found. In some cases it is best not to translate it.

Study the usage of הִנֵּה / הֵן in the following examples:

הִנֵּה הָאֵשׁ וְהָעֵצִים	*Here are* the fire and the wood (Gen. 22:7)
הִנֵּה בֵין־קָדֵשׁ וּבֵין בָּרֶד	*It is* between Kadesh and Bered (Gen. 16:14)
וַיֹּאמֶר לָבָן הֵן לוּ יְהִי כִדְבָרֶךָ	And Laban said: "*Good!* May it be according to your words" (Gen. 30:34)
גַּם הִנֵּה עַבְדְּךָ יַעֲקֹב אַחֲרֵינוּ	Moreover, your servant Jacob *is* (now) behind us (Gen. 32:21)
הִנְּךָ רֹאֶה בַּיּוֹם הַהוּא	*You will* (soon) see on that day (1 Kings 22:25)
הִנְּךָ יָפֶה דוֹדִי	*You are* handsome, my love (Song 1:16)

Vocabulary

Prepositions:

אֶת־ / אֵת	with, together with
סָבִיב	around. Also used as adjective (round about, around)
עִם	with

Verbs:

זָבַח	sacrifice. *Nouns:* מִזְבֵּחַ (pl מִזְבְּחוֹת) altar, זֶבַח sacrifice
כָּרַת	cut. Also used in idiom כָּרַת בְּרִית "cut a treaty" (= "make a covenant")
שָׁלַח	send, stretch out

Nouns:

אֵשׁ	(fs) fire
אִשֶּׁה	fire-offering
גִּבּוֹר	hero, warrior
דּוֹר	(pl. usually דּוֹרוֹת) generation
זֶרַע	seed. *Verb:* זָרַע sow
לֶחֶם	food, bread
מִדְבָּר	desert
מוֹעֵד	assembly, appointed feast

נָהָר (pl. נְהָרִים or נְהָרוֹת) river
עֵץ (pl. עֵצִים) tree, wood
שָׂדֶה (pl. שָׂדוֹת) field, country
שֵׁם (pl. שֵׁמוֹת) name
שָׁנָה (fp. שָׁנִים) year

Conjunction:

כִּי for, because, when, surely, indeed. כִּי־אָם but rather, unless

Exercise 8

A. Write the following in Hebrew:
1. I am with you
2. he is a prophet
3. you and they alike
4. I and you alike
5. I am sacrificing to YHWH
6. I am giving to them
7. they are alive (living)
8. I am doing a new thing
9. we are brothers
10. I am coming (about to come)
11. we were eating
12. stronger than us
13. indeed, you are a wise man
14. between you and me
15. she is the mother
16. she is coming
17. the thing was too difficult for me
18. he was coming (un)to me
19. evil is upon us
20. here am I

B. Translate the following into English:

1. He (this) is a prophet   נָבִיא הוּא   (Gen. 20:7)

2.   כָּבֵד מִמְּךָ הַדָּבָר   (Exod. 18:18)

3. I am a prophet like you   אֲנִי נָבִיא כָּמוֹךָ   (1 Kings 13:18)

4.   צַדִּיק אַתָּה יְהוָה   (Jer. 12:1)

5. Behold, I am with you   הִנֵּה אָנֹכִי עִמָּךְ   (Gen. 28:15)

6.   רִבְקָה אֹהֶבֶת אֶת־יַעֲקֹב   (Gen. 25:28)

7. I am God and not man   אֵל אָנֹכִי וְלֹא אִישׁ   (Hos. 11:9)

8.   צַדִּיק אַתָּה מִמֶּנִּי   (1 Sam. 24:18)

9. *am not a prophet and I am / a prophet's son*   לֹא־נָבִיא אָנֹכִי וְלֹא בֶן־נָבִיא [5] אָנֹכִי   (Amos 7:14)

10.   הִנֵּה אָנֹכִי שֹׁלֵחַ לָכֶם אֵת אֵלִיָּה הַנָּבִיא   (Mal. 3:23)

11. *standing upon them under the tree*   הוּא־עֹמֵד עֲלֵיהֶם תַּחַת הָעֵץ   (Gen. 18:8)

12.   אַחֲרָיו לֹא־קָם כָּמֹהוּ   (2 Kings 23:25)

13. We are brothers   אַחִים אֲנַחְנוּ   (Gen. 42:13)

14.   וְאַתָּה אָדָם וְלֹא־אֵל   (Ezek. 28:2)

15. *we the God / the heavens*   הָאֱלֹהִים בַּשָּׁמַיִם וְאַתָּה עַל־הָאָרֶץ   (Qol. 5:1)

16. *and upon the / earth*   וּמֵעוֹלָם עַד־עוֹלָם אַתָּה אֵל   (Ps. 90:2)

17.   עֹבְרִים אֲנַחְנוּ מִבֵּית־לֶחֶם   (Judg. 19:18)

18.   הִנֵּה חָכָם אַתָּה מִדָּנִיֵּאל   (Ezek. 28:3)

19.   כִּי עַם קָדוֹשׁ אַתָּה לַיהוָה   (Deut. 7:6)

20.   כִּי עִמָּנוּ אֵל   (Isa. 8:10)

21.   אֲנִי שׁוֹלֵחַ אוֹתְךָ אֲלֵיהֶם   (Ezek. 2:4)

22.   וְאַבְרָהָם הֹלֵךְ עִמָּם   (Gen. 18:16)

23.   וִיהוּדָה אֹהֵב אֶת־דָּוִד כִּי־הוּא יוֹצֵא וָבָא לִפְנֵיהֶם   (1 Sam. 18:16)

24.   צַדִּיק עִם־רָשָׁע   (Gen. 18:23)

25.   הַמַּיִם מִתַּחַת הַשָּׁמַיִם אֶל־מָקוֹם   (Gen. 1:9)

26.   הִנֵּה יָמִים בָּאִים   (Jer. 23:5)

27.   יְהוָה אֹהֵב מִשְׁפָּט   (Ps. 37:28)

28.   הִנֵּה אֲנַחְנוּ בָאִים בָּאָרֶץ   (Josh. 2:18)

29.   כָּמוֹךָ כְּפַרְעֹה   (Gen. 44:18)

30.   הִנֵּה הָאֵשׁ וְהָעֵצִים   (Gen. 22:7)

---

[5] בֶּן־נָבִיא son of a prophet.

LESSON IX

1. Demonstratives

ident.

ms	זֶה	this	mp	אֵלֶּה	these
fs	זֹאת	this	fp	אֵלֶּה	these

ms	הוּא	that	mp	הֵם	those
fs	הִיא	that	fs	הֵנָּה	those

a. The demonstratives may be used as pronouns. Hence, it is no surprise that one set of the demonstratives are identical to the third person independent personal pronouns.

A demonstrative pronoun agrees in gender and number with the referent noun, but it does not take the definite article.

זֶה־הַשַּׁעַר לַיהוָה	*this* is the gate of YHWH (Ps. 118:20)
זֹאת הַתּוֹרָה לָעֹלָה	*this* is the instruction regarding the burnt offering (Lev. 7:37)
אֵלֶּה הַמִּצְוֹת וְהַמִּשְׁפָּטִים	*these* are the commandments and ordinances (Num. 36:13)
אֲנִי יְהוָה הוּא שְׁמִי	I am YHWH, *that* is my name (Isa. 42:8)
הוּא הָעִיר הַגְּדֹלָה	*that* is the great city (Gen. 10:12)
וְהֵם בַּעֲלֵי בְרִית	and *those* were allies (Gen. 14:13)

If the referent is implicitly neuter, זֹאת is usually used instead of זֶה, but הוּא is used more frequently than הִיא.

בְּכָל־זֹאת לֹא־שָׁב אַפּוֹ	in all *this* his anger did not turn back (Isa. 5:25)
כֶּן־הוּא	so be *it*! (Josh. 2:21)

b. Demonstratives may also be used as attributive adjectives. When a demonstrative is used in this way, it takes the definite article and

60

agrees in gender and number with the noun it modifies. If other attributive adjectives are used, the demonstrative adjective will come after them.

נַעֲמָן הָאֲרַמִּי הַזֶּה	*this* Naaman the Syrian (2 Kings 5:20)
לָעִיר הַגְּדֹלָה הַזֹּאת	to *this* great city (Jer. 22:8)
הַשָּׁנִים הַטֹּבֹת הַבָּאֹת הָאֵלֶּה	*these* coming good years (Gen. 41:35)
כָּל־הַמִּדְבָּר הַגָּדוֹל וְהַנּוֹרָא הַהוּא	all *that* great and awesome desert (Deut 1:19)
בַּיָּמִים הָהֵם וּבָעֵת הַהִיא	in *those* days and at *that* time (Jer. 33:15)
וְהַמֹּפְתִים הַגְּדֹלִים הָהֵם	and *those* great wonders (Deut. 29:2)[1]

c. The demonstratives are sometimes added to a question or a statement to give emphasis and clarity to what is said. In such cases, it is frequently untranslatable.

אָנֹכִי אָנֹכִי הוּא מֹחֶה פְּשָׁעֶיךָ	I am, I am (indeed) the one who blots out your transgressions (Isa. 43:25)
מַה־זֹּאת עָשָׂה אֱלֹהִים לָנוּ	What (indeed) has God done to us? (Gen. 42:28)
הַאַתָּה זֶה עֲשָׂהאֵל	Is it (really) you Asahel? (2 Sam. 2:20)
וְהִנֵּה־זֶה מַלְאָךְ נֹגֵעַ בּוֹ	Just then, an angel touched him (1 Kings 19:5)
עַתָּה זֶה יָדַעְתִּי כִּי אִישׁ אֱלֹהִים אָתָּה	Now (at last) I know that you are a man of God! (1 Kings 17:24)

d. The repetition of the demonstrative, as in זֶה . . . זֶה, or זֹאת . . . זֹאת, may be translated "one . . . (the) other," or the like.

וְקָרָא זֶה אֶל־זֶה	and one said to another (Isa. 6:3)
אֵלֶּה מִזֶּה וְאֵלֶּה מִזֶּה	these were on this side, and those were on the other side (Josh. 8:22)

2. Relative Clauses

a. Relative clauses in biblical Hebrew prose (rarely in poetry) are usually introduced by the indeclinable particle אֲשֶׁר. The translation of

---

[1] The definite article before הֵם and הֵנָּה has the long vowel: הָהֵם, הָהֵנָּה. The singular הוּא and הִיא, on the other hand, correctly assume virtual doubling: הַהוּא, הַהִיא.

this word usually depends on the antecedent. According to the function of the antecedent, then, one translates אֲשֶׁר with one of the relative pronouns in English. Study the following examples carefully:

מֶלֶךְ־חָדָשׁ עַל־מִצְרָיִם אֲשֶׁר לֹא־יָדַע אֶת־יוֹסֵף	a new king over Egypt *who* did not know Joseph (Exod. 1:8)
אֶל־הָאָרֶץ אֲשֶׁר אָנֹכִי נֹתֵן לָהֶם	to the land *which* I am giving to them (Josh. 1:2)
הַמָּקוֹם אֲשֶׁר אַתָּה עוֹמֵד עָלָיו	the place on *which* you stand—lit.: the place where you are standing on it (Exod. 3:5)
הַיָּמִים אֲשֶׁר מָלַךְ דָּוִד	the days *when* David reigned (1 Kings 2:11)
הָאֱמֹרִי אֲשֶׁר אַתֶּם יוֹשְׁבִים בְּאַרְצָם	the Amorites in *whose* land you dwell—lit.: the Amorite (collective) who you are dwelling in their land (Judg. 6:10)
לְאִישׁ אֲשֶׁר־אֵלֶּה לֹּו אָנֹכִי הָרָה	by a certain man to *whom* these belong, I am pregnant (Gen. 38:25)
מִי יְהוָה אֲשֶׁר אֶשְׁמַע בְּקֹלוֹ	who is YHWH *that* I should obey his voice? (Exod. 5:2)

The particle אֲשֶׁר also occurs in combination with some prepositions. The following are the most common and should be committed to memory:

עֵקֶב אֲשֶׁר	because of
יַעַן אֲשֶׁר	because of
כַּאֲשֶׁר	as, even as, when
אַחֲרֵי אֲשֶׁר	after

b. In some portions of the Hebrew Bible, especially in Qohelet, the relative pronoun שֶׁ / שַׁ is used instead of אֲשֶׁר, with no difference in meaning. This relative pronoun is simply joined to the word following it, as a definite article would be:

כַּחוֹל שֶׁעַל־שְׂפַת הַיָּם	like sand *that* is on the shore of the sea (Judg. 7:12)
אוֹת שָׁאַתָּה מְדַבֵּר עִמִּי	a sign *that* you are speaking with me (Judg. 6:17)

c. In archaic or archaistic poetry, זֶה and the related forms זוּ and זֹו may be found instead of אֲשֶׁר. There is no clear semantic difference between these forms and אֲשֶׁר.

הַר־צִיּוֹן זֶה שָׁכַנְתָּ בּוֹ	Mount Zion *wherein* you dwell (Ps. 74:2)
שְׁמַע לְאָבִיךָ זֶה יְלָדֶךָ	Listen to your father *who* bore you (Prov. 23:22)
עַם־זוּ גָּאָלְתָּ	a people *whom* you redeemed (Exod. 15:13)
וְעֵדֹתִי ² זוֹ אֲלַמְּדֵם	and my covenant *which* I will teach them (Ps. 132:12)

d. The relative is sometimes expressed by a simple juxtaposition of clauses.

הַדֶּרֶךְ יֵלְכוּ בָהּ	the way *on which* they walk (Exod. 18:20)
יֹאבַד יוֹם אִוָּלֶד בּוֹ	Perish the day *in which* I was born! (Job 3:3)

3. Particle of Existence

a. To express the existence of something or someone, the particle יֵשׁ / יֶשׁ־ is used.

יֵשׁ נָבִיא בְּיִשְׂרָאֵל	*there is* a prophet in Israel (2 Kings 5:8)
אָכֵן יֵשׁ יְהוָה בַּמָּקוֹם הַזֶּה	Surely, YHWH *is* (*present*) in this place (Gen. 28:16)
אוּלַי יֵשׁ חֲמִשִּׁים צַדִּיקִם בְּתוֹךְ הָעִיר	Perhaps *there are* fifty righteous ones in the city (Gen. 18:24)

b. To express existence of a person or persons, Hebrew sometimes uses יֵשׁ with pronominal suffixes.

אִם־יֶשְׁכֶם עֹשִׂים חֶסֶד וֶאֱמֶת	If *you are* acting loyally and faithfully (Gen. 24:49)
אִם־יֶשְׁךָ מוֹשִׁיעַ בְּיָדִי אֶת־יִשְׂרָאֵל	if *you will* deliver into Israel by my hand (Judg. 6:36)

² The Masoretic text has וְעֵדֹתִי.

c. Possession is expressed by the idiom יֶשׁ לְ‑.

יֵשׁ אֱלֹהִים לְיִשְׂרָאֵל there is a God for Israel > Israel *has* a God (1 Sam. 17:46)

4. Particle of Absence

a. To express absence or nonexistence, the negative particle אֵין (אַיִן when stressed) is used.

אֵין כַּיהוָה אֱלֹהֵינוּ *there is none* like YHWH our God (Exod. 8:6)

b. אֵין may take pronominal suffixes like those appended to the inseparable prepositions בְּ and כְּ, or similar to those used with מִן.

אֵינֶנִּי נֹתֵן לָכֶם תֶּבֶן *I am not* giving you straw! (Exod. 5:10)

וְהִנֵּה אֵינֶנּוּ *He was not there!* (Ps. 37:36)

וּמִן־הַבְּהֵמָה אֲשֶׁר אֵינֶנָּה טְהוֹרָה and from the beasts that *are not clean* (Gen. 7:8)

The forms אֵינֶנּוּ and אֵינֶנָּה are derived from אֵינֶנְהוּ* and אֵינֶנְהָ*, respectively.

c. To express non-possession, the idiom אֵין לְ is used.

אֵין לוֹ בֵן there is not for him a son > he *has no* son   (Num. 27:4)

כַּצֹּאן אֲשֶׁר אֵין לָהֶם רֹעֶה like a flock that for them there is no shepherd > like a flock *without* a shepherd   (1 Kings 22:17)

5. Interrogative Clauses

a. Sometimes questions are asked simply by intonation and are, therefore, discernible as such only from context.

שָׁאוּל יִמְלֹךְ עָלֵינוּ Shall Saul reign over us?   (1 Sam 11:12)

b. Much more frequently, questions are introduced by an interrogative particle, which is found in the following forms:

i. Before most consonants it is הֲ.   *signifies a question*

הֲטוֹבָה הִוא אִם־רָעָה
Is it good or bad?   (Num. 13:19)

הֲיֵשׁ לָכֶם אָח

Do you have a brother? (Gen. 43:7)

ii. Before a consonant with the *šĕwā'* it is הֲ.

הַיְדַעְתֶּם אֶת־לָבָן בֶּן־נָחוֹר

Do you know Laban ben-Nahor? (Gen. 29:5)

Note: The interrogative הֲ does *not* call for the doubling of the following radical, as is the case with the definite article. In a few rare instances, however, an anomalous *dāḡēš forte* may appear, even in the letter ר:

הַרְּאִיתֶם הָאִישׁ הָעֹלֶה הַזֶּה

Have you seen this man who was going up? (1 Sam. 17:25)

iii. Before a guttural it is ordinarily הַ.

הַאַתָּה זֶה בְּנִי

Are you indeed my son? (Gen. 27:21)

הַאֶפְרָתִי אַתָּה

Are you an Ephraimite? (Judg. 12:5)

iv. Before a guttural with a ָ it is הֶ.

הֶאָנֹכִי הָרִיתִי אֵת כָּל־הָעָם הַזֶּה

Did I conceive all this people? (Num. 11:12)

c. The personal interrogative pronoun מִי is indeclinable.

מִי אַתָּה בְּנִי	*Who* are you, my son? (Gen. 27:18)
מִי הָאֲנָשִׁים הָאֵלֶּה עִמָּךְ	*Who* are these men with you? (Num. 22:9)
לְמִי־אַתָּה	*To whom* do you belong? (Gen. 32:18)
אֶת־מִי יוֹרֶה	*Whom* will he teach? (Isa. 28:9)

Less frequently, מִי may be translated by the indefinite "whoever, whosoever."

מִי לַיהוָה אֵלָי	*Whoever* is for YHWH (come) unto me! (Exod. 32:26)

A very common usage of מִי in the Hebrew Bible is the idiom מִי־יִתֵּן "if only" or "would that" (lit.: "who would grant").

מִי־יִתֵּן רֹאשִׁי מַיִם	*Would that* my head were water! (Jer. 8:23)
מִי יִתֵּן מִצִּיּוֹן יְשׁוּעוֹת יִשְׂרָאֵל	*If only* the salvation of Israel would come from Zion! (Ps. 53:7)

מִי־יִתֶּן־לִי אֵבֶר כַּיּוֹנָה   *If* I *only* had wings like a dove! (Ps. 55:7)

Occasionally מִי יִתֵּן is abbreviated to just מִי.

d. The impersonal interrogative pronoun מה is found with different vocalizations.

    i.   The form is ordinarily מַה־ plus doubling of the next radical.

        מַה־שְּׁמוֹ

        What is his name? (Exod. 3:13)

    ii.   Before א or ר it is מָה.

        מָה אַתֶּם עֹשִׂים

        What are you doing? (Judg. 18:18)

    iii.   Before ח or ע it is usually מֶה.

        מֶה עָשִׂיתָ

        What have you done? (Gen. 4:10)

    iv.   Before ה it is either מָה or מֶה.

        מָה הַחֲלוֹם הַזֶּה

        What is this dream? (Gen. 37:10)

        מֶה־הָיָה הַדָּבָר

        How was the matter? (2 Sam. 1:4)

e. The prepositions בְּ, כְּ, and לְ may be combined with מַה־:

בַּמֶּה־   in what?   = how?   (מַה־ by itself also "how?")

כַּמֶּה־   like what?   = how many, how much

לַמֶּה־   for what?   = why?   (also לָמָה, לָמֶה, etc.)

f. The interrogative pronouns are frequently strengthened by זֶה, which cannot be rendered in English.

בֶּן־מִי־זֶה הַנַּעַר   *Whose* son is the boy? (1 Sam. 17:55)

מַה־זֶּה הָיָה לְבֶן־קִישׁ   *What* (indeed) happened to the son of Kish? (1 Sam. 10:11)

מַה־זֹּאת עָשִׂיתָ   *What* (indeed) have you done? (Gen. 3:13)

מִי זֶה מֶלֶךְ הַכָּבוֹד   *Who* (really) is the king of glory? (Ps. 24:8)

g. The interrogative adverb אַיֵּה may also take the pronominal suffixes: אַיֶּכָּה "where are you?" אַיּוֹ "where is he?" and אַיָּם "where are they?"

Vocabulary

Nouns:

אוֹת	sign
אַף	(dual אַפַּיִם) anger, nose, face
בַּד	solitude. *Adverb:* לְבַדּוֹ by himself, etc.
גְּבוּל	territory, boundary
כִּסֵּא	(pl. כִּסְאוֹת) throne, chair
עֲבֹדָה	servitude, service
עֵת	time, season
קֶרֶב	midst, inside
שֶׁמֶשׁ	(usually regarded as fs.) sun
תּוֹרָה	instruction, law. *Verb:* יָרָה teach, instruct

Verbs:

בָּכָה	weep
מָשַׁל	govern. Takes object marked by בְּ. *Noun:* מֶמְשָׁלָה governing, government
נָפַל	fall
שָׁכַב	lie down
שָׁמַר	keep, watch. *Noun:* מִשְׁמֶרֶת obligation, custody

Adverbs:

אֵי / אַיֵּה	where
אֵיךְ / אֵיכָה	how
עוֹד	still, yet, once again. Takes pronominal suffixes like מִן
עַתָּה	now
שָׁם	there

Exercise 9

A. Translate the following into Hebrew:
1. this law which you keep
2. who is wise?
3. who is the woman?
4. he who is giving the law to you
5. those are the men who went down to Egypt (מִצְרַיִם)
6. after these things
7. this is the word which YHWH was saying
8. this is the great city
9. who are these wicked men?
10. he is not there
11. there is a covenant between me and you
12. who (indeed) is the king?
13. these are the names
14. we have no money
15. those great cities

B. Translate the following into English:

1. *This is a good man* אִישׁ־טוֹב זֶה (2 Sam. 18:27)
2. הֲלוֹא־זֶה דָוִד (1 Sam. 21:12)
3. *Who is this entering from Edom?* מִי־זֶה בָּא מֵאֱדוֹם (Isa. 63:1)
4. מָה־הַדָּבָר הַזֶּה אֲשֶׁר אַתָּה עֹשֶׂה לָעָם (Exod. 18:14)
5. *This is the great nation* הַגּוֹי הַגָּדוֹל הַזֶּה (Deut. 4:6)
6. מֵהַמִּדְבָּר וְהַלְּבָנוֹן הַזֶּה וְעַד־הַנָּהָר הַגָּדוֹל (Josh. 1:4)
7. *nothing new under the sun* וְאֵין כָּל־חָדָשׁ ³ תַּחַת הַשָּׁמֶשׁ ⁴ (Qoh. 1:9)
8. הֲזֹאת נָעֳמִי (Ruth 1:19)
9. וְלֹא אִתְּכֶם לְבַדְּכֶם אָנֹכִי כֹּרֵת אֶת־הַבְּרִית הַזֹּאת (Deut. 29:13)
10. יֵשׁ־אֱלֹהִים שֹׁפְטִים בָּאָרֶץ (Ps. 58:12)
11. הִנֵּה־אֵלֶּה רְשָׁעִים (Ps. 73:12)
12. עַל־אֵלֶּה אֲנִי בוֹכִיָּה עֵינִי עֵינִי יֹרְדָה מַּיִם (Lam. 1:16)

³ -כָּל anything
⁴ Pausal form. See Appendix C2.

13.	וְהַכְּנַעֲנִי⁵ הַיֹּשֵׁב בָּהָר הַהוּא	(Num. 14:45)
14.	הוּא וְהָאֲנָשִׁים אֲשֶׁר־עִמּוֹ	(Gen. 24:54)
15.	הָאָרֶץ אֲשֶׁר אַתָּה שֹׁכֵב עָלֶיהָ	(Gen. 28:13)
16.	בַּדֶּרֶךְ הַזֶּה אֲשֶׁר אָנֹכִי הוֹלֵךְ	(Gen. 28:20)
17.	הַעוֹד אֲבִיכֶם חַי הֲיֵשׁ לָכֶם אָח	(Gen. 43:7)
18.	יֵשׁ יְהוָה בַּמָּקוֹם הַזֶּה	(Gen. 28:16)
19.	לֹא־טוֹב הַדָּבָר אֲשֶׁר אַתָּה עֹשֶׂה	(Exod. 18:17)
20.	בַּת־מִי אַתְּ	(Gen. 24:23)
21.	יְהוָה מִי כָמוֹךָ	(Ps. 35:10)
22.	וְאִישׁ אֵין בָּאָרֶץ	(Gen. 19:31)
23.	אֵין מֶלֶךְ וְאֵין שָׂר	(Hos. 3:4)
24.	הִנֵּה אָנֹכִי שֹׁלֵחַ מַלְאָךְ לְפָנֶיךָ	(Exod. 23:20)
25.	חֲשֵׁכָה⁶ גְדֹלָה נֹפֶלֶת עָלָיו	(Gen. 15:12)

⁵ כְּנַעֲנִי Canaanite. Here used as collective. The final י is a gentilic ending. See Appendix A.24.

⁶ darkness

LESSON X

1. Genitival Relationships

There is no word in biblical Hebrew that functions in all cases like the English preposition "of." Genitival relationships are most frequently expressed by a juxtaposition of nouns in two states, *construct* and *absolute*. A noun in the construct state is "bound" to the following noun or nouns; its definiteness is dependent on the governing noun at the end of the construction, and its primary stress is often drawn to the governing noun. The absolute state is the free form of the noun standing at the end of the construct chain. In the following example, בֶּן־ and אִישׁ are said to be "in construct," bound to the absolute חַיִל in a genitival expression.

בֶּן־אִישׁ־חַיִל   a son *of* a man *of* valor (1 Chron. 11:22)

Nouns in construct do not, as a rule, take the definite article. Absolute nouns, on the other hand, may or may not take the definite article. The absolute is said to be definite if it is a proper name, has the definite article, or is specified by a possessive suffix. Otherwise it is said to be indefinite.

If several nouns are involved in a construct chain, only the absolute may be definite; all the other nouns must be in construct.

a. A noun construction is indefinite if the absolute is indefinite.

יְהוָה אִישׁ מִלְחָמָה   YHWH is *a* man of war (Exod. 15:3)

b. A noun construction is definite if the absolute is definite.

עֶבֶד אַבְרָהָם   *the* servant of Abraham (Gen. 24:34)

אֲרוֹן הַבְּרִית   *the* ark of the covenant (Josh. 4:9)

יַד־אָבִיו   *the* hand of his father (Gen. 48:17)

If a prefixed preposition is used with the noun in construct, that preposition will be indefinite in form.

בְּבֵית אָבִינוּ   in *the* house of our father (Gen. 31:14)

בְּאֶרֶץ־כְּנַעַן   in *the* land of Canaan (Gen. 13:12)

70

c. Since nouns in construct cannot take the definite article, genitival relationship between an indefinite noun and a definite noun can only be expressed by circumlocution involving the preposition לְ.

מִזְמוֹר לְדָוִד   a psalm (belonging) to David > a psalm of David (Ps. 3:1)

בֵּן לְיִשַׁי   a son (belonging) to Jesse > a son of Jesse (1 Sam. 16:18)

Since proper names are considered definite, the simple juxtaposition of the nouns without the intervening לְ would make the phrases definite. Thus, whereas בֶּן־יִשַׁי in 1 Sam. 20:27 means "*the* son of Jesse," בֵּן לְיִשַׁי in the above example means "*a* son of Jesse." By the same token, עֶבֶד אֲדֹנִי (Dan. 10:17) means "*the* servant of my lord," but עֶבֶד לַאדֹנִי (Gen. 44:33) means "*a* servant of my lord."

2. Nouns in Construct

Since nouns in construct are so closely bound to the absolute, they often lose their primary stress and/or undergo other morphological changes.

The following rules will suffice to account for most of the changes:

a. The vowel ֵ in monosyllabic nouns will frequently become ֶ when that noun is joined to the absolute by means of a *maqqēp̄*. But the construct of such nouns need not have the *maqqēp̄*, nor need the vowel be shortened.

Absolute	Construct	
בֵּן	בֶּן־ (rarely בֵּן־)	son
לֵב	לֶב־ / לֵב־	heart
עֵת	עֶת־ / עֵת־	time

b. The masculine plural and the dual endings are changed to ֵי.

Absolute	Construct	
אֲדֹנִים	אֲדֹנֵי	lords
מַיִם	מֵי	water
עֵינַיִם	עֵינֵי	eyes

c. The feminine ending הָ is changed to ת.

Absolute	Construct	
תּוֹרָה	תּוֹרַת	instruction
שִׂמְחָה	שִׂמְחַת	joy

d. ָ in a final closed syllable becomes ַ.

Absolute	Construct	
יָד	יַד	hand
מַלְאָךְ	מַלְאַךְ	angel

e. In an open syllable (i) *ā* reduces to *šĕwā'*, (ii) *ē* reduces to *šĕwā'*, but (iii) *ō* remains unchanged.

Absolute	Construct	
שָׁלוֹם	שְׁלוֹם	peace
שֵׁמוֹת	שְׁמוֹת	names
כֹּהֵן	כֹּהֵן	priest
דָּמִים	דְּמֵי	blood
דָּבָר	דְּבַר	word
עֵדָה	עֲדַת	congregation

f. Long vowels that have been compensatorily lengthened (e.g., the plural of monosyllabic nouns of geminate roots) cannot be reduced.

Absolute	Construct	
שָׂרִים	שָׂרֵי not שְׂרֵי	rulers
הָרִים	הָרֵי not הֲרֵי	mountains

The long vowel must be preserved since it indicates the geminate root (see IV.4). Occasionally, the geminate root is indicated not by compensatory lengthening of the vowel, but by duplication of the root. Thus, the plural construct of הַר is הָרֵי or הַרְרֵי.

g. Final הָ becomes הֵ.

Absolute	Construct	
מַעֲשֶׂה	מַעֲשֵׂה	deed
מִשְׁתֶּה	מִשְׁתֵּה	banquet

h. Original **aw* contracts to *ô* since the stress is lost (see IV.2.c.ii).

Absolute	Construct	
מָוֶת	מוֹת	death
תָּוֶךְ	תּוֹךְ	midst

i. Original **ay* contracts to *ê* since the stress is lost (see IV.2.c.iii)

Absolute	Construct	
בַּיִת	בֵּית	house
עַיִן	עֵין	eye

j. Segolate plurals retain their **qaṭl*, **qiṭl*, or **quṭl* (*qoṭl*) base in the construct state. Thus, the three different types are clearly discernible in the plural construct, although in the absolute they are not distinguished (see IV.5).

Absolute	Construct	
(i) *qaṭl*		
מְלָכִים	מַלְכֵי	kings
נְפָשׁוֹת	נַפְשׁוֹת	lives
(ii) *qiṭl*		
סְפָרִים	סִפְרֵי	books
(iii) *quṭl* (*qoṭl*)		
חֳדָשִׁים	חָדְשֵׁי	new moons
גְּרָנוֹת	גָּרְנוֹת	threshing floors

k. If the reduction of any vowel results in two vocal *šĕwā*'s in immediate succession, the first *šĕwā'* normally becomes *i*, the second becomes silent. But if the first *šĕwā'* is composite, it becomes the corresponding short vowel.

Absolute	Construct			
דְּבָרִים	דְּבָרֵי* >	דְּבְרֵי* >	דִּבְרֵי	words
אֲנָשִׁים	אֲנָשֵׁי* >	אֲנְשֵׁי* >	אַנְשֵׁי	men
אֲרָצוֹת	אֲרָצוֹת* >	אֲרְצוֹת* >	אַרְצוֹת	lands

l. Absolutes of the *qāṭēl* pattern will become *qĕṭal* in the construct.

Absolute	Construct	
זָקֵן	זְקַן	elder

כָּבֵד	כְּבַד	heavy
עָרֵל	עֲרַל	uncircumcised

It is of utmost importance that the student be able to reconstruct the absolute from the construct forms. Monosyllabic nouns should pose no problem. As for words with more than one syllable, the following summary should prove helpful in the recognition of their construct forms:

	Construct	Absolute
i.	Final יִ	יִם or יָם
ii.	Final תַ	ה ָ
iii.	Final ְ	ָ
iv.	Vocal ְ	ָ or ֻ
v.	Final הֶ	ה ֶ
vi.	קְטַל־	קְטָל־
	קִטְל־	קִטֶל־
	קְטֹל־	קְטֹל־

Study the following examples carefully:

	Construct		Absolute	
	בְּנֵי		בָּנִים	iv, i
years of (שְׁנֵי)		שְׁנַיִם or שָׁנִים	iv, i	*years*
heavens שְׁמֵי		שָׁמַיִם	iv, i	*heavens*
	דְּבַר		דָּבָר	iii, iv
	שְׁמוֹת		שֵׁמוֹת	iv	*names*
	שְׂדֵה		שָׂדֶה	iv, v
	דִּבְרֵי		דְּבָרִים	vi, i
	אַנְשֵׁי		אֲנָשִׁים	vi, i
elders of זִקְנֵי		זְקֵנִים	vi, i	*elders*
	בִּרְכַּת		בְּרָכָה	vi, ii
	אַרְצוֹת		אֲרָצוֹת	vi

A few nouns have construct forms that are unpredictable. The following should be committed to memory.

Absolute	Construct	
אִשָּׁה	אֵשֶׁת	wife
אָב	אֲבִי	father

אָח	אֲחִי	brother
אַחִים	אֲחֵי	brothers
יָרֵךְ	יֶרֶךְ	thigh
כָּתֵף	כֶּתֶף	shoulder
מִלְחָמָה	מִלְחֶמֶת	battle
מִשְׁפָּחָה	מִשְׁפַּחַת	family
עָרִים	עָרֵי	cities
פֶּה	פִּי	mouth
רָאשִׁים	רָאשֵׁי	heads

3. Participles and Adjectives in Construct

a. Since participles may function as substantives, they, too, may be in construct.

יְהוָה צְבָאוֹת יֹשֵׁב הַכְּרֻבִים	YHWH Ṣĕḇā'ôt, who *sits (enthroned)* on the cherubim (2 Sam. 6:2)
בְּנֵי שְׁלֹמֹה וּבֹנֵי חִירוֹם	Solomon's *builders* and Hiram's *builders* (1 Kings 5:32)

b. Adjectives may also be found in construct, although they are not as common as participles.

יְפֵה־תֹאַר וִיפֵה מַרְאֶה	*handsome* of form and *handsome* of appearance (Gen. 39:6)
כְּבַד־פֶּה וּכְבַד לָשׁוֹן אָנֹכִי	I am *heavy* of mouth and *heavy* of tongue (Exod. 4:10)

4. Special Uses of the Construct Chain

a. Construct noun with explicative absolute.

עֲצֵי־גֹפֶר	wood of gopher = gopher wood (Gen. 6:14)
בְּרִית עוֹלָם	covenant of eternity = eternal covenant (Gen. 9:16)
אֲרוֹן עֻזֶּךָ	the ark of your might = your mighty ark (Ps. 132:8)

b. The superlative may be expressed simply by making an adjective definite (e.g., הַקָּטֹן "the youngest," הַטּוֹב "the best") or by means of a construct chain.

שִׁיר הַשִּׁירִים   the song of songs = the best song
(Song 1:1)

5. Forms and Usage of כֹּל

a. The word כֹּל (any, all, each, every) may appear in three forms:

- i. Independent form, כֹּל;
- ii. A form attached to the following noun by a *maqqēp*, כָּל־ (*kol–*, not *kāl*); and
- iii. A form with pronominal suffix, כָּל־.

b. The precise translation of כֹּל is dependent on the definiteness of the noun it qualifies.

i. With a definite noun it is usually translated as "all" or "the whole."

כִּי כָל־הָעֵדָה כֻּלָּם קְדֹשִׁים   for the whole congregation, all of them are holy (Num. 16:3)

כֹּל גּוֹיֵי הָאָרֶץ   all the nations of the earth (Gen. 18:18)

ii. With the indefinite noun it may be translated as "each, every, any."

כֹּל אֲשֶׁר־בָּאָרֶץ   everything that is on earth (Gen. 6:17)

בְּכָל־יוֹם   on each day/every day (Ps. 7:12)

Vocabulary

Nouns:

בֶּגֶד	garment
בָּקָר	cattle
בֹּקֶר	morning
חוֹמָה	wall
חוּץ	street, outside
יַיִן	wine

כֹּל   all
כָּנָף   wing, skirt
מָוֶת   death
מְלָאכָה   (cs. מְלֶאכֶת) mission, work
מַרְאֶה   vision, appearance. *Verb:* רָאָה see
נְאֻם   oracle
סֵפֶר   book, scroll, letter
עֵדָה   congregation
עָפָר   dust
פֶּה   (cs. פִּי) mouth
צֹאן   flock, sheep
צָבָא   (pl. צְבָאוֹת) host
תָּוֶךְ   midst

Exercise 10

A. Give the construct forms of the following:

1.	מָקוֹם	11.	אָב	21.	שָׂרִים
2.	יָם	12.	אַחִים	22.	עֵדָה
3.	שָׂדֶה	13.	תָּוֶךְ	23.	יַיִן
4.	בָּתִּים	14.	שֵׁמוֹת	24.	מַעֲשֶׂה
5.	אֲנָשִׁים	15.	נְפָשׁוֹת	25.	עָפָר
6.	אֲרָצוֹת	16.	פָּנִים	26.	מְלָאכָה
7.	יָד	17.	רָאשִׁים	27.	צְדָקָה
8.	עֲבָדִים	18.	חֲרָבוֹת	28.	בָּנוֹת
9.	עַמִּים	19.	כֵּלִים	29.	נְבִיאִים
10.	חָכְמָה	20.	תּוֹרָה	30.	סְפָרִים

B. Give the absolute forms of the following. If you are uncertain about your answers, check the dictionary.

1.	אֲחֵי	3.	נְשֵׁי	5.	עָרֵי
2.	דִּבְרֵי	4.	מִלְחֶמֶת	6.	אֲחִי

7.	בְּנֵי	15.	יְמֵי	23.	הַרְרֵי
8.	דַּרְכֵי	16.	יְמֵי	24.	שְׁנֵי
9.	כַּנְפֵי	17.	מֵי	25.	שְׁמֵי
10.	דְּמֵי	18.	עֲצֵי	26.	פִּי
11.	צִדְקוֹת	19.	כְּלֵי	27.	אַנְשֵׁי
12.	אֵשֶׁת	20.	אָרְחוֹת	28.	רָאשֵׁי
13.	עַבְדֵּי	21.	חָדְשֵׁי	29.	יֶרֶךְ
14.	מוֹת	22.	אָהֳלֵי	30.	קָדְשֵׁי

C. Translate the following into English:

1. עֶבֶד עֲבָדִים (Gen. 9:25)
2. קֹדֶשׁ הַקֳּדָשִׁים (Num. 4:4)
3. מַעֲשֵׂה יְדֵי אָדָם (Deut. 4:28)
4. אַחֲרֵי מוֹת מֹשֶׁה עֶבֶד יְהוָה (Josh. 1:1)
5. הַר־קָדְשִׁי (Ps. 2:6)
6. יֹשְׁבֵי יְרוּשָׁלַם (Jer. 11:12)
7. עֵץ פְּרִי (Gen. 1:11)
8. מֹשֶׁה אִישׁ הָאֱלֹהִים (Deut. 33:1)
9. עֶבֶד לַאדֹנִי (Gen. 44:33)
10. אֶרֶץ מִצְרַיִם לְפָנֶיךָ הוּא (Gen. 47:6)
11. וְיֶשׁ־בָּם אַנְשֵׁי־חַיִל (Gen. 47:6)
12. הַמִּלְחָמָה חֲזָקָה עַל־פְּלִשְׁתִּים כֹּל יְמֵי שָׁאוּל (1 Sam. 14:52)
13. כִּי יוֹדֵעַ כָּל־שַׁעַר עַמִּי כִּי אֵשֶׁת חַיִל אָתְּ (Ruth 3:11)
14. לִמְלֶאכֶת אֹהֶל מוֹעֵד וּלְכָל־עֲבֹדָתוֹ וּלְבִגְדֵי הַקֹּדֶשׁ (Exod. 35:21)
15. אָנֹכִי אֱלֹהֵי אַבְרָהָם (Gen. 26:24)
16. כֹּל זִקְנֵי אֶרֶץ־מִצְרַיִם (Gen. 50:7)
17. אֵלֶּה שְׁמוֹת בְּנֵי יִשְׂרָאֵל (Exod. 1:1)
18. וּבְנוֹת אַנְשֵׁי הָעִיר יֹצְאֹת (Gen. 24:13)
19. כַּפּוֹת רַגְלֵי הַכֹּהֲנִים נֹשְׂאֵי אֲרוֹן יְהוָה אֲדוֹן כָּל־הָאָרֶץ (Josh. 3:13)
20. יְהוָה צְבָאוֹת אֱלֹהֵי יִשְׂרָאֵל יֹשֵׁב הַכְּרֻבִים (Isa. 37:16)
    אַתָּה־הוּא הָאֱלֹהִים לְבַדְּךָ לְכֹל מַמְלְכוֹת הָאָרֶץ
    אַתָּה עָשִׂיתָ¹ אֶת־הַשָּׁמַיִם וְאֶת־הָאָרֶץ׃

¹ you made

LESSON XI

1. Nouns with Pronominal Suffixes

a. Masculine nouns with suffixes.   *possessive(!) suffixes*

	Singular Noun		Plural Noun	
abs.	סוּס	horse	סוּסִים	horses
cs.	סוּס	horse of	סוּסֵי	horses of
3 ms	סוּסוֹ	his horse	סוּסָיו	his horses
3 fs	סוּסָהּ	her horse	סוּסֶיהָ	her horses
2 ms	סוּסְךָ	your horse	סוּסֶיךָ	your horses
2 fs	סוּסֵךְ	your horse	סוּסַיִךְ	your horses
1 cs	סוּסִי	my horse	סוּסַי	my horses
3 mp	סוּסָם	their horse	סוּסֵיהֶם	their horses
3 fp	סוּסָן	their horse	סוּסֵיהֶן	their horses
2 mp	סוּסְכֶם	your horse	סוּסֵיכֶם	your horses
2 fp	סוּסְכֶן	your horse	סוּסֵיכֶן	your horses
1 cp	סוּסֵנוּ	our horse	סוּסֵינוּ	our horses

Notes:

i. There is no distinction between the suffixes for the dual and the plural nouns; so, יָדָיו "his (two) hands," etc.

ii. A י standing before the suffix characterizes the paradigm for the plural (and dual) noun. Thus, סוּסֵינוּ "our horses," but סוּסֵנוּ "our horse."

79

b. Feminine nouns with suffixes.

	Singular Noun		Plural Noun	
abs.	סוּסָה	mare	סוּסוֹת	mares
cs.	סוּסַת	mare of	סוּסוֹת	mares of
3 ms	סוּסָתוֹ	his mare	סוּסוֹתָיו	his mares
3 fs	סוּסָתָהּ	her mare	סוּסוֹתֶיהָ	her mares
2 ms	סוּסָתְךָ	your mare	סוּסוֹתֶיךָ	your mares
2 fs	סוּסָתֵךְ	your mare	סוּסוֹתַיִךְ	your mares
1 cs	סוּסָתִי	my mare	סוּסוֹתַי	my mares
3 mp	סוּסָתָם	their mare	סוּסוֹתֵיהֶם	their mares
3 fp	סוּסָתָן	their mare	סוּסוֹתֵיהֶן	their mares
2 mp	סוּסַתְכֶם	your mare	סוּסוֹתֵיכֶם	your mares
2 fp	סוּסַתְכֶן	your mare	סוּסוֹתֵיכֶן	your mares
1 cp	סוּסָתֵנוּ	our mare	סוּסוֹתֵינוּ	our mares

Notes:

i.   The הָ ending of feminine nouns becomes תַ , but the ַ vowel is lengthened to ָ before all suffixes except the 2 mp and 2 fp.

ii. The plural nouns will have the feminine plural ending (וֹת-), but they will *also* have the י before the suffixes, as in the masculine plural.

2. Forms of the Noun before Suffixes

a. Words that have more than one syllable will reduce any propretonic ָ or ֵ in an open syllable. If the vowel in the propretonic syllable cannot be reduced, the pretonic vowel should be reduced, provided it is ֵ .

דָּבָר	word	דְּבָרוֹ	his word
אָדוֹן	lord	אֲדֹנִי	my lord
שָׁנָה	year	שְׁנָתוֹ	his year
לֵבָב	heart	לְבָבוֹ	his heart
חֵמָה	anger	חֲמָתוֹ	his anger

גֹּאֵל redeemer   גֹּאֲלוֹ his redeemer

מִשְׁפָּט judgment   מִשְׁפָּטוֹ his judgment

If, as a result of such a reduction, two vocal šĕwā's should stand in immediate succession, the rule of šĕwā' given in X.2.k applies.

דְּבָרֵיהֶם* > דִּבְרֵיהֶם* > דִּבְרֵיהֶם their words

צִדְקָתוֹ* > צִדְקָתוֹ* > צִדְקָתוֹ his righteousness

אַדְמָתוֹ* > אַדְמָתוֹ* > אַדְמָתוֹ his ground

אַנְשֵׁיהֶם* > אֲנְשֵׁיהֶם* > אַנְשֵׁיהֶם their men

The following are some examples of polysyllabic nouns with pronominal suffixes:

Singular Noun

cs.	דְּבַר	חֲצַר	צִדְקַת
3 ms	דְּבָרוֹ	חֲצֵרוֹ	צִדְקָתוֹ
3 fs	דְּבָרָהּ	חֲצֵרָהּ	צִדְקָתָהּ
2 ms	דְּבָרְךָ	חֲצֵרְךָ	צִדְקָתְךָ
2 fs	דְּבָרֵךְ	חֲצֵרֵךְ	צִדְקָתֵךְ
1 cs	דְּבָרִי	חֲצֵרִי	צִדְקָתִי
3 mp	דְּבָרָם	חֲצֵרָם	צִדְקָתָם
3 fp	דְּבָרָן	חֲצֵרָן	צִדְקָתָן
2 mp	דְּבַרְכֶם	חֲצַרְכֶם	צִדְקַתְכֶם
2 fp	דְּבַרְכֶן	חֲצַרְכֶן	צִדְקַתְכֶן
1 cp	דְּבָרֵנוּ	חֲצֵרֵנוּ	צִדְקָתֵנוּ

Plural Noun

cs.	דִּבְרֵי	חַצְרֵי	צִדְקוֹת
3 ms	דְּבָרָיו	חֲצֵרָיו	צִדְקוֹתָיו
3 fs	דְּבָרֶיהָ	חֲצֵרֶיהָ	צִדְקוֹתֶיהָ
2 ms	דְּבָרֶיךָ	חֲצֵרֶיךָ	צִדְקוֹתֶיךָ
2 fs	דְּבָרַיִךְ	חֲצֵרַיִךְ	צִדְקוֹתַיִךְ
1 cs	דְּבָרַי	חֲצֵרַי	צִדְקוֹתַי
3 mp	דִּבְרֵיהֶם	חַצְרֵיהֶם	צִדְקוֹתֵיהֶם

3 fp	דִּבְרֵיהֶן	חַצְרֵיהֶן	צִדְקוֹתֵיהֶן
2 mp	דִּבְרֵיכֶם	חַצְרֵיכֶם	צִדְקוֹתֵיכֶם
2 fp	דִּבְרֵיכֶן	חַצְרֵיכֶן	צִדְקוֹתֵיכֶן
1 cp	דִּבְרֵינוּ	חַצְרֵינוּ	צִדְקוֹתֵינוּ

b. Nouns that were originally *qall, qill,* or *qull* (see IV.4), and those that have become associated with nouns in this group by virtue of the assimilation of a נ radical (i.e., **qanl, *qinl,* and **qunl*), will show gemination when a suffix is added.

Singular Noun

	Qall	Qill	Qull
cs.	עַם	חֵץ	חֹק
3 ms	עַמּוֹ	חִצּוֹ	חֻקּוֹ
3 fs	עַמָּהּ	חִצָּהּ	חֻקָּהּ
2 ms	עַמְּךָ	חִצְּךָ	חֻקְּךָ
2 fs	עַמֵּךְ	חִצֵּךְ	חֻקֵּךְ
1 cs	עַמִּי	חִצִּי	חֻקִּי
3 mp	עַמָּם	חִצָּם	חֻקָּם
3 fp	עַמָּן	חִצָּן	חֻקָּן
2 mp	עַמְּכֶם	חִצְּכֶם	חֻקְּכֶם
2 fp	עַמְּכֶן	חִצְּכֶן	חֻקְּכֶן
1 cp	עַמֵּנוּ	חִצֵּנוּ	חֻקֵּנוּ

Plural Noun

cs.	עַמֵּי	חִצֵּי	חֻקֵּי
3 ms	עַמָּיו	חִצָּיו	חֻקָּיו
3 fs	עַמֶּיהָ	חִצֶּיהָ	חֻקֶּיהָ
2 ms	עַמֶּיךָ	חִצֶּיךָ	חֻקֶּיךָ
2 fs	עַמַּיִךְ	חִצַּיִךְ	חֻקַּיִךְ
1 cs	עַמַּי	חִצַּי	חֻקַּי

3 mp	עַמֵּיהֶם	חִצֵּיהֶם	חֻקֵּיהֶם
3 fp	עַמֵּיהֶן	חִצֵּיהֶם	חֻקֵּיהֶן
2 mp	עַמֵּיכֶם	חִצֵּיכֶם	חֻקֵּיכֶם
2 fp	עַמֵּיכֶן	חִצֵּיכֶן	חֻקֵּיכֶן
1 cp	עַמֵּינוּ	חִצֵּינוּ	חֻקֵּינוּ

c. Nouns that were originally *qaṭl*, *qiṭl*, or *quṭl* will always retain their base forms in the singular with suffixes (see X.2.j). The plural nouns will also have their base forms, but not with the singular suffixes.

Singular Noun

	Qaṭl	*Qiṭl*	*Quṭl*
cs.	מֶלֶךְ	נֶדֶר	חֹדֶשׁ
3 ms	מַלְכּוֹ	נִדְרוֹ	חָדְשׁוֹ
3 fs	מַלְכָּהּ	נִדְרָהּ	חָדְשָׁהּ
2 ms	מַלְכְּךָ	נִדְרְךָ	חָדְשְׁךָ
2 fs	מַלְכֵּךְ	נִדְרֵךְ	חָדְשֵׁךְ
1 cs	מַלְכִּי	נִדְרִי	חָדְשִׁי
3 mp	מַלְכָּם	נִדְרָם	חָדְשָׁם
3 fp	מַלְכָּן	נִדְרָן	חָדְשָׁן
2 mp	מַלְכְּכֶם	נִדְרְכֶם	חָדְשְׁכֶם
2 fp	מַלְכְּכֶן	נִדְרְכֶן	חָדְשְׁכֶן
1 cp	מַלְכֵּנוּ	נִדְרֵנוּ	חָדְשֵׁנוּ

Plural Noun

cs.	מַלְכֵי	נִדְרֵי	חָדְשֵׁי
3 ms	מְלָכָיו	נְדָרָיו	חֲדָשָׁיו
3 fs	מְלָכֶיהָ	נְדָרֶיהָ	חֲדָשֶׁיהָ
2 ms	מְלָכֶיךָ	נְדָרֶיךָ	חֲדָשֶׁיךָ
2 fs	מְלָכַיִךְ	נְדָרַיִךְ	חֲדָשַׁיִךְ
1 cs	מְלָכַי	נְדָרַי	חֲדָשַׁי
3 mp	מַלְכֵיהֶם	נִדְרֵיהֶם	חָדְשֵׁיהֶם

3 fp	מַלְכֵיהֶן	נִדְרֵיהֶן	חָדְשֵׁיהֶן
2 mp	מַלְכֵיכֶם	נִדְרֵיכֶם	חָדְשֵׁיכֶם
2 fp	מַלְכֵיכֶן	נִדְרֵיכֶן	חָדְשֵׁיכֶן
1 cp	מַלְכֵינוּ	נִדְרֵינוּ	חָדְשֵׁינוּ

Akin to these three types are a few penultimately stressed feminine nouns that end in ת ֶ or ת ֶ .

תִּפְאֶרֶת	glory	תִּפְאַרְתּוֹ	his glory
מִשְׁמֶרֶת	obligation	מִשְׁמַרְתּוֹ	his obligation
גְּבֶרֶת	mistress	גְּבִרְתִּי	my mistress
קְטֹרֶת	incense	קְטָרְתִּי	my incense
נְחֹשֶׁת	bronze	נְחָשְׁתִּי	my bronze
		נְחָשְׁתָּם	their bronze

d. Diphthongs in nouns will contract according to the principles given in IV.2.c.ii-iii, thus:

מָוֶת	death	מוֹתוֹ	his death
בַּיִת	house	בֵּיתוֹ	his house

e. There are several noun types that have י or ו as the original third radical of the root.

i. The nouns אָב (father) and אָח (brother) belong to this group. Hence the construct forms אֲבִי and אֲחִי. Together with the noun פֶּה (mouth), whose construct is פִּי, they take the suffixes that differ slightly with those used on nouns ending with consonants.

Singular Noun

cs.	אֲבִי	אֲחִי	פִּי
3 ms	אָבִיו	אָחִיו	פִּיו
	אָבִיהוּ	אָחִיהוּ	פִּיהוּ
3 fs	אָבִיהָ	אָחִיהָ	פִּיהָ
2 ms	אָבִיךְ	אָחִיךְ	פִּיךְ

2 fs	אָבִיךְ	אָחִיךְ	פִּיךָ
1 cs	אָבִי	אָחִי	פִּי
3 mp	אֲבִיהֶם	אֲחִיהֶם	פִּיהֶם
3 fp	אֲבִיהֶן	אֲחִיהֶן	פִּיהֶן
2 mp	אֲבִיכֶם	אֲחִיכֶם	פִּיכֶם
2 fp	אֲבִיכֶן	אֲחִיכֶן	פִּיכֶן
1 cp	אָבִינוּ	אָחִינוּ	פִּינוּ

ii. Nouns that end in הָ will simply lose the הָ ending and take the suffixes regularly (like סוּס), but the 3 ms suffix for the singular noun will almost always be הוּ ֵ instead of וֹ.

מַעֲשֶׂה deed   מַעֲשֵׂהוּ his deed
                     מַעֲשֵׂנוּ our deed
                     מַעֲשֵׂינוּ our deeds

שָׂדֶה field   שָׂדֵהוּ his field
                     שָׂדִי my field
                     שְׂדֹתֵינוּ our fields
                     שָׂדֵינוּ our fields

פָּנִים face   פָּנָיו his face
                     פְּנֵיהֶם their faces

iii. III-*Yōḏ* nouns like חֲצִי (half), פְּרִי (fruit), and עֳנִי (affliction) treat the final י as a consonant whenever the suffix is added. They take the suffixes like those appended to סוּס, not like those with אָב, אָח, and פֶּה. When the suffix is added, the vowel in the first syllable is difficult to predict. The following are the attested forms of the pronominal suffixes with nouns in this group.

Singular Noun

3 ms	חֶצְיוֹ	פִּרְיוֹ	עָנְיוֹ
3 fs	חֶצְיָהּ	פִּרְיָהּ	עָנְיָהּ
2 ms		פִּרְיְךָ	
2 fs		פִּרְיֵךְ	עָנְיֵךְ
1 cs		פִּרְיִי	עָנְיִי

3 mp	חִצֵּיהֶם	פִּרְיָם	עֲנָיָם
3 fp		פִּרְיָן	
2 mp		פִּרְיְכֶם	
1 cp	חִצֵּינוּ		

The alternate פִּרְיֵהֶם (their fruit) and פִּרְיֵהֶן (with 3 fp suffix) are attested, as is the 2 mp suffixal form for שְׁבִיכֶם (your captive).

f. The nouns בֵּן (son) and שֵׁם (name) reduce the stem vowel (ֵ) before the suffix. If, as a result of this reduction, two vocal *šĕwā*'s stand in immediate succession, the rule given in V.2.b.i applies. Thus,

בֵּן son	בְּנוֹ his son
	בִּנְךָ > בְּנְךָ* your son
שֵׁם name	שְׁמוֹ his name
	שִׁמְךָ > שְׁמְךָ* your name

g. The suffixal forms of אִשָּׁה (wife) and בַּת (daughter) are אֵשֶׁת– and בַּת–, respectively. Thus,

אִשָּׁה wife	אִשְׁתּוֹ his wife
בַּת daughter	בִּתּוֹ his daughter

Vocabulary

Nouns:

חֵמָה	heat, rage
חֲצִי	half, middle
חָצֵר	(pl. חֲצֵרוֹת) court
חֹק	(also חֻקָּה) statute
כֹּחַ	strength, power
מִגְדָּל	tower
מִנְחָה	gift, offering
מִצְוָה	(fp מִצְוֺת) commandment

מִשְׁפָּחָה   family, clan

נֶדֶר   vow. *Verb:* נָדַר vow

נַחֲלָה   inheritance

עֹז   strength, might. *Adjective:* עַז strong, mighty

עָנָן   cloud

רֵעַ   friend

רֵעֶה   friend, companion

שֵׁן   (fs) tooth, ivory

תִּפְאֶרֶת   glory, beauty, splendor

Verbs:

חָנָה   camp, encamp. *(Noun:* מַחֲנֶה (mp מַחֲנוֹת ,מַחֲנִים) camp, army

נָטָה   stretch out, extend, spread (pitch a tent). *Nouns:* מַטֶּה rod, staff, tribe; מִטָּה couch, bed

Conjunction

לֵאמֹר   saying (introduces a quote)

Exercise 11

A. Write the following in Hebrew:

1. her nose	11. his wife	21. your (mp) spirit
2. your (ms) seed	12. his wives	22. your cities
3. his camp	13. my daughter	23. my name
4. her garments	14. my people	24. our king
5. his staff	15. our father	25. your (ms) brother
6. your (ms) staff	16. his hands	26. your (ms) brothers
7. her strength	17. his field	27. his men
8. a heavy cloud	18. our deeds	28. their fruit
9. her field	19. my fruit	29. your (ms) son
10. cloud of YHWH	20. his mouth	30. his house

B. Translate the following into English:

1.	רוּחַ חַיִּים בְּאַפָּיו	11.	רוּחַ אַחֶרֶת
2.	בְּגְדֵי תִפְאַרְתֵּךְ	12.	כִּסֵּא־שֵׁן גָּדוֹל
3.	זֶרַע זֶרַע	13.	אֹהֶל מוֹעֵד
4.	זַרְעֲךָ אַחֲרֶיךָ	14.	רוּחַ חָכְמָה
5.	בִּגְדֵי הַקֹּדֶשׁ	15.	מִגְדַּל־עֹז
6.	עֲנָנְךָ עֹמֵד עֲלֵיהֶם	16.	אִמֹּתָם הַיֹּלְדוֹת אֹתָם
7.	בָּתֵּי הַשֵּׁן	17.	כְּמִגְדַּל הַשֵּׁן
8.	רוּחַ אַפֵּינוּ	18.	רֵיחַ בְּגָדָיו
9.	אָבִינוּ זָקֵן	19.	כָּל־אַנְשֵׁי בֵיתוֹ
10.	אֱלֹהִים אֲבוֹתֵינוּ	20.	כָּל־יְמֵי חַיָּי

C. Translate the following into English:

1.	מִי־יוֹדֵעַ עֹז אַפֶּךָ	(Ps. 90:11)
2.	זֶרַע לַזֹּרֵעַ וְלֶחֶם לָאֹכֵל	(Isa. 55:10)
3.	אַפֵּךְ כְּמִגְדַּל הַלְּבָנוֹן	(Song 7:5)
4.	מִפִּיךָ וּמִפִּי זַרְעֲךָ וּמִפִּי זֶרַע זַרְעֲךָ	(Isa. 59:21)
5.	וְחַסְדְּכֶם כַּעֲנַן־בֹּקֶר	(Hos. 6:4)
6.	אֵין־כָּמוֹךָ בָאֱלֹהִים אֲדֹנָי וְאֵין כְּמַעֲשֶׂיךָ	(Ps. 86:8)
7.	כִּי־טוֹב חַסְדְּךָ מֵחַיִּים	(Ps. 63:4)
8.	אֶל־הַמִּדְבָּר אֲשֶׁר־הוּא חֹנֶה שָׁם הַר הָאֱלֹהִים	(Exod. 18:5)
9.	כִּי־חַסְדְּךָ גָּדוֹל עָלָי	(Ps. 86:13)
10.	מַחֲנֵה אֱלֹהִים זֶה	(Gen. 32:3)
11.	אֵין־נֹטֶה עוֹד אָהֳלִי	(Jer. 10:20)
12.	מִגְדַּל־עֹז שֵׁם יְהוָה	(Prov. 18:10)
13.	זֶה דְּבַר־יְהוָה אֶל־זְרֻבָּבֶל לֵאמֹר	(Zech 4:6)
	לֹא בְחַיִל וְלֹא בְכֹחַ כִּי אִם־בְּרוּחִי	
14.	וְרוּחִי עֹמֶדֶת בְּתוֹכְכֶם	(Hagg. 2:5)
15.	אָנֹכִי יְהוָה עֹשֶׂה כֹּל	(Isa. 44:24)
	נֹטֶה שָׁמַיִם לְבַדִּי	
16.	נֶפֶשׁ בְּנֶפֶשׁ עַיִן בְּעַיִן שֵׁן בְּשֵׁן יָד בְּיָד רֶגֶל בְּרָגֶל	(Deut. 19:21)

17.   הִנְנִי נֹתֵן דְּבָרַי בְּפִיךָ לְאֵשׁ   (Jer. 5:14)

18.   בִּשְׁנַת־מוֹת הַמֶּלֶךְ   (Isa. 6:1)

19.   הִנֵּה אֲרוֹן הַבְּרִית אֲדוֹן כָּל־הָאָרֶץ עֹבֵר לִפְנֵיכֶם   (Josh. 3:11)

20.   כָּל־עַבְדֵי פַרְעֹה זִקְנֵי בֵיתוֹ וְכֹל זִקְנֵי אֶרֶץ־מִצְרָיִם   (Gen. 50:7)

LESSON XII

1. Afformatives of the Perfect

The first full inflection of the finite verb in Hebrew is called the *Perfect*. Gender, number, and person, are, in the perfect, indicated by afformatives.

The same set of afformatives can be found in the perfect verb of all the *binyānîm* (see Appendix B.1)

3 ms	קָטַל	3 cp	‒וּ
3 fs	‒ ָ ה		
2 ms	‒תָּ	2 mp	‒תֶּם
2 fs	‒תְּ	2 fp	‒תֶּן
1 cs	‒תִּי	1 cp	‒נוּ

Notes:

i. Compare the afformatives for the second person with their corresponding forms in the independent personal pronouns (VIII.1).

ii. An archaic afformative ‒תִּי is attested for the 2 fs, as in the 2 fs of the independent personal pronoun, אַתִּי/אַתְּ (see VIII.1.a.iii).

iii. The afformatives of the second person plural are always stressed.

iv. There is no distinction between the masculine and the feminine gender in the third person plural.

2. G Perfect

There are three basic types of G Perfect (sometimes called Qal) verbs: *qāṭal*, *qāṭēl*, and *qāṭōl*. The *qāṭal* type is by far the most dominant of the three. Verbs belonging to this group are typically active-transitive; for example, כָּתַב (write), שָׁמַר (keep), נָתַן (give).

90

The *qāṭēl* and *qāṭōl* types are much smaller groups of typically stative-intransitive verbs: e.g., כָּבֵד (be fat, weighty, important), זָקֵן (be old), יָרֵא (be afraid, fearful), קָטֹן (be small). As the 3 ms forms of these types suggest, such verbs are related to the adjectives. Thus, the word כָּבֵד in the phrase הוּא כָּבֵד may be considered a stative verb or a predicative adjective; one cannot tell by form or syntax which is correct. The 3 fs form כָּבְדָה, on the other hand, can be distinguished from the fs. form of the adjective (כְּבֵדָה).

A rigid semantic categorization of the types must be avoided, however. Many stative verbs which may originally have belonged to the *qāṭēl* group have been assimilated into the *qāṭal* group due to the presence of a guttural in the root. A few others, though originally of the *qāṭal* pattern, are stative verbs. Moreover, the formal distinction between the *qāṭal* and *qāṭēl* types is no longer maintained beyond the 3 ms forms.

The inflection of the G perfect (*qāṭal*) is as follows:

3 ms	קָטַל	3 cp	קָטְלוּ
3 fs	קָטְלָה		
2 ms	קָטַלְתָּ	2 mp	קְטַלְתֶּם
2 fs	קָטַלְתְּ	2 fp	קְטַלְתֶּן
1 cs	קָטַלְתִּי	1 cp	קָטַלְנוּ

The inflection of the G perfect of שָׁמַר (keep), כָּבֵד (be heavy), and קָטֹן (be small) are as follows:

	qāṭal	*qāṭēl*	*qāṭōl*
3 ms	שָׁמַר	כָּבֵד	קָטֹן
3 fs	שָׁמְרָה	כָּבְדָה	קָטְנָה
2 ms	שָׁמַרְתָּ	כָּבַדְתָּ	קָטֹנְתָּ
2 fs	שָׁמַרְתְּ	כָּבַדְתְּ	קָטֹנְתְּ
1 cs	שָׁמַרְתִּי	כָּבַדְתִּי	קָטֹנְתִּי
3 cp	שָׁמְרוּ	כָּבְדוּ	קָטְנוּ

2 mp	שְׁמַרְתֶּם	כְּבַדְתֶּם	קְטָנְתֶּם
2 fp	שְׁמַרְתֶּן	כְּבַדְתֶּן	קְטָנְתֶּן
1 cp	שְׁמַרְנוּ	כְּבַדְנוּ	קָטֹנוּ

Notes:

i. The original characteristic vowel in the *qāṭēl* perfect is preserved only in the 3 ms; elsewhere the forms cannot be distinguished from the *qāṭal* perfect.

ii. The *qāṭōl* type preserves the characteristic vowel whenever the second syllable is stressed. In the 2 mp and 2 fp forms, the vowel is shortened (thus, *qĕṭontem* and *qĕṭonten*).

iii. If the final radical of the stem is the same as the consonant of the suffix, the consonantal Hebrew text frequently shows the consonant only once, but in pointed texts, the doubling in indicated by a *dāḡēš forte*. Thus,

קָטְנוּ they were small   קָטֹנּוּ we were small

נָתְנוּ they gave   נָתַנּוּ we gave

Verbs with final radical ת will show, by a *dāḡēš forte*, the doubling of ת in all afformatives beginning with ת. Thus,

כָּרְתָה she cut   כָּרַתָּ you cut

כָּרַתִּי I cut

The verb נָתַן not only shows doubling in the 1 cp form, the final *nûn* also assimilates whenever it precedes the consonant ת. Thus,

נָתַתָּ>נָתַנְתָּ* you gave

נָתַתִּי>נָתַנְתִּי* I gave

3. The Meaning of the Perfect

a. The perfect is most commonly used to express action that is actually *completed*, or thought by the speaker or writer to be completed. Hence, we usually render the perfect with the English simple past or present perfect.

עָמַדְתָּ לִפְנֵי יְהוָה אֱלֹהֶיךָ   *you stood* before YHWH your God

(Deut. 4:10)

נָתַ֫תִּי בְיָדְךָ אֶת־סִיחֹן מֶ֫לֶךְ־   *I have given* into your hand Sihon, the

חֶשְׁבּוֹן הָאֱמֹרִי וְאֶת־אַרְצוֹ   king of Heshbon, the Amorite, and his

land (Deut. 2:24)

b. The perfect of stative verbs may indicate the present state or condition of the subject. In such instances one may translate the perfect by the English present of the verb "to be."

צָֽדְקָה מִמֶּ֫נִּי   *she is* more *righteous* than I (Gen. 38:26)

וַאֲנִי זָקַ֫נְתִּי   *I am old* (Gen. 18:13)

c. The perfect of verbs that concern a subject's attitude, perception, or experience may also be rendered by the English present.

יָדַ֫עְתִּי כִּי־נָתַן יְהוָה לָכֶם   *I know* that YHWH has given the land

אֶת־הָאָ֫רֶץ   to you (Josh. 2:9)

זָכַ֫רְתִּי לָךְ חֶ֫סֶד נְעוּרַ֫יִךְ   *I remember*, regarding you, the devotion of your youth (Jer. 2:2)

אָהַ֫בְתִּי אֶת־אֲדֹנִי אֶת־אִשְׁתִּי   *I love* my master, my wife, and my

וְאֶת־בָּנָי   children (Exod. 21:5)

d. Some verbs suggesting instantaneous action (i.e., action that is perceived as completed as soon as the speaker or author mentioned it) are regularly rendered by the English present tense. Perhaps the best example of this use of the perfect is in the prophetic formula, כֹּה אָמַר יְהוָה "thus *says* YHWH."

כֹּה־אָמַר יְהוָה מְשַׁחְתִּ֫יךָ   thus *says* YHWH, *I (hereby) anoint* you

לְמֶ֫לֶךְ אֶל־יִשְׂרָאֵל   as king over Israel (2 Kings 9:3)

e. In some instances, the certainty of an imminent event in the mind of the speaker is enough to justify the use of the perfect. This usage of the perfect is especially common in prophecies, promises, and threats. In such cases, one should render the Hebrew perfect by the English present, or even future.

נָתַ֫תִּי רוּחִי עָלָיו   *I will put* my spirit upon him (Isa. 42:1)

הֵן גָּוַ֫עְנוּ אָבַ֫דְנוּ כֻּלָּ֫נוּ אָבָ֫דְנוּ   We are doomed, we are ruined, we are all ruined (Num. 17:27)

[handwritten: o.d. — o.i — S — V — emit.]

4. Syntax

a. Normal Word Order

In Hebrew prose, the normal word order in a verbal sentence is as follows:

   i.   *Time Frame.* Any expression of time that places a narrative in a proper context ("then," "now," "at that time," "in those days," "after these events," etc.) will ordinarily come first.

   ii. *Verb.* The verb normally stands before the nominal subject, if any. Apart from expressions of time, the verb normally stands in the first position. The interrogative pronoun, however, may stand before the verb.

   iii. *Subject.* Since the subject of a verb is often indicated in the verb itself, it is possible that neither noun nor independent pronoun may be stated. When a nominal subject is explicitly named, however, it ordinarily comes after the verb.

   iv. *Indirect Object.* When the indirect object (usually indicated by the prepositions לְ or אֶל־) is involved, it usually comes after the subject but occasionally before it.

   v.   *Direct Object.* When there is a direct object, it will normally come after the verb and after the indirect object, if any.

Study the following examples carefully:

	Word Order
אָז שָׁמַע הַמֶּלֶךְ אֲלֵיהֶם	i, ii, iii, iv
then the king listened to them (2 Chron. 24:17)	
נָתַן יְהוָה לָכֶם אֶת־הָאָרֶץ	ii, iii, iv, v
YHWH has given you the land (Josh. 2:9)	
אַחַר זֶה שָׁלַח סַנְחֵרִיב מֶלֶךְ־אַשּׁוּר עֲבָדָיו	i,ii,iii,v
after this, Sennacherib, the king of Assyria, sent his servants (2 Chron. 32:9)	
נָתַן יְהוָה אֵלַי אֶת־שְׁנֵי לֻחֹת הָאֲבָנִים	ii, iii, iv, v
YHWH gave the two stone tablets to me (Deut. 9:11)	

b. Disrupted Word Order

Although the rules for proper word order are not strictly adhered to in every instance, they do provide a norm. A "normal" word order may be disrupted for various reasons. If the conjunction וְ is involved in this "disruption," and it stands before a word that is not a verb, that ‌וֹ is likely to be *disjunctive*, and may be translated "but," "now," or the like.

i. When a *new subject* is introduced, the normal order of verb-subject may be reversed.

וְהָאָדָם יָדַע אֶת־חַוָּה אִשְׁתּוֹ

Now Adam knew Eve, his wife (Gen. 4:1)

ii. A redundant independent personal pronoun is frequently put before a verb, particularly in *parenthetical comments.*

וְהֵם לֹא יָדְעוּ כִּי שֹׁמֵעַ יוֹסֵף

now they did not know that Joseph was listening (Gen. 42:23)

iii. Sometimes the normal word order is disrupted for *emphasis.*

אֹתוֹ אָהַב אֲבִיהֶם מִכָּל־אֶחָיו

their father loved *him* above all his brothers (Gen. 37:4)

וְהוּא עָבַר לִפְנֵיהֶם

Now he *himself* crossed over before them (Gen. 33:3)

iv. Sometimes the word order is intended to highlight *contrast.*

וְאָבִיו שָׁמַר אֶת־הַדָּבָר

but his father kept the matter (to himself) (Gen. 37:11)

וְלוֹט יָשַׁב בְּעָרֵי הַכִּכָּר

but Lot dwelled in the cities of the plain (Gen. 13:12)

c. Agreement of Subject

i. When more than one nominal subject is named *after* a verb, the verb is frequently in the singular.

וּמָשַׁח אֹתוֹ שָׁם צָדוֹק הַכֹּהֵן וְנָתָן הַנָּבִיא

Zadok the priest and Nathan the prophet *anointed* him there (1 Kings 1:34)

ii. Collectives frequently take the plural verb.

וְאַחַר נָסְעוּ הָעָם מֵחֲצֵרוֹת

Later the people *journeyed* from Hazeroth (Num. 12:16)

iii. Nouns that occur in the plural of majesty (e.g., אֱלֹהִים, אֲדֹנִים)
take the singular verb.

בָּרָא אֱלֹהִים אֵת הַשָּׁמַיִם וְאֵת הָאָרֶץ

God *created* the heaven and the earth (Gen. 1:1)

5. Negation of Finite Verbs

Finite verbs are negated by the adverb לֹא placed before the verb.

לֹא שָׁמַעְתָּ בְּקוֹל יְהוָה אֱלֹהֶיךָ

you did *not* obey the voice of YHWH your God (Deut. 28:45)

6. The Directive ָה

To indicate direction, Hebrew frequently uses a *unaccented* final ָה
appended to the common noun (with or without the definite article) or
proper noun. When the noun receives the directive ָה, it may be vocalized slightly differently:

a. Common Nouns

בַּיִת	house	הַבַּיְתָה/בַּיְתָה	to the house
אֶרֶץ	land	אַרְצָה	to the land
הַר	mountain	הָהָרָה/הֶרָה	to the mountain

b. Directions

צָפוֹן	Zaphon, north	צָפוֹנָה	to the north
קֶדֶם	front, east	קֵדְמָה	to the east
יָם	sea, west	יָמָּה	to the west
תֵּימָן	Teman, south	תֵּימָנָה	to the south

c. Place Names

אַשּׁוּר	Assyria	אַשּׁוּרָה	to Assyria
בָּבֶל	Babel	בָּבֶלָה	to Babylon
נֶגֶב	Negeb	נֶגְבָּה	to the Negeb

d. Adverbs

אָן	where?	אָנָה	whither
שָׁם	there	שָׁמָּה	thither

7. Interrupted Construct Chains

A construct chain may be interrupted by the directive ה ָ , or a pronominal suffix.

אַרְצָה מִצְרַיִם	to the land of Egypt (Exod. 4:20)
בֵּיתָה יוֹסֵף	into the house of Joseph (Gen. 44:14)
בְּרִיתִי שָׁלוֹם	my covenant of peace (Num. 25:12)

Vocabulary

Nouns:

אֶבְיוֹן	poor
אֹיֵב	enemy
מִשְׁכָּן	tabernacle. *Verb:* שָׁכַן dwell
עֳנִי	affliction
פַּר	bull
צָפוֹן	north, Zaphon
קֶדֶם	east, antiquity, front
רֹעֶה	shepherd. *Verb:* רָעָה tend, feed
שָׁכֵן	neighbor
תֵּימָן	south, Teman

Verbs:

זָכַר	remember. *Noun:* זִכָּרוֹן memorial
חָזַק	prevail, be(come) strong
יָרֵא	fear, be afraid
כָּבֵד	be(come) weighty, important, rich
כָּתַב	write
לָקַח	receive, take
מָשַׁח	anoint. *Noun:* מָשִׁיחַ anointed
עָזַב	abandon, leave, forsake

Adverbs:

אָז	then, at that time
אַיִן	where
אָן	where
כֹּה	thus, here

Exercise 12

A. Write the following G perfect forms in Hebrew:

1. 3 fs of זכר	11. 2 ms of שמר
2. 2 fs of שמר	12. 1 cs of זקן
3. 1 cp of זכר	13. 1 cs of כרת
4. 1 cp of נתן	14. 3 cp of נתן
5. 2 ms of כרת	15. 3 fs of כבד
6. 1 cp of כתב	16. 2 mp of זכר
7. 1 cs of לקח	17. 3 cp of מלך
8. 3 cp of משח	18. 3 fs of חזק
9. 1 cs of כתב	19. 1 cs of הלך
10. 3 cp of לקח	20. 1 cs of נתן

B. Translate the following into English:

1.	אָהַבְתִּי אֶתְכֶם אָמַר יְהוָה	(Mal. 1:2)
2.	הוּא הַלֶּחֶם אֲשֶׁר נָתַן יְהוָה לָכֶם	(Exod. 16:15)
3.	אָכְלוּ מַצּוֹת בְּתוֹךְ אֲחֵיהֶם	(2 Kings 23:9)
4.	כִּי אָמַרְתֶּם כָּרַתְנוּ בְרִית אֶת־מָוֶת	(Isa. 28:15)
5.	הִנֵּה שָׁמַעְתִּי בְקֹלְכֶם לְכֹל אֲשֶׁר־אֲמַרְתֶּם לִי	(1 Sam. 12:1)
6.	הֲזֶה אֲחִיכֶם הַקָּטֹן אֲשֶׁר אֲמַרְתֶּם אֵלָי	(Gen. 43:29)
7.	זָכַר לְעוֹלָם בְּרִיתוֹ	(Ps. 105:8)
8.	עַתָּה יָדַעְתִּי כִּי־יְרֵא אֱלֹהִים	(Gen. 22:12)
9.	זָכְרָה יְרוּשָׁלַיִם יְמֵי עָנְיָהּ	(Lam. 1:7)
10.	הִנֵּה נָתַתִּי לְךָ לֵב חָכָם	(1 Kings 3:12)

11. לֹא אָכַל לֶחֶם כָּל־הַיּוֹם וְכָל־הַלָּיְלָה (1 Sam. 28:20)

12. שָׁמַע כִּי אֹתוֹ מָשְׁחוּ לְמֶלֶךְ תַּחַת אָבִיהוּ (1 Kings 5:15)

13. אָז יָדַע מָנוֹחַ כִּי־מַלְאַךְ יְהוָה הוּא (Judg. 13:21)

14. הִנֵּה יָרְדָה אֵשׁ מִן־הַשָּׁמַיִם (2 Kings 1:14)

15. הֲשָׁלוֹם אֲבִיכֶם הַזָּקֵן אֲשֶׁר אֲמַרְתֶּם הַעוֹדֶנּוּ חָי (Gen. 43:27)

16. מָלַךְ אֱלֹהִים עַל־גּוֹיִם אֱלֹהִים יָשַׁב עַל־כִּסֵּא (Ps. 47:9)
קָדְשׁוֹ:

17. זָקַנְתִּי לֹא יָדַעְתִּי יוֹם מוֹתִי (Gen. 27:2)

18. וְאֵלֶּה שְׁמוֹת בְּנֵי יִשְׂרָאֵל הַבָּאִים מִצְרָיְמָה אֵת (Exod. 1:1)
יַעֲקֹב

19. כִּי־כָבְדָה הָעֲבֹדָה עַל־הָעָם הַזֶּה (Neh. 5:18)

20. אֶל־הַמָּקוֹם אֲשֶׁר־עָמַד שָׁם אֶת־פְּנֵי יְהוָה (Gen. 19:27)

21. אָהַבְתָּ רָע מִטּוֹב (Ps. 52:5)

22. בַּיּוֹם הַהוּא כָּרַת יְהוָה אֶת־אַבְרָם בְּרִית לֵאמֹר (Gen. 15:18)
לְזַרְעֲךָ נָתַתִּי אֶת־הָאָרֶץ הַזֹּאת מִנְּהַר מִצְרַיִם
עַד־הַנָּהָר הַגָּדֹל נְהַר־פְּרָת:

LESSON XIII

1. G Perfect of I-Guttural Verbs

a. Whenever a *šĕwā'* is expected under a first radical that is a guttural, we get ֲ instead of ְ. In the G perfect, this situation occurs only in the 2 mp and 2 fp. Thus,

2 mp	עֲמַדְתֶּם	not	עְמַדְתֶּם*
2 fp	עֲמַדְתֶּן	not	עְמַדְתֶּן*

b. The inflection of the G perfect of עָמַד (stand) is as follows:

3 ms	עָמַד	3 cp	עָמְדוּ
3 fs	עָמְדָה		
2 ms	עָמַדְתָּ	2 mp	עֲמַדְתֶּם
2 fs	עָמַדְתְּ	2 fp	עֲמַדְתֶּן
1 cs	עָמַדְתִּי	1 cp	עָמַדְנוּ

c. The verbs הָיָה (be, become) and חָיָה (live) always have ֱ instead of ֲ in the 2 mp and 2 fp forms. See 5.c below.

2. G Perfect of II-Guttural Verbs

a. Whenever a vocal *šĕwā'* is expected under a *second* radical that is a guttural, we get ֲ instead of ְ. Thus,

3 fs	בָּחֲרָה	not	בָּחְרָה*
3 cp	בָּחֲרוּ	not	בָּחְרוּ*

b. The inflection of the G perfect of בָּחַר (choose) is as follows:

3 ms	כָּחַר	3 cp	כָּחֲרוּ
3 fs	כָּחֲרָה		
2 ms	כָּחַרְתָּ	2 mp	כְּחַרְתֶּם
2 fs	כָּחַרְתְּ	2 fp	כְּחַרְתֶּן
1 cs	כָּחַרְתִּי	1 cp	כָּחַרְנוּ

3. G Perfect of III-ה, ח, and ע Verbs

a. Perfect verbs of this type behave as strong verbs do—even to the extent of retaining the silent šĕwā' under the guttural. The only exception is the unique form in the 2 fs, where we have שָׁמַעַתְּ instead of *שָׁמְעַתְּ.

b. The inflection of the G perfect of שָׁמַע (hear) is as follows:

3 ms	שָׁמַע	3 cp	שָׁמְעוּ
3 fs	שָׁמְעָה		
2 ms	שָׁמַעְתָּ	2 mp	שְׁמַעְתֶּם
2 fs	שָׁמַעַתְּ	2 fp	שְׁמַעְתֶּן
1 cs	שָׁמַעְתִּי	1 cp	שָׁמַעְנוּ

4. G Perfect of III-א Verbs

a. Since א normally quiesces whenever it closes a syllable, any short vowel preceding it is lengthened, and the second person suffix is spirantized.

b. The inflection of the G perfect of מָצָא (find) is as follows:

3 ms	מָצָא	3 cp	מָצְאוּ
3 fs	מָצְאָה		
2 ms	מָצָאתָ	2 mp	מְצָאתֶם
2 fs	מָצָאת	2 fp	מְצָאתֶן
1 cs	מָצָאתִי	1 cp	מָצָאנוּ

Note: The 3 fs form of קָרָא (call) in one instance is קָרָאת. For a second root קָרָה/קָרָא (encounter), the 3 fs form is always קָרָאת.

c. In verbs like מָלֵא (be full), the ֵ (being already long) is retained; otherwise such verbs are inflected like מָצָא. Thus, מָלֵאתִי, מָלֵאתָ, etc.

d. Occasionally, the א is omitted in spelling: מָצָתִי, מָצָאתִי for מָלֵתִי, and so forth. This is true not only in the G perfect, but also elsewhere.

5. G Perfect of III-ה Verbs

a. As we have previously noted, most verbs listed in the dictionaries and grammars as III-ה did not originally have ה as the third radical (IV.2.c.iv); those that did are, in this grammar, always designated III-ה. III-ה verbs are mostly original III-*Yōd*, or are treated as such, although there are isolated examples of III-*Wāw* forms. In the perfect, all such verbs are characterized by the presence of the original third radical י in the first and second person forms.

b. The inflection of the G perfect of גָּלָה (uncover) is as follows:

3 ms	גָּלָה	3 cp	גָּלוּ
3 fs	גָּלְתָה		
2 ms	גָּלִיתָ	2 mp	גְּלִיתֶם
2 fs	גָּלִית	2 fp	גְּלִיתֶן
1 cs	גָּלִיתִי	1 cp	גָּלִינוּ

Notes:

i. In the 3 ms form, original *גָּלִי is inexplicably replaced by גָּלָה. The final ה ָ , therefore, is *not* a marker of feminine gender.

ii. Perhaps because of the possible confusion of the 3 ms (with the anomalous ה ָ) with the feminine, the 3 fs form takes an additional feminine marker, ת.

c. The verbs הָיָה (be, become) and חָיָה (live) are at once I-Guttural *and* III-ה; but the vocal *šewā'* expected in the 2 mp and 2 fp forms is not ֲ (as in עֲמַדְתֶּן, עֲמַדְתֶּם) but ֱ . The inflection of הָיָה (be, become), therefore, is as follows:

3 ms	הָיָה	3 cp	הָיוּ
3 fs	הָיְתָה		
2 ms	הָיִיתָ	2 mp	הֱיִיתֶם
2 fs	הָיִית	2 fp	הֱיִיתֶן
1 cs	הָיִיתִי	1 cp	הָיִינוּ

6. G Perfect of II-*Wāw/Yōḏ* Verbs

a. Verbs with II-*Wāw/Yōḏ* show only two radicals in the G perfect.[1] The weak middle radical disappears, so that there is no distinction between II-*Wāw* and II-*Yōḏ* in the transitive verbs.

b. The inflections קוּם (arise), שִׂים (set), and בּוֹא (come, enter) are as follows:

3 ms	קָם	שָׂם	בָּא
3 fs	קָמָה	שָׂמָה	בָּאָה
2 ms	קַמְתָּ	שַׂמְתָּ	בָּאתָ
2 fs	קַמְתְּ	שַׂמְתְּ	בָּאת
1 cs	קַמְתִּי	שַׂמְתִּי	בָּאתִי
3 cp	קָמוּ	שָׂמוּ	בָּאוּ
2 mp	קַמְתֶּם	שַׂמְתֶּם	בָּאתֶם
2 fp	קַמְתֶּן	שַׂמְתֶּן	בָּאתֶן
1 cp	קַמְנוּ	שַׂמְנוּ	בָּאנוּ

Notes:

i. The verb בּוֹא also shows the characteristics of a III-א verb (see 4 above).

ii. There is no formal difference between the 3 ms and the G active participle in ms. The proper understanding of the form will depend on context, although the order in which the form

---

[1] But we have examples of the middle "weak" radical treated as strong, for example, גָּוְעוּ they expired, גָּוַעְנוּ we expired, etc.

appears *may* be instructive. If the form stands *before* a nominal subject, it is more likely to be the perfect 3 ms (see XII.4.a); if it stands *after* the named subject, it is more likely the participle.

iii. The formal difference between the 3 fs perfect (קָמָה) and the G act. ptc. fs. (קָמָה) lies in the accent.

iv. The accent in the 3 cp is on the first syllable. This distinguishes it from the 3 cp of a III-ה verb. Thus, for example, שָׁבוּ (3 cp of שׁוּב) means "they returned," but שָׁבוּ (3 cp of שָׁבָה) means "they captured."

v. The inflections of the G perfect of the statives מוּת (die) and בּושׁ are as follows:

3 ms	מֵת	בֹּשׁ
3 fs	מֵתָה	בֹּושָׁה
2 ms	מַתָּה	בֹּשְׁתָּ
2 fs	מַתְּ	בֹּשְׁתְּ
1 cs	מַתִּי	בֹּשְׁתִּי
3 cp	מֵתוּ	בֹּשׁוּ
2 mp	מַתֶּם	בָּשְׁתֶּם
2 fp	מַתֶּן	בָּשְׁתֶּן
1 cp	מַתְנוּ	בֹּשְׁנוּ

Note: The assimilation of the third radical ת to the ת occurs in the suffix. Thus, מֵתָה, but מַתָּה (*máttā*).

7. Stative Participles

a. The G participle of stative verbs like יָרֵא (be afraid) and מָלֵא (be full) cannot be distinguished from the forms of the adjective. Thus, the inflection of the G (stative) participle of יָרֵא is as follows:

ms	יָרֵא	mp	יְרֵאִים
fs	יְרֵאָה	fp	יְרֵאוֹת

b. The inflection of the G participle of the stative verb מוּת (die) is as follows:

ms	מֵת	mp	מֵתִים
fs	מֵתָה	fp	מֵתוֹת

c. Stative participles are used to indicate on-going situations.

מֶלֶךְ בָּבֶל אֲשֶׁר־אַתֶּם יְרֵאִים מִפָּנָיו   the king of Babylon whose presence you *fear* (Jer. 42:11)

וְשׁוּלָיו מְלֵאִים אֶת־הַהֵיכָל   and his train *filled* the temple (Isa. 6:1)

וְאִם־אַיִן מֵתָה אָנֹכִי   if not, I *will die* (Gen. 30:1)

Stative participles may, of course, also be substantives:

יְרֵא אֱלֹהִים אַתָּה   you are a God fearer (Gen. 22:12)

8. Uses of הָיָה

There is no present tense verb "to be" in Hebrew. Simple predication is accomplished by juxtaposition of words (see VI.4). Existence of someone or something in the present time is expressed by the particle יֵשׁ (IX.3); absence is expressed by the particle אַיִן (IX.4).

a. Although a simple juxtaposition of words may also be adequate to state a past fact, Hebrew properly uses the perfect of the verb הָיָה for it.

עֲבָדִים הָיִינוּ לְפַרְעֹה   we *were* slaves of Pharaoh (Deut. 6:21)

b. To indicate the existence of someone or something in the past, the verb הָיָה is used.

אִישׁ יְהוּדִי הָיָה בְּשׁוּשָׁן   *there was* a Jew in Susa (Esth. 2:5)

c. To indicate the absence of something or someone in the past, the verb הָיָה is simply negated by the negative particle לֹא.

וּבַגּוֹיִם הָרַבִּים לֹא־הָיָה מֶלֶךְ כָּמֹהוּ   among the great nations *there was no* king like him (Neh. 13:26)

d. To indicate possession in a past time, the idiom הָיָה לְ is used:

וּלְכָל־בְּנֵי יִשְׂרָאֵל הָיָה אוֹר בְּמוֹשְׁבֹתָם   but all the Israelites *had* light in their residences (Exod. 10:23)

וְלוֹ־הָיָה בֵן וּשְׁמוֹ שָׁאוּל[2]   and he *had* a son whose name was Saul
(1 Sam. 9:2)

e. הָיָה may also be translated "come," "come to pass," "become," "happen," or the like.

הָיָה דְבַר־יְהוָה אֶל־אַבְרָם   the word of YHWH *came* to Abram
(Gen. 15:1)

מֶה־הָיָה הַדָּבָר בְּנִי   How *did* the matter *go,* my son?
(1 Sam. 4:16)

וְהוּא הָיָה לְאָבֶן   and he *became* as a stone (1 Sam. 25:37)

Vocabulary

Nouns:

אֹרֶךְ   length. *Verb:* אָרַךְ be long

רֹחַב   width, breadth. *Verb:* רָחַב be wide, broad

קוֹמָה   height

Verbs:

בּוֹשׁ   be ashamed. The only participle attested is mp בֹּשִׁים.
Noun: בֹּשֶׁת shame

בָּחַר   choose. Object usually indicated by marker or בְּ

גּוּר   sojourn. *Nouns:* מָגוֹר (mp מְגוּרִים) sojourning place,
sojourning. גֵּר sojourner

הָיָה   be, come to pass, come about, happen

חָטָא   sin. חָטָא לְX "sin against X"

חָיָה   live

מוּת   die

מָלֵא   be full

נָשָׂא   lift up, raise, bear, forgive. *Noun:* נָשִׂיא leader

סוּר   turn aside

[2] For the syntax, see XXX.3.

שִׂים   place, put, set

שׁוּב   turn, return, repent

Conjunctions:

אוֹ   or

אִם   if, or, either

Adverbs:

אַךְ   however, surely, indeed

גַּם   also, even. גַּם הוּא "he himself," etc. גַּם . . . גַּם "both . . . and"

Exercise 13

A. Write the following forms in Hebrew:

1. G perf. 3 fs of חזק
2. G perf. 3 fs of בוא
3. G perf. 2 ms of בוא
4. G act. ptc. mp cs. of בוא
5. G perf. 1 cs of גור
6. G perf. 3 fs of היה
7. G perf. 2 ms of היה
8. G act. ptc. mp cs. of גור
9. G act. ptc. fs of בוא
10. G perf. 3 fs of בושׁ
11. G perf. 2 mp of חזק
12. G perf. 3 cp of גור
13. G perf. 2 fs of היה
14. G act. ptc. fs of היה
15. G perf. 1 cs of חטא
16. G perf. 3 cp of מות

17. G perf. 1 cp of מות
18. G perf. 3 cp of היה
19. G perf. 3 cp of בוש
20. G stat. ptc. mp cs. of מות
21. G perf. 3 cp of חטא
22. G perf. 2 ms of חזק
23. G perf. 2 mp of היה
24. G perf. 2 mp of חטא
25. G perf. 2 mp of עלה
26. G perf. 1 cp of עשׂה
27. G perf. 3 cp of קום
28. G perf. 3 cp of ראה
29. G stat. ptc. fs of מות
30. G perf. 1 cp of חטא
31. G perf. 1 cp of בכה
32. G perf. 3 cp of שׁאל
33. G perf. 3 fs of חיה
34. G act. ptc. fs of שׁוב
35. G perf. 3 fs of שׁבה
36. G perf. 1 cs of ראה
37. G perf. 2 mp of שׁוב
38. G perf. 1 cs of מצא
39. G perf. 1 cs of שׁוב
40. G perf. 3 fs of עלה

B. Translate the following into English:

1. אַיֵּה הָאֲנָשִׁים אֲשֶׁר־בָּאוּ אֵלֶיךָ הַלָּיְלָה (Gen. 19:5)

2. בּוֹנֵה יְרוּשָׁלַ͏ִם יְהוָה (Ps. 147:2)

3. בֹּשְׁנוּ מְאֹד כִּי־עָזַבְנוּ אָרֶץ (Jer. 9:18)

4. וְאַבְרָהָם שָׁב לִמְקֹמוֹ (Gen. 18:33)

5. לֹא יָדַעְנוּ מֶה־הָיָה לוֹ (Exod. 32:1)

6.	הֶן־כֹּל רָאֲתָה עֵינִי שָׁמְעָה אָזְנִי	(Job 13:1)
7.	אַתֶּם רְאִיתֶם אֲשֶׁר עָשִׂיתִי לְמִצְרָיִם	(Exod. 19:4)
8.	מַה־זֶּה רוּחֲךָ סָרָה וְאֵינְךָ אֹכֵל לָחֶם׃	(1 Kings 21:5)
9.	הֶהָיְתָה זֹּאת בִּימֵיכֶם וְאִם בִּימֵי אֲבֹתֵיכֶם׃	(Joel 1:2)
10.	וּלְמִיכַל בַּת־שָׁאוּל לֹא־הָיָה לָהּ יָלֶד עַד יוֹם	(2 Sam. 6:23)
	מוֹתָהּ׃	
11.	וְרוּחַ יְהוָה סָרָה מֵעִם שָׁאוּל	(1 Sam. 16:14)
12.	וְזֹאת הַתּוֹרָה אֲשֶׁר־שָׂם מֹשֶׁה לִפְנֵי בְּנֵי יִשְׂרָאֵל׃	(Deut. 4:44)
13.	עֲבָדִים הָיִינוּ לְפַרְעֹה בְּמִצְרָיִם	(Deut. 6:21)
14.	אֲדֹנִי שָׁאַל אֶת־עֲבָדָיו לֵאמֹר הֲיֵשׁ־לָכֶם אָב	(Gen. 44:19)
	אוֹ־אָח׃	
15.	עַל נַהֲרוֹת בָּבֶל שָׁם יָשַׁבְנוּ גַּם־בָּכִינוּ	(Ps. 137:1)
16.	מֶה־עָשִׂיתָ לָּנוּ וּמֶה־חָטָאתִי לָךְ	(Gen. 20:9)
17.	כִּי יָדַע עַבְדְּךָ כִּי אֲנִי חָטָאתִי וְהִנֵּה־בָאתִי הַיּוֹם	(2 Sam. 19:21)
18.	נָשְׂאוּ נְהָרוֹת יְהוָה נָשְׂאוּ נְהָרוֹת קוֹלָם	(Ps. 93:3)
19.	כֹּל אֲשֶׁר הָיָה לְשָׁאוּל וּלְכָל־בֵּיתוֹ נָתַתִּי	(2 Sam. 9:9)
	לְבֶן־אֲדֹנֶיךָ׃	
20.	וְאַתֶּם יְדַעְתֶּם אֶת־נֶפֶשׁ הַגֵּר כִּי־גֵרִים הֱיִיתֶם	(Exod. 23:9)
	בְּאֶרֶץ מִצְרָיִם׃	
21.	וְלֹא־קָם נָבִיא עוֹד בְּיִשְׂרָאֵל כְּמֹשֶׁה אֲשֶׁר יְדָעוֹ[3]	(Deut. 34:10)
	יְהוָה פָּנִים אֶל־פָּנִים׃	
22.	וְעַתָּה הִנֵּה הַמֶּלֶךְ אֲשֶׁר בְּחַרְתֶּם אֲשֶׁר שְׁאֶלְתֶּם[4]	(1 Sam. 12:13)
	וְהִנֵּה נָתַן יְהוָה עֲלֵיכֶם מֶלֶךְ׃	
23.	אִישׁ הָיָה בְאֶרֶץ־עוּץ אִיּוֹב שְׁמוֹ וְהָיָה הָאִישׁ	(Job 1:1)
	הַהוּא תָּם[5] וְיָשָׁר וִירֵא אֱלֹהִים וְסָר מֵרָע׃	

---

[3] יָדַע אֹתוֹ = יְדָעוֹ

[4] An alternate form of שְׁאֶלְתֶּם

[5] blameless

24.   וַיֹּאמֶר⁶ יְהוָה אֶל־הַשָּׂטָן הֲשַׂמְתָּ לִבְּךָ עַל־עַבְדִּי   (Job 1:8)
אִיּוֹב כִּי אֵין כָּמֹהוּ בָּאָרֶץ אִישׁ תָּם⁵ וְיָשָׁר
יְרֵא אֱלֹהִים וְסָר מֵרָע:

25.   וְכָמֹהוּ לֹא־הָיָה לְפָנָיו מֶלֶךְ אֲשֶׁר־שָׁב אֶל־יְהוָה   (2 Kings 23:25)
בְּכָל־לְבָבוֹ וּבְכָל־נַפְשׁוֹ וּבְכָל־מְאֹדוֹ כְּכֹל תּוֹרַת
מֹשֶׁה וְאַחֲרָיו לֹא־קָם כָּמֹהוּ:

26.   אַךְ בַּת־פַּרְעֹה עָלְתָה מֵעִיר דָּוִד אֶל־בֵּיתָהּ   (1 Kings 9:24)
אֲשֶׁר בָּנָה־לָהּ

27.   אָנֹכִי עֹמֵד בֵּין־יְהוָה וּבֵינֵיכֶם בָּעֵת הַהִוא   (Deut. 5:5)
לְהַגִּיד⁷ לָכֶם אֶת־דְּבַר יְהוָה כִּי יְרֵאתֶם מִפְּנֵי
הָאֵשׁ וְלֹא־עֲלִיתֶם בָּהָר

28.   וַאֲנִי זֹאת בְּרִיתִי אוֹתָם אָמַר יְהוָה רוּחִי אֲשֶׁר   (Isa. 59:21)
עָלֶיךָ וּדְבָרַי אֲשֶׁר־שַׂמְתִּי בְּפִיךָ לֹא־יָמוּשׁוּ⁸
מִפִּיךָ וּמִפִּי זַרְעֲךָ וּמִפִּי זֶרַע זַרְעֲךָ
אָמַר יְהוָה מֵעַתָּה וְעַד־עוֹלָם:

---

⁶ and he said
⁷ to tell
⁸ shall not depart

LESSON XIV

1. D Perfect

a. The D *binyān* is characterized by the doubling of the second radical. Unlike the perfect in G, where we have three classes (*qāṭal*, *qāṭēl*, *qāṭōl*), there is only one class in D. The vowel under the first radical of the root is *i* in the perfect, but elsewhere it is always *a* (see Appendix B.1).

b. The D perfect of קטל is inflected as follows:

3 ms	קִטֵּל	3 cp	קִטְּלוּ
3 fs	קִטְּלָה		
2 ms	קִטַּלְתָּ	2 mp	קִטַּלְתֶּם
2 fs	קִטַּלְתְּ	2 fp	קִטַּלְתֶּן
1 cs	קִטַּלְתִּי	1 cp	קִטַּלְנוּ

Notes:

i. The ֵ vowel in the 3 ms is typical of the D *binyān*, but, as in the G perfect of the *qāṭēl* type, this vowel is preserved only in the 3 ms. Moreover, for some verbs the 3 ms form is always קִטַּל (including many that are "strong" — e.g., קִדַּשׁ, לִמַּד, יִסַּר, גִּדַּל), while others (mostly with final ר) frequently have ַ instead of ֵ in the second syllable (e.g., כִּפֶּר, דִּבֶּר).

ii. In a few instances, the doubling of the middle radical is lost when a *šĕwā'* stands under it (cf. V.6); e.g.,

3 fs	בִּקְשָׁה	>	בִּקְּשָׁה
3 cp	בִּקְשׁוּ	>	בִּקְּשׁוּ

2. Meaning of D Verbs

Most D verbs fall into one of five semantic categories, though some defy classification.

111

a. Some verbs are *factitive*—that is, they make transitive verbs that in G are stative or intransitive.   *i.e. with d.o.*

Root		G	D		
טהר	be clean	make clean	=	cleanse
ירא	be afraid	make afraid	=	terrify
קדש	be holy	make holy	=	consecrate
חיה	live	make live	=	sustain, resuscitate

b. Some verbs are *causative*—that is, they cause the action suggested by the G verb.

Root		G	*somewhat* D		
למד	learn	cause to learn	=	teach
מכר	buy	cause to buy *somebody*	=	sell

c. Some verbs are *denominative*—they are derived from nouns.

	Noun		D Verb	
דָּבָר	word	דִּבֶּר	speak
זִמְרָה	song	זִמֵּר	sing
קְטֹרֶת	smoke	קִטֵּר	offer (burn) sacrifice
קִנְאָה	jealousy	קִנֵּא	be jealous
תְּהִלָּה	praise	הִלֵּל	praise, boast

d. Many verbs are *pluralic, iterative,* or *intensive*—that is, they suggest multiple, repeated, or busy action. Here, again, it is best to compare the verbs in G and D.

Root		G	D
הלך	walk	walk around
כתב	write	keep writing
קבר	bury	bury many
שאל	ask	beg
שבר	break	shatter

Not all pluralic, iterative, and intensive verbs have corresponding G forms, however: בקש seek, מאן refuse, שרת serve, minister.

e. A few verbs in D are *declarative*—that is, they concern some kind of proclamation:

נָקִי innocent   נִקָּה declare innocent > exonerate

צַדִּיק righteous   צִדֵּק declare righteous > justify

It must be admitted that one is sometimes unable to fit a D verb in one of these categories; often there is no apparent reason for a verb being in D. Frequently, too, a verb may occur in both G and D with no discernible difference in meaning.

3. D Perfect of II-Guttural and II-ר Verbs

a. Since gutturals and ר cannot be doubled, such verbs will not show any doubling in the second radical. Instead,

    i. א and ר will cause the compensatory lengthening of the preceding ִ to ֵ.

         mi''ēn > מֵאֵן   he refused

         birrak > בֵּרַךְ   he blessed

    ii. ה, ח, and ע will be "virtually doubled."

         mihhar > מִהַר   he hastened

         šihhēt > שִׁחֵת   he ruined

         bi''ēr > בִּעֵר   he burned

b. When a vocal *šĕwā'* is expected under a guttural, one would get ֲ instead of ְ. Even ר will sometimes get ֲ. Thus, the 3 cp for ברך is either בֵּרֲכוּ or בֵּרְכוּ (cf. II.5.b, XIII.2.a).

c. The inflections of the D perfect of מאן (refuse) and מהר (hasten), representing the type with compensatory lengthening and the type with virtual doubling respectively, are as follows:

3 ms	מֵאֵן	מִהַר
3 fs	מֵאֲנָה	מִהֲרָה
2 ms	מֵאַנְתָּ	מִהַרְתָּ
2 fs	מֵאַנְתְּ	מִהַרְתְּ
1 cs	מֵאַנִי	מִהַרְתִּי

3 cp	מֵאֲנוּ	מִהֲרוּ
2 mp	מֵאַנְתֶּם	מִהַרְתֶּם
2 fp	מֵאַנְתֶּן	מִהַרְתֶּן
1 cp	מֵאַ֫נּוּ	מִהַ֫רְנוּ

4. D Perfect of III-א Verbs

Verbs of this type show the expected quiescence of א, the lengthening of the preceding vowel, and the spirantization of the ת of the suffixes (see XIII.4). It should be noted, however, that the original *i* vowel does not become *a*, as it does in other verb types, but remains in the same vowel class, only lengthening to —ֵ.

The inflection of the D perfect of מלא (fill) is as follows:

3 ms	מִלֵּא	3 cp	מִלְּאוּ
3 fs	מִלְּאָה		
2 ms	מִלֵּאתָ	2 mp	מִלֵּאתֶם
2 fs	מִלֵּאת	2 fp	מִלֵּאתֶן
1 cs	מִלֵּאתִי	1 cp	מִלֵּאנוּ

5. D Perfect of III-ה Verbs

Apart from the characteristic doubling of the second radical, and the *i* vowel in the first syllable, the D perfect of III-ה verbs is inflected like its G perfect counterpart (see XIII.5).

The inflection of the D perfect of גלה (uncover) is as follows:

3 ms	גִּלָּה	3 cp	גִּלּוּ
3 fs	גִּלְּתָה		
2 ms	גִּלִּיתָ	2 mp	גִּלִּיתֶם
2 fs	גִּלִּית	2 fp	גִּלִּיתֶן
1 cs	גִּלִּיתִי	1 cp	גִּלִּינוּ

Note: An alternative 1 cs form like גְּלֵיתִי is often found.

6. D of II-*Wāw/Yōḏ* Verbs

Such verbs are rather uncommon in the regular D *binyān*. Verbs that may be in D are usually found in the *qōlēl* and *qilqēl* stems instead (see XXIX.1-2). A few forms are found, however.

> עִוֵּר he blinded
>
> עִוְּדֻנִי they surrounded me

Curiously, the middle radical of קוּם changes from ו to י in the few attested D forms: קִיְּמוּ, קִיֵּם.

7. D Participle

a. The D participle is marked by a prefix -מְ, the characteristic *a* vowel under the first radical, and the doubling of the second radical.

b. The D participle is inflected as follows:

ms	מְקַטֵּל	mp	מְקַטְּלִים
fs	מְקַטֶּלֶת	fp	מְקַטְּלוֹת

The doubling in the second radical may be lost when it is followed by ְ (see 1.b.ii in this lesson).

> מְבַקְשִׁים* > מְבַקְשִׁים *mĕbaqšîm*

c. A synopsis of the forms of the D participles is presented below. The student should review VII.2 if not already thoroughly familiar with the material there.

Synopsis of Forms of the D Participle

Root	ms	mp	fs	fp
קטל	מְקַטֵּל	מְקַטְּלִים	מְקַטֶּלֶת	מְקַטְּלוֹת
מאן	מְמָאֵן	מְמָאֲנִים	מְמָאֶנֶת	מְמָאֲנוֹת
מהר	מְמַהֵר	מְמַהֲרִים	מְמַהֶרֶת	מְמַהֲרוֹת
שלח	מְשַׁלֵּחַ	מְשַׁלְּחִים	מְשַׁלַּחַת	מְשַׁלְּחוֹת
מלא	מְמַלֵּא	מְמַלְּאִים	מְמַלֵּאת	מְמַלְּאוֹת

| מְנֻלּוֹת | מְנֻלָּה | מְנֻלִּים | מְנֻלֶּה | גלה |
| מְיֻלָּדוֹת | מְיֻלֶּדֶת | מְיֻלָּדִים | מְיֻלֵּד | ילד |

Vocabulary

Verbs:

בקש	(D) seek
ברך	(D) bless. *Noun:* בְּרָכָה blessing. G (passive) ptc. בָּרוּךְ blessed
גדל	be great
דבר	(D) speak
הלל	(D) praise, boast. *Noun:* תְּהִלָּה praise, song of praise
כלה	(G) be complete, be finished; (D) complete, finish
כסה	(D) cover, conceal
מאן	(D) refuse
מהר	(D) hurry, hasten
ספר	(G) count, write; (D) recount, relate, tell. *Noun:* מִסְפָּר number. *Idioms:* אֵין מִסְפָּר innumerable, infinite; יֵשׁ מִסְפָּר numerable
פעל	(G) work, perform, accomplish. *Noun:* פֹּעַל deed
צוה	(D) command, charge, appoint
קדש	(G) be holy, consecrated; (D) sanctify, consecrate. *Noun:* מִקְדָּשׁ sanctuary
שרת	(D) serve, minister

Nouns:

בָּשָׂר	flesh
נַחַל	wadi, stream
נְחֹשֶׁת	bronze, copper
עֵמֶק	valley

Adverb:

כֵּן   so, thus, therefore, accordingly

Exercise 14

Translate the following into English:

1.	מַעֲשֵׂה יָדָיו בֵּרַכְתָּ	(Job 1:10)
2.	מְבָרֲכֶיךָ בָרוּךְ	(Num. 24:9)
3.	בִּקֵּשׁ יְהוָה לוֹ אִישׁ כִּלְבָבוֹ	(1 Sam. 13:14)
4.	וַיהוָה בֵּרַךְ אֶת־אֲדֹנִי מְאֹד	(Gen. 24:35)
5.	אָבִיךָ צִוָּה לִפְנֵי מוֹתוֹ	(Gen. 50:16)
6.	חָטָאנוּ כִּי־דִבַּרְנוּ בַיהוָה וָבָךְ	(Num. 21:7)
7.	וְהַנַּעַר הָיָה מְשָׁרֵת אֶת־יְהוָה אֶת־פְּנֵי עֵלִי הַכֹּהֵן	(1 Sam. 2:11)
8.	כִּי־מֵתוּ כָּל־הָאֲנָשִׁים הַמְבַקְשִׁים אֶת־נַפְשֶׁךָ:	(Exod. 4:19)
9.	אַתֶּם רְאִיתֶם כִּי מִן־הַשָּׁמַיִם דִּבַּרְתִּי עִמָּכֶם:	(Exod. 20:22)
10.	זְכָר־נָא ¹ אֶת־הַדָּבָר אֲשֶׁר צִוִּיתָ אֶת־מֹשֶׁה עַבְדְּךָ	(Neh. 1:8)
11.	וְאַחֲרֵי כֵן דִּבְּרוּ אֶחָיו אִתּוֹ:	(Gen. 45:15)
12.	הַשָּׁמַיִם מְסַפְּרִים כְּבוֹד־אֵל	(Ps. 19:2)
13.	כַּאֲשֶׁר צִוָּה יְהוָה אֹתָם כֵּן עָשׂוּ:	(Exod. 7:6)
14.	הֲלֹא־זֶה הַדָּבָר אֲשֶׁר דִּבַּרְנוּ אֵלֶיךָ בְמִצְרַיִם	(Exod. 14:12)
15.	וְהוּא לֹא־אוֹיֵב לוֹ וְלֹא מְבַקֵּשׁ רָעָתוֹ:	(Num. 35:23)
16.	הַאַתָּה הָאִישׁ אֲשֶׁר־דִּבַּרְתָּ אֶל־הָאִשָּׁה	(Judg. 13:11)
17.	בֵּאלֹהִים הִלַּלְנוּ כָל־הַיּוֹם	(Ps. 44:9)
18.	כִּי מִי כָל־בָּשָׂר אֲשֶׁר שָׁמַע קוֹל אֱלֹהִים חַיִּים מְדַבֵּר מִתּוֹךְ־הָאֵשׁ כָּמֹנוּ	(Deut. 5:26)

---

¹ Remember!

19. (1 Kings 10:24) וְכָל־הָאָרֶץ מְבַקְשִׁים אֶת־פְּנֵי שְׁלֹמֹה לִשְׁמֹעַ[2]
 אֶת־חָכְמָתוֹ אֲשֶׁר־נָתַן אֱלֹהִים בְּלִבּוֹ:

20. (2 Sam. 4:8) הִנֵּה־רֹאשׁ אִישׁ־בֹּשֶׁת בֶּן־שָׁאוּל אֹיִבְךָ
 אֲשֶׁר בִּקֵּשׁ אֶת־נַפְשֶׁךָ

21. (Song 3:1) עַל־מִשְׁכָּבִי[3] בַּלֵּילוֹת בִּקַּשְׁתִּי אֵת שֶׁאָהֲבָה
 נַפְשִׁי בִּקַּשְׁתִּיו[4] וְלֹא מְצָאתִיו[5]:

22. (Qoh. 7:28) אֲשֶׁר עוֹד־בִּקְשָׁה נַפְשִׁי וְלֹא מָצָאתִי אָדָם אֶחָד
 מֵאֶלֶף[6] מָצָאתִי וְאִשָּׁה בְכָל־אֵלֶּה לֹא מָצָאתִי:

23. (Ps. 44:2) אֱלֹהִים בְּאָזְנֵינוּ שָׁמַעְנוּ אֲבוֹתֵינוּ
 סִפְּרוּ־לָנוּ פֹּעַל פָּעַלְתָּ בִימֵיהֶם בִּימֵי קֶדֶם:

24. (Ps. 85:3) נָשָׂאתָ עֲוֹן עַמֶּךָ כִּסִּיתָ כָל־חַטָּאתָם

25. (Deut. 33:1) וְזֹאת הַבְּרָכָה אֲשֶׁר בֵּרַךְ מֹשֶׁה אִישׁ הָאֱלֹהִים
 אֶת־בְּנֵי יִשְׂרָאֵל לִפְנֵי מוֹתוֹ:

26. (Gen. 24:1) וְאַבְרָהָם זָקֵן בָּא בַּיָּמִים[7] וַיהוָה בֵּרַךְ
 אֶת־אַבְרָהָם בַּכֹּל:

27. (Jer. 36:2) כָּל־הַדְּבָרִים אֲשֶׁר־דִּבַּרְתִּי אֵלֶיךָ עַל־יִשְׂרָאֵל
 וְעַל־יְהוּדָה וְעַל־כָּל־הַגּוֹיִם מִיּוֹם דִּבַּרְתִּי
 אֵלֶיךָ מִימֵי יֹאשִׁיָּהוּ וְעַד הַיּוֹם הַזֶּה:

28. (Gen. 18:17) וַיהוָה אָמָר הַמְכַסֶּה אֲנִי מֵאַבְרָהָם אֲשֶׁר
 אֲנִי עֹשֶׂה:

29. (Gen. 27:8) וְעַתָּה בְנִי שְׁמַע[8] בְּקֹלִי לַאֲשֶׁר אֲנִי מְצַוָּה אֹתָךְ:

30. (1 Sam. 20:1) מֶה עָשִׂיתִי מֶה־עֲוֹנִי וּמֶה־חַטָּאתִי לִפְנֵי אָבִיךָ
 כִּי מְבַקֵּשׁ אֶת־נַפְשִׁי:

---

[2] to hear
[3] מִשְׁכָּב bed
[4] בִּקַּשְׁתִּי אֹתוֹ =
[5] מָצָאתִי אֹתוֹ =
[6] אֶחָד מֵאֶלֶף one among a thousand
[7] זָקֵן בָּא בַּיָּמִים *Idiom:* was getting old
[8] hear!

31. (1 Sam. 20:23) וְהַדָּבָר אֲשֶׁר דִּבַּרְנוּ אֲנִי וָאָתָּה הִנֵּה
יְהוָה בֵּינִי וּבֵינְךָ עַד־עוֹלָם:

32. (2 Kings 6:33) עוֹדֶנּוּ מְדַבֵּר עִמָּם וְהִנֵּה הַמַּלְאָךְ יֹרֵד
אֵלָיו וַיֹּאמֶר[9] הִנֵּה־זֹאת הָרָעָה מֵאֵת יְהוָה

33. (1 Kings 1:22) וְהִנֵּה עוֹדֶנָּה מְדַבֶּרֶת עִם־הַמֶּלֶךְ וְנָתָן
הַנָּבִיא בָּא:

34. (2 Sam. 24:10) וַיֹּאמֶר[9] דָּוִד אֶל־יְהוָה חָטָאתִי מְאֹד אֲשֶׁר עָשִׂיתִי

35. (2 Chron. 20:26) כִּי־שָׁם בֵּרֲכוּ אֶת־יְהוָה עַל־כֵּן קָרְאוּ אֶת־שֵׁם
הַמָּקוֹם הַהוּא עֵמֶק בְּרָכָה עַד־הַיּוֹם:

36. (Dan. 9:6) וְלֹא שָׁמַעְנוּ אֶל־עֲבָדֶיךָ הַנְּבִיאִים אֲשֶׁר
דִּבְּרוּ בְּשִׁמְךָ אֶל־מְלָכֵינוּ שָׂרֵינוּ וַאֲבֹתֵינוּ
וְאֶל כָּל־עַם הָאָרֶץ:

37. (Prov. 29:26) רַבִּים מְבַקְשִׁים פְּנֵי־מוֹשֵׁל וּמֵיְהוָה מִשְׁפַּט־אִישׁ:

38. (Ezra 8:22) כִּי־אָמַרְנוּ לַמֶּלֶךְ לֵאמֹר יַד־אֱלֹהֵינוּ
עַל־כָּל־מְבַקְשָׁיו

39. (Jer. 44:30) כֹּה אָמַר יְהוָה הִנְנִי נֹתֵן אֶת־פַּרְעֹה
חָפְרַע מֶלֶךְ־מִצְרַיִם בְּיַד אֹיְבָיו וּבְיַד
מְבַקְשֵׁי נַפְשׁוֹ כַּאֲשֶׁר נָתַתִּי אֶת־צִדְקִיָּהוּ
מֶלֶךְ־יְהוּדָה בְּיַד נְבוּכַדְרֶאאצַּר מֶלֶךְ־בָּבֶל
אֹיְבוֹ וּמְבַקֵּשׁ נַפְשׁוֹ:

40. (1 Kings 8:23-24) וַיֹּאמַר[9] יְהוָה אֱלֹהֵי יִשְׂרָאֵל אֵין־כָּמוֹךָ אֱלֹהִים
בַּשָּׁמַיִם מִמַּעַל וְעַל הָאָרֶץ מִתָּחַת שֹׁמֵר הַבְּרִית
וְהַחֶסֶד לַעֲבָדֶיךָ הַהֹלְכִים לְפָנֶיךָ
בְּכָל־לִבָּם:
אֲשֶׁר שָׁמַרְתָּ לְעַבְדְּךָ דָוִד אָבִי אֵת
אֲשֶׁר־דִּבַּרְתָּ לוֹ וַתְּדַבֵּר[10] בְּפִיךָ וּבְיָדְךָ
מִלֵּאתָ כַּיּוֹם הַזֶּה:

---

[9] and he said
[10] and you spoke

LESSON XV

1. H Perfect

The H *binyān* is characterized by a prefixed or syncopated ה. In the perfect, the ה prefix has become הִ through a complex phonological process. The second vowel, said to be "thematic" for the H *binyān,* was originally *i* but now appears as *i* only in the third person forms; elsewhere it is *a*.

The H perfect of קטל is inflected as follows:

3 ms	הִקְטִיל	3 cp	הִקְטִילוּ
3 fs	הִקְטִילָה		
2 ms	הִקְטַלְתָּ	2 mp	הִקְטַלְתֶּם
2 fs	הִקְטַלְתְּ	2 fp	הִקְטַלְתֶּן
1 cs	הִקְטַלְתִּי	1 cp	הִקְטַלְנוּ

2. Meaning of H Verbs

Most H verbs fall into one of five semantic categories, but others cannot be easily classified.

a. Many verbs in H are *causative* of the corresponding verb in G.

Root	G	H _someboby_	
אכל	eat	cause to eat	= feed
בוא	come	cause to come	= bring
הלך	go	cause to go	= lead
מות	die	cause to die	= kill
ראה	see	cause to see	= show
שוב	return	cause to return	= restore
שמע	hear	cause to hear	= declare

120

הִמְלַכְתָּ אֶת־עַבְדְּךָ תַּחַת דָּוִד אָבִי   you *caused* your servant *to reign* instead of David, my father (1 Kings 3:7)

הִבְטַחְתָּ אֶת־הָעָם הַזֶּה עַל־שָׁקֶר   you *caused* this people *to trust* a lie (Jer. 28:15)

The nature of causative verbs is such that many will take two accusatives.

הֶרְאָה אֹתִי אֱלֹהִים גַּם אֶת־זַרְעֶךָ   God has shown *me* even *your seed* (Gen. 48:11)

מִן־הַשָּׁמַיִם הִשְׁמִיעֲךָ אֶת־קֹלוֹ   from the heavens he caused *you* to hear *his voice* (Deut. 4:36)

The last two examples may also be taken as *permissive* — that is, "he *allowed* me to see your seed," and "he *allowed* you to hear his voice."

b. Some verbs in H are, like many D verbs, also *factitive* — that is, they transitivize verbs that are stative or intransitive in G.

Root	G	H	
גבה	be high	make high	= raise
גדל	be great	make great	= exalt
יבש	be dry	make dry	= dry up
רחב	be wide	make wide	= widen

c. As many D verbs, some H verbs are *denominative.*

Noun		H Verb	
אֹזֶן	ear	הֶאֱזִין	pay attention, listen
יָמִין	right (hand)	הֵימִין	go to the right

d. Some H verbs are related to adjectives but are, even in H, still *intransitive* or *stative.*

Adjective		H Verb	
זָקֵן	old	הִזְקִין	become old
טוֹב	good	הֵיטִיב	do well
רַע	wicked	הֵרַע	act wickedly

Some verbs in this group are, curiously, transitive as well as intransitive.

	Intransitive	Transitive
הֵיטִיב	do well	make (something) good
הֵרַע	act wickedly	bring evil

e. Like some D verbs, a few H verbs are *declarative.*

	Adjective		H Verb
צַדִּיק	righteous	הִצְדִּיק	declare righteous
רָשָׁע	wicked	הִרְשִׁיעַ	declare criminal

There is obviously some semantic overlap between verbs in D and those in H. Hence, some verbs are found in both D and H with no apparent difference in meaning. Other verbs are in H for no discernible reason, and cannot be classified under one of the above categories.

3. H Perfect of I-Guttural Verbs

Whereas the *šĕwā'* under the first radical of the strong verb is silent, it is ָ when the first radical is a guttural. The vowel with the prefixed ה, moreover, is influenced by the ָ, so that it is changed from ִ to ֶ. The inflection of the H perfect of עמד (stand) is as follows:

3 ms	הֶעֱמִיד	3 cp	הֶעֱמִידוּ
3 fs	הֶעֱמִידָה		
2 ms	הֶעֱמַדְתָּ	2 mp	הֶעֱמַדְתֶּם
2 fs	הֶעֱמַדְתְּ	2 fp	הֶעֱמַדְתֶּן
1 cs	הֶעֱמַדְתִּי	1 cp	הֶעֱמַדְנוּ

4. H Perfect of III-ה, ח, ע Verbs

In verbs of this type, the *furtive pátaḥ* appears as expected (II.9) whenever the final ה, ח, or ע stands at the end of the form. In the perfect, this situation occurs only in the 3 ms form.

The inflection of the H perfect of שמע (hear) is as follows:

3 ms	הִשְׁמִיעַ	3 cp	הִשְׁמִיעוּ
3 fs	הִשְׁמִיעָה		
2 ms	הִשְׁמַעְתָּ	2 mp	הִשְׁמַעְתֶּם
2 fs	הִשְׁמַעַתְּ	2 fp	הִשְׁמַעְתֶּן
1 cs	הִשְׁמַעְתִּי	1 cp	הִשְׁמַעְנוּ

5. H Perfect of III-א Verbs

Verbs of this type show the expected quiescence of the א, lengthening of the vowel preceding the א, and spirantization of the ת of the suffix. As in the D *binyān*, the original *i* vowel in the second syllable does not become *a*, but is lengthened to *ē*.

The inflection of the H Perfect of מצא (find) is as follows:

3 ms	הִמְצִיא	3 cp	הִמְצִיאוּ
3 fs	הִמְצִיאָה		
2 ms	הִמְצֵאתָ	2 mp	הִמְצֵאתֶם
2 fs	הִמְצֵאת	2 fp	הִמְצֵאתֶן
1 cs	הִמְצֵאתִי	1 cp	הִמְצֵאנוּ

6. H Perfect of the III-ה Verbs

The inflection of the III-ה perfect is comparable to those of the G and D perfects, except that the second person singular and plural, as well as the 1 cs, have alternate forms with *ê* in the second syllable.

The inflection of the H perfect of גלה is as follows:

uncover

3 ms	הֶגְלָה/הִגְלָה	3 cp	הִגְלוּ
3 fs	הִגְלְתָה		
2 ms	הִגְלִיתָ/הִגְלֵיתָ	2 mp	הִגְלִיתֶם/הִגְלֵיתֶם
2 fs	הִגְלֵית/הִגְלִית	2 fp	הִגְלִיתֶן/הִגְלֵיתֶן
1 cs	הִגְלִיתִי/הִגְלֵיתִי	1 cp	הִגְלִינוּ

Note: The alternate 3 ms form הָגְלָה is actually more common for this root.

7. H Perfect of I-*Nûn* Verbs

The נ is assimilated into the following consonant as expected (IV.2.b).

הִגִּיד > *הִנְגִיד*

הִטָּה > *הִנְטָה*

I-*Nûn* verbs that are also II-Guttural are extremely rare; the attested roots do not show any assimilation—whether virtual or explicit.

נחל	הִנְחַלְתִּי	I bequeathed
נחה	הִנְחַנִי	he led me

The inflection of the H perfect of נגד (tell) is as follows:

3 ms	הִגִּיד	3 cp	הִגִּידוּ
3 fs	הִגִּידָה		
2 ms	הִגַּדְתָּ	2 mp	הִגַּדְתֶּם
2 fs	הִגַּדְתְּ	2 fp	הִגַּדְתֶּן
1 cs	הִגַּדְתִּי	1 cp	הִגַּדְנוּ

8. H Perfect of I-*Wāw* Verbs

a. The *a* vowel of the original causative prefix הַ (see XV.1) forms a diphthong *aw* with the radical ו. But unaccented *aw* as a rule contracts to *ô* (see IV.2.c.ii). Thus, for example, הוֹשִׁיב>הַוְשִׁיב*.

The inflection of ישׁב (original *ושׁב dwell) is as follows:

3 ms	הוֹשִׁיב	3 cp	הוֹשִׁיבוּ
3 fs	הוֹשִׁיבָה		
2 ms	הוֹשַׁבְתָּ	2 mp	הוֹשַׁבְתֶּם
2 fs	הוֹשַׁבְתְּ	2 fp	הוֹשַׁבְתֶּן
1 cs	הוֹשַׁבְתִּי	1 cp	הוֹשַׁבְנוּ

b. The verb הָלַךְ (walk) behaves as if it were *וָלַךְ in all inflections of the H *binyān*. Thus, הוֹלִיךְ, הוֹלִיכָה, etc.

c. A small group of verbs (almost always with צ as the second radical) regularly behave like I-*Nûn* verbs—that is, the initial radical is assimilated. The following verbs are the most important.

יצג	set down	הִצִּיג, הִצִּיגָה, הַצַּגְתָּ, etc.
יצק	pour out	הִצִּיק, הִצִּיקָה, הַצַּקְתָּ, etc.
יצת	kindle	הִצִּית, הִצִּיתָה, הַצַּתָּ, etc.

9. H Perfect of I-*Yōḏ* Verbs

a. The *a* vowel of the original prefix הַ- forms a diphthong with the radical י. But unaccented *ay* contracts to *ê* (see IV.2.c.iii). Thus, *הַיְטִיב > הֵיטִיב.

The inflection of the H perfect of יטב (be good) is as follows:

3 ms	הֵיטִיב	3 cp	הֵיטִיבוּ
3 fs	הֵיטִיבָה		
2 ms	הֵיטַבְתָּ	2 mp	הֵיטַבְתֶּם
2 fs	הֵיטַבְתְּ	2 fp	הֵיטַבְתֶּן
1 cs	הֵיטַבְתִּי	1 cp	הֵיטַבְנוּ

b. Verbs of this type are extremely rare; most verbs listed as I-*Yōḏ* in the dictionaries are original I-*Wāw*. The only genuine I-*Yōḏ* verbs occurring in H are:

Root	**G**	**H**
יטב	please, fare well	treat well, make good
ינק	suck	suckle, nurse
ילל	–not attested–	wail, howl
ימן	–not attested–	go to the right
ישר	be level	level

The verb יבשׁ (be dry) behaves like I-*Yōḏ* in G, but it is like original I-*Wāw* in H.

10. H Perfect of II-*Wāw/Yōḏ* Verbs

There is no distinction between II-*Wāw* and II-*Yōḏ* verbs in the H perfect.

The inflection of the H perfect of קוּם (arise) is as follows:

3 ms	הֵקִים	3 cp	הֵקִימוּ
3 fs	הֵקִימָה		
2 ms	הֲקִימֹותָ	2 mp	הֲקִימֹותֶם
2 fs	הֲקִימֹות	2 fp	הֲקִימֹותֶן
1 cs	הֲקִימֹותִי	1 cp	הֲקִימֹונוּ

Notes:

i. The characteristic –הֵ prefix becomes –הֵ, which, in the second and first person forms reduces to –הֲ. In some instances, however, we may have ֵ instead of ֲ.

ii. A superfluous וֹ precedes every consonantal suffix, thus opening the syllable and causing the spirantization of suffixal ת. Not infrequently, however, the וֹ is omitted.

הֵבֵאתָ	instead of	הֲבִיאֹותָ
הֵבֵאתִי	instead of	הֲבִיאֹותִי
הֲמֵתֶם	instead of	הֲמִיתֹותֶם

11. H Participle

a. H participles are typically marked by a prefixed מַ (*ma–*). The original causative marker *ha–* has apparently been syncopated: that is, **muha–* > *ma–*.

The H participle is inflected as follows:

ms	מַקְטִיל	mp	מַקְטִילִים
fs	מַקְטֶלֶת	fp	מַקְטִילֹות

b. A synopsis of the H participles is presented below:

Root	ms	mp	fs	fp
קטל	מַקְטִיל	מַקְטִילִים	מַקְטֶלֶת	מַקְטִילוֹת
עמד	מַעֲמִיד	מַעֲמִידִים	מַעֲמֶדֶת	מַעֲמִידוֹת
שלח	מַשְׁלִיחַ	מַשְׁלִיחִים	מַשְׁלַחַת	מַשְׁלִיחוֹת
גלה	מַגְלֶה	מַגְלִים	מַגְלָה	מַגְלוֹת
נגד	מַגִּיד	מַגִּידִים	מַגֶּדֶת	מַגִּידוֹת
ישב	מוֹשִׁיב	מוֹשִׁיבִים	מוֹשֶׁבֶת	מוֹשִׁיבוֹת
יטב	מֵיטִיב	מֵיטִיבִים	מֵיטֶבֶת	מֵיטִיבוֹת
קום	מֵקִים	מְקִימִים	מְקִימָה	מְקִימוֹת

Notes:

i. Apart from the II-*Wāw*/*Yōd* verbs, the proper fs participle is of the מַקְטֶלֶת pattern. The fp forms are all regular.

ii. The prefix is -מַ in most H participles, but I-*Wāw* has מוֹ (contracted from מַו*), I-*Yōd* has -מֵי (contracted from מַי*), and II-*Wāw*/*Yōd* has -מֵ which is reduced to -מְ in all forms except the ms.

Vocabulary

Nouns:

בְּכוֹר	first-born
פֶּתַח	door
רֶכֶב	chariotry, *cf.* מֶרְכָּבָה chariot. *Verb:* ride, mount
רָעָב	famine, hunger. *Verb:* רָעֵב be hungry, starve
שֶׁקֶר	deception, falsehood

Verbs:

דרשׁ	inquire, demand
הרג	kill
יטב	(G) please, fare well; (H) make good, treat well

יָרַד	go down, descend
יָשַׁע	(H) save, deliver. *Nouns:* תְּשׁוּעָה ,יֶשַׁע ,יְשׁוּעָה deliverance, salvation
נָגַד	(H) tell, announce, report
נָחַל	inherit, possess. *Cf.* נַחֲלָה possession, inheritance
נָטַע	plant
נָכָה	(H) strike, smite, defeat. *Noun:* מַכָּה blow, strike
נָצַל	(H) rescue, snatch, deliver
צָעַק	cry out. *Noun:* צְעָקָה cry
רָבָה	(G) be(come) great, numerous; (H) multiply, increase. *Adverb:* הַרְבֵּה copiously, abundantly
שָׁחַת	(D, H) ruin, destroy
שָׁלַךְ	(H) throw, cast
שָׁתָה	drink. *Noun:* מִשְׁתֶּה banquet

Exercise 15

1.	אָנֹכִי הִגַּדְתִּי וְהוֹשַׁעְתִּי וְהִשְׁמַעְתִּי	(Isa. 43:12)
2.	וְאֵלֶּה מַלְכֵי הָאָרֶץ אֲשֶׁר הִכּוּ בְנֵי־יִשְׂרָאֵל	(Josh. 12:1)
3.	עַתָּה יָדַעְתִּי כִּי הוֹשִׁיעַ יְהוָה מְשִׁיחוֹ	(Ps. 20:7)
4.	וְלֹא הִגִּיד לְאָבִיו וּלְאִמּוֹ אֵת אֲשֶׁר עָשָׂה:	(Judg. 14:6)
5.	הִגִּיד לְךָ אָדָם מַה־טּוֹב וּמָה־יְהוָה דּוֹרֵשׁ מִמְּךָ	(Mic. 6:8)
6.	וַיהוָה הִשְׁלִיךְ עֲלֵיהֶם אֲבָנִים גְּדֹלוֹת מִן־הַשָּׁמַיִם	(Josh. 10:11)
7.	מַה־זֹּאת עָשִׂיתָ לִּי לָמָּה לֹא־הִגַּדְתָּ לִּי כִּי אִשְׁתְּךָ הִוא:	(Gen. 12:18)
8.	וּלְכָל־הָעָם הִגִּידוּ לֵאמֹר הִנֵּה הַמֶּלֶךְ יוֹשֵׁב בַּשַּׁעַר	(2 Sam. 19:9)
9.	וַיהוָה הִכָּה כָל־בְּכוֹר בְּאֶרֶץ מִצְרַיִם	(Exod. 12:29)
10.	הִגִּידוּ הַשָּׁמַיִם צִדְקוֹ וְרָאוּ כָל־הָעַמִּים כְּבוֹדוֹ:	(Ps. 97:6)

11. (2 Sam. 22:1) וַיְדַבֵּר¹ דָּוִד לַיהוָה אֶת־דִּבְרֵי הַשִּׁירָה² הַזֹּאת

בְּיוֹם³ הִצִּיל יְהוָה אֹתוֹ מִכַּף כָּל־אֹיְבָיו וּמִכַּף שָׁאוּל:

12. (Num. 17:6) אַתֶּם הֲמִתֶּם אֶת־עַם יְהוָה:

13. (Num. 14:3) וְלָמָה יְהוָה מֵבִיא אֹתָנוּ אֶל־הָאָרֶץ הַזֹּאת

14. (Isa. 43:3) כִּי אֲנִי יְהוָה אֱלֹהֶיךָ קְדוֹשׁ יִשְׂרָאֵל מוֹשִׁיעֶךָ

15. (Deut. 7:8) הוֹצִיא יְהוָה אֶתְכֶם בְּיָד חֲזָקָה וַיִּפְדְּךָ⁴

מִבֵּית עֲבָדִים מִיַּד פַּרְעֹה מֶלֶךְ־מִצְרָיִם:

16. (2 Kings 19:12) הַהִצִּילוּ אֹתָם אֱלֹהֵי הַגּוֹיִם אֲשֶׁר שִׁחֲתוּ אֲבוֹתַי

17. (1 Sam. 4:8) אֵלֶּה הֵם הָאֱלֹהִים הַמַּכִּים אֶת־מִצְרַיִם

בְּכָל־מַכָּה בַּמִּדְבָּר:

18. (Jon. 1:9-10) וַיֹּאמֶר⁵ אֲלֵיהֶם עִבְרִי אָנֹכִי וְאֶת־יְהוָה אֱלֹהֵי

הַשָּׁמַיִם אֲנִי יָרֵא אֲשֶׁר־עָשָׂה אֶת־הַיָּם וְאֶת־

הַיַּבָּשָׁה:⁶

וַיִּירְאוּ⁷ הָאֲנָשִׁים יִרְאָה גְדוֹלָה וַיֹּאמְרוּ⁸

אֵלָיו

מַה־זֹּאת עָשִׂיתָ כִּי־יָדְעוּ הָאֲנָשִׁים כִּי־מִלִּפְנֵי

יְהוָה הוּא בֹרֵחַ⁹ כִּי הִגִּיד לָהֶם:

19. (Gen. 9:8-9) וַיֹּאמֶר⁵ אֱלֹהִים אֶל־נֹחַ וְאֶל־בָּנָיו אִתּוֹ לֵאמֹר:

וַאֲנִי הִנְנִי מֵקִים אֶת־בְּרִיתִי אִתְּכֶם

וְאֶת־זַרְעֲכֶם אַחֲרֵיכֶם:

20. (Gen. 44:8) הֵן כֶּסֶף אֲשֶׁר מָצָאנוּ בְּפִי אַמְתְּחֹתֵינוּ¹⁰

הֱשִׁיבֹנוּ אֵלֶיךָ מֵאֶרֶץ כְּנָעַן

21. (Gen. 41:28) הוּא הַדָּבָר אֲשֶׁר דִּבַּרְתִּי אֶל־פַּרְעֹה אֲשֶׁר

הָאֱלֹהִים עֹשֶׂה הֶרְאָה אֶת־פַּרְעֹה:

---

¹ spoke
² שִׁירָה song
³ when
⁴ and he redeemed you
⁵ and he said
⁶ the dry ground
⁷ and they were afraid
⁸ and they said
⁹ ברח flee
¹⁰ our sack

22. (Gen. 9:17) וַיֹּאמֶר⁵ אֱלֹהִים אֶל־נֹחַ זֹאת אוֹת־הַבְּרִית
אֲשֶׁר הֲקִמֹתִי בֵּינִי וּבֵין כָּל־בָּשָׂר אֲשֶׁר
עַל־הָאָרֶץ:

23. (2 Sam. 12:9) אֵת אוּרִיָּה הַחִתִּי הִכִּיתָ בַחֶרֶב וְאֶת־אִשְׁתּוֹ
לָקַחְתָּ לְּךָ לְאִשָּׁה וְאֹתוֹ הָרַגְתָּ בְּחֶרֶב בְּנֵי עַמּוֹן:

24. (1 Kings 3:7) וְעַתָּה יְהוָה אֱלֹהָי אַתָּה הִמְלַכְתָּ אֶת־עַבְדְּךָ
תַּחַת דָּוִד אָבִי וְאָנֹכִי נַעַר קָטֹן

25. (Jer. 2:6) וְלֹא אָמְרוּ אַיֵּה יְהוָה הַמַּעֲלֶה אֹתָנוּ
מֵאֶרֶץ מִצְרָיִם
הַמּוֹלִיךְ אֹתָנוּ בַּמִּדְבָּר

26. (Gen. 19:13) כִּי־מַשְׁחִתִים אֲנַחְנוּ אֶת־הַמָּקוֹם הַזֶּה
כִּי־גָדְלָה צַעֲקָתָם אֶת־פְּנֵי יְהוָה

27. (Deut. 26:10) וְעַתָּה הִנֵּה הֵבֵאתִי אֶת־רֵאשִׁית פְּרִי
הָאֲדָמָה אֲשֶׁר־נָתַתָּה לִּי יְהוָה

28. (Ps. 18:51) מַגְדִּל יְשׁוּעוֹת מַלְכּוֹ וְעֹשֶׂה חֶסֶד לִמְשִׁיחוֹ
לְדָוִד וּלְזַרְעוֹ עַד־עוֹלָם:

29. (Qoh. 2:4) הִגְדַּלְתִּי מַעֲשָׂי בָּנִיתִי לִי בָתִּים נָטַעְתִּי
לִי כְּרָמִים:¹¹

30. (Esth. 8:1) בַּיּוֹם הַהוּא נָתַן הַמֶּלֶךְ אֲחַשְׁוֵרוֹשׁ לְאֶסְתֵּר
הַמַּלְכָּה אֶת־בֵּית הָמָן צֹרֵר¹² הַיְּהוּדִיים
וּמָרְדֳּכַי בָּא לִפְנֵי הַמֶּלֶךְ כִּי־הִגִּידָה אֶסְתֵּר
מָה הוּא־לָהּ:

---

¹¹ כֶּרֶם vineyard
¹² enemy

LESSON XVI

1. Perfect with Object Suffixes

a. In addition to the marker of the definite accusative with pro-nominal suffixes (VIII.3), the pronominal object of a verb may be indicated by an object suffix appended to the verb. These are merely alternate ways of indicating "personal" objects; no difference in meaning may be discerned between the two ways. Thus,

יְדַעְתִּיךָ = יָדַ֫עְתִּי אֹתְךָ I knew you

הִצִּילָם = הִצִּיל אֹתָם he delivered them

b. Since the object suffix tends to draw the accent toward it, the verb form may undergo vowel reduction, first in the propretonic syllable, but otherwise in the pretonic syllable, if that is possible. Neither the propre-tonic nor the pretonic syllable may be reduced, however, if that vowel

    i.   is unchangeably long (i.e., with a *mater*),
   ii. is in a closed syllable,
  iii. has been compensatorily lengthened, or
  iv. stands before a consonant that is virtually doubled.

Any short vowel that stands in an open syllable after the addition of the suffix will be lengthened.

Verb + Suffix			Remarks
יָדַ֫עְתִּי ךָ	>	יְדַעְתִּ֫יךָ	propretonic reduction
עָבַד ךָ	>	עֲבָדְךָ	propretonic reduction
דִּבֶּר וֹ	>	דִּבְּרוֹ	ii, pretonic reduction
בֵּרַךְ וֹ	>	בֵּרְכוֹ	iii, pretonic reduction
בֵּרַךְ ךָ	>	בֵּרַכְךָ	iii, ii, no reduction
שִׁחֵת הָ	>	שִׁחֲתָהּ	iv, pretonic reduction
הִשְׁמִיד וֹ	>	הִשְׁמִידוֹ	ii, i, no reduction

c. There may also be some morphological changes to the affor-matives of the perfect verb before the suffix.

131

    i.   The 3 fs ending הָ , > ת ָ

    ii. The 2 ms ending תָּ- > ת-

    iii. The 2 fs ending תְּ- > תִי-

    iv. The 2 mp ending תֶּם- > תוּ-

    v. The 2 fp ending תֶּן- > תוּ-

d. With the proper vowel reductions and changes to the afformatives, the forms of the G, D, and H perfects (of קְטֹל) before the object suffixes are as follows:

	G	D	H
3 ms	קְטָל-	קִטְּל-	הִקְטִיל-
3 fs	קְטָלַת-	קִטְּלַת-	הִקְטִילַת-
2 ms	קְטַלְתְּ-	קִטַּלְתְּ-	הִקְטַלְתְּ-
2 fs	קְטַלְתִּי-	קִטַּלְתִּי-	הִקְטַלְתִּי-
1 cs	קְטַלְתִּי-	קִטַּלְתִּי-	הִקְטַלְתִּי-
3 cp	קְטָלוּ-	קִטְּלוּ-	הִקְטִילוּ-
2 mp	קְטַלְתּוּ-	קִטַּלְתּוּ-	הִקְטַלְתּוּ-
2 fp	קְטַלְתּוּ-	קִטַּלְתּוּ-	הִקְטַלְתּוּ-
1 cp	קְטַלְנוּ-	קִטַּלְנוּ-	הִקְטַלְנוּ-

Notes:

    i.   The student should take care not to confuse the ת of the 3 fs form with the ת afformative in the second person forms.

    ii. The תִי- ending in the 2 fs form is related to the תִי- ending on the 2 fs independent personal pronoun (VIII.1.a.ii) and, occasionally, on the 2 fs perfect without suffix (XII.1.ii). The 2 fs form is identical to the 1 cs form. One must depend upon the context for the proper translation of the word.

e. The attested object suffixes used with the perfects are as follows:

		I	II	III	IV	V	VI	VII	VIII	IX
		3 ms	3 fs	2 ms	2 fs	1 cs	3 cp	3 fp	2 mp	1 cp
A	3 ms	הוֹ/וֹ ָ	ה ָ	ְךָ	ֵךְ	נִי ֵ	ָם	ָן		נוּ ֵ
B	3 fs	הוֹ/תוּ	תָה	ְךָ	ֵךְ	נִי	ָם			נוּ
C	2 ms	הוֹ/וֹ ָ	ה ָ			נִי ַ	ָם			נוּ ָ
D	2 fs	הוּ	ָה			נִי ַ	ם			נוּ
E	1 cs	הוֹ/וֹ ָ	ָה	ְךָ	ֵךְ		ם	ָן	ֶכֶם	
F	3 cp	הוּ	ָה	ְךָ	ֵךְ	נִי	ם	ָן		נוּ
G	2 mp	הוּ				נִי				נוּ
H	2 fp	הוּ				נִי				נוּ
I	1 cp	הוּ	ָה	ְךָ	ֵךְ		ם		ֶכֶם	

Notes:

i. The 2 fp object suffix is not attested.

ii. The 3 ms object suffix used with the 3 fs perfect is הו, as expected, but also תו. The latter is apparently developed from –*áthû*: that is, –*áthû* > –*áttû*. The 3 fs object suffix used with the 3 fs perfect is –*áthā(h)* > –*áttā(h)*.

f. The following examples will suffice to illustrate the translation of the perfect with object suffixes:

i. 3 ms perfect: שָׁמַר–

שְׁמָרוֹ/שְׁמָרָהוּ	he observed him/it	A-I
שְׁמָרָהּ	he observed her/it	A-II
שְׁמָרְךָ	he observed you	A-III
שְׁמָרֵךְ	he observed you	A-IV
שְׁמָרַנִי	he observed me	A-V
שְׁמָרָם	he observed them	A-VI
שְׁמָרָן	he observed them	A-VII
שְׁמָרָנוּ	he observed us	A-IX

ii. 3 fs perfect: שָׁמְרַת–

שְׁמָרַתְהוּ/שְׁמָרַתּוּ	she observed him/it	B-I
שְׁמָרַתָּה	she observed her/it	B-II
שְׁמָרַתֶךָ	she observed you	B-III
שְׁמָרַתֶךְ	she observed you	B-IV
שְׁמָרַתְנִי	she observed me	B-V
שְׁמָרָתָם	she observed them	B-VI
שְׁמָרַתְנוּ	she observed us	B-IX

iii. 2 ms perfect: שְׁמַרְתָּ–

שְׁמַרְתָּהוּ/שְׁמַרְתּוֹ	you observed him/it	C-I
שְׁמַרְתָּהּ	you observed her/it	C-II
שְׁמַרְתַּנִי	you observed me	C-V
שְׁמַרְתָּם	you observed them	C-VI
שְׁמַרְתָּנוּ	you observed us	C-IX

iv. 2 fs perfect: שְׁמַרְתִּי–

שְׁמַרְתִּיהוּ	you observed him/it	D-I
שְׁמַרְתִּיהָ	you observed her/it	D-II
שְׁמַרְתִּינִי	you observed me	D-V
שְׁמַרְתִּים	you observed them	D-VI
שְׁמַרְתִּינוּ	you observed us	D-IX

v. 1 cs perfect: שְׁמַרְתִּי–

שְׁמַרְתִּיהוּ/שְׁמַרְתִּיו	I observed him/it	E-I
שְׁמַרְתִּיהָ	I observed her/it	E-II
שְׁמַרְתִּיךָ	I observed you	E-III
שְׁמַרְתִּיךְ	I observed you	E-IV
שְׁמַרְתִּים	I observed them	E-VI
שְׁמַרְתִּין	I observed them	E-VII
שְׁמַרְתִּיכֶם	I observed you	E-VIII

2. Perfect of III-ה Verbs with Suffixes

a. In the 3 ms perfect of all *binyānîm,* the final weak radical is lost before the suffix.

רָאָה	he saw	רָאָהוּ	he saw him/it
צִוָּה	he commanded	צִוָּהוּ	he commanded him
הֶרְאָה	he showed	הֶרְאֲךָ	he showed you

b. The 3 fs perfect is doubly marked for gender in the form of the verb without object suffix (XIII.5.b.ii). When the verb takes an object suffix, however, the 3 fs perfect is marked as feminine only once.

רָאֲתָה	she saw	רָאַתְךָ	she saw you
צִוְּתָה	she commanded	צִוַּתָּה	she commanded her

c. Apart from the 3 ms and 3 fs, the perfect of III-ה verbs are regular for their type.

רָאִיתִי	I saw	רְאִיתִיךָ	I saw you
רָאוּ	they saw	רָאוּךָ	they saw you

3. G Perfect Verbs with Anomalous "i" or "ē" Vowels

In a few instances, the G perfect with object suffix will have either *i* (ִ) or *ē* (ֵ) instead of *a* (ַ) in the second syllable. This is true even for verbs that have *a* as the "thematic" vowel (i.e., the *qāṭal* type).

ילד	יְלִדְתִּינִי	you (fs) have begotten me
	יְלִדְתִּיךָ	I have begotten you
	יְלִדְתִּיהוּ	I have begotten him
ירשׁ	יְרִשְׁתָּהּ	you possessed it
	יְרֵשׁוּךָ	they possessed you
שׁאל	שְׁאִלְתִּיו	I asked him
	שְׁאֵלוּנוּ	they asked us

Note: We have the form שְׁאֶלְתֶּם (i.e., without any object suffix) attested a few times in the Hebrew Bible.

4. Redundant Object Suffixes

Sometimes an object suffix may be resumptive and need not be translated in English.

בְּתוּלָה וְאִישׁ לֹא יְדָעָהּ   a virgin whom no man had known (*her*)
(Gen 24:16)

Vocabulary

Nouns:

יָמִין	right side
לָשׁוֹן	tongue
שָׂפָה	lip, edge, language
שִׁפְחָה	maid servant
תּוֹעֵבָה	abomination

Verbs:

בטח	trust
ברח	flee
לבשׁ	clothe
למד	(G) learn; (D) teach
מלט	(N) escape; (D) save
ענה	answer, reply
שָׂנֵא	hate. *Noun:* שִׂנְאָה hatred
שׁבר	break
שׁכח	forget

Adjectives:

רָחוֹק	far
רַק	thin. *Adverb:* רַק only

Adverbs:

יַחְדָּו/יַחַד	together

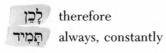

לָכֵן therefore

תָּמִיד always, constantly

Exercise 16

1. (Deut. 2:7) כִּי יְהוָה אֱלֹהֶיךָ בֵּרַכְךָ בְּכֹל מַעֲשֵׂה יָדֶךָ
2. (Hos. 13:5) אֲנִי יְדַעְתִּיךָ בַּמִּדְבָּר
3. (Jer. 20:14) יוֹם אֲשֶׁר־יְלָדַתְנִי אִמִּי
4. (Gen. 24:7) יְהוָה אֱלֹהֵי הַשָּׁמַיִם אֲשֶׁר לְקָחַנִי

   מִבֵּית אָבִי וּמֵאֶרֶץ מוֹלַדְתִּי[1] וַאֲשֶׁר דִּבֶּר־לִי
5. (Gen. 37:20) חַיָּה רָעָה אֲכָלָתְהוּ
6. (Jer. 50:7) כָּל־מוֹצְאֵיהֶם אֲכָלוּם
7. (Ps. 2:7) אָמַר אֵלַי בְּנִי אַתָּה אֲנִי הַיּוֹם יְלִדְתִּיךָ:
8. (Gen. 45:9) כֹּה אָמַר בִּנְךָ יוֹסֵף שָׂמַנִי אֱלֹהִים

   לְאָדוֹן לְכָל־מִצְרָיִם
9. (Exod. 3:12) וְזֶה־לְּךָ הָאוֹת כִּי אָנֹכִי שְׁלַחְתִּיךָ
10. (Num. 20:5) וְלָמָה הֶעֱלִיתֻנוּ מִמִּצְרַיִם לְהָבִיא[2] אֹתָנוּ

    אֶל־הַמָּקוֹם הָרָע הַזֶּה
11. (Jer. 28:15-16) וַיֹּאמֶר[3] יִרְמְיָה הַנָּבִיא אֶל־חֲנַנְיָה הַנָּבִיא

    שְׁמַע־נָא[4] חֲנַנְיָה לֹא־שְׁלָחֲךָ יְהוָה וְאַתָּה

    הִבְטַחְתָּ אֶת־הָעָם הַזֶּה עַל־שָׁקֶר:

    לָכֵן כֹּה אָמַר יְהוָה הִנְנִי מְשַׁלֵּחֲךָ

    מֵעַל פְּנֵי הָאֲדָמָה הַשָּׁנָה אַתָּה מֵת

    כִּי־סָרָה[5] דִבַּרְתָּ אֶל־יְהוָה:
12. (Jer. 14:14) וַיֹּאמֶר[3] יְהוָה אֵלַי שֶׁקֶר הַנְּבִאִים נִבְּאִים[6]

    בִּשְׁמִי לֹא שְׁלַחְתִּים וְלֹא צִוִּיתִים וְלֹא

    דִבַּרְתִּי אֲלֵיהֶם

---

[1] מוֹלֶדֶת kindred
[2] to bring
[3] said
[4] hear!
[5] rebellion
[6] are prophesying

13.   (Song. 5:6) נַפְשִׁי יָצְאָה בְדַבְּרוֹ[7] בִּקַּשְׁתִּיהוּ וְלֹא
מְצָאתִיהוּ קְרָאתִיו וְלֹא עָנָנִי:

14.   (Josh. 12:6) מֹשֶׁה עֶבֶד־יְהוָה וּבְנֵי יִשְׂרָאֵל הִכּוּם

15.   (Ps. 22:2) אֵלִי אֵלִי לָמָה עֲזַבְתָּנִי רָחוֹק מִישׁוּעָתִי
דִּבְרֵי שַׁאֲגָתִי[8]:

16.   (2 Sam. 19:10-11) הַמֶּלֶךְ הִצִּילָנוּ מִכַּף אֹיְבֵינוּ וְהוּא
מִלְּטָנוּ מִכַּף פְּלִשְׁתִּים וְעַתָּה בָּרַח
מִן־הָאָרֶץ מֵעַל אַבְשָׁלוֹם:
וְאַבְשָׁלוֹם אֲשֶׁר מָשַׁחְנוּ עָלֵינוּ מֵת בַּמִּלְחָמָה

17.   (Isa. 49:14) וַתֹּאמֶר צִיּוֹן עֲזָבַנִי יְהוָה וַאדֹנָי שְׁכֵחָנִי:

18.   (Ps. 119:12) בָּרוּךְ אַתָּה יְהוָה לַמְּדֵנִי[9] חֻקֶּיךָ:

19.   (Isa. 65:11) וְאַתֶּם עֹזְבֵי יְהוָה הַשְּׁכֵחִים אֶת־הַר קָדְשִׁי

20.   (Song. 2:4) הֱבִיאַנִי אֶל־בֵּית הַיָּיִן וְדִגְלוֹ[10] עָלַי אַהֲבָה:

21.   (1 Sam. 1:15) לֹא אֲדֹנִי אִשָּׁה קְשַׁת־רוּחַ אָנֹכִי
וְיַיִן וְשֵׁכָר[11] לֹא שָׁתִיתִי

22.   (1 Sam. 18:12) וַיִּרָא[12] שָׁאוּל מִלִּפְנֵי דָוִד כִּי־הָיָה יְהוָה
עִמּוֹ וּמֵעִם שָׁאוּל סָר:

23.   (1 Kings 15:5) עָשָׂה דָוִד אֶת־הַיָּשָׁר בְּעֵינֵי יְהוָה
וְלֹא־סָר מִכֹּל אֲשֶׁר־צִוָּהוּ כֹּל יְמֵי חַיָּיו
רַק בִּדְבַר אוּרִיָּה הַחִתִּי:

24.   (2 Sam. 13:15) כִּי גְדוֹלָה הַשִּׂנְאָה אֲשֶׁר שְׂנֵאָהּ מֵאַהֲבָה אֲשֶׁר
אֲהֵבָהּ

25.   (2 Sam. 12:7) וַיֹּאמֶר[3] נָתָן אֶל־דָּוִד אַתָּה הָאִישׁ כֹּה־אָמַר יְהוָה
אֱלֹהֵי יִשְׂרָאֵל אָנֹכִי מְשַׁחְתִּיךָ לְמֶלֶךְ
עַל־יִשְׂרָאֵל וְאָנֹכִי הִצַּלְתִּיךָ מִיַּד שָׁאוּל:

---

[7] when he spoke
[8] שְׁאָגָה roaring, groaning
[9] teach me!
[10] דֶּגֶל signal, banner
[11] beer
[12] was afraid

26. ‏כְּכָל־מִצְוָתְךָ אֲשֶׁר צִוִּיתָנִי לֹא־עָבַרְתִּי (Deut. 26:13)
    ‏מִמִּצְוֺתֶיךָ וְלֹא שָׁכָחְתִּי:

27. ‏וְלֹא הִטִּיתֶם אֶת־אָזְנְכֶם וְלֹא שְׁמַעְתֶּם אֵלָי: (Jer. 35:15–17)
    ‏כִּי הֵקִימוּ בְּנֵי יְהוֹנָדָב בֶּן־רֵכָב אֶת־מִצְוַת
    ‏אֲבִיהֶם אֲשֶׁר צִוָּם וְהָעָם הַזֶּה לֹא שָׁמְעוּ אֵלָי:
    ‏לָכֵן כֹּה־אָמַר יְהוָה אֱלֹהֵי צְבָאוֹת אֱלֹהֵי
    ‏יִשְׂרָאֵל הִנְנִי מֵבִיא אֶל־יְהוּדָה וְאֶל כָּל־יוֹשְׁבֵי
    ‏יְרוּשָׁלַם אֵת כָּל־הָרָעָה אֲשֶׁר דִּבַּרְתִּי עֲלֵיהֶם
    ‏יַעַן[13] דִּבַּרְתִּי אֲלֵיהֶם וְלֹא שָׁמֵעוּ וָאֶקְרָא[14] לָהֶם
    ‏וְלֹא עָנוּ:

28. ‏עַבְדְּךָ יוֹאָב הוּא צִוָּנִי וְהוּא שָׂם בְּפִי שִׁפְחָתְךָ (2 Sam 14:19)
    ‏אֵת כָּל־הַדְּבָרִים הָאֵלֶּה:

29. ‏זֶה מֹשֶׁה הָאִישׁ אֲשֶׁר הֶעֱלָנוּ מֵאֶרֶץ מִצְרַיִם לֹא (Exod. 32:1)
    ‏יָדַעְנוּ מֶה־הָיָה לוֹ:

30. ‏וַיְדַבֵּר[15] אֱלֹהִים אֵת כָּל־הַדְּבָרִים הָאֵלֶּה לֵאמֹר: (Exod. 20:1–2)
    ‏אָנֹכִי יְהוָה אֱלֹהֶיךָ אֲשֶׁר הוֹצֵאתִיךָ
    ‏מֵאֶרֶץ מִצְרַיִם מִבֵּית עֲבָדִים:

---

[13] ‏יַעַן אֲשֶׁר‎ = (see IX.2.a)
[14] and I called
[15] and spoke

LESSON XVII

1. Preformatives and Afformatives of the Imperfect

a. Whereas the gender, number, and person of a verb are indicated in the perfect by afformatives, in the imperfect they are marked by preformatives and afformatives.

b. The following set of preformatives and afformatives are found in the imperfects of all the *binyānîm* (see Appendix B.1):

3 ms	◌ַ—יִ	3 mp	יִ—◌ֵ—וּ
3 fs	תִ—◌ַ	3 fp	תִ—◌ֵ—נָה
2 ms	תִ—◌ַ	2 mp	תִ—◌ֵ—וּ
2 fs	תִ—◌ֵ—יִ	2 fp	תִ—◌ֵ—נָה
1 cs	אֶ—◌ַ	1 cp	נִ—◌ַ

Notes:

i. Whereas no distinction is made in the perfect between masculine and feminine of the third person plural, gender is clearly distinguished in the imperfect.

ii. The 3 mp and 2 mp forms frequently have an additional *nûn* at the end, i.e., וּן– instead of וּ.

2. G Imperfect

a. In the perfect we recognize three types: *qāṭal, qāṭēl,* and *qāṭōl.* In the imperfect, only two types are discernible: *yiqṭōl* and *yiqṭal.* Verbs that are transitive, like שׁמר (watch, keep), generally belong to the first type; stative-intransitive verbs, like כבד (be heavy) and קטן (be small), generally belong to the second type. Thus we have a situation like this:

i. *qāṭal — yiqṭōl*
ii. *qāṭēl — yiqṭal*
iii. *qāṭōl — yiqṭal*

A rigid classification of the verb types is, however, impossible. Verbs with II- or III-Guttural tend to be assimilated into perfect or imperfect types with *a*; i.e., *qāṭal* and *yiqṭal*. Moreover, a small group of transitive verbs inexplicably take the *a* thematic vowel in the imperfect.

   b. The inflections of the G imperfect of שמר (keep, watch) and כבד (be heavy) are as follows:

3 ms	יִשְׁמֹר	יִכְבַּד
3 fs	תִּשְׁמֹר	תִּכְבַּד
2 ms	תִּשְׁמֹר	תִּכְבַּד
2 fs	תִּשְׁמְרִי	תִּכְבְּדִי
1 cs	אֶשְׁמֹר	אֶכְבַּד
3 mp	יִשְׁמְרוּ	יִכְבְּדוּ
3 fp	תִּשְׁמֹרְנָה	תִּכְבַּדְנָה
2 mp	תִּשְׁמְרוּ	תִּכְבְּדוּ
2 fp	תִּשְׁמֹרְנָה	תִּכְבַּדְנָה
1 cp	נִשְׁמֹר	נִכְבַּד

Notes:

i.   The thematic vowel is reduced whenever it is in the pretonic position. Even the *ō* vowel, which normally cannot be reduced, is reduced to ְ . When the form is in pause, however, the full vowel is retained. Thus, the 3 mp forms of שמר and כבד, when in pause, are יִשְׁמֹרוּ and יִכְבָּדוּ, respectively. When the afformative is ‏וּן‏–, the thematic vowel may or may not be reduced. Thus, יִשְׁמְרוּן or יִשְׁמֹרוּן, יִכְבְּדוּן or יִכְבָּדוּן.

ii.   When the imperfect is linked to the following word by a *maqqēp̄*, the *ō* vowel becomes *o*.

   יִשְׁמֹר but יִשְׁמָר־לוֹ (*yišmor-lô*)

3. Meaning of the Imperfect

   Whereas the perfect indicates completed action or present state, the imperfect indicates incomplete action or state.

a. In most instances, the imperfect indicates an action in the *future*—from the standpoint of the speaker, or from any other point.

שָׁאוּל יִמְלֹךְ עָלֵינוּ   Saul *will reign* over us (1 Sam. 11:12)

וֶאֱלִישָׁע חָלָה אֶת־חָלְיוֹ אֲשֶׁר   Now Elisha was sick with the sickness
יָמוּת בּוֹ   by which *he was to die* (2 Kings 13:14)

After the particle טֶרֶם (not yet, before), or the preposition עַד (until), the imperfect could also be rendered by the English past or perfect, but it should be stressed that the imperfect in such cases still represents action that is not completed from some point of reference.

עַד־יִגְדַּל שֵׁלָה בְנִי   until Shelah my son *has grown up* (Gen. 38:11)

וְכֹל־עֵשֶׂב הַשָּׂדֶה טֶרֶם יִצְמָח   Now, as for all the plants of the field, *they had* not yet *sprouted* (Gen. 2:5)

b. The imperfect may have reference to *habitual* or *customary* action either in the present or in the past. This usage of the imperfect is common especially in proverbial sayings and statements of universal truth.

עַל־כֵּן יֹאמְרוּ הַמֹּשְׁלִים   therefore, the bards *used to say* (Num. 21:27)

הָאָדָם יִרְאֶה לַעֵינַיִם וַיהוָה   humans *look* in regards to the eyes, but
יִרְאֶה לַלֵּבָב   YHWH *looks* in regard to the heart (1 Sam. 16:7)

חֲכָמִים יִצְפְּנוּ־דָעַת   wise men *store up* knowledge (Prov. 10:14)

This use of the imperfect is particularly common after particles like כַּאֲשֶׁר (as, even as), כֵּן (thus, so), כָּכָה (thus), or the like.

כַּאֲשֶׁר יִשָּׂא הָאֹמֵן אֶת־הַיֹּנֵק   as the nurse *carries* the infant (Num. 11:12)

לֹא־יֵעָשֶׂה כֵן בִּמְקוֹמֵנוּ   *it is* not *done so* in our place (Gen. 29:26)

כָּכָה יַעֲשֶׂה אִיּוֹב כָּל־הַיָּמִים   thus Job *would do* all the time (Job 1:5)

c. The imperfect is frequently rendered by the English *modal*.

▽
should
would

יֹאמְרוּ פְּלִיטֵי אֶפְרַיִם אֶעֱבֹרָה	the fugitives of Ephraim *would say*, "Let us pass" (Judg. 12:5)
מִי יְהוָה אֲשֶׁר אֶשְׁמַע בְּקֹלוֹ	Who is YHWH that *I should heed* his voice? (Exod. 5:2)

This modal use of the imperfect is especially common after particles like אֵיךְ (how), אוּלַי (perhaps), or the interrogatives מַה (what), מִי (who), לָמָּה (why), and so forth.

וְאֵיךְ יִשְׁמַע אֵלַי פַּרְעֹה	but how *shall* Pharaoh *listen* to me? (Exod. 6:30)
לָמָה אֶשְׁכַּל גַּם־שְׁנֵיכֶם יוֹם אֶחָד	why *should I be bereft* of you both in one day? (Gen. 27:45)
אוּלַי יִשְׁמַע יְהוָה אֱלֹהֶיךָ אֵת כָּל־דִּבְרֵי רַב־שָׁקֵה	perhaps YHWH your God *would hear* the words of Rabshakeh (2 Kings 19:4)

The imperfect is also commonly used after *telic* (final) particles like פֶּן (lest), לְמַעַן (so that, in order that), כִּי (that), or the like.

פֶּן־יִשְׁלַח יָדוֹ	lest *he should stretch forth* his hand (Gen. 3:22)
לְמַעַן יִשְׁמְעוּ כָּל־עֲדַת בְּנֵי יִשְׂרָאֵל	so that all the congregation of Israel *may obey* (Num. 27:20)

d. With the *interrogative*, the imperfect may be translated by the English present tense.

לָמָּה זֶּה תִּשְׁאַל לִשְׁמִי	Why *do you ask* for my name? (Gen. 32:30)

e. The imperfect may be used to express an *injunction*.

וְאֶת־מִצְוֹתַי תִּשְׁמֹרוּ	*You shall keep* my commandments! (Lev. 26:3)

4. Jussive

To express desire for action from a *third person* or *second person* subject, Hebrew uses the jussive. In the strong verb there is no formal distinction between the jussives and the corresponding imperfect forms. Thus, for example, יִשְׁמֹר could mean "he will keep" or "may he keep" or "let him keep."

וְעַתָּה יִשְׁמַע־נָא אֲדֹנִי הַמֶּלֶךְ now, *let* my lord the king *hear* the
אֵת דִּבְרֵי עַבְדּוֹ words of his servant (1 Sam. 26:19)

מִי־חָכָם וְיִשְׁמָר־אֵלֶּה whoever is wise, *let him observe* these
things (Ps. 107:43)

יִשָּׂא יְהוָה פָּנָיו אֵלֶיךָ *may* YHWH *lift up* his face unto you
(Num. 6:26)

5. Cohortative

a. To express the speaker's desire or intention to act, the cohortative is used. Thus, the cohortative will occur only in the 1 cs and 1 cp.

b. The cohortative is often marked by a volitive element, הָ ֭, appended to the 1 cs or 1 cp or the imperfect. Since this volitive הָ ֭ is stressed, the thematic vowel is ordinarily reduced. When the verb is in pause, however, the thematic vowel may be retained.

אֶעְבְּרָה בְאַרְצֶךָ *let me pass* through your land
(Num. 21:22)

וְנִקְרְבָה בְּאַחַד הַמְּקֹמוֹת and *let us draw near* to one of the
places (Judg. 19:13)

6. Negation of the Imperfect, Jussive, and Cohortative

a. The imperfect is regularly negated by לֹא.

וְלֹא־יִשְׁמַע אֲלֵכֶם פַּרְעֹה Pharaoh *will not listen* to you (Exod. 7:4)

b. The negative particle לֹא is used with the second person imperfect forms to express *prohibition*.

לֹא תֹאכְלוּ מִמֶּנּוּ וְלֹא תִגְּעוּ בּוֹ you *shall not eat* from it, and you *shall
not touch* it (Gen. 3:3)

c. Negative command is expressed by the negative particle אַל (do not) with the appropriate second person imperfect form.

אַל־תִּשְׁלַח יָדְךָ אֶל־הַנַּעַר *do not stretch out* your hand against
the boy! (Gen. 22:12)

d. The cohortative and jussive are also negated by the negative particle אַל.

אַל־נָא נֹאבְדָה *Do not let us perish!* (Jon. 1:14)

Vocabulary

Nouns:

מָחֳרָה	the morrow. מָחָר tomorrow
עֶצֶם	bone
עֶרֶב	evening

Verbs:

בלע	swallow
בער	burn
ברא	create
גאל	redeem
זעק	cry out
ידה	(G) throw; (H) confess, give thanks. *Noun:* תּוֹדָה thanksgiving
כפר	cover; (D) cover, atone. *Nouns:* כֹּפֶר atonement; כַּפֹּרֶת cover (for the ark of covenant)
פקד	visit, appoint, inspect
קבץ	gather (*cf.* Kibbutz)
קבר	bury. *Noun:* קֶבֶר grave; קְבוּרָה burial site
קטר	(D) burn. *Noun:* קְטֹרֶת incense
רדף	pursue, follow
שׂמח	rejoice. *Noun:* שִׂמְחָה joy (*cf.* שִׂמְחַת תּוֹרָה)
שׂרף	burn. *Noun:* שָׂרָף Saraph (a winged-cobra)
שׁפך	pour out

Conjunctions:

לְמַעַן	in order that, so that
פֶּן־	lest

Exercise 17

Translate the following into English:

1.   (Ps. 14:1)   אָמַר נָבָל¹ בְּלִבּוֹ אֵין אֱלֹהִים

2.   (Ps. 15:1)   מִי־יִשְׁכֹּן בְּהַר קָדְשֶׁךָ:

3.   (1 Sam. 23:17)   וְאַתָּה תִּמְלֹךְ עַל־יִשְׂרָאֵל

4.   (Ps. 18:38)   אֶרְדּוֹף אוֹיְבַי

5.   (2 Sam. 7:26)   וְיִגְדַּל שִׁמְךָ עַד־עוֹלָם

6.   (Deut. 33:19)   שָׁם יִזְבְּחוּ זִבְחֵי־צֶדֶק

7.   (Ps. 104:34)   אָנֹכִי אֶשְׂמַח בַּיהוָה:

8.   (Ps. 111:5)   יִזְכֹּר לְעוֹלָם בְּרִיתוֹ:

9.   (Gen. 24:7)   יִשְׁלַח מַלְאָכוֹ לְפָנֶיךָ

10.   (1 Sam. 9:16)   כָּעֵת מָחָר אֶשְׁלַח אֵלֶיךָ אִישׁ מֵאֶרֶץ בִּנְיָמִן

11.   (1 Kings 8:42)   כִּי יִשְׁמְעוּן אֶת־שִׁמְךָ הַגָּדוֹל וְאֶת־יָדְךָ הַחֲזָקָה

12.   (Gen. 17:10)   זֹאת בְּרִיתִי אֲשֶׁר תִּשְׁמְרוּ בֵּינִי
                                            וּבֵינֵיכֶם וּבֵין זַרְעֲךָ אַחֲרֶיךָ

13.   (Jer. 28:4)   וְאֶת־כָּל־גָּלוּת² יְהוּדָה הַבָּאִים בָּבֶלָה אֲנִי
                מֵשִׁיב אֶל־הַמָּקוֹם הַזֶּה נְאֻם־יְהוָה כִּי
                אֶשְׁבֹּר אֶת־עֹל³ מֶלֶךְ בָּבֶל:

14.   (Isa. 30:21)   וְאָזְנֶיךָ תִּשְׁמַעְנָה דָבָר מֵאַחֲרֶיךָ לֵאמֹר זֶה הַדֶּרֶךְ

15.   (Ps. 116:17)   לְךָ־אֶזְבַּח זֶבַח תּוֹדָה וּבְשֵׁם יְהוָה אֶקְרָא:

16.   (Job 7:21)   כִּי־עַתָּה לֶעָפָר אֶשְׁכָּב וְשִׁחַרְתַּנִי⁴ וְאֵינֶנִּי:

17.   (Judg. 14:15)   פֶּן־נִשְׂרֹף אוֹתָךְ וְאֶת־בֵּית־אָבִיךְ בָּאֵשׁ

18.   (Ps. 119:101)   מִכָּל־אֹרַח רָע כָּלִאתִי⁵ רַגְלָי לְמַעַן
                אֶשְׁמֹר דְּבָרֶךָ:

19.   (Ezek. 22:20)   כֵּן אֶקְבֹּץ בְּאַפִּי וּבַחֲמָתִי

---

¹ a fool
² גָּלוּת exiled community
³ yoke
⁴ שׁחר (D) seek diligently
⁵ כלא withhold

20.   (Josh. 1:17) כְּכֹל אֲשֶׁר־שָׁמַעְנוּ אֶל־מֹשֶׁה כֵּן נִשְׁמַע
אֵלֶיךָ רַק יִהְיֶה יְהוָה אֱלֹהֶיךָ עִמָּךְ
כַּאֲשֶׁר הָיָה עִם־מֹשֶׁה:

21.   (Prov. 8:15) בִּי מְלָכִים יִמְלֹכוּ

22.   (Neh. 6:11) הַאִישׁ כָּמוֹנִי יִבְרָח

23.   (Exod. 30:30) וְאֶת־אַהֲרֹן וְאֶת־בָּנָיו תִּמְשָׁח

24.   (Deut. 13:4) לֹא תִשְׁמַע אֶל־דִּבְרֵי הַנָּבִיא הַהוּא אוֹ
אֶל־חוֹלֵם הַחֲלוֹם הַהוּא

25.   (Jer. 31:33) כִּי זֹאת הַבְּרִית אֲשֶׁר אֶכְרֹת אֶת־בֵּית
יִשְׂרָאֵל אַחֲרֵי הַיָּמִים הָהֵם

26.   (1 Sam. 26:24) וְהִנֵּה כַּאֲשֶׁר גָּדְלָה נַפְשְׁךָ הַיּוֹם הַזֶּה
בְּעֵינָי כֵּן תִּגְדַּל נַפְשִׁי בְּעֵינֵי יְהוָה

27.   (Josh. 4:6) לְמַעַן תִּהְיֶה זֹאת אוֹת בְּקִרְבְּכֶם כִּי־
יִשְׁאָלוּן בְּנֵיכֶם מָחָר לֵאמֹר מָה הָאֲבָנִים
הָאֵלֶּה לָכֶם:

28.   (Judg. 8:23) וַיֹּאמֶר אֲלֵהֶם גִּדְעוֹן לֹא־אֶמְשֹׁל
אֲנִי בָּכֶם וְלֹא־יִמְשֹׁל בְּנִי בָּכֶם
יְהוָה יִמְשֹׁל בָּכֶם:

29.   (1 Kings 19:16) וְאֵת יֵהוּא בֶן־נִמְשִׁי תִּמְשַׁח לְמֶלֶךְ עַל־יִשְׂרָאֵל
וְאֶת־אֱלִישָׁע בֶּן־שָׁפָט מֵאָבֵל מְחוֹלָה תִּמְשַׁח
לְנָבִיא תַּחְתֶּיךָ:

30.   (Num. 34:17) אֵלֶּה שְׁמוֹת הָאֲנָשִׁים אֲשֶׁר־יִנְחֲלוּ לָכֶם
אֶת־הָאָרֶץ אֶלְעָזָר הַכֹּהֵן וִיהוֹשֻׁעַ בִּן־נוּן:

31.   (Job 6:8) מִי־יִתֵּן תָּבוֹא שֶׁאֱלָתִי [6] וְתִקְוָתִי [7] יִתֵּן אֱלוֹהַּ:

32.   (Ps. 77:4) אֶזְכְּרָה אֱלֹהִים

33.   (Isa. 55:3) וְאֶכְרְתָה לָכֶם בְּרִית עוֹלָם

34.   (Gen. 31:44) נִכְרְתָה בְרִית אֲנִי וָאָתָּה

35.   (Gen. 30:15) יִשְׁכַּב עִמָּךְ הַלָּיְלָה

---

[6] שְׁאֵלָה request
[7] תִּקְוָה hope

LESSON XVIII

1. G Imperfect of I-Guttural Verbs

a. As in the strong verb, there are two basic types in the G imperfect of I-Guttural verbs: (i) the type with the thematic vowel *ō*, and (ii) the type with the thematic vowel *a*.

b. Since gutturals generally prefer the composite *šĕwā'* instead of under the first radical we have ֲ for verbs with the thematic vowel *ō* and ֱ for verbs with the thematic vowel *a*. Not infrequently, however, the silent *šĕwā'* may be retained (e.g., יֶעְתַּר, יֶחְמֹל, יַחְבֹּשׁ, יַחְשֹׁךְ).

c. I-א verbs behave normally, except for the following: אמר (say), אכל (eat), אבד (perish), אפה (bake), אבה (be willing). For these verbs, the vowel in the preformative is always *ō*, and the א quiesces.

d. The inflections of the G imperfect of עמד (stand), חזק (be strong), and אכל (eat) are as follows:

3 ms	יַעֲמֹד	יֶחֱזַק	יֹאכַל
3 fs	תַּעֲמֹד	תֶּחֱזַק	תֹּאכַל
2 ms	תַּעֲמֹד	תֶּחֱזַק	תֹּאכַל
2 fs	תַּעַמְדִי	תֶּחֶזְקִי	תֹּאכְלִי
1 cs	אֶעֱמֹד	אֶחֱזַק	אֹכַל
3 mp	יַעַמְדוּ	יֶחֶזְקוּ	יֹאכְלוּ
3 fp	תַּעֲמֹדְנָה	תֶּחֱזַקְנָה	תֹּאכַלְנָה
2 mp	תַּעַמְדוּ	תֶּחֶזְקוּ	תֹּאכְלוּ
2 fp	תַּעֲמֹדְנָה	תֶּחֱזַקְנָה	תֹּאכַלְנָה
1 cp	נַעֲמֹד	נֶחֱזַק	נֹאכַל

Notes:

i. When a composite *šĕwā'* precedes a simple vocal *šĕwā'*, the former becomes the corresponding short vowel, and the latter becomes silent. Thus,

148

תַּעַמְדִי < תַּעֲמְדִי*

תֶּחֱזְקִי < תֶּחֱזְקִי*

יַעַמְדוּ < יַעֲמְדוּ*

יֶחֱזְקוּ < יֶחֱזְקוּ*

תַּעַמְדוּ < תַּעֲמְדוּ*

תֶּחֱזְקוּ < תֶּחֱזְקוּ*

ii. I-א verbs of the אכל type frequently have ֶ instead of ֲ (thus, תֹּאכֵל, יֹאכֵל, etc.)

iii. The 1 cs of I-א verbs of the אכל type shows the development אֹכֵל < אֹאכֵל* < אֹאֱכֵל*, and .

2. G Imperfect of III-א Verbs

a. Since the א quiesces when it closes a syllable, the preceding vowel is lengthened. The 3 fp/2 fp form, however, is תִּמְצֶאנָה not תִּמְצָאנָה, as one might expect.

b. The inflection of the G imperfect of מצא (find) is as follows:

3 ms	יִמְצָא	3 mp	יִמְצְאוּ
3 fs	תִּמְצָא	3 fp	תִּמְצֶאנָה
2 ms	תִּמְצָא	2 mp	תִּמְצְאוּ
2 fs	תִּמְצְאִי	2 fp	תִּמְצֶאנָה
1 cs	אֶמְצָא	1 cp	נִמְצָא

3. G Imperfect of III-ה Verbs

The inflections of נלה (uncover) and היה (be) are as follows:

3 ms	יִגְלֶה	יִהְיֶה
3 fs	תִּגְלֶה	תִּהְיֶה
2 ms	תִּגְלֶה	תִּהְיֶה
2 fs	תִּגְלִי	תִּהְיִי
1 cs	אֶגְלֶה	אֶהְיֶה

3 mp	יִגְלוּ	יִהְיוּ
3 fp	תִּגְלֶינָה	תִּהְיֶינָה
2 mp	תִּגְלוּ	תִּהְיוּ
2 fp	תִּגְלֶינָה	תִּהְיֶינָה
1 cp	נִגְלֶה	נִהְיֶה

Note: The verbs היה (be) and חיה (live) do not behave like I-Guttural verbs in the imperfect.

4. G Imperfect of I-*Nûn* Verbs

a. The נ is typically assimilated into the following radical unless the second radical happens to be a guttural. Thus, (יִפֹּל > יִנְפֹּל*) יִפֹּל — נָפַל but יִנְחַל — נָחַל.

b. Verbs with strong radicals almost always have $\bar{o}$ as the thematic vowel. Verbs with II- or III-Guttural have *a* as the thematic vowel. The verb נתן (give) is an exception in that the thematic vowel is $\bar{e}$.

c. The inflections of the G imperfect of נפל (fall), נחל (inherit), נסע (set out), and נתן (give) are as follows:

3 ms	יִפֹּל	יִנְחַל	יִסַּע	יִתֵּן
3 fs	תִּפֹּל	תִּנְחַל	תִּסַּע	תִּתֵּן
2 ms	תִּפֹּל	תִּנְחַל	תִּסַּע	תִּתֵּן
2 fs	תִּפְּלִי	תִּנְחֲלִי	תִּסְּעִי	תִּתְּנִי
1 cs	אֶפֹּל	אֶנְחַל	אֶסַּע	אֶתֵּן
3 mp	יִפְּלוּ	יִנְחֲלוּ	יִסְּעוּ	יִתְּנוּ
3 fp	תִּפֹּלְנָה	תִּנְחַלְנָה	תִּסַּעְנָה	תִּתֵּנָּה
2 mp	תִּפְּלוּ	תִּנְחֲלוּ	תִּסְּעוּ	תִּתְּנוּ
2 fp	תִּפֹּלְנָה	תִּנְחַלְנָה	תִּסַּעְנָה	תִּתֵּנָּה
1 cp	נִפֹּל	נִנְחַל	נִסַּע	נִתֵּן

d. The verb לקח (take) behaves like a I-*Nûn* verb in the G imperfect. Thus, it is inflected like נסע, with the assimilation of ל (תִּקַּח, יִקַּח, etc.).

5. G Imperfect of I-*Wāw* Verbs

a. Three important features characterize the G imperfect of most I-*Wāw* verbs:

  i.   Aphaeresis (loss) of the *wāw* radical,
  ii. The vowel of the preformative is *ē*,
  iii. The thematic vowel is ordinarily *ē*, except in the 3 fp/2 fp form where it is *a*. III-ה, ח, ע verbs will also have *a* as the thematic vowel.

b. The inflections of יֹשֵׁב (sit, dwell) and ירע (know) are as follows:

3 ms	יֵשֵׁב	יֵדַע
3 fs	תֵּשֵׁב	תֵּדַע
2 ms	תֵּשֵׁב	תֵּדַע
2 fs	תֵּשְׁבִי	תֵּדְעִי
1 cs	אֵשֵׁב	אֵדַע
3 mp	יֵשְׁבוּ	יֵדְעוּ
3 fp	תֵּשַׁבְנָה	תֵּדַעְנָה
2 mp	תֵּשְׁבוּ	תֵּדְעוּ
2 fp	תֵּשַׁבְנָה	תֵּדַעְנָה
1 cp	נֵשֵׁב	נֵדַע

c. The verb הלך (walk, go) behaves like an original I-*Wāw* verb in the G and H *binyānîm* (cf. XV.8.b). The G imperfect, therefore, is inflected like יֹשֵׁב (i.e., with aphaeresis [loss] of the first radical). Forms without aphaeresis (e.g., אֶהֱלֹךְ, יַהֲלֹךְ) are attested but quite rare.

d. A smaller group of original I-*Wāw* verbs may retain the first radical — but as *yōḏ*, not *wāw*. The thematic vowel of such verbs is regularly *a*, not *ē*. For example, the forms of the imperfect of ירשׁ are יִירַשׁ, אִירַשׁ, תִּירַשׁ, and so forth. The forms are actually not surprising, since one would expect *יִירַשׁ to become יִירַשׁ, even as *בִּיהוּדָה* > בִּיהוּדָה >

בְּיהוּדָה (see V.2.b.i). The following are the most common verbs in this group:

Perfect	Imperfect	
יָגַע	יִיגַע	become weary
יָעַץ	יִיעַץ	advise
יָרֵא	יִירָא	be afraid
יָרַשׁ	יִירַשׁ	possess, dispossess
יָשֵׁן	יִישַׁן	sleep

The imperfects of such verbs are frequently written defectively (i.e., without the *mater*). In such cases, a *métẹḡ* is added after the vowel of the preformative to indicate that it is long: יִרַשׁ (for יִירַשׁ), יִגְעוּ (for יִירְגְעוּ), יִרְאוּ (for יִירְאוּ), and so forth. The defective form יִרְאוּ (they were afraid) may be confused with יִרְאוּ (they saw), except that the *métẹḡ* in the former indicates that it is a defective spelling for יִירְאוּ.

e. I-*Wāw* verbs that behave like I-*Nûn* (see XV.7.d) are sporadically attested: for example, יָצַת, but יִצַּת, תִּצַּתְנָה, and so on.

6. G Imperfect of I-Yōḏ Verbs

a. Original I-*Yōḏ* verbs are treated like any strong verb with the *a* thematic vowel, except that the silent *šẹwā'* under the first radical is lost (cf. V.2.b.i). Thus, for example, יִיטַב > יִיטַב.

b. The inflection of the G imperfect of יטב (be good) is as follows:

3 ms	יִיטַב	3 mp	יִיטְבוּ
3 fs	תִּיטַב	3 fp	תִּיטַבְנָה
2 ms	תִּיטַב	2 mp	תִּיטְבוּ
2 fs	תִּיטְבִי	2 fp	תִּיטַבְנָה
1 cs	אִיטַב	1 cp	נִיטַב

7. G Imperfect of II-Wāw/Yōḏ Verbs

a. The vowel of the preformative in the G imperfect of II-*Wāw/Yōḏ* verbs is normally ָ , which is reduced when it is propretonic. Only very rarely is it ֻ instead of ָ (e.g., יָבוֹשׁ—בּוֹשׁ, יָאוֹר—אוֹר, יֵבוֹשׁ).

b. The distinction between II-*Wāw* and II-*Yōd* is clear in the G imperfect.

c. The inflections of the G imperfect of קוּם (arise), שִׂים (place), and בּוֹא (come) are as follows:

3 ms	יָקוּם	יָשִׂים	יָבוֹא
3 fs	תָּקוּם	תָּשִׂים	תָּבוֹא
2 ms	תָּקוּם	תָּשִׂים	תָּבוֹא
2 fs	תָּקוֹמִי	תָּשִׂימִי	תָּבוֹאִי
1 cs	אָקוּם	אָשִׂים	אָבוֹא
3 mp	יָקוּמוּ	יָשִׂימוּ	יָבוֹאוּ
3 fp	תְּקוּמֶינָה	תְּשִׂימֶינָה	תְּבֹאֶינָה
2 mp	תָּקוּמוּ	תָּשִׂימוּ	תָּבוֹאוּ
2 fp	תְּקוּמֶינָה	תְּשִׂימֶינָה	תְּבֹאֶינָה
1 cp	נָקוּם	נָשִׂים	נָבוֹא

Note: The variant forms תָּקֹמְנָה (instead of תְּקוּמֶינָה), and תָּבֹאנָה (instead of תְּבֹאֶינָה) are also attested.

8. יָכֹל

The verb יָכֹל (be able), which sometimes precedes an infinitive (see XXII.3.b), behaves regularly in the G perfect, that is, like a *qātōl* stative.

The G imperfect of יָכֹל, however, is unique. The following forms are attested.

3 ms	יוּכַל	3 mp	יוּכְלוּ
3 fs	תּוּכַל	3 fp	–not attested–
2 ms	תּוּכַל	2 mp	תּוּכְלוּ
2 fs	תּוּכְלִי	2 fp	–not attested–
1 cs	אוּכַל	1 cp	נוּכַל

Vocabulary

Nouns:

חֵן	grace, favor. *Verb:* חנן be gracious, favor
עֵצָה	counsel, plan, advice. *Verb:* יעץ advise. *Noun:* יֹעֵץ counsellor, advisor
שֵׁבֶט	rod, tribe

Verbs:

אבה	be willing
אחז	seize
אמן	(N) be faithful, believe; (H) believe, trust
אסר	bind. *Noun:* אָסִיר prisoner
חדל	cease, stop (doing something)
חלק	divide, apportion. *Noun:* חֵלֶק portion, lot
חפץ	delight, desire. *Noun:* חֵפֶץ desire, pleasure
חשב	think, reckon. *Noun:* מַחֲשֶׁבֶת thought
יכל	be able (to do something), prevail
ירש	possess, dispossess
נום	flee
נסע	set out, travel, depart
רוץ	run
שאר	remain
שלם	(G) be whole, healthy, complete, at peace; (D) make whole, make amends, recompense (*cf.* שָׁלוֹם)

Exercise 18

Translate the following into English:

1. (Exod. 3:11) מִי אָנֹכִי כִּי אֵלֵךְ אֶל־פַּרְעֹה

2. (Exod. 3:12) כִּי־אֶהְיֶה עִמָּךְ וְזֶה־לְּךָ הָאוֹת כִּי אָנֹכִי שְׁלַחְתִּיךָ

3. (Exod. 3:12) תַּעַבְדוּן אֶת־הָאֱלֹהִים עַל הָהָר הַזֶּה:

4. (Exod. 3:14) אֶהְיֶה אֲשֶׁר אֶהְיֶה

5. (Exod. 3:14) כֹּה תֹאמַר לִבְנֵי יִשְׂרָאֵל אֶהְיֶה שְׁלָחַנִי אֲלֵיכֶם:

6. (Exod. 4:16–17) הוּא יִהְיֶה־לְּךָ לְפֶה וְאַתָּה תִּהְיֶה־לּוֹ לֵאלֹהִים:
וְאֶת־הַמַּטֶּה הַזֶּה תִּקַּח בְּיָדֶךָ אֲשֶׁר
תַּעֲשֶׂה־בּוֹ אֶת־הָאֹתֹת:

7. (Jer. 18:18) לֹא־תֹאבַד תּוֹרָה מִכֹּהֵן וְעֵצָה מֵחָכָם וְדָבָר
מִנָּבִיא

8. (Amos 7:10–11) קָשַׁר¹ עָלֶיךָ עָמוֹס בְּקֶרֶב בֵּית יִשְׂרָאֵל
לֹא־תוּכַל הָאָרֶץ לְהָכִיל² אֶת־כָּל־דְּבָרָיו:
כִּי־כֹה אָמַר עָמוֹס בַּחֶרֶב יָמוּת יָרָבְעָם

9. (Gen. 34:21) הָאֲנָשִׁים הָאֵלֶּה שְׁלֵמִים הֵם אִתָּנוּ
וְיֵשְׁבוּ בָאָרֶץ וְיִסְחֲרוּ³ אֹתָהּ וְהָאָרֶץ
הִנֵּה רַחֲבַת־יָדַיִם⁴ לִפְנֵיהֶם אֶת־בְּנֹתָם
נִקַּח־לָנוּ לְנָשִׁים וְאֶת־בְּנֹתֵינוּ נִתֵּן לָהֶם:

10. (2 Kings 22:16) כֹּה אָמַר יְהוָה הִנְנִי מֵבִיא רָעָה אֶל־הַמָּקוֹם
הַזֶּה וְעַל־יֹשְׁבָיו אֵת כָּל־דִּבְרֵי הַסֵּפֶר אֲשֶׁר
קָרָא מֶלֶךְ יְהוּדָה:

11. (1 Sam. 14:45) וַיֹּאמֶר⁵ הָעָם אֶל־שָׁאוּל הֲיוֹנָתָן יָמוּת
אֲשֶׁר עָשָׂה הַיְשׁוּעָה הַגְּדוֹלָה הַזֹּאת בְּיִשְׂרָאֵל

12. (Isa. 2:3) כִּי מִצִּיּוֹן תֵּצֵא תוֹרָה וּדְבַר־יְהוָה מִירוּשָׁלָ͏ִם:

13. (Ps. 56:12) בֵּאלֹהִים בָּטַחְתִּי לֹא אִירָא מַה־יַּעֲשֶׂה אָדָם לִי:

14. (Jer. 8:4) הֲיִפְּלוּ וְלֹא יָקוּמוּ אִם־יָשׁוּב וְלֹא יָשׁוּב:

15. (Ps. 121:1–2) אֶשָּׂא עֵינַי אֶל־הֶהָרִים
מֵאַיִן יָבֹא עֶזְרִי:⁶
עֶזְרִי מֵעִם יְהוָה עֹשֵׂה שָׁמַיִם וָאָרֶץ:

---

¹ קָשַׁר conspire
² to endure
³ they may ply (trade in) it
⁴ broad of both hands, an idiom = extended on both sides, or the like
⁵ said
⁶ עֵזֶר help

16.   (Deut. 1:30–32) יְהוָה אֱלֹהֵיכֶם הַהֹלֵךְ לִפְנֵיכֶם הוּא יִלָּחֵם⁷
לָכֶם כְּכֹל אֲשֶׁר עָשָׂה אִתְּכֶם בְּמִצְרַיִם
לְעֵינֵיכֶם:
וּבַמִּדְבָּר אֲשֶׁר רָאִיתָ אֲשֶׁר נְשָׂאֲךָ יְהוָה
אֱלֹהֶיךָ כַּאֲשֶׁר יִשָּׂא־אִישׁ אֶת־בְּנוֹ בְּכָל־
הַדֶּרֶךְ אֲשֶׁר הֲלַכְתֶּם עַד־בֹּאֲכֶם⁸ עַד־הַמָּקוֹם
הַזֶּה:
וּבַדָּבָר הַזֶּה אֵינְכֶם מַאֲמִינִם בַּיהוָה
אֱלֹהֵיכֶם:

17.   (Gen. 47:5–6) וַיֹּאמֶר⁵ פַּרְעֹה אֶל־יוֹסֵף לֵאמֹר אָבִיךָ
וְאַחֶיךָ בָּאוּ אֵלֶיךָ:
אֶרֶץ מִצְרַיִם לְפָנֶיךָ הִוא בְּמֵיטַב⁹
הָאָרֶץ הוֹשֵׁב¹⁰ אֶת־אָבִיךָ וְאֶת־אַחֶיךָ יֵשְׁבוּ
בְּאֶרֶץ גֹּשֶׁן

18.   (2 Kings 21:7) בַּבַּיִת הַזֶּה וּבִירוּשָׁלִַם אֲשֶׁר בָּחַרְתִּי מִכֹּל
שִׁבְטֵי יִשְׂרָאֵל אָשִׂים אֶת־שְׁמִי לְעוֹלָם:

19.   (Num. 9:17) וְאַחֲרֵי־כֵן יִסְעוּ בְּנֵי יִשְׂרָאֵל וּבִמְקוֹם
אֲשֶׁר יִשְׁכָּן־שָׁם הֶעָנָן שָׁם יַחֲנוּ בְּנֵי יִשְׂרָאֵל:

20.   (Ruth 3:11) וְעַתָּה בִּתִּי אַל־תִּירְאִי כֹּל אֲשֶׁר־תֹּאמְרִי
אֶעֱשֶׂה־לָּךְ כִּי יוֹדֵעַ כָּל־שַׁעַר עַמִּי כִּי אֵשֶׁת
חַיִל אָתְּ:

21.   (Gen. 43:8) וַיֹּאמֶר⁵ יְהוּדָה אֶל־יִשְׂרָאֵל אָבִיו שִׁלְחָה¹¹
הַנַּעַר אִתִּי וְנָקוּמָה וְנֵלֵכָה וְנִחְיֶה
וְלֹא נָמוּת גַּם־אֲנַחְנוּ גַם־אַתָּה גַּם־טַפֵּנוּ:¹²

---

⁷ will fight
⁸ your coming
⁹ מֵיטַב best portion
¹⁰ settle! (cause to dwell)
¹¹ send!
¹² טַף children

22. (1 Kings 13:8-9) וַיֹּאמֶר⁵ אִישׁ־הָאֱלֹהִים אֶל־הַמֶּלֶךְ אִם־תִּתֶּן־לִי
אֶת־חֲצִי בֵיתֶךָ לֹא אָבֹא עִמָּךְ וְלֹא־אֹכַל לֶחֶם
וְלֹא אֶשְׁתֶּה־מַּיִם בַּמָּקוֹם הַזֶּה:
כִּי־כֵן צִוָּה אֹתִי בִּדְבַר יְהוָה לֵאמֹר
לֹא־תֹאכַל לֶחֶם וְלֹא תִשְׁתֶּה־מָּיִם וְלֹא תָשׁוּב
בַּדֶּרֶךְ אֲשֶׁר הָלָכְתָּ:

LESSON XIX

1. *Yqṭl* Preterite

We have learned so far that the simple past as well as the perfect are generally expressed by the *qāṭal* inflection, while the present or future is expressed by the *yiqṭōl* inflection. This is only partially correct, however.

In Hebrew, as in other Semitic languages, the simple past (preterite) was originally expressed by a *yqṭl* (**yaqṭul*) inflection, which is to be distinguished from the *yqṭl* imperfect (originally **yaqṭulu*). With the loss of final short vowels in Hebrew, probably toward the close of the second millennium B.C.E., the imperfect **yaqṭulu* became **yaqṭul*, thus coinciding with the preterite. Hebrew *yiqṭōl*, therefore, may be traced to original **yaqṭulu* (imperfect) or **yaqṭul* (preterite); there is no formal distinction between the imperfect and the preterite in the strong verb.

Since the function of the preterite in Hebrew is taken over by the perfect, the original preterite forms do not appear as often as expected. Nevertheless, they are still evident in the following situations:

a. In poetic, and especially archaic texts. Example:

$$\text{יִשְׁלַח דְּבָרוֹ וְיִרְפָּאֵם}$$ he *sent forth* his word and *healed* them
(Ps. 107:20)

The preterite sense of the *yiqṭōl* verb is often ascertained by its usage together with another verb in the *qāṭal* inflection;

$$\text{שָׁמְעוּ עַמִּים יִרְגָּזוּן}$$ the people heard, *they trembled*
(Exod. 15:14)

b. after the adverb אָז (then, at that time);

$$\text{אָז תִּפְשַׁע לִבְנָה}$$ then, Libnah *revolted* (2 Kings 8:22)

c. in the "*wāw*-conversive" forms.

The so-called "*wāw*-conversive" or "*wāw*-consecutive" form (where the *yiqṭōl* form follows a perfect and *wa–*) is, in fact, an original *yqṭl* preterite (see the discussion below).

158

2. Past Tense Narration

a. In past tense narration, the sequence *qātal* + *wayyiqtōl* is used. When following the perfect, every *wayyiqtōl* form is said to be "converted" and is translated as one would translate a perfect.

הוּא נָתְנָה־לִּי מִן־הָעֵץ וָאֹכֵל   she gave to me from the tree and *I ate* (Gen. 3:12)

וְנֹבַח הָלַךְ וַיִּלְכֹּד אֶת־קְנָת   Then, Nobah went *and captured* Kenath

וְאֶת־בְּנוֹתֶיהָ וַיִּקְרָא לָה   and it villages and *he called* it Nobah,

נֹבַח בִּשְׁמוֹ   in his name (Num. 32:42)

The aspect of the *wyqtl* form is not necessarily tied to a preceding *qātal* form. Even without following a *qātal* form, the *wyqtl* form must be translated by the English past or present perfect.

In this sequence the *yqtl* form must be immediately preceded by ו. If the conjunction is separated from the verb for any reason (e.g., negative), the sequence is broken. Past tense narration may be continued only in the perfect inflection, and any *yqtl* form that remains must be translated as an imperfect.

וַיִּקְרָא אֱלֹהִים לָאוֹר יוֹם   God *called* the light "Day," but the

וְלַחֹשֶׁךְ קָרָא לָיְלָה   darkness he *called* "Night" (Gen. 1:5)

b. The conjunction of the consecutive form is written as follows:

i.   It is normally ו (*wa–*) + doubling of the next radical: וַיִּקְרָא and he called.

ii.   If the next radical has a *šewā'*, it is ו without doubling (*cf.* V.6): וַיְדַבֵּר and he spoke.

iii.   If the preformative of the verb is א, it is ו without doubling: וָאֹכֵל and I ate.

3. Other Consecutions

a. The *qātal* + *wayyiqtōl* sequence is used in past tense narration. By analogy the *yiqtōl* + *weqātal* sequence is perceived as the logical opposite. Thus, since the *wayyiqtōl* form in a *qātal* + *wayyiqtōl* sequence is translated as if it were a perfect, then the *wĕqāṭal* form in a *yiqṭōl* + *wĕqāṭal* sequence must be translated as if it were an imperfect.[1]

תִּשְׁמֹר אֶת־מִצְוֹת יְהוָה	you shall keep the commandments of
אֱלֹהֶיךָ וְהָלַכְתָּ בִּדְרָכָיו	YHWH your God, and *you shall walk* in his ways (Deut. 28:9)
אֵצֵא וְהָיִיתִי רוּחַ שֶׁקֶר	I will go forth, and *I will be* a lying spirit (1 Kings 22:22)

b. A *wĕqāṭal* following a participle may also have reference to the future.

| אֲנִי מֵבִיא בָכֶם רוּחַ וִחְיִיתֶם | I will cause a spirit to enter you and *you will live* (Ezek. 37:5) |

4. *Wyqṭl* Forms

a. There is no formal distinction between the imperfect (*yiqṭōl*) and the *wyqṭl* forms in most verbs:

Imperfect	*wyqṭl*	
יִשְׁמֹר	וַיִּשְׁמֹר	keep
יַעֲמֹד	וַיַּעֲמֹד	stand
יִבְחַר	וַיִּבְחַר	choose
יִשְׁלַח	וַיִּשְׁלַח	send
יִמְצָא	וַיִּמְצָא	find
יִפֹּל	וַיִּפֹּל	fall

b. In the *wyqṭl* forms of I-א verbs like אכל and אמר (see XVIII.1.c), the accent tends to retract from the ultima in the imperfect and shift to the penultima.

Imperfect	*wyqṭl*	
יֹאמַר	וַיֹּאמֶר	say
יֹאכַל	וַיֹּאכַל	eat

---

[1] In this sequence there is a shift of stress in the 2 ms and 1 cs forms of the perfect in consecution.

| הָלַכְתִּי | but | וְהָלַכְתִּי |
| הָלַכְתָּ | but | וְהָלַכְתָּ |

Other I-א verbs behave normally (i.e., like any I-Guttural verb).

Imperfect	*wyqtl*	
יֶאֱהַב	וַיֶּאֱהַב	love
יֶאֱרֹב	וַיֶּאֱרֹב	lie in wait

c. In the *wyqtl* forms of the I-*Wāw* verbs, the accent usually retracts, which requires the shortening of the final vowel from ֵ to ֶ .

Imperfect	*wyqtl*	
יֵשֵׁב	וַיֵּשֶׁב	dwell, sit
תֵּלֵד	וַתֵּלֶד	bear
נֵדַע	וַנֵּדַע	know
יֵלֵךְ	וַיֵּלֶךְ	go, walk

Original I-*Yōd* verbs and I-*Wāw* verbs that retain the first radical (XVIII.5.d) show no change in the *wyqtl* forms.

Imperfect	*wyqtl*	
יִיטַב	וַיִּיטַב	be good
יִירַשׁ	וַיִּירַשׁ	possess

d. The *wyqtl* forms of II-*Wāw*/*Yōd* verbs generally show retraction of the accent and the consequent shortening of the vowels when possible.

Imperfect	*wyqtl*	
יָקוּם	וַיָּקָם	(*wayyā́qom*) arise
יָשִׂים	וַיָּשֶׂם	(*wayyā́śem*) place

There is no retraction of accent, however, in the *wyqtl* form of בוֹא: וַיָּבֹא-יָבוֹא; enter, come

A few verbs with III-ה, ע, or ר show retraction of accent, but the final vowel is shortened to *a*, not to the corresponding short vowel (i.e., *û* > *o*, *î* > *e*).

Imperfect	*wyqtl*	
יָנוּחַ	וַיָּנַח	rest
יָנוּעַ	וַיָּנַע	shake, wander
יָסוּר	וַיָּסַר	turn aside

e. The *wyqtl* forms of III-ה verbs are characterized by (i) the apocope (cutting off) of the ה, (ii) the retraction of the accent to the preformative, and (iii) usually, but not always, a short vowel inserted to prevent a consonant cluster at the end of the form.

Imperfect	**wyqtl**		
יִגְלֶה	*יִגְל >	וַיִּגֶל	uncover
יִבְנֶה	*יִבְן >	וַיִּבֶן	build
יִכְלֶה	*יִכְל >	וַיִּכֶל	be complete, done
תִּזְנֶה	*תִּזְן >	וַתִּזֶן	be a harlot

Beyond these basic characteristics, the *wyqtl* forms of III-ה verbs are quite unpredictable. Even within the same root there may be differences in vocalization.

Some III-ה verbs have the ֵ in the preformative of all *wyqtl* forms.

Imperfect	**wyqtl**		
יִבְכֶּה	*יִבְךְּ >	וַיֵּבְךְּ	weep
תִּבְכֶּה	*תֵּבְךְּ >	וַתֵּבְךְּ	
יִשְׁתֶּה	*יִשְׁתְּ >	וַיֵּשְׁתְּ	drink
תִּשְׁתֶּה	*תֵּשְׁתְּ >	וַתֵּשְׁתְּ	

III-ה verbs with I-Guttural will generally have *a* as the helping vowel, though there is some variation in the vocalization of the preformative.

Imperfect	**wyqtl**		
יַעֲנֶה	*יַעַן >	וַיַּעַן	answer
יַעֲשֶׂה	*יַעַשׂ >	וַיַּעַשׂ	make, do
נַעֲשֶׂה	*נַעַשׂ >	וַנַּעַשׂ	
יַחֲנֶה	*יַחַן >	וַיִּחַן	camp

The verbs הָיָה (be) and חָיָה (live) are peculiar in their *wyqtl* forms; because of their frequent occurrence they should be memorized.

Imperfect	**wyqtl**	
יִחְיֶה	וַיְחִי	live
יִהְיֶה	וַיְהִי	be
תִּהְיֶה	וַתְּהִי	

אֶהְיֶה	וָאֱהִי
נִהְיֶה	וַנְּהִי

III-ה verbs that are also I-*Nûn* may pose a problem to the beginning student for, in addition to the apocope, the form may also lose the gemination (doubling) of the second radical (i.e., indicating the assimilated נ).

Imperfect		*wyqtl*	
יַטֶּה > יִנְטֶה*	וַיֵּט	stretch out
יַזֶּה > יִנְזֶה*	וַיַּז	sprinkle

Finally, it should be noted that the *wyqtl* form of רֹאה (see) is וַיַּרְא. As this form occurs most frequently, the student should commit it to memory.

For other variations in the *wyqtl* forms, the student should consult the dictionaries.

Vocabulary

Nouns:

בְּהֵמָה	animal, beast (*cf.* Behemoth)
יֶתֶר	remainder, excess
כֶּבֶשׂ	ram
מִגְרָשׁ	pasture land
קָצֶה	(also קֵצָה) extremity, end
שַׂק	sack
שֶׁמֶן	oil, fat

Verbs:

אבד	perish
זנה	commit fornication. *Noun:* זֹנָה promiscuous woman
חזה	see a (prophetic) vision. *Noun:* חָזוֹן vision
מאס	reject, refuse

נָגַע   touch, strike (with plague). *Note:* object of the verb
usually indicated by בְּ. *Idiom:* ־נָגַע אֶל reach. *Noun:*
נֶגַע plague, stroke

צוֹם   fast. *Noun:* צוֹם fast, fasting

קָרַב   come near, approach. *Adjective:* קָרוֹב near

Prepositions:

בַּעֲבוּר   for the sake of, on account of

לִקְרָאת   before, against

Exercise 19

Translate the following into English:

1.   (Jon. 3:5–6) וַיַּאֲמִינוּ² אַנְשֵׁי נִינְוֵה בֵּאלֹהִים וַיִּקְרְאוּ־־צוֹם
וַיִּלְבְּשׁוּ שַׂקִּים מִגְּדוֹלָם וְעַד־קְטַנָּם:
וַיִּגַּע הַדָּבָר אֶל־מֶלֶךְ נִינְוֵה וַיָּקָם מִכִּסְאוֹ

2.   (Gen. 26:17) ✓ וַיֵּלֶךְ מִשָּׁם יִצְחָק וַיִּחַן בְּנַחַל־
גְּרָר וַיֵּשֶׁב שָׁם:

3.   (Gen. 26:24–25) וַיֵּרָא³ אֵלָיו יְהוָה בַּלַּיְלָה הַהוּא
וַיֹּאמֶר אָנֹכִי אֱלֹהֵי אַבְרָהָם אָבִיךָ
אַל־תִּירָא כִּי־אִתְּךָ אָנֹכִי וּבֵרַכְתִּיךָ
וְהִרְבֵּיתִי אֶת־זַרְעֲךָ בַּעֲבוּר אַבְרָהָם עַבְדִּי:
וַיִּבֶן שָׁם מִזְבֵּחַ וַיִּקְרָא בְּשֵׁם יְהוָה
וַיֶּט־שָׁם אָהֳלוֹ וַיִּכְרוּ⁴־שָׁם עַבְדֵי־יִצְחָק בְּאֵר⁵:

4.   (Isa. 41:8–9) וְאַתָּה יִשְׂרָאֵל עַבְדִּי יַעֲקֹב אֲשֶׁר בְּחַרְתִּיךָ
זֶרַע אַבְרָהָם אֹהֲבִי:
אֲשֶׁר הֶחֱזַקְתִּיךָ מִקְצוֹת הָאָרֶץ וּמֵאֲצִילֶיהָ⁶

---

² and (the people) believed
³ and (YHWH) appeared
⁴ כרה dig
⁵ a well
⁶ אָצִיל corner

קְרָאתִ֫יךָ וָאֹ֫מַר לְךָ עַבְדִּי־אַ֫תָּה בְּחַרְתִּ֫יךָ
וְלֹא מְאַסְתִּ֫יךָ:

5. (Gen. 21:34) וַיָּ֫גָר אַבְרָהָם בְּאֶ֫רֶץ פְּלִשְׁתִּים יָמִים רַבִּים: ✓

6. (Gen. 18:22) וַיִּפְנוּ מִשָּׁם הָאֲנָשִׁים וַיֵּלְכוּ
סְדֹ֫מָה וְאַבְרָהָם עוֹדֶ֫נּוּ עֹמֵד לִפְנֵי יְהוָה:

7. (Deut. 16:7) בַּמָּקוֹם אֲשֶׁר יִבְחַר יְהוָה אֱלֹהֶ֫יךָ בּוֹ ✓
וּפָנִ֫יתָ בַבֹּ֫קֶר וְהָלַכְתָּ לְאֹהָלֶ֫יךָ:

8. (Deut. 3:1–3) וַנֵּ֫פֶן וַנַּ֫עַל דֶּ֫רֶךְ הַבָּשָׁן וַיֵּצֵא עוֹג מֶ֫לֶךְ־הַבָּשָׁן
לִקְרָאתֵ֫נוּ[7] הוּא וְכָל־עַמּוֹ לַמִּלְחָמָה אֶדְרֶֽעִי:
וַיֹּ֫אמֶר יְהוָה אֵלַי אַל־תִּירָא אֹתוֹ כִּי בְיָדְךָ
נָתַ֫תִּי אֹתוֹ וְאֶת־כָּל־עַמּוֹ וְאֶת־אַרְצוֹ וְעָשִׂ֫יתָ
לּוֹ כַּאֲשֶׁר עָשִׂ֫יתָ לְסִיחֹן מֶ֫לֶךְ הָאֱמֹרִי
אֲשֶׁר יוֹשֵׁב בְּחֶשְׁבּֽוֹן:
וַיִּתֵּן יְהוָה אֱלֹהֵ֫ינוּ בְּיָדֵ֫נוּ גַּם אֶת־עוֹג
מֶ֫לֶךְ־הַבָּשָׁן וְאֶת־כָּל־עַמּוֹ

9. (Exod. 19:2–4) וַיִּסְעוּ מֵרְפִידִים וַיָּבֹ֫אוּ מִדְבַּר סִינַי
וַיַּחֲנוּ בַּמִּדְבָּר וַיִּחַן־שָׁם יִשְׂרָאֵל נֶ֫גֶד הָהָר:
וּמֹשֶׁה עָלָה אֶל־הָאֱלֹהִים וַיִּקְרָא אֵלָיו יְהוָה
מִן־הָהָר לֵאמֹר כֹּה תֹאמַר לְבֵית יַעֲקֹב וְתַגֵּיד[8]
לִבְנֵי יִשְׂרָאֵל:
אַתֶּם רְאִיתֶם אֲשֶׁר עָשִׂ֫יתִי לְמִצְרָ֑יִם וָאֶשָּׂא
אֶתְכֶם עַל־כַּנְפֵי נְשָׁרִים[9] וָאָבִא[10] אֶתְכֶם אֵלָי:

10. (Gen. 6:2) וַיִּרְאוּ בְנֵי־הָאֱלֹהִים אֶת־בְּנוֹת הָאָדָם
כִּי טֹבֹת הֵ֫נָּה וַיִּקְחוּ לָהֶם נָשִׁים מִכֹּל
אֲשֶׁר בָּחָֽרוּ:

[7] "to meet us"; see XXI.2.
[8] tell
[9] eagles
[10] and I brought

11. (Ps. 78:67–68) וַיִּמְאַס בְּאֹהֶל יוֹסֵף וּבְשֵׁבֶט אֶפְרַיִם לֹא בָחָר:
וַיִּבְחַר אֶת־שֵׁבֶט יְהוּדָה אֶת־הַר צִיּוֹן אֲשֶׁר
אָהֵב:

12. (Gen. 3:2–3) וַתֹּאמֶר הָאִשָּׁה אֶל־הַנָּחָשׁ[11] מִפְּרִי
עֵץ־הַגָּן נֹאכֵל:
וּמִפְּרִי הָעֵץ אֲשֶׁר בְּתוֹךְ־הַגָּן
אָמַר אֱלֹהִים לֹא תֹאכְלוּ מִמֶּנּוּ וְלֹא
תִגְּעוּ בּוֹ פֶּן־תְּמֻתוּן:

13. (Gen. 3:9–10) וַיִּקְרָא יְהוָה אֱלֹהִים אֶל־הָאָדָם וַיֹּאמֶר
לוֹ אַיֶּכָּה:
וַיֹּאמֶר אֶת־קֹלְךָ שָׁמַעְתִּי בַּגָּן וָאִירָא

14. (1 Sam. 3:3–5) וְנֵר[12] אֱלֹהִים טֶרֶם יִכְבֶּה[13] וּשְׁמוּאֵל שֹׁכֵב
בְּהֵיכַל יְהוָה אֲשֶׁר־שָׁם אֲרוֹן אֱלֹהִים:
וַיִּקְרָא יְהוָה אֶל־שְׁמוּאֵל וַיֹּאמֶר הִנֵּנִי:
וַיָּרָץ אֶל־עֵלִי וַיֹּאמֶר הִנְנִי כִּי־קָרָאתָ לִּי
וַיֹּאמֶר לֹא־קָרָאתִי שׁוּב שְׁכָב[14] וַיֵּלֶךְ וַיִּשְׁכָּב:

15. (Exod. 12:28–30) וַיֵּלְכוּ וַיַּעֲשׂוּ בְּנֵי יִשְׂרָאֵל כַּאֲשֶׁר צִוָּה
יְהוָה אֶת־מֹשֶׁה וְאַהֲרֹן כֵּן עָשׂוּ:
וַיְהִי בַּחֲצִי הַלַּיְלָה וַיהוָה הִכָּה כָל־בְּכוֹר
בְּאֶרֶץ מִצְרַיִם מִבְּכֹר פַּרְעֹה הַיֹּשֵׁב עַל־כִּסְאוֹ
עַד בְּכוֹר הַשְּׁבִי[15] אֲשֶׁר בְּבֵית הַבּוֹר[16] וְכֹל
בְּכוֹר בְּהֵמָה:
וַיָּקָם פַּרְעֹה לַיְלָה הוּא וְכָל־עֲבָדָיו
וְכָל־מִצְרַיִם וַתְּהִי צְעָקָה גְדֹלָה בְּמִצְרָיִם
כִּי־אֵין בַּיִת אֲשֶׁר אֵין־שָׁם מֵת:

[11] the snake
[12] נֵר lamp
[13] כבה be quenched, extinguished
[14] שׁוּב שְׁכָב lie down again!
[15] שְׁבִי captive, prisoner
[16] בּוֹר pit, dungeon

LESSON XX

1. Forms of the G Jussive

a. The G jussives can be clearly distinguished from the corresponding imperfects only in III-ה and II-*Wāw/Yōd* verbs.

In III-ה verbs, the jussives are usually identical to the corresponding *wyqtl* forms without the conjunctive *wāw*.

Root	Imperfect	*wyqtl*	Jussive	
בנה	יִבְנֶה	וַיִּבֶן	יִבֶן	build
גלה	יִגְלֶה	וַיִּגֶל	יִגֶל	uncover
היה	יִהְיֶה	וַיְהִי	יְהִי	be, become
חיה	יִחְיֶה	וַיְחִי	יְחִי	live
חרה	יֶחֱרֶה	וַיִּחַר	יִחַר	be angry
נטה	יִטֶּה	וַיֵּט	יֵט	stretch
עלה	יַעֲלֶה	וַיַּעַל	יַעַל	go up
עשׂה	יַעֲשֶׂה	וַיַּעַשׂ	יַעַשׂ	do, make
שתה	יִשְׁתֶּה	וַיֵּשְׁתְּ	יֵשְׁתְּ	drink

For the verb רֹאה, however, there is a slight difference between *wyqtl* and 3 ms forms: וַיַּרְא and he saw, יֵרֶא let him see.

b. In II-*Wāw/Yōd* verbs, the jussives are normally distinguished from the *wyqtl* forms.

Root	Imperfect	*wyqtl*	Jussive	
מות	יָמוּת	וַיָּמָת	יָמֹת	die
רום	יָרוּם	וַיָּרָם	יָרֹם	be exalted
שׁוב	יָשׁוּב	וַיָּשָׁב	יָשֹׁב	return
גיל	יָגִיל	וַיָּגֶל	יָגֵל	rejoice
ריב	יָרִיב	וַיָּרֶב	יָרֵב	quarrel
שׂים	יָשִׂים	וַיָּשֶׂם	יָשֵׂם	place, set

167

2. Cohortative Forms of Weak Verbs

a. The G cohortative forms of weak verbs are as follows:

Root	1 cs	1 cp	
עמד	אֶעֶמְדָה	נַעַמְדָה	stand
אכל	אֹכְלָה	נֹאכְלָה	eat
בחר	אֶבְחֲרָה	נִבְחֲרָה	choose
שלח	אֶשְׁלְחָה	נִשְׁלְחָה	send
נפל	אֶפְּלָה	נִפְּלָה	fall
ישׁב	אֵשְׁבָה	נֵשְׁבָה	dwell
קום	אָקוּמָה	נָקוּמָה	arise
שׂים	אָשִׂימָה	נָשִׂימָה	place

Notes:

i. When the cohortative is in pause the thematic vowel will not be reduced.

אֶעֱמֹדָה but אֶעֶמְדָה

אֶפֹּלָה but אֶפְּלָה

ii. *אֶעֶמְדָה > אֶעֶמְדָה; *נַעַמְדָה > נַעֲמֹדָה (see XVIII.1.d.i).

iii. *אֹאכְלָה > אֹכְלָה.

b. Instead of special cohortative forms, III-ה verbs use the appropriate imperfect forms—that is, without the volitive ה ָ.

3. Forms of the G Imperative

a. Imperatives occur only in the second person. Third person commands are expressed by the jussives.

b. It is easier at this point to think of the imperatives as forms related to the corresponding imperfects. Observe:

	Imperfect	**Imperative**
2 ms	תִּקְטֹל	קְטֹל
2 fs	תִּקְטְלִי	קִטְלִי > *קְטְלִי
2 mp	תִּקְטְלוּ	קִטְלוּ > *קְטְלוּ
2 fp	תִּקְטֹלְנָה	קְטֹלְנָה

c. The inflections of the G imperative of the strong verbs שָׁמַר (keep) and שָׁכַב (lie down) are as follows:

2 ms	שְׁמֹר	שְׁכַב
2 fs	שִׁמְרִי	שִׁכְבִי
2 mp	שִׁמְרוּ	שִׁכְבוּ
2 fp	שְׁמֹרְנָה	שְׁכַבְנָה

d. The inflections of the G imperative of the I-Guttural verbs עָמַד (stand), חָזַק (be strong), and אָכַל (eat) are as follows:

2 ms	עֲמֹד	חֲזַק	אֱכֹל
2 fs	עִמְדִי	חִזְקִי	אִכְלִי
2 mp	עִמְדוּ	חִזְקוּ	אִכְלוּ
2 fp	עֲמֹדְנָה	חֲזַקְנָה	אֱכֹלְנָה

Notes:

i. Although the imperfect of חָזַק is תֶּחֱזַק, the imperative is חֲזַק, not *חֱזַק.

ii. In the imperative, all I-אֵ verbs prefer ֱ to ֲ .

iii. Regardless of the guttural, the 2 fs and 2 mp forms have *i* in the first syllable; we expect *עֲמְדִי > עִמְדִי, etc. (see XVIII.1.d.i).

e. The inflection of the G imperative of the II-Guttural verb בָּחַר (choose) is as follows:

2 ms	בְּחַר
2 fs	בַּחֲרִי
2 mp	בַּחֲרוּ
2 fp	בְּחַרְנָה

Notes:

i. *בַּחֲרוּ > *בְּחֲרוּ; בַּחֲרִי > *בְּחֲרִי (*cf.* V.2.b.ii)

ii.   Forms with I-א, however, will prefer ֳ to ֲ (*cf.* 3.d.ii above): אֱחֹזוּ, אֱהֱבוּ.

f. The inflections of the G imperative of the III-ה verbs בנה (build), עשׂה (do), and היה (be) are as follows:

2 ms	בְּנֵה	עֲשֵׂה	הֱיֵה
2 fs	בְּנִי	עֲשִׂי	הֱיִי
2 mp	בְּנוּ	עֲשׂוּ	הֱיוּ
2 fp	בְּנֶינָה	עֲשֶׂינָה	הֱיֶינָה

Notes:

i.   The ending in the 2 ms is always ה ֵ, not ה ֶ, as in the imperfect 2 ms.

ii.   For the verbs היה (be) and חיה (live), the first syllable is always ֱ, not ֲ.

g. The inflections of the G imperative of the I-*Wāw* verbs ישׁב (dwell) and ידע (know), and the verb הלך, are as follows:

2 ms	שֵׁב	דַּע	לֵךְ
2 fs	שְׁבִי	דְּעִי	לְכִי
2 mp	שְׁבוּ	דְּעוּ	לְכוּ
2 fp	שֵׁבְנָה	דַּעְנָה	לֵכְנָה

Notes:

i.   As previously noted (XVIII.5.c), the verb הלך behaves like an original I-*Wāw* verb in some forms of the G and in all forms of the H *binyānim.*

ii.   As in the imperfect, the first radical does not appear anywhere in the imperative.

iii.   Note the imperf. תֵּשַׁבְנָה but impv. שֵׁבְנָה; תֵּלַכְנָה but לֵכְנָה.

iv.   Although ירשׁ behaves like an original I-*Yōd* verb in the imperfect (see XVIII.5.d), the imperatives are, with one exception, typical of I-*Wāw* verbs (i.e., רַשׁ, רְשׁוּ). The verb ירא (be afraid), on the other hand, shows no aphaeresis in the imperative (יִרְאוּ ;יְרָא). The imperative of original I-*Yōḏ* verbs is unattested, although one would expect the קְטַל pattern; that is, with no aphaeresis.

h. The inflections of the G imperatives of the I-*Nûn* verbs נפל (fall), נסע (set out), and נתן (give) are as follows:

2 ms	נְפֹל	סַע	תֵּן
2 fs	נִפְלִי	סְעִי	תְּנִי
2 mp	נִפְלוּ	סְעוּ	תְּנוּ
2 fp	נְפֹלְנָה	סַעְנָה	תֵּנָּה

Notes:
i. There are two basic types of I-*Nûn* verbs in the G imperative: those with the first radical, and those with aphaeresis of the first radical. With the exception of נתן (give), verbs with aphaeresis of the נ in the imperative always have the *a* thematic vowel in the imperfect and imperative.
ii. The verb לקח (take) behaves like a I-*Nûn* verb; thus קַח, קְחִי, קְחוּ (the 2 fp form is unattested).
iii. The I-*Wāw* verb יצק (pour out) has both יְצֹק and צַק in the imperative (cf. XV.8.c; XVIII.5.e).

i. The inflections of the G imperative of the II-*Wāw* verbs קוּם and בוא, and the II-*Yōḏ* verb שׂים are as follows:

2 ms	קוּם	בּוֹא	שִׂים
2 fs	קוּמִי	בֹּאִי	שִׂימִי
2 mp	קוּמוּ	בֹּאוּ	שִׂימוּ
2 fp	קֹמְנָה	——	——

Notes:
i. II-*Wāw* verbs are clearly distinguished from II-*Yōḏ* verbs.
ii. The 2 fp form of קוּם is קֹמְנָה even though the 2 fp imperfect is usually תְּקוּמֶינָה.

j. The imperatives may be vocalized slightly differently in certain situations.

   i.   When linked to a following word or particle by means of a *maqqēp̄*, the imperative becomes proclitic and the last syllable may be shortened.

   שְׁמֹר but שְׁמָר־לְךָ Keep!

   שֵׁב but שֶׁב־שָׁם Stay there!

   ii. When the imperative is in pause, the thematic vowel may not be reduced; it may, in fact, be lengthened.

   שְׁבוּ but שֵׁבוּ Stay!

   שִׁמְעַ but שְׁמָע Hear!

   אִכְלוּ but אֱכֹלוּ Eat!

4. Imperative Forms with Volitive הָ

a. The 2 ms of the imperative may take the volitive הָ, like the cohortative (XVII.5.b). When it does, the base form is shortened, contracted, or reduced before the volitive הָ, unless it is a II-*Wāw/Yōd* verb, in which case it remains unchanged.

b. The following are the forms of the G imperative with volitive הָ:

שְׁמֹר	שָׁמְרָה	Keep!
עֲמֹד	עָמְדָה	Stand!
אֱכֹל	אָכְלָה	Eat!
שְׁלַח	שִׁלְחָה	Send!
גְּלֵה	–not attested–	Uncover! (cf. 2.b above)
שֵׁב	שְׁבָה	Sit!
דַּע	דְּעָה	Know!
נְפֹל	נָפְלָה	Fall!
סַע	סְעָה	Set out!
תֵּן	תְּנָה	Give!
קוּם	קוּמָה	Arise!
בּוֹא	בֹּאָה	Come!
שִׂים	שִׂימָה	Place!

5. Negative Commands

a. The imperative forms are *not* negated in Hebrew.

b. To express a negative command, the particle לֹא or אַל is used with the appropriate imperfect form (see XVII.6.b,c).

i. לֹא תִקְטֹל is used to express prohibition.

לֹא תַעֲשֶׂה־לְךָ פֶסֶל

you shall not (ever) *make* an idol for yourself! (Exod. 20:4)

ii. אַל תִקְטֹל is used to express dissuasion or warning.

אַל־תִּירָא כִּי־אִתְּךָ אָנֹכִי

do not be afraid, for I am with you! (Gen. 26:24)

6. נָא — → emphasizes a command, not translated

a. The particle נָא is found most frequently after jussives, cohortatives, imperatives, or an interjection, probably for emphasis or to express urgency or immediacy. It is often impossible to render it in English.

הִנֵּה־נָא יָדַעְתִּי כִּי אִשָּׁה   I *(do)* know that you are a beautiful

יְפַת־מַרְאֶה אָתְּ   woman (Gen. 12:11)

אוֹי־נָא לִי   *Woe* to me! (Jer. 45:3)

סְלַח־נָא   *Forgive (please)!* (Amos 7:2)

When a word is linked to the particle by a *maqqēp̄,* the final vowel may, of course, be shortened or reduced as needed.

לֶךְ־נָא אֶל־הַצֹּאן   *Go (now)* to the flock! (Gen. 27:9)

b. In dissuasion and warning, the נָא particle may be appended immediately after אַל.

אַל־נָא תַעֲזֹב אֹתָנוּ   Please *don't* abandon us! (Num. 10:31)

The נָא particle is never used with לֹא.

7. Imperatives as Interjections

A few imperative forms are used as interjections and should not be taken literally. When so used, the "imperative" form may be masculine singular even though the subject may be feminine or plural.

a. רָאָה (see)

רְאֵה רֵיחַ בְּנִי כְּרֵיחַ שָׂדֶה   *Behold!* The smell of my son is like a
אֲשֶׁר בֵּרֲכוֹ יְהוָה   field which YHWH has blessed!
                           (Gen. 27:27)

b. קוּם (arise)

In many instances, the verb קוּם indicates the initiation of an action.

קוּם־נָא שְׁבָה וְאָכְלָה   *Come on!* Sit down and eat!
                         (Gen. 27:19)

c. יהב (give)

הָבָה־נָּה אָבוֹא אֵלַיִךְ   *Come!* Let me come into you!
                       (Gen. 38:16)

d. הלך (go)

לְכָה נִכְרְתָה בְרִית   *Come on!* Let us make a covenant!
                     (Gen. 31:44)

8. Redundant Dative with Imperative

After the imperative, the preposition לְ with the second person pronominal suffix may occur redundantly to affirm the significance of the command for the subject. This redundant dative is normally not translated in English.

לֶךְ־לְךָ מֵאַרְצְךָ   *Go* from your country (Gen. 12:1)

וְקוּם בְּרַח־לְךָ אֶל־לָבָן אָחִי   *Go on! Flee* to Laban my brother
                                  (Gen. 27:43)

9. Imperative in Narrative Sequence

a. *qĕṭōl* + *wĕqāṭal* (impv. + *wĕ*-Perfect). By analogy to other narrative sequences one should translate the *wĕqāṭal* form as if it were an imperative.

לֵךְ וּבָאתָ־לְּךָ אֶרֶץ יְהוּדָה   Go on and *enter* the land of Judah
                           (1 Sam. 22:5)

שְׁמַע בְּקוֹלָם וְהִמְלַכְתָּ לָהֶם   Hear their voice and *cause* a king *to*
מֶלֶךְ   *reign* for them (1 Sam. 8:22)

b. *qĕṭōl* + *wĕyiqṭōl* (impv. + *wĕ*-Imperfect/Jussive). In this case, *wĕ*– begins a purpose or result clause.

שִׂים לֶחֶם וָמַיִם לִפְנֵיהֶם place food and water before them *so*

וְיֹאכְלוּ וְיִשְׁתּוּ *that* they may eat and drink
(2 Kings 6:22)

שִׁמְעוּ וּתְחִי נַפְשְׁכֶם Hear *that* you may live (Isa. 55:3)

The imperative + *wĕ*-cohortative likewise indicates result or purpose. Moreover, since the jussive and cohortative function like the imperative, a *wĕyiqṭōl* (not to be confused with the *wayyiqṭōl* form) form standing in sequence with that jussive or cohortative will also indicate result or purpose.

יָבֹא־נָא אֵלַי וְיֵדַע כִּי יֵשׁ let him come to me *that* he may know

נָבִיא בְּיִשְׂרָאֵל that there is a prophet in Israel
(2 Kings 5:8)

Finally, it should be noted that the imperative following the jussive in sequence may again indicate result or purpose.

יִתֵּן יְהוָה לָכֶם וּמְצֶאןָ מְנוּחָה May YHWH grant *that* you may find a
resting place (Ruth 1:9)

Vocabulary

Nouns:

אֶרֶז   cedar

חֲמוֹר   ass

יְאֹר   river, Nile

לוּחַ   (pl. לוּחוֹת) tablet

Verbs:

חוּל   writhe, tremble, dance

חָשַׂךְ   restrain, withhold

טָהֵר   be clean. *Adjective:* טָהוֹר clean, pure

יהב   give, ascribe. Occurs most frequently in the
imperative form. The ms imperative with volitive
ה ָ, is always הָבָה.

יָצַק	pour out
יָצַר	form
כבס	(D) wash, clean
כָּשַׁל	stumble
נוּחַ	rest
נָצַר	watch
עָרַךְ	arrange, set in order
שִׁיר	sing. *Noun:* שִׁיר song

Adverbs:

אֵיפֹה	where?
פֹּה	here

Preposition:

מֵעַל	above

Exercise 20

1. (Ps. 96:1) שִׁירוּ לַיהוָה שִׁיר חָדָשׁ שִׁירוּ לַיהוָה כָּל־הָאָרֶץ:

2. (Gen. 13:12–14) אַבְרָם יָשַׁב בְּאֶרֶץ־כְּנָעַן וְלוֹט יָשַׁב
בְּעָרֵי הַכִּכָּר[1] וַיֶּאֱהַל עַד־סְדֹם:
וְאַנְשֵׁי סְדֹם רָעִים וְחַטָּאִים לַיהוָה מְאֹד:
וַיהוָה אָמַר אֶל־אַבְרָם אַחֲרֵי הִפָּרֶד־לוֹט[2]
מֵעִמּוֹ שָׂא נָא עֵינֶיךָ וּרְאֵה
מִן־הַמָּקוֹם אֲשֶׁר־אַתָּה שָׁם צָפֹנָה וָנֶגְבָּה
וָקֵדְמָה וָיָמָּה:

3. (Gen. 11:4) וַיֹּאמְרוּ הָבָה נִבְנֶה־לָּנוּ עִיר וּמִגְדָּל
וְרֹאשׁוֹ בַשָּׁמַיִם וְנַעֲשֶׂה־לָּנוּ שֵׁם

---

[1] the plain
[2] Lot's separation

4.   (Exod. 7:17) כֹּה אָמַר יְהוָה בְּזֹאת תֵּדַע כִּי אֲנִי יְהוָה

הִנֵּה אָנֹכִי מַכֶּה בַּמַּטֶּה אֲשֶׁר־בְּיָדִי עַל־הַמַּיִם

אֲשֶׁר בַּיְאֹר וְנֶהֶפְכוּ[3] לְדָם:

5.   (Exod. 7:19–20) וַיֹּאמֶר יְהוָה אֶל־מֹשֶׁה אֱמֹר אֶל־אַהֲרֹן קַח

מַטְּךָ וּנְטֵה־יָדְךָ עַל־מֵימֵי מִצְרַיִם עַל־נַהֲרֹתָם

עַל־יְאֹרֵיהֶם וְעַל־אַגְמֵיהֶם[4] וְעַל כָּל־מִקְוֵה

מֵימֵיהֶם וְיִהְיוּ־דָם וְהָיָה דָם בְּכָל־אֶרֶץ

מִצְרַיִם וּבָעֵצִים וּבָאֲבָנִים:

וַיַּעֲשׂוּ־כֵן מֹשֶׁה וְאַהֲרֹן כַּאֲשֶׁר צִוָּה יְהוָה

6.   (2 Kings 22:15-16) וַתֹּאמֶר אֲלֵיהֶם כֹּה־אָמַר יְהוָה אֱלֹהֵי יִשְׂרָאֵל

אִמְרוּ לָאִישׁ אֲשֶׁר־שָׁלַח אֶתְכֶם אֵלָי:

כֹּה אָמַר יְהוָה הִנְנִי מֵבִיא רָעָה אֶל־הַמָּקוֹם

הַזֶּה וְעַל־יֹשְׁבָיו אֵת כָּל־דִּבְרֵי הַסֵּפֶר אֲשֶׁר

קָרָא מֶלֶךְ יְהוּדָה:

7.   (Exod. 24:12–14) וַיֹּאמֶר יְהוָה אֶל־מֹשֶׁה עֲלֵה אֵלַי הָהָרָה

וֶהְיֵה־שָׁם וְאֶתְּנָה לְךָ אֶת־לֻחֹת הָאֶבֶן וְהַתּוֹרָה

וְהַמִּצְוָה אֲשֶׁר כָּתַבְתִּי לְהוֹרֹתָם:[5]

וַיָּקָם מֹשֶׁה וִיהוֹשֻׁעַ מְשָׁרְתוֹ וַיַּעַל מֹשֶׁה

אֶל־הַר הָאֱלֹהִים:

וְאֶל־הַזְּקֵנִים אָמַר שְׁבוּ־לָנוּ בָזֶה עַד

אֲשֶׁר־נָשׁוּב אֲלֵיכֶם

8.   (Ps. 96:7–8) הָבוּ לַיהוָה מִשְׁפְּחוֹת עַמִּים הָבוּ לַיהוָה

כָּבוֹד וָעֹז:

הָבוּ לַיהוָה כְּבוֹד שְׁמוֹ שְׂאוּ־מִנְחָה וּבֹאוּ

לְחַצְרוֹתָיו:

9.   (Gen. 44:33–34) וְעַתָּה יֵשֶׁב־נָא עַבְדְּךָ תַּחַת הַנַּעַר

עֶבֶד לַאדֹנִי וְהַנַּעַר יַעַל עִם־אֶחָיו:

כִּי־אֵיךְ אֶעֱלֶה אֶל־אָבִי וְהַנַּעַר

---

[3] they will be turned
[4] their reed pools
[5] for their instruction

אֵינֶנּוּ אִתִּי פֶּן אֶרְאֶה בְרָע אֲשֶׁר

יִמְצָא אֶת־אָבִי:

10. (Gen. 22:3–6) וַיָּקָם וַיֵּלֶךְ אֶל־הַמָּקוֹם אֲשֶׁר־אָמַר־לוֹ

הָאֱלֹהִים:

בַּיּוֹם הַשְּׁלִישִׁי [6] וַיִּשָּׂא אַבְרָהָם אֶת־

עֵינָיו וַיַּרְא אֶת־הַמָּקוֹם מֵרָחֹק:

וַיֹּאמֶר אַבְרָהָם אֶל־נְעָרָיו שְׁבוּ־לָכֶם

פֹּה עִם־הַחֲמוֹר וַאֲנִי וְהַנַּעַר

נֵלְכָה עַד־כֹּה וְנִשְׁתַּחֲוֶה [7] וְנָשׁוּבָה אֲלֵיכֶם:

וַיִּקַּח אַבְרָהָם אֶת־עֲצֵי הָעֹלָה וַיָּשֶׂם

עַל־יִצְחָק בְּנוֹ וַיִּקַּח בְּיָדוֹ אֶת־הָאֵשׁ

וְאֶת־הַמַּאֲכֶלֶת [8] וַיֵּלְכוּ שְׁנֵיהֶם [9] יַחְדָּו:

[6] third

[7] worship

[8] knife

[9] two of them

LESSON XXI

1. Imperfect and Imperative with Object Suffixes

a. As in the perfect, the imperfect and imperative may have object suffixes appended to them. Thus,

אֶשְׁלַח אֹתְךָ = אֶשְׁלָחֲךָ   "I will send you"

שְׁלַח אֹתִי = שְׁלָחֵנִי   "Send me!"

b. The imperfect may undergo certain vowel changes before the object suffix:

    i.   The unreduced *ō* thematic vowel is reduced to *ĕ*: יִשְׁמֹר but יִשְׁמְרֵנִי "he will keep me." Before the 2 ms and 2 mp suffixes, however, *ō* will usually be shortened to *o*. Thus, יִשְׁמָרְךָ and יִשְׁמָרְכֶם.

    ii.   The unreduced *ē* thematic vowel is reduced to *ĕ*: יִתֵּן but יִתְּנֵנִי "he will give me." Before the 2 ms and 2 mp suffixes, however, *ē* will usually be shortened to *e*. Thus, יִתֶּנְךָ; יִתֶּנְכֶם.

    iii.   The unreduced *a* thematic vowel is lengthened to *ā*:

יִשְׁמַע but יִשְׁמָעֵנִי   he will hear me

אֶקַּח but אֶקָּחֲךָ   I will take you

c. The imperative may undergo certain changes before the object suffixes:

    i.   The G imperative ms, קְטֹל becomes – קָטְל (*qoṭl*–) before the suffix (cf. the קָטְלָה imperative; XX.4.b): שָׁמְרֵנִי "Keep me!" The mp קִטְלוּ and fs קִטְלִי remain unchanged: e.g., דִּרְשׁוּנִי "Seek me!"

    ii.   The G imperative of קְטַל type will be – קְטָל before the object suffix.

שְׁמָעֵנִי   Hear me!

שְׁמָעוּנִי   Hear me! (not שִׁמְעוּנִי)

As a rule, the *a* vowel in the imperative of any type will be lengthened.

דָּעֵהוּ   Know him!

קָחֵהוּ   Take him!

There are a few exceptions, however: e.g.,

אָכְלֵם but אֹכַל, not *אָכְלֵם

iii. In the imperative of any *binyān,* any *ē* vowel will be reduced to *ĕ*:

תֵּן   Give!

תְּנֵהוּ   Give it!

תְּנֵם   Give them up!

d. The object suffixes used with the imperfect and imperative are as follows:

3 ms	הוּ ָ –	3 mp	ם ָ –
3 fs	הָ ָ –	3 fp	ן ָ –
2 ms	ךָ–	2 mp	כֶם–
2 fs	ךְ ָ –	2 fp	–not attested–
1 cs	נִי ָ –	1 cp	נוּ ָ –

If the imperfect or imperative ends in a vowel, the "connecting vowel" (ָ or ֶ) is omitted before the suffix. Thus, the 2 fs, 2 mp, and 3 mp forms will all take suffixes without the connecting vowel. The תִּקְטֹלְנָה and קְטֹלְנָה forms will be replaced by תִּקְטְלוּ and קִטְלוּ, respectively. Study the following carefully:

i. יִשְׁמֹר he will keep

יִשְׁמְרֵהוּ he will keep him/it

יִשְׁמְרֶהָ he will keep her/it

יִשְׁמָרְךָ he will keep you (ms)

יִשְׁמְרֵךְ he will keep you (fs)

יִשְׁמְרֵנִי he will keep me

יִשְׁמְרֵם he will keep them

יִשְׁמְרֵן he will keep them

יִשְׁמָרְכֶם he will keep you (mp)

יִשְׁמְרֵנוּ he will keep us

ii. יִשְׁמְרוּ they will keep

יִשְׁמְרוּהוּ they will keep him/it

יִשְׁמְרוּהָ they will keep her/it

יִשְׁמְרוּךְ they will keep you (ms)

יִשְׁמְרוּךְ they will keep you (fs)

יִשְׁמְרוּנִי they will keep me

יִשְׁמְרוּם they will keep them

יִשְׁמְרוּן they will keep them

יִשְׁמְרוּכֶם they will keep you (mp)

יִשְׁמְרוּנוּ they will keep us

e. Very frequently, there will be an additional *nûn* before the actual suffix. The following forms are attested:

3 ms	־ֶנּוּ	(*-énhû > -énnû)
3 fs	־ֶנָּה	(*-énhā > -énnā[h])
2 ms	־ֶךָּ	(*-énkā > -ekkā)
1 cs	־ֶנִּי	(-énnî)
1 cp	־ֶנּוּ	(-énnû)

There is no difference in meaning between the suffixes with the additional *nûn* and those without. Thus, יִשְׁלָחֵהוּ is similar in meaning to יִשְׁלָחֶנּוּ "he will send him/it."

f. III—ה verbs drop the final ה *mater* before the object suffix.

אֶבְנֶךָ	I will build you
יִרְאֵנִי	he will see me
תַּעֲשֵׂנּוּ	you shall make it
עֲנֵנִי	Answer me!

g. The distinction between the imperfect and the jussive/*wyqtl* forms is not maintained when the forms take suffixes.

תַּעֲנֵנִי	you will answer me
וַתַּעֲנֵנִי	and you answered me

2. G Infinitive Absolute

a. The regular form of the G infinitive absolute is קָטוֹל, or, more accurately, קָטֹל.

b. The G infinitive absolute of the III-ה verb בנה is either בָּנוֹ or בָּנֹה.

c. There is no difference in the infinitive absolute between II-*Wāw* and II-*Yōd* verbs:

Root	Inf. Abs.
קוֹם	קוֹם
בוֹא	בּוֹא
שִׂים	שׂוֹם

3. Uses of the Infinitive Absolute

The infinitive absolute is used in the following ways:

a. As a *verbal noun.*

שָׂשׂוֹן וְשִׂמְחָה הָרֹג בָּקָר וְשָׁחֹט צֹאן	joy and gladness, *slaying* cattle and *slaughtering* sheep (Isa. 22:13)
לְדַעְתּוֹ מָאוֹס בָּרָע וּבָחוֹר בַּטּוֹב	when he knows *to refuse* evil and *to choose* good (Isa. 7:15)
אָכֹל דְּבַשׁ הַרְבּוֹת לֹא־טוֹב	It is not good *to eat* much honey (Prov. 25:27)

b. Most commonly the infinitive absolute stands before a finite verb of the same root to emphasize the certainty, force, or decisiveness of the verbal idea.

מוֹת תָּמוּת	You shall *certainly* die (Gen. 2:17)
אִם־שָׁכֹחַ תִּשְׁכַּח אֶת־יְהוָה אֱלֹהֶיךָ	If *indeed* you forget YHWH your God (Deut. 8:19)
שָׁמוֹר תִּשְׁמְרוּן אֶת־מִצְוֹת יְהוָה אֱלֹהֵיכֶם	You will *diligently* keep the commandments of YHWH your God (Deut. 6:17)

Occasionally the infinitive may also come after the finite verb apparently without any difference in meaning.

c. The infinitive absolute may come after an imperative to strengthen or intensify it.

הָרְגֵנִי נָא הָרֹג	Kill me *right away!* (Num. 11:15)
שִׁמְעוּ שָׁמוֹעַ אֵלַי	*Really* listen to me! (Isa. 55:2)

d. It may stand after any verb to indicate continuance or repetition.

שִׁמְעוּ שָׁמוֹעַ וְאַל־תָּבִינוּ וּרְאוּ רָאוּ וְאַל־תֵּדָעוּ	*Keep on* listening but do not understand, *keep on* looking but do not know (Isa. 6:9)
לַשָּׁוְא צָרַף צָרוֹף	One *goes on* refining for nothing (Jer. 6:29)

Frequently following such a construction comes a second infinitive indicating another action occurring simultaneously.

הָלְכוּ הָלֹךְ וְגָעוֹ	they went along *lowing (as they went)* (1 Sam. 6:12)
וַיֵּצֵא יָצוֹא וָשׁוֹב	and it went *back and forth* (Gen. 8:7)
יֹצֵא יָצוֹא וּמְקַלֵּל	he came out *cursing* (2 Sam. 16:5)

Probably because of the frequent use of הָלוֹךְ in this construction, this infinitive has become an idiomatic term indicating continuance.

| וְהַמַּיִם הָיוּ הָלוֹךְ וְחָסוֹר | the water was *diminishing continually* (Gen. 8:5) |
| וַיִּסַּע אַבְרָם הָלוֹךְ וְנָסוֹעַ הַנֶּגְבָּה | Abram *kept on journeying* southward (Gen. 12:9) |

In some instances, the participle of הלך is used in place of the infinitive, with no discernible difference in meaning. Compare the following:

| וַיֵּלֶךְ הָלוֹךְ וְקָרֵב | he *kept* approaching (2 Sam. 18:25) |
| וַיֵּלֶךְ הַפְּלִשְׁתִּי הֹלֵךְ וְקָרֵב | the Philistine *kept* approaching (1 Sam. 17:41) |

e. The infinitive absolute is frequently used in place of an imperative.

| זָכוֹר אֶת־יוֹם הַשַּׁבָּת | *Remember* the sabbath day (Exod. 20:8) |
| שָׁמוֹר אֶת־יוֹם הַשַּׁבָּת | *Observe* the sabbath day! (Deut. 5:12) |

f. Less frequently the infinitive absolute is used in place of a *finite verb*, whether perfect or imperfect.

| וְנָתוֹן אֹתוֹ עַל כָּל־אֶרֶץ מִצְרָיִם | and he *set* him over all the land of Egypt (Gen. 41:43) |
| יִקְנוּ וְכָתוֹב בַּסֵּפֶר | they will buy and will *write* in the book (Jer. 32:44) |

Vocabulary

Nouns:

אָוֶן wickedness, trouble

אֹמֶר   (also אִמְרָה) word, saying

אֱמֶת   truth. Also אֱמוּנָה faithfulness. *Verb: cf.* אמן

בִּינָה   understanding, perception. *Verb:* בין understand

בַּעַל   lord, master, husband, owner; frequently used as
proper name, Baal (a Canaanite god). *Verb:* בעל
rule, be lord, marry

חֹזֶק   strength

יָרֵךְ   thigh

צָרָה   distress. *Verbs:* צור oppress, press hard. צרר be hard-
pressed, be in distress

רֶחֶם   (fs.) womb, mercy. *Verb:* רחם (D) have compassion

Verbs:

בזז   plunder, prey. *Noun:* בַּז plunder, prey

הרה   conceive, become pregnant. *Adjective:* הָרָה pregnant

חגר   gird

לכד   capture

סגר   close

עזר   help. *Noun:* עֵזֶר help

פתח   open. *Cf.* פֶּתַח door

קנה   acquire, buy, create. *Nouns:* מִקְנֶה possession,
property; קִנְיָן property

קרע   rend, tear

ריב   dispute, quarrel. *Noun:* רִיב lawsuit

שחט   slaughter

שית   put, place

שקה   (H) give drink, irrigate

Exercise 21

1.   (Isa. 22:13) אָכוֹל וְשָׁתוֹ כִּי מָחָר נָמוּת:

2.

(Exod. 13:3) וַיֹּאמֶר מֹשֶׁה אֶל־הָעָם זָכוֹר אֶת־הַיּוֹם הַזֶּה
אֲשֶׁר יְצָאתֶם מִמִּצְרַיִם מִבֵּית עֲבָדִים כִּי
בְּחֹזֶק יָד הוֹצִיא יְהוָה אֶתְכֶם מִזֶּה

3.

(Prov. 4:5-7) קְנֵה חָכְמָה קְנֵה בִינָה אַל־תִּשְׁכַּח וְאַל־תֵּט
מֵאִמְרֵי־פִי:
אַל־תַּעַזְבֶהָ וְתִשְׁמְרֶךָּ אֱהָבֶהָ וְתִצְּרֶךָּ:
רֵאשִׁית חָכְמָה קְנֵה חָכְמָה וּבְכָל־קִנְיָנְךָ
קְנֵה בִינָה:

4.

(Gen. 47:29-30) וַיִּקְרְבוּ יְמֵי־יִשְׂרָאֵל לָמוּת וַיִּקְרָא
לִבְנוֹ לְיוֹסֵף וַיֹּאמֶר לוֹ אִם־נָא מָצָאתִי
חֵן בְּעֵינֶיךָ שִׂים־נָא יָדְךָ תַּחַת יְרֵכִי
וְעָשִׂיתָ עִמָּדִי חֶסֶד וֶאֱמֶת אַל־נָא
תִקְבְּרֵנִי בְּמִצְרָיִם:
וְשָׁכַבְתִּי עִם־אֲבֹתַי וּנְשָׂאתַנִי
מִמִּצְרַיִם וּקְבַרְתַּנִי בִּקְבֻרָתָם
וַיֹּאמַר אָנֹכִי אֶעֱשֶׂה כִדְבָרֶךָ:

5.

(Amos 5:4-5) √ כִּי כֹה אָמַר יְהוָה לְבֵית יִשְׂרָאֵל דִּרְשׁוּנִי
וִחְיוּ:
וְאַל־תִּדְרְשׁוּ בֵּית־אֵל וְהַגִּלְגָּל לֹא תָבֹאוּ
וּבְאֵר שֶׁבַע לֹא תַעֲבֹרוּ כִּי הַגִּלְגָּל גָּלֹה יִגְלֶה
וּבֵית־אֵל יִהְיֶה לְאָוֶן:

6.

(Gen. 29:31-33) וַיַּרְא יְהוָה כִּי־שְׂנוּאָה[1] לֵאָה וַיִּפְתַּח
אֶת־רַחְמָהּ וְרָחֵל עֲקָרָה:[2]
וַתַּהַר לֵאָה וַתֵּלֶד בֵּן וַתִּקְרָא שְׁמוֹ
רְאוּבֵן כִּי אָמְרָה כִּי־רָאָה יְהוָה
בְּעָנְיִי כִּי עַתָּה יֶאֱהָבַנִי אִישִׁי:
וַתַּהַר עוֹד וַתֵּלֶד בֵּן וַתֹּאמֶר
כִּי־שָׁמַע יְהוָה כִּי־שְׂנוּאָה[1] אָנֹכִי וַיִּתֶּן־לִי
גַּם־אֶת־זֶה וַתִּקְרָא שְׁמוֹ שִׁמְעוֹן:

[1] (Leah) was hated
[2] was barren

7.   (Jer. 31:31–33) הִנֵּה יָמִים בָּאִים נְאֻם־יְהוָה וְכָרַתִּי אֶת־בֵּית

יִשְׂרָאֵל וְאֶת־בֵּית יְהוּדָה בְּרִית חֲדָשָׁה:

לֹא כַבְּרִית אֲשֶׁר כָּרַתִּי אֶת־אֲבוֹתָם בְּיוֹם

הֶחֱזִיקִי[3] בְיָדָם לְהוֹצִיאָם[4] מֵאֶרֶץ מִצְרָיִם

אֲשֶׁר־הֵמָּה הֵפֵרוּ[5] אֶת־בְּרִיתִי וְאָנֹכִי

בָּעַלְתִּי בָם נְאֻם־יְהוָה:

כִּי זֹאת הַבְּרִית אֲשֶׁר אֶכְרֹת אֶת־בֵּית

יִשְׂרָאֵל אַחֲרֵי הַיָּמִים הָהֵם נְאֻם־יְהוָה

נָתַתִּי אֶת־תּוֹרָתִי בְּקִרְבָּם וְעַל־לִבָּם

אֶכְתֲּבֶנָּה וְהָיִיתִי לָהֶם לֵאלֹהִים וְהֵמָּה

יִהְיוּ־לִי לְעָם:

8.   (Ps. 99:6) מֹשֶׁה וְאַהֲרֹן בְּכֹהֲנָיו וּשְׁמוּאֵל בְּקֹרְאֵי

שְׁמוֹ קֹרִאים אֶל־יְהוָה וְהוּא יַעֲנֵם:

9.   (Deut. 1:38–41) יְהוֹשֻׁעַ בִּן־נוּן הָעֹמֵד לְפָנֶיךָ הוּא יָבֹא שָׁמָּה

אֹתוֹ חַזֵּק[6] כִּי־הוּא יַנְחִלֶנָּה[7] אֶת־יִשְׂרָאֵל:

וְטַפְּכֶם[8] אֲשֶׁר אֲמַרְתֶּם לָבַז יִהְיֶה וּבְנֵיכֶם

אֲשֶׁר לֹא־יָדְעוּ הַיּוֹם טוֹב וָרָע הֵמָּה יָבֹאוּ

שָׁמָּה וְלָהֶם אֶתְּנֶנָּה וְהֵם יִירָשׁוּהָ:

וְאַתֶּם פְּנוּ לָכֶם וּסְעוּ הַמִּדְבָּרָה דֶּרֶךְ

יַם־סוּף:[9]

וַתַּעֲנוּ וַתֹּאמְרוּ אֵלַי חָטָאנוּ לַיהוָה

אֲנַחְנוּ נַעֲלֶה וְנִלְחַמְנוּ[10] כְּכֹל אֲשֶׁר־צִוָּנוּ יְהוָה

אֱלֹהֵינוּ וַתַּחְגְּרוּ אִישׁ אֶת־כְּלֵי מִלְחַמְתּוֹ

---

[3] my holding fast
[4] to bring them
[5] they broke
[6] D imperative of חזק
[7] will cause (Israel) to possess it
[8] טַף children
[9] Sea of Reeds
[10] and we will fight

LESSON XXII

1. G Infinitive Construct

a. The regular form of the G infinitive construct is קְטֹל. Thus,

שְׁמֹר	to keep, keeping
עֲמֹד	to stand, standing
אֱכֹל	to eat, eating
בְּחֹר	to choose, choosing
שְׁלֹחַ	to send, sending

b. As a verbal noun, the infinitive construct may take a pronominal suffix—the same as those appended to singular nouns (see XI.1).

Before a pronominal suffix, the infinitive קְטֹל becomes –קָטְל (*qoṭl–*) in most instances. Before the 2 ms and 2 mp suffixes it is –קְטָל (*qĕṭol–*). For III-ה, ח, ע verbs, it is usually *qoṭl–*. Thus,

שָׁמְרִי	my keeping	שָׁמְרְךָ	your keeping
עָמְדִי	my standing	עָמְדְךָ	your standing
אָכְלִי	my eating	אָכְלְךָ	your eating
בָּחֳרִי	my choosing	בָּחָרְךָ	your choosing
שָׁלְחִי	my sending	שָׁלְחֲךָ	your sending

Infrequently, the infinitive construct form before the suffix is *qiṭl–* or *qaṭl–* instead of *qoṭl–*.

בִּטְחֵךְ	your trusting
זַעֲקֵךְ	your crying

Since suffixes appended to nouns only indicate possession, one must decide from the context if the infinitive is subjective or objective. In the following examples, the 2 fs suffix in the first instance indicates the subject (the one who abandons), but in the second instance the 2 fs suffix indicates the object (the one abandoned).

עָזְבֵךְ אֶת־יְהוָה   *your abandoning* YHWH (Jer. 2:17)

187

לְעָזְבֵךְ לָשׁוּב מֵאַחֲרָיִךְ   *to abandon you*, to turn from following you (Ruth 1:16)

Occasionally, clarity is achieved when a verbal object suffix is used instead.

לְהָרְגֵנִי   to kill me

לְדָרְשֵׁנִי   to seek me

2. G Infinitive Construct of Weak Verbs

a. The infinitive construct of III-ה verbs always has an anomalous ‑וֹת ending:

בְּנוֹת   to build, building

עֲשׂוֹת   to make, making

הֱיוֹת   to be, being

b. The infinitive construct of I-*Wāw* verbs generally shows aphaeresis of the initial radical, and takes an anomalous ה‑ ending. The form acts like a *qiṭl‑* segolate. But since the first radical is lost and the anomalous ה is added, the original pattern is properly **ṭilt*, which develops to *ṭélet* (cf. IV.5). With the pronominal suffix, then, the original *ṭilt* pattern is retained (cf. XI.2.c). Verbs with III-ה, ח, ע tend to have infinitives of the *ṭalt* pattern, instead of *ṭilt*.

שֶׁבֶת	to dwell, dwelling	שִׁבְתִּי	my dwelling
לֶדֶת	to bear, bearing	לִדְתִּי	my bearing
צֵאת	to go out, going out	צֵאתִי	my going out
רֶשֶׁת	to possess, possessing	רִשְׁתִּי	my possessing
דַּעַת	to know, knowing	דַּעְתִּי	my knowing

Notes:

i.   The verb הלך behaves like a I-*Wāw* verb. Hence, the infinitive construct is usually לֶכֶת. With suffixes it is always ‑לֶכְת, not *‑לְכְת. The form הֲלֹךְ is also attested.

ii. Original *צְאֵת > צֵאת with quiescence of א and compensatory lengthening of ֵ to ֵ .

iii. ירש is regular even though the imperfect is יִירַשׁ and the imperative is רֵשׁ.

iv. The G infinitive construct of I-*Yōd* verbs is not attested, but יָשֵׁן (sleep), which behaves like I-*Yōd* in the imperfect, has יְשֹׁן. The verb ירא, which behaves like a I-*Yōd* verb in the imperfect and imperative, has יְרֹא twice as the infinitivé construct, but in most instances the function of the infinitive is taken by the noun יִרְאָה (fear, fearing).

v. The G infinitive construct of יכל (be able) is יְכֹלֶת.

c. As there are two basic types of I-*Nûn* verbs in the G imperfect, so there are two types in the G infinitive: those that retain the first radical, and those that may show aphaeresis of the first radical and take an anomalous ת ending (i.e., *tilt/talt* types).

i. Most verbs are regular—i.e., they retain the first radical.

Root	Inf. Cs.	Inf. with Suffix	
נפל	נְפֹל	נָפְלוֹ	fall
נגף	נְגֹף	נָגְפוֹ	strike
נסע	נְסֹעַ	נָסְעוֹ	set out

ii. A few verbs may lose the initial נ in the G infinitive construct. These are mainly verbs with III-א, ח, ע; otherwise, only נתן and [נגשׁ]—a verb not attested in the G perfect and whose G imperative forms show some confusion with the imperative of a geminate root—lose the initial נ in the G infinitive construct. The verb לקח also loses the initial radical in the infinitive construct.

Root	Inf. Cs.	Inf. with Suff.	
נגע	גַּעַת/נְגֹעַ	נָגְעוֹ, נָגְעֵךְ	strike
נטע	טַעַת/נְטֹעַ	–not attested–	plant
נפח	פֹּחַת	–not attested–	blow
נשׂא	נְשֹׂא/שְׂאֵת/שֵׂאת	נָשְׂאִי; שְׂאֵתוֹ, שְׂאֵתִי	lift
נתן	נְתֹן/תֵּת	תִּתּוֹ, תִּתִּי	give
[נגשׁ]	גֶּשֶׁת	גִּשְׁתָּם, גִּשְׁתּוֹ	draw near
לקח	קַחַת	קָחְתּוֹ, קַחְתִּי	take

Notes:

α. שֵׂאת>*שְׂאֵת* (*cf.* 2.b.ii in this lesson); שְׂאֵת is a "hyper-correct" variant.

β. תֵּת is derived from original *tint (i.e., *tint > *titt > *tēt* [*cf.* IV.4]).

d. Whereas no distinction is made between II-*Wāw* and II-*Yōḏ* verbs in the infinitive absolute, they are distinguished in the infinitive construct.

Inf. Cs.	Inf. with Suffix	
קוּם	קוּמִי	arise
בּוֹא	בּוֹאִי	come
שִׁית	שִׁיתִי	put

3. Uses of the Infinitive Construct

The infinitive construct may be used in the following ways:

a. As a subject or object of a sentence:

שְׁמֹעַ מִזֶּבַח טוֹב	*Obeying* is better than sacrifice (1 Sam. 15:22)
לֹא אֵדַע צֵאת וָבֹא	I do not know how *to go out* or *come in* (1 Kings 3:7)

b. Most commonly it stands after לְ to express purpose:

וַיֵּצְאוּ לָלֶכֶת אַרְצָה כְּנַעַן	they set out *to go* to the land of Canaan (Gen. 12:5)
סָר לִרְאוֹת	he had turned aside *to see* (Exod. 3:4)

c. With לְ as a gerund:

הִנֵּה הָעָם חֹטְאִים לַיהוָה לֶאֱכֹל עַל־הַדָּם	The people are sinning against YHWH *by eating* blood (1 Sam. 14:33)
צִוִּיתִיךָ לֵאמֹר לֹא תֹאכַל מִמֶּנּוּ	I commanded you (by) *saying*, "You shall not eat from it! (Gen. 3:17)

d. It is used very frequently in temporal clauses.

בְּיוֹם עֲשׂוֹת יְהוָה אֱלֹהִים
אֶרֶץ וְשָׁמָיִם

When YHWH-God *made* earth and heaven [literally: In the day of YHWH-God's making of earth and heaven] (Gen. 2:4)

בְּיוֹם אֲכָלְךָ מִמֶּנּוּ מוֹת תָּמוּת

When you eat from it, you will certainly die (Gen. 2:17)

4. Negation of Infinitives

Construct infinitives are negated by בִּלְתִּי, usually preceded by לְ.

צִוִּיתִיךָ לְבִלְתִּי אֲכָל־מִמֶּנּוּ

I commanded you *not to eat* from it (Gen. 3:11)

פֶּן־תִּשְׁכַּח אֶת־יְהוָה אֱלֹהֶיךָ
לְבִלְתִּי שְׁמֹר מִצְוֹתָיו
וּמִשְׁפָּטָיו וְחֻקֹּתָיו

lest you forget YHWH your God *by not keeping* his commandments, his ordinances, and his statutes (Deut. 8:11)

5. Temporal Clauses

a. Past Events

Discourse on past events is usually introduced by וַיְהִי, literally, "it came to pass" (cf. XIX.2). Since other indications of time usually follow, it appears that וַיְהִי is redundant.

The event that happened is introduced by וַ. Thus, the sequence וַיְהִי . . . וַ means, literally, "it happened . . . that." The student should avoid a rigid translation, however.

The text may provide the narrative context in any of the following ways:

    i.   Some specific reference to the time may be provided.

וַיְהִי בָעֶרֶב וַיִּקַּח אֶת־לֵאָה בִתּוֹ וַיָּבֵא אֹתָהּ אֵלָיו

In the evening, he took Leah his daughter, and he brought her to him (Gen. 29:23)

וַיְהִי בָּעֵת הַהִוא וַיֵּרֶד יְהוּדָה מֵאֵת אֶחָיו

At that time, Judah went down from his brothers (Gen. 38:1)

וַיְהִי בַּחֲצִי הַלַּיְלָה וַיהוָה הִכָּה כָל־בְּכוֹר
בְּאֶרֶץ מִצְרַיִם

At midnight, YHWH smote all the first-born in the land of
Egypt (Exod. 12:29)

ii. Temporal clauses may be introduced by כַּאֲשֶׁר, כְּמוֹ, or כִּי
with a finite verb.

וַיְהִי כִּי־בָאנוּ אֶל־הַמָּלוֹן וַנִּפְתְּחָה אֶת־אַמְתְּחֹתֵינוּ
When we came to the lodge, we opened our sacks
(Gen. 43:21)

iii. Temporal clauses are very frequently introduced by בְּ or כְּ
with the infinitive construct.

וַיְהִי בִּשְׁכֹּן יִשְׂרָאֵל בָּאָרֶץ הַהִוא וַיֵּלֶךְ רְאוּבֵן
וַיִּשְׁכַּב אֶת־בִּלְהָה

When Israel *dwelled* in that land, Reuben went and slept
with Bilhah (Gen. 35:22)

וַיְהִי כְּבוֹא אַבְרָם מִצְרָיְמָה וַיִּרְאוּ הַמִּצְרִים
אֶת־הָאִשָּׁה כִּי־יָפָה הִוא מְאֹד

As Abram *was entering* Egypt, the Egyptians saw that the
woman was very beautiful (Gen. 12:14)

b. Future Events

Discourse on future happenings is usually introduced by וְהָיָה,
literally, "and it shall be" (*cf.* XIX.3). As in the introductory וַיְהִי, it is best
to leave וְהָיָה untranslated.

וְהָיָה כִּי־תָבֹאוּ אֶל־הָאָרֶץ	*When you enter* the land which YHWH
אֲשֶׁר יִתֵּן יְהוָה לָכֶם	will give to you, even as he has
כַּאֲשֶׁר דִּבֵּר וּשְׁמַרְתֶּם אֶת־	spoken, you shall keep this service
הָעֲבֹדָה הַזֹּאת	(Exod. 12:25)
וְהָיָה בַּיּוֹם הַהוּא וְקָרָאתִי	*On that day,* I will summon my servant
לְעַבְדִּי לְאֶלְיָקִים בֶּן־	Eliakim ben-Hilkiah (Isa. 22:20)
חִלְקִיָּהוּ	

6. Synopsis of Verbs in G

The following is a synopsis of verbs in G, reconstructed to the best of our knowledge. These are provided as a pedagogical tool to aid the student in learning the various forms. Some of the forms below are not actually attested (for the particular root) but are reconstructed by analogy to other verbs of the same class.

Root	Perf.	Impf.	Juss.	Impv.	Inf. Abs.	Inf. Cs.	Ptc.
שמר	שָׁמַר	יִשְׁמֹר	יִשְׁמֹר	שְׁמֹר	שָׁמוֹר	שְׁמֹר	שֹׁמֵר
כבד	כָּבֵד	יִכְבַּד	יִכְבַּד	כְּבַד	כָּבוֹד	כְּבֹד	כָּבֵד
קטן	קָטֹן	יִקְטַן	יִקְטַן	קְטַן	קָטוֹן	קְטֹן	קָטֹן
עמד	עָמַד	יַעֲמֹד	יַעֲמֹד	עֲמֹד	עָמוֹד	עֲמֹד	עֹמֵד
חזק	חָזַק	יֶחֱזַק	יֶחֱזַק	חֲזַק	חָזוֹק	חֲזֹק	חָזֵק
אכל	אָכַל	יֹאכַל	יֹאכַל	אֱכֹל	אָכוֹל	אֱכֹל	אֹכֵל
בחר	בָּחַר	יִבְחַר	יִבְחַר	בְּחַר	בָּחוֹר	בְּחֹר	בֹּחֵר
שלח	שָׁלַח	יִשְׁלַח	יִשְׁלַח	שְׁלַח	שָׁלוֹחַ	שְׁלֹחַ	שֹׁלֵחַ
מצא	מָצָא	יִמְצָא	יִמְצָא	מְצָא	מָצוֹא	מְצֹא	מֹצֵא
גלה	גָּלָה	יִגְלֶה	יֶגֶל	גְּלֵה	גָּלֹה/גָּלוֹ	גְּלוֹת	גֹּלֶה
נפל	נָפַל	יִפֹּל	יִפֹּל	נְפֹל	נָפוֹל	נְפֹל	נֹפֵל
נסע	נָסַע	יִסַּע	יִסַּע	סַע	נָסוֹעַ	[סֹעַת]/נְסֹעַ	נֹסֵעַ
נתן	נָתַן	יִתֵּן	יִתֵּן	תֵּן	נָתוֹן	תֵּת	נֹתֵן
ישב	יָשַׁב	יֵשֵׁב	יֵשֵׁב	שֵׁב	יָשׁוֹב	שֶׁבֶת	יֹשֵׁב
יטב	יָטַב	יִיטַב	יִיטַב	יְטַב	יָטוֹב	יְטֹב	יֹטֵב
קום	קָם	יָקוּם	יָקֹם	קוּם	קוֹם	קוּם	קָם
בוא	בָּא	יָבוֹא	יָבֹא	בּוֹא	בּוֹא	בּוֹא	בָּא
שית	שָׁת	יָשִׁית	יָשֵׁת	שִׁית	שׁוֹת	שִׁית	שָׁת
מות	מֵת	יָמוּת	יָמֹת	מוּת	מוֹת	מוֹת	מֵת

Vocabulary

Nouns:

אֶחָד	one. אֲחֵרִים few
כַּף	palm (of hand), sole (of foot)
שָׂטָן	adversary
שֻׁלְחָן	table

Verbs:

אסף	gather, collect
הפך	turn
יָבֵשׁ	be dry. *Noun:* יַבָּשָׁה dry ground
יכח	(H) reprove
כעס	be irritated, angry
לין/לון	lodge. *Noun:* מָלוֹן lodging place
עור	awake, arouse
פגע	meet, befall, encounter. *Noun:* פֶּגַע happening
פדה	ransom
פרץ	break, breach, increase
פרשׂ	spread out
צלח	succeed, prosper
רפא	heal
רצה	be pleased
צחק/שׂחק	(G) laugh; (D) play, jest
שכם	(H) do something early, arise early
תפשׂ	catch, seize

Exercise 22

1.   עֵת לָלֶדֶת וְעֵת לָמוּת עֵת לָטַעַת (Qoh. 3:2–4)

וְעֵת לַעֲקוֹר נָטוּעַ: [1]

עֵת לַהֲרוֹג וְעֵת לִרְפּוֹא

עֵת לִפְרוֹץ וְעֵת לִבְנוֹת:

עֵת לִבְכּוֹת וְעֵת לִשְׂחוֹק

2. (2 Sam. 9:7–9) וַיֹּאמֶר לוֹ דָוִד אַל־תִּירָא כִּי עָשֹׂה אֶעֱשֶׂה

עִמְּךָ חֶסֶד בַּעֲבוּר יְהוֹנָתָן אָבִיךָ וַהֲשִׁבֹתִי

לְךָ אֶת־כָּל־שְׂדֵה שָׁאוּל אָבִיךָ וְאַתָּה תֹּאכַל לֶחֶם

עַל־שֻׁלְחָנִי תָּמִיד:

וַיִּשְׁתַּחוּ [2] וַיֹּאמֶר מֶה עַבְדֶּךָ כִּי פָנִיתָ

אֶל־הַכֶּלֶב [3] הַמֵּת אֲשֶׁר כָּמוֹנִי:

וַיִּקְרָא הַמֶּלֶךְ אֶל־צִיבָא נַעַר שָׁאוּל וַיֹּאמֶר

אֵלָיו כֹּל אֲשֶׁר הָיָה לְשָׁאוּל וּלְכָל־בֵּיתוֹ

נָתַתִּי לְבֶן־אֲדֹנֶיךָ:

3. (1 Kings 5:14–18) וַיָּבֹאוּ מִכָּל־הָעַמִּים לִשְׁמֹעַ אֵת חָכְמַת

שְׁלֹמֹה מֵאֵת כָּל־מַלְכֵי הָאָרֶץ אֲשֶׁר שָׁמְעוּ

אֶת־חָכְמָתוֹ:

וַיִּשְׁלַח חִירָם מֶלֶךְ־צוֹר אֶת־עֲבָדָיו אֶל־שְׁלֹמֹה

כִּי שָׁמַע כִּי אֹתוֹ מָשְׁחוּ לְמֶלֶךְ תַּחַת אָבִיהוּ

כִּי אֹהֵב הָיָה חִירָם לְדָוִד כָּל־הַיָּמִים:

וַיִּשְׁלַח שְׁלֹמֹה אֶל־חִירָם לֵאמֹר:

אַתָּה יָדַעְתָּ אֶת־דָּוִד אָבִי כִּי לֹא יָכֹל

לִבְנוֹת בַּיִת לְשֵׁם יְהוָה אֱלֹהָיו מִפְּנֵי

הַמִּלְחָמָה אֲשֶׁר סְבָבֻהוּ [4] עַד תֵּת־יְהוָה אֹתָם

תַּחַת כַּפּוֹת רַגְלָיו:

וְעַתָּה הֵנִיחַ יְהוָה אֱלֹהַי לִי מִסָּבִיב

אֵין שָׂטָן וְאֵין פֶּגַע רָע:

---

[1] to uproot what is planted

[2] then he bowed down

[3] כֶּלֶב dog

[4] surrounded him

4.   (Gen. 3:9–13) וַיִּקְרָא יְהוָה אֱלֹהִים אֶל־הָאָדָם וַיֹּאמֶר
לוֹ אַיֶּכָּה:
וַיֹּאמֶר אֶת־קֹלְךָ שָׁמַעְתִּי בַּגָּן וָאִירָא
כִּי־עֵירֹם⁵ אָנֹכִי וָאֵחָבֵא:⁶
וַיֹּאמֶר מִי הִגִּיד לְךָ כִּי עֵירֹם⁵ אָתָּה
הֲמִן־הָעֵץ אֲשֶׁר צִוִּיתִיךָ לְבִלְתִּי
אֲכָל־מִמֶּנּוּ אָכָלְתָּ:
וַיֹּאמֶר הָאָדָם הָאִשָּׁה אֲשֶׁר נָתַתָּה
עִמָּדִי הִוא נָתְנָה־לִּי מִן־הָעֵץ וָאֹכֵל:
וַיֹּאמֶר יְהוָה אֱלֹהִים לָאִשָּׁה מַה־זֹּאת עָשִׂית
וַתֹּאמֶר הָאִשָּׁה הַנָּחָשׁ⁷ הִשִּׁיאַנִי⁸
וָאֹכֵל:

5.   (Gen. 29:18–22) וַיֶּאֱהַב יַעֲקֹב אֶת־רָחֵל וַיֹּאמֶר
אֶעֱבָדְךָ⁹ שֶׁבַע⁹ שָׁנִים בְּרָחֵל¹⁰ בִּתְּךָ
הַקְּטַנָּה:
וַיֹּאמֶר לָבָן טוֹב תִּתִּי אֹתָהּ לָךְ
מִתִּתִּי אֹתָהּ לְאִישׁ אַחֵר שְׁבָה עִמָּדִי:
וַיַּעֲבֹד יַעֲקֹב בְּרָחֵל שֶׁבַע⁹ שָׁנִים
וַיִּהְיוּ בְעֵינָיו כְּיָמִים אֲחָדִים
בְּאַהֲבָתוֹ אֹתָהּ:
וַיֹּאמֶר יַעֲקֹב אֶל־לָבָן הָבָה אֶת־אִשְׁתִּי
כִּי מָלְאוּ יָמָי וְאָבוֹאָה אֵלֶיהָ:
וַיֶּאֱסֹף לָבָן אֶת־כָּל־אַנְשֵׁי הַמָּקוֹם
וַיַּעַשׂ מִשְׁתֶּה:

6.   (Josh. 1:1–5) וַיְהִי אַחֲרֵי מוֹת מֹשֶׁה עֶבֶד יְהוָה וַיֹּאמֶר
יְהוָה אֶל־יְהוֹשֻׁעַ בִּן־נוּן מְשָׁרֵת מֹשֶׁה לֵאמֹר:

---

⁵ naked
⁶ and I hid myself
⁷ the snake
⁸ נשׁא (H) deceive, trick
⁹ seven
¹⁰ עבד בְּ X work for (the sake of) X

מֹשֶׁה עַבְדִּי מֵת וְעַתָּה קוּם עֲבֹר אֶת־הַיַּרְדֵּן
הַזֶּה אַתָּה וְכָל־הָעָם הַזֶּה אֶל־הָאָרֶץ אֲשֶׁר
אָנֹכִי נֹתֵן לָהֶם לִבְנֵי יִשְׂרָאֵל:
כָּל־מָקוֹם אֲשֶׁר תִּדְרֹךְ¹¹ כַּף־רַגְלְכֶם בּוֹ
לָכֶם נְתַתִּיו כַּאֲשֶׁר דִּבַּרְתִּי אֶל־מֹשֶׁה:
מֵהַמִּדְבָּר וְהַלְּבָנוֹן הַזֶּה וְעַד־הַנָּהָר
הַגָּדוֹל נְהַר־פְּרָת כֹּל אֶרֶץ הַחִתִּים וְעַד־
הַיָּם הַגָּדוֹל מְבוֹא¹² הַשָּׁמֶשׁ יִהְיֶה גְּבוּלְכֶם:¹³
לֹא־יִתְיַצֵּב¹⁴ אִישׁ לְפָנֶיךָ כֹּל יְמֵי חַיֶּיךָ
כַּאֲשֶׁר הָיִיתִי עִם־מֹשֶׁה אֶהְיֶה עִמָּךְ לֹא אַרְפְּךָ¹⁵
וְלֹא אֶעֶזְבֶךָ:

11 דרך tread, step
12 מָבוֹא entrance, entering
13 your territory
14 shall stand
15 I will (not) let go of you

LESSON XXIII

1. D Imperfect

a. The D imperfect of קִטֵּל is inflected as follows:

3 ms	יְקַטֵּל	3 mp	יְקַטְּלוּ
3 fs	תְּקַטֵּל	3 fp	תְּקַטֵּֽלְנָה
2 ms	תְּקַטֵּל	2 mp	תְּקַטְּלוּ
2 fs	תְּקַטְּלִי	2 fp	תְּקַטֵּֽלְנָה
1 cs	אֲקַטֵּל	1 cp	נְקַטֵּל

Notes:

In a few verbs, gemination may be lost if it is followed by a šĕwā' (*cf.* V.6).

תְּבַקְשִׁי not תְּבַקְּשִׁי

יְבַקְשׁוּ not יְבַקְּשׁוּ

This is also the case when object suffixes are added.

אֲבַקְשֶׁנּוּ but אֲבַקֵּשׁ

תְּבַקְשֵׁם but תְּבַקֵּשׁ

b. The inflections of the D imperfect of מֵאֵן (refuse) and מִהַר (hasten) are as follows (*cf.* XIV.3):

3 ms	יְמָאֵן	יְמַהֵר
3 fs	תְּמָאֵן	תְּמַהֵר
2 ms	תְּמָאֵן	תְּמַהֵר
2 fs	תְּמָאֲנִי	תְּמַהֲרִי
1 cs	אֲמָאֵן	אֲמַהֵר

198

3 mp	יְמָאֲנוּ	יְמַהֲרוּ
3 fp	תְּמָאֵנָה	יְמַהֵרְנָה
2 mp	תְּמָאֲנוּ	תְּמַהֲרוּ
2 fp	תְּמָאֵנָה	תְּמַהֵרְנָה
1 cp	נְמָאֵן	נְמַהֵר

c. The D imperfect of III-א verbs is regular, except that we get תְּמַלֵּאנָה, not *תְּמַלֶּאנָה, in the 3 fp and 2 fp.

d. The D imperfect of III-ה, ח, ע usually has the *yĕqaṭṭal* pattern: for example, יְבַקַּע, יְשַׁלַּח.[1]

e. The inflection of the D imperfect of גלה (uncover, reveal) is as follows (*cf.* XVIII.3).

3 ms	יְגַלֶּה	3 mp	יְגַלּוּ
3 fs	תְּגַלֶּה	3 fp	תְּגַלֶּינָה
2 ms	תְּגַלֶּה	2 mp	תְּגַלּוּ
2 fs	תְּגַלִּי	2 fp	תְּגַלֶּינָה
1 cs	אֲגַלֶּה	1 cp	נְגַלֶּה

f. Original I-*Wāw* verbs merge with verbs of I-*Yōd* type, even though the ו radical is no longer in initial position (*cf.* IV.2.c.ii; XV.8). We expect *יְוַסֵּר instead of יְיַסֵּר, *יְוַחֵל instead of יְיַחֵל, and so forth; but we get the forms with the *yōd*. Thus, in the D imperfect, I-*Wāw* and I-*Yōd* verbs are both inflected "regularly" (i.e. analogously to קטל).

g. The D jussive (and *wyqṭl*) forms are similar to the corresponding imperfect, except that for III-ה verbs we find the ה apocopated (see XIX.4.e) and the loss of the gemination of what has become the final consonant (namely, the original second radical):

$$\text{יְגַל} > \text{*יְגַלּ but יְגַלֶּה}$$

[1] However, in pause it is always *yĕqaṭṭēl*: יְבַקֵּעַ, יְשַׁלֵּחַ. The verb זבח (sacrifice) is an exception to the rule.

Also, gemination in the preformative is lost in the *wyqtl* forms (see V.6): וַיְבַקֵּשׁ > וַיְבַקֵּשׁ.

2. D Imperative

Root	ms	fs	mp	fp
בקשׁ	בַּקֵּשׁ	בַּקְשִׁי	בַּקְשׁוּ	בַּקֵּשְׁנָה
מאן	מָאֵן	מָאֲנִי	מָאֲנוּ	מָאֵנָּה
מהר	מַהֵר	מַהֲרִי	מַהֲרוּ	מַהֵרְנָה
שׁלח	שַׁלַּח	שַׁלְּחִי	שַׁלְּחוּ	שַׁלַּחְנָה
מלא	מַלֵּא	מַלְּאִי	מַלְּאוּ	מַלֶּאנָה
יסר	יַסֵּר	יַסְּרִי	יַסְּרוּ	יַסֵּרְנָה

Notes:

i. In some verbs, gemination may be lost in accordance with V.6. Thus, מַלְּאוּ>מַלְּאוּ. On the other hand, we have שַׁלְּחוּ, never *שַׁלְּחוּ.

ii. The D imperative 2 ms may also take the volitive הָ ָ–; for example, סַפְּרָה tell!, מַהֲרָה hurry!

3. D Infinitives

Abs.	Cs.	Cs. with Suffixes
גַּדֵּל	גַּדֵּל	גַּדֶּלְךָ, גַּדְּלוֹ
בָּרֵךְ	בָּרֵךְ	בָּרֶכְךָ, בָּרְכוֹ
בַּעֵר	בַּעֵר	בַּעֶרְךָ, בַּעֲרוֹ
שַׁלֵּחַ	שַׁלֵּחַ	שַׁלֵּחֲךָ, שַׁלְּחוֹ
קַנֹּא	קַנֵּא	קַנַּאֲךָ, קַנְּאוֹ
צַוֵּה	צַוֹּות	צַוֹּותְךָ, צַוֹּותוֹ
יַסֹּר	יַסֵּר	יַסֶּרְךָ, יַסְּרוֹ

Notes:

i.   Essentially, the D infinitive absolute may be *qaṭṭōl* or *qaṭṭēl*. The former is actually quite uncommon, though we have a few examples: קַנֹּא, יַסֹּר, רַפֹּא, etc. For most verbs, the form of the infinitive, both construct and absolute, is *qaṭṭēl*.

ii.   The infinitive construct of III-ה, ח, ע verbs is usually like שַׁלַּח, but the form for זבח is זַבֵּחַ.

iii.   In addition to the infinitive absolute of the צַוֵּה type, we also get the type like קֹּה for III-ה verbs.

4. Synopsis of Verbs in D

Root	Perf.	Impf.	Juss.	Impv.	Inf. Abs.	Inf. Cs.	Ptc.
בקש	בִּקֵּשׁ	יְבַקֵּשׁ	יְבַקֵּשׁ	בַּקֵּשׁ	בַּקֵּשׁ	בַּקֵּשׁ	מְבַקֵּשׁ
מאן	מֵאֵן	יְמָאֵן	יְמָאֵן	מָאֵן	מָאֵן	מָאֵן	מְמָאֵן
מהר	מִהַר	יְמַהֵר	יְמַהֵר	מַהֵר	מַהֵר	מַהֵר	מְמַהֵר
שלח	שִׁלַּח	יְשַׁלַּח	יְשַׁלַּח	שַׁלַּח	שַׁלֵּחַ	שַׁלַּח	מְשַׁלֵּחַ
מלא	מִלֵּא	יְמַלֵּא	יְמַלֵּא	מַלֵּא	מַלֵּא	מַלֵּא	מְמַלֵּא
גלה	גִּלָּה	יְגַלֶּה	יְגַל	גַּלֵּה	גַּלֵּה/גַּלֹּו	גַּלּוֹת	מְגַלֶּה
יסר	יִסַּר	יְיַסֵּר	יְיַסֵּר	יַסֵּר	יַסֹּר	יַסֵּר	מְיַסֵּר

5. Cardinal Numbers

	Masc. Abs.	Masc. Cs.	Fem. Abs.	Fem. Cs.
one	אֶחָד	אַחַד	אַחַת	אַחַת
two	שְׁנַיִם	שְׁנֵי	שְׁתַּיִם	שְׁתֵּי
three	שָׁלֹשׁ	שְׁלֹשׁ	שְׁלֹשָׁה	שְׁלֹשֶׁת
four	אַרְבַּע	אַרְבַּע	אַרְבָּעָה	אַרְבַּעַת
five	חָמֵשׁ	חֲמֵשׁ	חֲמִשָּׁה	חֲמֵשֶׁת
six	שֵׁשׁ	שֵׁשׁ	שִׁשָּׁה	שֵׁשֶׁת

seven	שֶׁבַע	שְׁבַע	שִׁבְעָה	שִׁבְעַת
eight	שְׁמֹנֶה	שְׁמֹנֶה	שְׁמֹנָה	שְׁמֹנַת
nine	תֵּשַׁע	תְּשַׁע	תִּשְׁעָה	תִּשְׁעַת
ten	עֶשֶׂר	עֶשֶׂר	עֲשָׂרָה	עֲשֶׂרֶת

a. One to Ten

   i. The numeral "1" is most frequently used as an attributive adjective. It usually follows the noun and agrees with it in gender and definiteness.

      אִישׁ אֶחָד   one man, a man

      הָאִישׁ הָאֶחָד   the one man

      אִשָּׁה אַחַת   one woman, a woman

      הָאִשָּׁה הָאַחַת   the one woman

This numeral may also be used as a substantive, standing in construct state before a plural noun.

      אַחַד הָאֲנָשִׁים   one of the men

      אַחַת הַנָּשִׁים   one of the women

  ii. The numeral "2" is a substantive, and it either stands in construct before the noun or as an absolute in apposition. In both cases, there is agreement of gender.

      שְׁנֵי אֲנָשִׁים   two men

      שְׁנֵי הָאֲנָשִׁים   the two men

      שְׁנֵי אֲנָשָׁיו   his two men

      שְׁתֵּי נָשִׁים   two women

      שְׁתֵּי הַנָּשִׁים   the two women

      שְׁתֵּי נָשָׁיו   his two women

      שְׁנַיִם אֲנָשִׁים   two men

      שְׁתַּיִם נָשִׁים   two women

Note: שְׁנֵי and שְׁתֵּי may take the pronominal suffix. Thus: שְׁנֵיהֶם two of them, שְׁנֵיכֶם two of you, שְׁנֵינוּ two of us, and so forth.

iii. The numerals "3" through "10" are treated as substantives like the numeral "2," but there is no agreement in gender. In fact, the feminine form of the number is always used with the masculine noun, and the masculine form is always used with the feminine noun.

שְׁלֹשֶׁת אֲנָשִׁים	three men
שְׁלֹשֶׁת הָאֲנָשִׁים	the three men
שְׁלֹשֶׁת אֲנָשָׁיו	his three men
שְׁלֹשׁ נָשִׁים	three women
שְׁלֹשׁ הַנָּשִׁים	the three women
שְׁלֹשׁ נָשָׁיו	his three women
שְׁלֹשָׁה אֲנָשִׁים	three men

b. Teens

	With mp. Nouns	With fp. Nouns
eleven	אַחַד עָשָׂר	אַחַת עֶשְׂרֵה
	עַשְׁתֵּי עָשָׂר	עַשְׁתֵּי עֶשְׂרֵה
twelve	שְׁנֵים עָשָׂר	שְׁתֵּים עֶשְׂרֵה
	שְׁנֵי עָשָׂר	שְׁתֵּי עֶשְׂרֵה
thirteen	שְׁלֹשָׁה עָשָׂר	שְׁלֹשׁ עֶשְׂרֵה
fourteen	אַרְבָּעָה עָשָׂר	אַרְבַּע עֶשְׂרֵה
fifteen	חֲמִשָּׁה עָשָׂר	חֲמֵשׁ עֶשְׂרֵה . . . etc.

c. Tens

twenty	עֶשְׂרִים	("tens")
thirty	שְׁלֹשִׁים	
forty	אַרְבָּעִים	
fifty	חֲמִשִּׁים . . . etc.	

d. Hundreds

| one hundred | מֵאָה | (cs. מְאַת) |
| two hundred | מָאתַיִם | |

three hundred	שְׁלֹשׁ מֵאוֹת
four hundred	אַרְבַּע מֵאוֹת
five hundred	חֲמֵשׁ מֵאוֹת ... etc.

e. Thousands

one thousand	אֶלֶף
two thousand	אַלְפַּיִם
three thousand	שְׁלֹשֶׁת אֲלָפִים
four thousand	אַרְבַּעַת אֲלָפִים
five thousand	חֲמֵשֶׁת אֲלָפִים ... etc.

ten thousand	רִבּוֹת/רְבָבָה
twenty thousand	רִבּוֹתַיִם
thirty thousand	שְׁלֹשׁ רִבּוֹת
forty thousand	אַרְבַּע רִבּוֹת ... etc.

6. Ordinal Numbers

a. The first ten ordinal numbers are as follows:

	Masculine	Feminine
first	רִאשׁוֹן	רִאשׁוֹנָה
second	שֵׁנִי	שֵׁנִית
third	שְׁלִישִׁי	שְׁלִישִׁיָּה / שְׁלִישִׁית
fourth	רְבִיעִי	רְבִיעִית
fifth	חֲמִישִׁי	חֲמִישִׁית
sixth	שִׁשִּׁי	שִׁשִּׁית
seventh	שְׁבִיעִי	שְׁבִיעִית
eighth	שְׁמִינִי	שְׁמִינִית
ninth	תְּשִׁיעִי	תְּשִׁיעִית
tenth	עֲשִׂירִי	עֲשִׂירִיָּה / עֲשִׂירִית

The ordinal numbers are treated as attributive adjectives. They stand after the noun and agree with it in gender and, usually, in definiteness.

בֵּן שֵׁנִי   a second son

בַּיּוֹם הַשֵּׁנִי   on the second day

בַּת שֵׁנִית   a second daughter

בַּשָּׁנָה הַשֵּׁנִית   in the second year

The cardinal number "1" (אֶחָד) may occasionally be used instead of רִאשׁוֹן.

b. Beyond the first ten ordinal numbers, Hebrew uses the cardinal numbers to serve the function of ordinal numbers.

7. Distributive

a. The distributive is expressed by repetition of the substantive in various ways.

שְׁנַיִם שְׁנַיִם   two each = two by two

יוֹם יוֹם   day by day

שֵׁשׁ כְּנָפַיִם שֵׁשׁ כְּנָפַיִם   six wings each

יָמִים יָמִימָה   every year

חֶדֶר בְּחֶדֶר   room by room

b. The preposition ל may also be used to indicate the distributive.

לִשְׁלֹשֶׁת יָמִים   every three days

לְשָׁלֹשׁ שָׁנִים   every three years

c. Idiomatic use of אִישׁ.

אִישׁ־אִישׁ מִמְּלַאכְתּוֹ   each one from his task

אִישׁ לִלְשֹׁנוֹ   each one by his own language

אִישׁ חֲלֹמוֹ   each his own dream

When so used, אִישׁ may refer not only to men but also to women and inanimate objects. Less frequently, אִשָּׁה is also used in this manner.

Related to this use of אִישׁ are the expressions of reciprocity: אִישׁ . . . אָחִיו (literally: each . . . his brother) and אִישׁ . . . רֵעֵהוּ (literally: each . . . his friend).

וַיֹּאמְרוּ אִישׁ אֶל־אָחִיו מָן הוּא   And they said *one to another*, "What is that?" (Exod. 16:15)

וְכָשְׁלוּ אִישׁ־בְּאָחִיו And they shall stumble over *one another* (Lev. 26:37)

Vocabulary

Nouns:

אַלְמָנָה	widow
אָמָה	(irreg. pl. אֲמָהוֹת) female slave
אֹרַח	path
אַרְיֵה/אֲרִי	lion
בֶּטֶן	belly
גָּאוֹן	pride. *Verb:* גאה be proud, arrogant
גִּבְעָה	hill
גּוֹרָל	lot
גַּיְא/גֵּי	(pl. גֵּאָיוֹת) valley
זָכָר	male
חֲלוֹם	dream. *Verb:* חלם dream
מוֹפֵת	sign, omen
עוֹר	skin, hide
עָרְלָה	foreskin. *Adjective:* עָרֵל uncircumcised (having foreskin)
שְׂמֹאל	left (hand)

Verbs:

חרה	be(come) angry. *Idioms:* חָרָה אַף ל X, X became angry (literally: the nose of X became hot); hence, also חרה ל X, X became angry; but חרה ב X, be/become angry with X
נשק	kiss (object marked by ל)
פגש	meet
קוה	wait, expect, hope. *Noun:* תִּקְוָה hope

Exercise 23

A. Translate Ruth 1:1–16.

v. 1 שְׂדֵי = שָׂדֶה cs.

v. 3 וַתִּשָּׁאֵר and she was left

v. 6 כַּלָּה daughter-in-law

v. 8 יַעֲשֶׂה *Kĕṯîḇ–Qĕrē'* —that is, written (in consonantal text) one way but suggested to read (in vocalization) another way. Here, the consonants suggest imperfect, but vocalization suggests jussive. See Appendix C.5.

v. 13 לָהֵן therefore

שׂבר (D) wait

תֵּעָגֵנָה keep withdrawn

מַר־לִי I am distressed

v. 14 וַתִּשֶּׂנָה See XIII.4.d

חָמוֹת mother-in-law

דָּבְקָה cling

v. 15 יְבִמְתֵּךְ your sister-in-law

v. 16 פגע בּ X urge X

B. Translate Exod. 4:14–25.

v. 18 חֹתֵן in-law

v. 24 הֲמִיתוֹ to kill him

v. 25 צֹר flint

תַּגַּע she touched

חָתָן husband, bridegroom, one related in marriage

LESSON XXIV

1. H Imperfect

As in the H participle (see XV.11.a), the "ה" causative marker is not apparent in the H imperfect. Original *yuha– has been syncopated to the ya– of the preformative (but see 3 in this lesson).

a. The H imperfect of קטל is inflected as follows:

3 ms	יַקְטִיל	3 mp	יַקְטִֽילוּ
3 fs	תַּקְטִיל	3 fp	תַּקְטֵֽלְנָה
2 ms	תַּקְטִיל	2 mp	תַּקְטִֽילוּ
2 fs	תַּקְטִֽילִי	2 fp	תַּקְטֵֽלְנָה
1 cs	אַקְטִיל	1 cp	נַקְטִיל

b. The H imperfect of עמד is inflected as follows:

3 ms	יַעֲמִיד	3 mp	יַעֲמִֽידוּ
3 fs	תַּעֲמִיד	3 fp	תַּעֲמֵֽדְנָה
2 ms	תַּעֲמִיד	2 mp	תַּעֲמִֽידוּ
2 fs	תַּעֲמִֽידִי	2 fp	תַּעֲמֵֽדְנָה
1 cs	אַעֲמִיד	1 cp	נַעֲמִיד

Notes:

i.   There is no distinction in the H imperfect between verbs of the עמד type and those of the חזק and אכל types (*cf.* XVIII.1). Thus, יַאֲכִיל, יַחֲזִיק, יַעֲמִיד, etc.

ii. Even though the G imperfect of עמד also has *a* in the preformative, there should be no confusion between the G and H imperfects: G יַעֲמֹד, תַּעֲמֹדְנָה; H יַעֲמִיד, תַּעֲמֵֽדְנָה. Note also

208

the different vocalization of the preformative in the 1 cs: G אֶעֱמֹד; H אַעֲמִיד.

c. The H imperfect of שׁלח (send) is inflected as follows:

3 ms	יַשְׁלִיחַ	3 mp	יַשְׁלִיחוּ
3 fs	תַּשְׁלִיחַ	3 fp	תַּשְׁלַחְנָה
2 ms	תַּשְׁלִיחַ	2 mp	תַּשְׁלִיחוּ
2 fs	תַּשְׁלִיחִי	2 fp	תַּשְׁלַחְנָה
1 cs	אַשְׁלִיחַ	1 cp	נַשְׁלִיחַ

d. The H imperfect fp of מצא is תַּמְצֶאנָה.

e. The inflections of the H imperfect of גלה (remove) and עלה (go up) are as follows (*cf.* XVIII.3):

3 ms	יַגְלֶה	יַעֲלֶה
3 fs	תַּגְלֶה	תַּעֲלֶה
2 ms	תַּגְלֶה	תַּעֲלֶה
2 fs	תַּגְלִי	תַּעֲלִי
1 cs	אַגְלֶה	אַעֲלֶה
3 mp	יַגְלוּ	יַעֲלוּ
3 fp	תַּגְלֶינָה	תַּעֲלֶינָה
2 mp	תַּגְלוּ	תַּעֲלוּ
2 fp	תַּגְלֶינָה	תַּעֲלֶינָה
1 cp	נַגְלֶה	נַעֲלֶה

Note: Since the endings on the imperfect are consistent for all the *binyānîm* of III-ה verbs, and since the G preformative of I-Guttural verbs may have *a*, the H imperfect forms of verbs like עלה will be identical to the corresponding forms in G, except for the 1 cs.

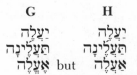

G	H
וַיַּעַל	וַיַּעַל
תַּעֲלֶינָה	תַּעֲלֶינָה
אֶעֱלֶה but	אַעֲלֶה

f. The *a* vowel of the preformative forms a diphthong with the original first radical *w*. But unaccented *yawšíḇ > *yôšíḇ*, etc.

The inflection of the H imperfect of יֹשֵׁב (dwell) is as follows:

3 ms	יוֹשִׁיב	3 mp	יוֹשִׁיבוּ
3 fs	תּוֹשִׁיב	3 fp	תּוֹשֵׁבְנָה
2 ms	תּוֹשִׁיב	2 mp	תּוֹשִׁיבוּ
2 fs	תּוֹשִׁיבִי	2 fp	תּוֹשֵׁבְנָה
1 cs	אוֹשִׁיב	1 cp	נוֹשִׁיב

Notes:

i. The verb הלך behaves like a I-*Wāw* verb in the H *binyān*: תּוֹלִיךְ, יוֹלִיךְ, etc.

ii. The I-*Yōḏ* verb יבשׁ behaves like a I-*Wāw* verb in H. The 1 cs אוֹבִישׁ is the only H imperfect form attested.

g. The *a* vowel of the preformative forms a diphthong with the original first radical *y*. But unaccented *ay contracts to *ê* in accordance with IV.2.c.iii. Thus, *yaytíḇ > *yêtíḇ*.

The inflection of H imperfect of יטב (be good) is as follows:

3 ms	יֵיטִיב	3 mp	יֵיטִיבוּ
3 fs	תֵּיטִיב	3 fp	תֵּיטֵבְנָה
2 ms	תֵּיטִיב	2 mp	תֵּיטִיבוּ
2 fs	תֵּיטִיבִי	2 fp	תֵּיטֵבְנָה
1 cs	אֵיטִיב	1 cp	נֵיטִיב

h. I-*Nûn* verbs show the expected assimilation of *nûn*: *יַנְגִּיד > יַגִּיד.

The inflections of נגד (tell) and the I-*Nûn*/III-ה verb נכה (smite) are as follows:

3 ms	יַגִּיד	יַכֶּה
3 fs	תַּגִּיד	תַּכֶּה
2 ms	תַּגִּיד	תַּכֶּה
2 fs	תַּגִּידִי	תַּכִּי
1 cs	אַגִּיד	אַכֶּה
3 mp	יַגִּידוּ	יַכּוּ
3 fp	תַּגֵּדְנָה	תַּכֶּינָה
2 mp	תַּגִּידוּ	תַּכּוּ
2 fp	תַּגֵּדְנָה	תַּכֶּינָה
1 cp	נַגִּיד	נַכֶּה

i. The inflections of H imperfect of קוּם (arise) and שִׂים (place) are as follows:

3 ms	יָקִים	יָשִׂים
3 fs	תָּקִים	תָּשִׂים
2 ms	תָּקִים	תָּשִׂים
2 fs	תָּקִימִי	תָּשִׂימִי
1 cs	אָקִים	אָשִׂים
3 mp	יָקִימוּ	יָשִׂימוּ
3 fp	תְּקִימֶינָה	תְּשִׂימֶינָה
2 mp	תָּקִימוּ	תָּשִׂימוּ
2 fp	תְּקִימֶינָה	תְּשִׂימֶינָה
1 cp	נָקִים	נָשִׂים

Notes:

i. Occasionally, a shorter form of the fp is found; for example, תָּקִמְנָה instead of תְּקִימֶינָה.

ii. The vowel of the preformative is normally ִ , but when it is propretonic, it reduces to ְ . Thus, תָּקִים but תְּקִימֶ֫ינָה, and when suffixes are added: יָקִים but יְקִימֵ֫נוּ; אָבִיא but אֲבִיאֶ֫נּוּ.

iii. The H imperfect is clearly distinguished from the G in II-*Wāw* verbs, but not II-*Yōḏ:* G יָשִׂים, H יָשִׂים: G יָקוּם but H יָקִים.

2. H *wyqṭl*/Jussive

The H *wyqṭl* and jussive forms are distinguished from the corresponding forms in the imperfect.

a. In most cases, the difference is merely a shift from *yaqṭîl > yaqṭēl*.

Root	Impf.	Jussive	*wyqṭl*	
שׁמד	יַשְׁמִיד	יַשְׁמֵד	וַיַּשְׁמֵד	destroy
נגד	יַגִּיד	יַגֵּד	וַיַּגֵּד	tell
קום	יָקִים	יָקֵם	וַיָּ֫קֶם	arise

b. III-ה, ח, ע verbs will, of course, prefer *a* instead of *ē*.

Root	Impf.	Jussive	*wyqṭl*	
שׁלח	יַשְׁלִיחַ	יַשְׁלַח	וַיַּשְׁלַח	send
נגע	יַגִּ֫יעַ	יַגַּע	וַיַּגַּע	touch
נוח	יָנִ֫יחַ	יָנַח	וַיָּ֫נַח	rest

c. III-ה verbs show apocope of ה and retraction of accent.

Root	Impf.	Jussive	*wyqṭl*	
גלה	יַגְלֶה	יֶ֫גֶל	וַיֶּ֫גֶל	remove
עלה	יַעֲלֶה	יַ֫עַל	וַיַּ֫עַל	go up
נכה	יַכֶּה	יַךְ	וַיַּךְ	smite

Notes:

i. The form יֶ֫גֶל is developed analogously to מֶ֫לֶךְ: *מַלְךְ > מֶ֫לֶךְ*, so *יַגְלְ > יֶ֫גֶל*. By the same token, יַ֫עַל is developed analogously to נַ֫עַר. The H jussive/*wyqṭl* form is often distinguished from the corresponding G form: G יִ֫גֶל but H יֶ֫גֶל. However, many forms cannot be so distinguished:

G	H
וַיַּ֫עַל	וַיַּ֫עַל

וַיִּרָא   וַיֵּרָא

וַיַּשְׁק   וַיִּשַּׁק

ii.   יַךְ is developed from original *yank — that is, *yank > *yakk > yak (cf. IV.4). Compare the development in the G jussive form יֵט (from נטה): *yinṭ > *yiṭṭ > yēṭ.

d. I-Wāw verbs generally show retraction of accent in the *wyqṭl* forms, but not the jussive. Examples:

Root	Impf.	Jussive	*wyqṭl*	
ישׁב	יוֹשִׁיב	יוֹשֵׁב	וַיּוֹשֶׁב	dwell
ידע	יוֹדִיעַ	יוֹדַע	וַיּוֹדַע	know
ירה	יוֹרֶה	יוֹר	וַיּוֹר	teach

3. H Imperative

As we have already noted, the imperative is closely related in form to the corresponding imperfect. In fact, it looks as if the imperative form is the imperfect without the preformative and with the application of the rules of *šĕwā'* in the resulting form (cf. V.2.b; XX.3.b). Thus:

	Impf.	Impv.
G	תִּקְטֹל	קְטֹל
D	תְּקַטֵּל	קַטֵּל

The H imperative may be thought of in the same manner; but one should remember that the causative marker "h" has been lost in syncope. For example, since תַּקְטֵלְנָה is derived from *תְּהַקְטֵלְנָה (unsyncopated form), the fp imperative is הַקְטֵלְנָה. Thus, the H imperative is still marked by the ה causative marker:

2 ms	הַקְטֵל	2 mp	הַקְטִילוּ
2 fs	הַקְטִילִי	2 fp	הַקְטֵלְנָה

Note that the 2 ms imperative is הַקְטֵל, though the 2 ms imperfect is תַּקְטִיל. The inflections of the H imperative are as follows:

Root	ms	fs	mp	fp	
שׁמד	הַשְׁמֵד	הַשְׁמִידִי	הַשְׁמִידוּ	הַשְׁמֵדְנָה	destroy
עמד	הַעֲמֵד	הַעֲמִידִי	הַעֲמִידוּ	הַעֲמֵדְנָה	stand
שׁלח	הַשְׁלַח	הַשְׁלִיחִי	הַשְׁלִיחוּ	הַשְׁלַחְנָה	send
מצא	הַמְצֵא	הַמְצִיאִי	הַמְצִיאוּ	הַמְצֶאנָה	find
גלה	הַגְלֵה	הַגְלִי	הַגְלוּ	הַגְלֶינָה	remove
נגד	הַגֵּד	הַגִּידִי	הַגִּידוּ	הַגֵּדְנָה	tell
ישׁב	הוֹשֵׁב	הוֹשִׁיבִי	הוֹשִׁיבוּ	הוֹשֵׁבְנָה	dwell
יטב	הֵיטֵב	הֵיטִיבִי	הֵיטִיבוּ	הֵיטֵבְנָה	be good
קום	הָקֵם	הָקִימִי	הָקִימוּ	הָקֵמְנָה	arise

4. Synopsis of Verbs in H

Root	Perf.	Impf.	Juss.	Impv.	Inf. Abs.	Inf. Cs.	Ptc.
שׁמד	הִשְׁמִיד	יַשְׁמִיד	יַשְׁמֵד	הַשְׁמֵד	הַשְׁמֵד	הַשְׁמִיד	מַשְׁמִיד
עמד	הֶעֱמִיד	יַעֲמִיד	יַעֲמֵד	הַעֲמֵד	הַעֲמֵד	הַעֲמִיד	מַעֲמִיד
שׁלח	הִשְׁלִיחַ	יַשְׁלִיחַ	יַשְׁלַח	הַשְׁלַח	הַשְׁלֵחַ	הַשְׁלִיחַ	מַשְׁלִיחַ
מצא	הִמְצִיא	יַמְצִיא	יַמְצֵא	הַמְצֵא	הַמְצֵא	הַמְצִיא	מַמְצִיא
גלה	הִגְלָה	יַגְלֶה	יֶגֶל	הַגְלֵה	הַגְלֵה	הַגְלוֹת	מַגְלֶה
נגד	הִגִּיד	יַגִּיד	יַגֵּד	הַגֵּד	הַגֵּד	הַגִּיד	מַגִּיד
ישׁב	הוֹשִׁיב	יוֹשִׁיב	יוֹשֵׁב	הוֹשֵׁב	הוֹשֵׁב	הוֹשִׁיב	מוֹשִׁיב
יטב	הֵיטִיב	יֵיטִיב	יֵיטֵב	הֵיטֵב	הֵיטֵב	הֵיטִיב	מֵיטִיב
קום	הֵקִים	יָקִים	יָקֵם	הָקֵם	הָקֵם	הָקִים	מֵקִים

5. G Passive Participle

a. The G passive participle is formed on the קָטוּל pattern. The "u-class" vowel here marks the passive.

b. The following is a synopsis of forms of the G passive participle:

Root	ms	mp	fs	fp	
שׁמר	שָׁמוּר	שְׁמוּרִים	שְׁמוּרָה	שְׁמוּרוֹת	keep
אסר	אָסוּר	אֲסוּרִים	אֲסוּרָה	אֲסוּרוֹת	bind
בחר	בָּחוּר	בְּחוּרִים	בְּחוּרָה	בְּחוּרוֹת	choose
שׁלח	שָׁלוּחַ	שְׁלוּחִים	שְׁלוּחָה	שְׁלוּחוֹת	send
קרא	קָרוּא	קְרוּאִים	קְרוּאָה	קְרוּאוֹת	call
גלה	גָּלוּי	גְּלוּיִם	גְּלוּיָה	גְּלוּיוֹת	uncover
נתן	נָתוּן	נְתוּנִים	נְתוּנָה	נְתוּנוֹת	give
ידע	יָדוּעַ	יְדוּעִים	יְדוּעָה	יְדוּעוֹת	know

Notes:

i. III-ה verbs retain the final *yōd*.

ii. II-*Wāw/Yōd* verbs are extremely rare in the passive participle. But note:

Root   **G Passive Ptc.**

מול   מוּלִים ,מוּל   circumcision

שׂים   שִׂימָה ,שִׂים   put

c. Like the active participle, the passive participle is a verbal adjective. But unlike the active participle, the passive participle seldom denotes ongoing activity. Rather, it is used most frequently like an adjective, either predicative or attributive.

מִשְׁפָּט כָּתוּב   *written* judgment (Ps. 149:9)

כָּתוּב בְּתוֹרַת מֹשֶׁה   *it is written* in the law of Moses (Dan. 9:13)

בִּזְרוֹעַ נְטוּיָה   with *outstretched* arm (Exod. 6:6)

Passive participles can also be used as substantives.

כָּל־הַכָּתוּב בַּסֵּפֶר הַזֶּה   all *which is written* in this book (Jer. 25:13)

לַעֲקוֹר נָטוּעַ   to uproot *what is planted* (Qoh. 3:2)

Hence, the third portion of Hebrew Scriptures is called כְּתָבִים "writings," and the Hebrew Bible is called the *TNK* (TaNaK)—from the first letter of each of the three parts of the Bible: תּוֹרָה, נְבִיאִים, כְּתָבִים (Law, Prophets, Writings).

Vocabulary

Nouns:

זְרוֹעַ	arm
חַג	festival
חֵלֶב	fat
חָמָס	violence
חֵץ	arrow
יָרֵחַ	moon
כּוֹכָב	star
מִזְרָח	sunrise, east
מְעַט	little, few
מָרוֹם	height, high place
עוֹף	(no pl.; ms. may be used collectively) bird. *Verb:* עוּף fly

Verbs:

אור	become bright, become light. *Nouns:* אוֹר light; מָאוֹר luminary, lamp
בדל	(H) divide, separation
דמה	(G) be like, be alike; (D) liken, compare. *Noun:* דְּמוּת likeness
הגה	mumble, meditate
יסף	(G) add, continue; (H) add, continue, enhance
סלח	forgive
פרה	be fruitful. Cf. פְּרִי fruit

Exercise 24

Translate Gen. 1:1–31.

v. 2   תֹּהוּ וָבֹהוּ emptiness and waste

   תְּהוֹם abyss, primeval deep

   רחף (D) hover, soar

v. 6   רָקִיעַ firmament

v. 9   וְתֵרָאֶה let . . . appear

v. 10   קוה II, collect. *Noun:* מִקְוֶה collection

v. 11   דֶּשֶׁא grass. *Verb:* דשא (H) cause to sprout

   עֵשֶׂב herb, vegetation

   מִין kind, type, species

v. 16   מֶמְשָׁלָה dominion, authority. *Cf.* משל govern

v. 20   *Verb:* שרץ teem, swarm. *Noun:* שֶׁרֶץ teeming (things)

   יְעוֹפֵף flies

v. 21   תַּנִּין sea-monster, dragon

   Verb: רמש creep, crawl. *Noun:* רֶמֶשׂ creeping (things)

v. 24   חַיְתוֹ (its) living thing

v. 26   צֶלֶם image

   רדה tread, dominate, rule

   דָּגָה fish

v. 27   נְקֵבָה female

v. 28   כבשׁ subject, harness

v. 30   יֶרֶק greenery, vegetation

LESSON XXV

1. N *binyān*

The N *binyān* is characterized by the presence of a prefixed, or infixed and assimilated, נ in all inflections.

a. In the perfect and the participle, the נ is prefixed.

b. In the imperfect, imperative, and infinitive, the נ is usually infixed and assimilated.

2. Meaning of Verbs in N

Most verbs fall into one of the following semantic categories, though a few cannot be easily classified.

a. *Reflexive*

The reflexive verb indicates action for, or concerning, oneself. In many languages a reflexive pronoun is added to clarify the object, but in the Hebrew "N" verb no reflexive pronoun is needed.

נִמְכַּר	he sold himself
נֶחְבָּא	he hid himself
נִסְגַּר	he shut himself in

Verbs suggesting emotional turmoil within oneself are, therefore, regularly in N.

נֶאֱנַח	he moaned
נִחַם	he was sorry

A sub-group in this category are verbs that are sometimes called *tolerative.*

נִזְהַר	he let himself be warned
נִדְרַשׁ	he let himself be sought

b. *Middle*

Verbs that are normally used in passive constructions may be used in a quasi-active sense, but with the object as the subject of the verb.

Compare the uses of the English verb "open" in the three following examples.

> Active:　The man *opened* the door.
> Passive:　The door *was opened* by the man.
> Middle:　The door *opened*.

In the third example, the subject of the verb is the door, normally the object of the verb "open." The statement is not that somebody opened the door, nor that the door was opened (by someone), but that the door opened (itself). The verb "opened" in this third example is said to be a "middle" verb.

The N verb is frequently used in this "middle" sense.

וְנִפְקְחוּ עֵינֵיכֶם	and your eyes *will open* (Gen. 3:5)
נִפְתְּחוּ הַשָּׁמַיִם	the heavens *opened* (Ezek. 1:1)
נִקְהֲלוּ הַיְּהוּדִים בְּעָרֵיהֶם	the Jews *gathered* in their cities (Esth. 9:2)

c. *Passive*

The N is frequently used as the passive of the verb in G.

Root	G	N
קבר	bury	be buried
אכל	eat	be eaten
כרת	cut	be cut
עזב	abandon	be abandoned

In many instances, the N passive is impersonal and no subject is explicitly stated: נֶאֱמַר it was said; נֶאֱכַל it was eaten.

d. *Stative*

From the impersonal use of the N passives it is easy to see how some N verbs would function like stative verbs: נֶאֱכָל is eaten > is edible; נִרְאָה is seen > is visible > appeared.

Not surprisingly, then, many N participles function practically as adjectives.

Root		N Ptc	
בחר	choose	נִבְחָר	choice
חמד	desire	נֶחְמָד	desirable

יָרֵא	be afraid	נוֹרָא	awesome
בִּין	perceive	נָבוֹן	perceptive, intelligent
אָמֵן	be firm	נֶאֱמָן	firm

e. Reciprocal

In some instances, the N verb suggests reciprocity or mutuality: נִדְבְּרוּ they spoke with one another; נִלְחֲמוּ they fought with one another.

3. N Perfect

a. The inflection of the N perfect of קְטֹל is as follows:

3 ms	נִקְטַל	3 cp	נִקְטְלוּ
3 fs	נִקְטְלָה		
2 ms	נִקְטַלְתָּ	2 mp	נִקְטַלְתֶּם
2 fs	נִקְטַלְתְּ	2 fp	נִקְטַלְתֶּן
1 cs	נִקְטַלְתִּי	1 cp	נִקְטַלְנוּ

Notes:
i. The *niqtal* pattern is dissimilated from an earlier *naqtal.
ii. Whereas in the G *binyān* there are three classes of verbs (*qātal, qātēl, qātōl*), in the N there is only one class.

b. In I-Guttural verbs, –נְ > –נֶ, even as the –הְ prefix becomes –הֶ in the H perfect. The inflection of the N perfect of עזב is as follows:

3 ms	נֶעֱזַב	3 cp	נֶעֶזְבוּ
3 fs	נֶעֶזְבָה		
2 ms	נֶעֱזַבְתָּ	2 mp	נֶעֱזַבְתֶּם
2 fs	נֶעֱזַבְתְּ	2 fp	נֶעֱזַבְתֶּן
1 cs	נֶעֱזַבְתִּי	1 cp	נֶעֱזַבְנוּ

Notes:
i. *נֶעֱזָבָה > נֶעֶזְבָה and נֶעֶזְבוּ > נֶעֶזְבוּ in accordance with XVIII.1.d.i.

ii. Some verbs with I-Guttural will tolerate a silent *šĕwāʾ* under the guttural, for example, נֶחְשַׁב ,נֶחְבָּא.

iii. Occasionally, the original *na*– prefix will prevail; e.g., נַחְבֵּאתָ not נֶחְבֵּאתָ.

c. In I-*Wāw* verbs, earlier *nawlad > *nôlad* in accordance with IV.2.c.ii.

The inflection of ילד (beget) is as follows:

3 ms	נוֹלַד	3 cp	נוֹלְדוּ
3 fs	נוֹלְדָה		
2 ms	נוֹלַדְתָּ	2 mp	נוֹלַדְתֶּם
2 fs	נוֹלַדְתְּ	2 fp	נוֹלַדְתֶּן
1 cs	נוֹלַדְתִּי	1 cp	נוֹלַדְנוּ

d. There is no distinction between II-*Wāw* and II-*Yōd* verbs in the N perfect. The inflection of the N perfect of כון (prepare) is as follows:

3 ms	נָכוֹן	3 cp	נָכוֹנוּ
3 fs	נָכוֹנָה		
2 ms	נְכוּנוֹתָ	2 mp	נְכוּנוֹתֶם
2 fs	נְכוּנוֹת	2 fp	נְכוּנוֹתֶן
1 cs	נְכוּנוֹתִי	1 cp	נְכוּנוֹנוּ

e. The N perfects of other weak verbs are regular for their types.

   i.   I-*Nûn* verbs will show the assimilation of נ: *nintan > *nittan*. If, however, the second radical is ח, we will get virtual doubling of ח: *nḥam > נֶחַם. For נער (shake), the N perfect נִנְעַרְתִּי (with an unassimilated נ) is found. There are no other examples of N perfects of I-*Nûn* verbs that are also II-Guttural/ר.

   ii. III-א verbs show the characteristic lengthening of the vowel before the quiescent ʾ*ālep̄*, and the spirantization of suffixal ת. It should be noted, however, that the vowel before the second and first person forms is always *ē*, not *ā*. Thus, נִמְצָא but נִמְצֵאתָ, etc.

4. N Imperfect

a. The N imperfect is characterized by the infixed and assimilated
נ. Thus, earlier **yinqaṭil > yiqqāṭēl*. The inflection of the N imperfect of
קטל, therefore, is as follows:

3 ms	יִקָּטֵל	3 mp	יִקָּטְלוּ
3 fs	תִּקָּטֵל	3 fp	תִּקָּטַלְנָה
2 ms	תִּקָּטֵל	2 mp	תִּקָּטְלוּ
2 fs	תִּקָּטְלִי	2 fp	תִּקָּטַלְנָה
1 cs	אֶקָּטֵל	1 cp	נִקָּטֵל

b. Since gutturals and ר cannot take the *dāgēš forte,* the *i* vowel in
the preformative is always compensatorily lengthened. The inflection of
the N imperfect of עזב is as follows:

3 ms	יֵעָזֵב	3 mp	יֵעָזְבוּ
3 fs	תֵּעָזֵב	3 fp	תֵּעָזַבְנָה
2 ms	תֵּעָזֵב	2 mp	תֵּעָזְבוּ
2 fs	תֵּעָזְבִי	2 fp	תֵּעָזַבְנָה
1 cs	אֵעָזֵב	1 cp	נֵעָזֵב

c. In I-*Wāw* verbs, the initial ו is retained; I-*Yōd* verbs are not
attested in N. The inflection of the N imperfect of ילד is as follows:

3 ms	יִוָּלֵד	3 mp	יִוָּלְדוּ
3 fs	תִּוָּלֵד	3 fp	תִּוָּלַדְנָה
2 ms	תִּוָּלֵד	2 mp	תִּוָּלְדוּ
2 fs	תִּוָּלְדִי	2 fp	תִּוָּלַדְנָה
1 cs	אִוָּלֵד	1 cp	נִוָּלֵד

d. There is no distinction between II-*Wāw* and II-*Yōḏ* verbs. The N imperfect of כּוּן (prepare) is inflected as follows:

3 ms	יִכּוֹן	3 mp	יִכּוֹנוּ
3 fs	תִּכּוֹן	3 fp	–not attested–
2 ms	תִּכּוֹן	2 mp	תִּכּוֹנוּ
2 fs	תִּכּוֹנִי	2 fp	–not attested–
1 cs	אֶכּוֹן	1 cp	נִכּוֹן

5. N Imperative

a. In the N imperative there is an anomalous *hi–* prefix which should not be confused with the *hi–* prefix in the H perfect.

b. The following is a synopsis of the inflections of the N imperative:

Root	ms	fs	mp	fp
שׁמר	הִשָּׁמֵר	הִשָּׁמְרִי	הִשָּׁמְרוּ	הִשָּׁמַרְנָה
אסף	הֵאָסֵף	הֵאָסְפִי	הֵאָסְפוּ	הֵאָסַפְנָה
שׁבע	הִשָּׁבַע	הִשָּׁבְעִי	הִשָּׁבְעוּ	הִשָּׁבַעְנָה
מלא	הִמָּלֵא	הִמָּלְאִי	הִמָּלְאוּ	הִמָּלֶאנָה
גלה	הִגָּלֵה	הִגָּלִי	הִגָּלוּ	הִגָּלֶינָה
נתן	הִנָּתֵן	הִנָּתְנִי	הִנָּתְנוּ	הִנָּתַנָּה
ילד	הִוָּלֵד	הִוָּלְדִי	הִוָּלְדוּ	הִוָּלַדְנָה
כון	הִכּוֹן	הִכּוֹנִי	הִכּוֹנוּ	———

6. N Participle

The N participle of קטל is inflected as follows:

ms		mp	
ms	נִקְטָל	mp	נִקְטָלִים
fs	נִקְטֶלֶת/נִקְטָלָה	fp	נִקְטָלוֹת

Notes:

i.   The ms. participle נִקְטָל is not to be confused with the perfect 3 ms נִקְטַל (note the short "a").

ii. Since the vowel before III-א is lengthened (so נִמְצָא*‎>נִמְצָא*), the participle of III-א verbs cannot be distinguished from the perfect 3 ms.

iii. The participle of II-*Wāw/Yōd* verbs also cannot be distinguished from the perfect 3 ms.

iv. The participle of the III-ה verb גלה is inflected as follows:

ms	נִגְלֶה	mp	נִגְלִים
fs	נִגְלָה	fp	נִגְלוֹת

7. Synopsis of Verbs in N

Root	Perf.	Impf.	Impv.	Inf. Abs.	Inf. Cs.	Ptc.
שמר	נִשְׁמַר	יִשָּׁמֵר	הִשָּׁמֵר	הִשָּׁמֹר/נִשְׁמֹר	הִשָּׁמֵר	נִשְׁמָר
עזב	נֶעֱזַב	יֵעָזֵב	הֵעָזֵב	הֵעָזֹב/נַעֲזֹב	הֵעָזֵב	נֶעֱזָב
שבע	נִשְׁבַּע	יִשָּׁבַע	הִשָּׁבַע	הִשָּׁבֵעַ/נִשְׁבֹּעַ	הִשָּׁבַע	נִשְׁבָּע
מלא	נִמְלָא	יִמָּלֵא	הִמָּלֵא	הִמָּלֵא/נִמְלֹא	הִמָּלֵא	נִמְלָא
גלה	נִגְלָה	יִגָּלֶה	הִגָּלֵה	הִגָּלֵה/נִגְלֹה	הִגָּלוֹת	נִגְלֶה
נתן	נִתַּן	יִנָּתֵן	הִנָּתֵן	הִנָּתֵן/נִתּוֹן	הִנָּתֵן	נִתָּן
ילד	נוֹלַד	יִוָּלֵד	הִוָּלֵד	not attested	הִוָּלֵד	נוֹלָד
כון	נָכוֹן	יִכּוֹן	הִכּוֹן	הִכּוֹן/נָכוֹן	הִכּוֹן	נָכוֹן

Vocabulary

Nouns:

אֵצֶל   side. Also used as preposition: beside, near

בָּמָה   high place

זָר   stranger, foreigner, another person

חֶרְפָּה   reproach

כֶּרֶם   vineyard

עֹשֶׁר   wealth, riches. *Verb:* עשׁר be rich

Verbs:

ינק   suckle. *Noun:* יוֹנֵק infant, child

יָשֵׁן   sleep. *Noun:* שֵׁנָה sleep

כון   (N) be prepared, established, firm; (H) prepare,
install, establish. *Noun:* מָכוֹן place, support

לחם   (N) fight. *Cf.* מִלְחָמָה war, battle

מנה   count. *Noun:* מָנֶה Mina (a measure of silver or gold)

נבא   (N) prophesy. *Cf.* נָבִיא prophet

נדח   thrust away, banish

סתר   (N) to hide oneself

פוץ   be dispersed, scattered

פלא   (N) be marvelous, extraordinary. *Ptc.* נִפְלָאוֹת wonders.
Noun: פֶּלֶא wonder

שׁבע   (N) swear. *Noun:* שְׁבוּעָה oath

Preposition/Conjunction

זוּלַת/זוּלָתִי   except

Idiom:

בִּי אֲדֹנִי   "Excuse me, my lord!" A formula used to begin
conversation with a superior

Exercise 25

Translate 1 Kings 3:1–28.

v. 1   וַיִּתְחַתֵּן (Solomon) became related by marriage

v. 3   קטר (H) burn incense. *Cf.* קְטֹרֶת incense, smoke

v. 15 יָקַץ be awake, wake up

v. 20 חֵיק bosom

v. 21 וָאֶתְבּוֹנֵן and I looked closely

v. 25 גזר cut

v. 26 כמר (N) be agitated

גְּזֹרוּ G impv 2 mp (pausal form) of גזר to cut

LESSON XXVI

1. HtD *binyān*

The HtD *binyān* is characterized by a prefixed or infixed *(h)it–* and the doubling of the second radical of the root.

2. Meaning of Verbs in HtD

Verbs in HtD generally fall into one of the following semantic categories:

a. *Reflexive*

הִתְגַּדֵּל	magnify oneself
הִתְחַבֵּא	hide oneself
הִתְקַדֵּשׁ	sanctify oneself

In all these examples, the direct object, though unspecified, is the subject. But there are some reflexives which represent acts not on oneself but acts for or in regard to oneself.

הִתְפַּשֵּׁט	strip (clothes from) oneself
הִתְפָּרֵק	tear off from oneself
הִתְפַּתַּח	loosen for oneself

Also subsumed under this category are a few verbs that may be regarded as *tolerative:* הִתְמַכֵּר let oneself to be sold.

b. *Reciprocal*

הִתְקַשֵּׁר	conspire
הִדַּבֵּר	converse
הִתְרָאָה	look at one another

c. *Iterative*

הִתְהַלֵּךְ	walk back and forth
הִתְהַפֵּךְ	turn back and forth

227

d. *Denominative*

הִתְנַבֵּא   prophesy (*Noun:* נָבִיא)

הִתְיַהֵד   pretend to be a Jew (*Noun:* יְהוּדִי)

הִתְיַלֵּד   declare one's pedigree (*Noun:* תּוֹלֵדוֹת)

3. Inflections of the HtD

a. Perfect

3 ms	הִתְקַטֵּל	3 cp	הִתְקַטְּלוּ
3 fs	הִתְקַטְּלָה		
2 ms	הִתְקַטַּלְתָּ	2 mp	הִתְקַטַּלְתֶּם
2 fs	הִתְקַטַּלְתְּ	2 fp	הִתְקַטַּלְתֶּן
1 cs	הִתְקַטַּלְתִּי	1 cp	הִתְקַטַּלְנוּ

b. Imperfect

3 ms	יִתְקַטֵּל	3 mp	יִתְקַטְּלוּ
3 fs	תִּתְקַטֵּל	3 fp	תִּתְקַטֵּלְנָה
2 ms	תִּתְקַטֵּל	2 mp	תִּתְקַטְּלוּ
2 fs	תִּתְקַטְּלִי	2 fp	תִּתְקַטֵּלְנָה
1 cs	אֶתְקַטֵּל	1 cp	נִתְקַטֵּל

c. Imperative

2 ms	הִתְקַטֵּל	2 mp	הִתְקַטְּלוּ
2 fs	הִתְקַטְּלִי	2 fp	הִתְקַטֵּלְנָה

d. Infinitive

Absolute   הִתְקַטֵּל

Construct   הִתְקַטֵּל

e. Participle

ms	מִתְקַטֵּל	mp	מִתְקַטְּלִים
fs	מִתְקַטֶּלֶת	fp	מִתְקַטְּלוֹת

The verb פָּקַד (visit), though a strong verb, never shows doubling of the second radical (e.g., וַיִּתְפָּקֵד).

4. Peculiar Treatment of the Infixed *t*

will switch place with ת

a. Roots with one of the sibilants ס, צ, שׁ, or שׂ as the first radical will show *metathesis* of the infixed ת and that sibilant.

מִסְתַּתֵּר > מִתְסַתֵּר*   hiding oneself

מִשְׂתַּכֵּר > מִתְשַׂכֵּר*   hiring oneself out

יִשְׁתַּמֵּר > יִתְשַׁמֵּר*   he will be on guard

In addition to the metathesis, the emphatic sibilant צ will cause the ת to change to ט.

נִצְטַדֵּק > נִתְצַדֵּק*   we will show ourselves innocent

הִצְטַיַּדְנוּ > הִתְצַיַּדְנוּ*   we took provisions

b. Verbs with one of the dentals ד, ט, or ת as the first radical will show assimilation of the infixed ת into that dental.

מִדַּבֵּר > מִתְדַּבֵּר*   conversing

מִטַּהֵר > מִתְטַהֵר*   purifying oneself

תִּתַּמָּם > תִּתְתַּמָּם*   you show yourself blameless

Similar assimilations also occur sporadically with other dentals.

יִנַּשֵּׂא > יִתְנַשֵּׂא*   he shall exalt himself

הִנַּבְּאוּ > הִתְנַבְּאוּ*   they prophesied

יִזַּכּוּ > יִתְזַכּוּ*   clean yourselves!

5. HtD of Weak Verbs

a. There are few surprises in the inflection of weak verbs in the HtD *binyān*:

  i. Since gutturals and ר cannot take the *dāḡēš forte*, the preceding vowel is usually lengthened.

  יִתְבָּרֵךְ   he will bless himself

  יִתְגָּאֵל   he will defile himself

  הִתְרָחַצְתִּי   I washed myself

But we also get virtual doubling in some instances.

  הִטַּהַרְנוּ   we cleansed ourselves

  ii. I-*Wāw* verbs preserve the original ו in some verbs, but ו > י in others: הִתְוַדָּה, הִתְוַדַּע, but also הִתְיַלְדוּ (for loss of gemination in the ל, see V.6), תְּתִיַפִּי, יִתְיַעֲצוּ. I-*Yōd* verbs are not attested in HtD.

b. The following is a synopsis of verbs in HtD:

Root	Perf.	Impf.	Juss./*wyqtl*	Impv.	Inf.	Ptc.
שמר	הִשְׁתַּמֵּר	יִשְׁתַּמֵּר	יִשְׁתַּמֵּר	הִשְׁתַּמֵּר	הִשְׁתַּמֵּר	מִשְׁתַּמֵּר
ברך	הִתְבָּרֵךְ	יִתְבָּרֵךְ	יִתְבָּרֵךְ	הִתְבָּרֵךְ	הִתְבָּרֵךְ	מִתְבָּרֵךְ
גלה	הִתְגַּלָּה	יִתְגַּלֶּה	יִתְגַּל	הִתְגַּלֵּה	הִתְגַּלּוֹת	מִתְגַּלֶּה
ידע	הִתְוַדַּע	יִתְוַדַּע	יִתְוַדַּע	הִתְוַדַּע	הִתְוַדַּע	מִתְוַדַּע

6. *št* Verb חוה

The *št* (causative-reflexive) *binyān* occurs in the Hebrew Bible only for the verb חוה (bow down, worship). No other *binyān* contains this verb. Prior to the discovery of the Ugaritic tablets in 1929, forms of this verb were incorrectly analyzed as HtD forms of שׁחה (i.e., with metathesis), though we would still expect *הִשְׁתַּחְתָה not הִשְׁתַּחֲוָה, and so on. In Ugaritic, the forms *yšthwy*, *tšthwy*, and *yšthwyn* are attested, all indicating that the root is *ḥwy* (thus, Hebrew חוה).

The following forms are attested in the Hebrew Bible:

a. Perfect

3 ms	הִשְׁתַּחֲוָה	3 cp	הִשְׁתַּחֲווּ
2 ms	הִשְׁתַּחֲוִיתָ	2 mp	הִשְׁתַּחֲוִיתֶם
1 cs	הִשְׁתַּחֲוֵיתִי		

b. Imperfect

3 ms	יִשְׁתַּחֲוֶה	3 mp	יִשְׁתַּחֲווּ
		3 fp	תִּשְׁתַּחֲוֶינָה
2 ms	תִּשְׁתַּחֲוֶה	2 mp	תִּשְׁתַּחֲווּ
1 cs	אֶשְׁתַּחֲוֶה	1 cp	נִשְׁתַּחֲוֶה

c. Imperative and Jussive/*wyqṭl*

	Impv.	Jussive/*wyqṭl*
3 ms		יִשְׁתַּחוּ
2 ms		תִּשְׁתַּחוּ
2 fs	הִשְׁתַּחֲוִי	
2 mp	הִשְׁתַּחֲווּ	

d. Infinitive

הִשְׁתַּחֲוֹת

e. Participle

ms מִשְׁתַּחֲוֶה   mp מִשְׁתַּחֲוִים

The second radical ו, it should be noted, is immediately evident in all forms except the jussive/*wyqṭl* forms. The student should take care not to confuse the endings in the latter with the plural endings. Compare the following:

וַיִּשְׁתַּחוּ אָרְצָה   and *he* bowed down to the ground
  (Gen. 18:2)

וַיִּשְׁתַּחֲווּ־לוֹ   and *they* bowed down to him
  (Gen. 42:6)

7. Imprecations and Oaths

In most imprecations and oaths there are two parts: the imprecatory/oath formula and the action desired or not desired.

a. *Imprecations*

i. Imprecations are occasionally introduced by one of the following formulae:

כֹּה־יַעֲשֶׂה אֱלֹהִים וְכֹה יוֹסִף

Thus God will do and add more (1 Sam. 14:44)

כֹּה־יַעֲשׂוּן אֱלֹהִים וְכֹה יוֹסִפוּן

The gods will do and add more (1 Kings 19:2)

Very frequently we get כֹּה יַעֲשֶׂה לX יְהוָה/אֱלֹהִים "thus YHWH/God will do to X." The formula apparently invokes curses upon someone, usually the subject, if such and such is done or not done. For example:

כֹּה־יַעֲשֶׂה אֱלֹהִים   Thus God will do and add more: You
וְכֹה יוֹסִף כִּי־מוֹת תָּמוּת   will surely die! (1 Sam. 14:44)

That is, "You will surely die—*or curses be (on me)*."

ii. If the imprecation is affirmative, the second part of the imprecation is introduced by כִּי, once by אִם לֹא.

כֹּה יַעֲשֶׂה יְהוָה לִי וְכֹה יֹסִיף כִּי הַמָּוֶת יַפְרִיד בֵּינִי וּבֵינֵךְ

Thus YHWH will do to me and add more: (Only) death will separate us! (Ruth 1:17)

כֹּה יַעֲשֶׂה־לִּי אֱלֹהִים וְכֹה יוֹסִיף אִם־לֹא שַׂר־צָבָא תִּהְיֶה לְפָנַי

Thus God will do to me and add more: You will become commander of the army before me (2 Sam. 19:14). (Literally, "I'll be damned if you do not become

commander . . ."="you will certainly become
commander. . . .")

   iii.   If the imprecation is negative, it is introduced by אִם.

כֹּה יַעֲשֶׂה־לְּךָ אֱלֹהִים וְכֹה יוֹסִיף אִם־תְּכַחֵד מִמֶּנִּי דָּבָר

Thus God will do to you and add more: You
shall not hide anything from me (1 Sam. 3:17)

b. *Oaths*

   i.   Oaths are usually introduced by an oath formula.

חַי יְהוָה	As YHWH lives . . .
חַי אֱלֹהִים	As God lives . . .
חַי אֵל	As God lives . . .
חַי אָנִי	As I live . . .
חֵי נַפְשְׁךָ	By your life . . .
חֵי פַרְעֹה	By Pharaoh's life . . .
חַי יְהוָה וְחֵי נַפְשְׁךָ	As YHWH lives and by your life . . .

   ii.   If the oath is affirmative, the second part of the oath is
introduced by כִּי אִם, or אִם לֹא.

חַי־יְהוָה . . . כִּי כֵן אֶעֱשֶׂה הַיּוֹם הַזֶּה

As YHWH lives . . . I will do so today (1 Kings 1:29–30)

חַי־יְהוָה כִּי אִם־יְהוָה יִגָּפֶנּוּ

As YHWH lives, YHWH will smite him (1 Sam. 26:10)

חַי־אָנִי נְאֻם־יְהוָה אִם־לֹא כַּאֲשֶׁר דִּבַּרְתֶּם בְּאָזְנָי כֵּן אֶעֱשֶׂה לָכֶם

As I live—says YHWH—surely what you have spoken into
my ears I will do to you! (Num. 14:28)

In a few instances, the desired action is introduced without
כִּי or אִם־לֹא:

חַי־יְהוָה . . . וְנִבְנוּ

As YHWH lives . . . they shall be built (Jer. 12:16)

   iii.   If the oath is negative, the second part is introduced by אִם
or כִּי לֹא.

חֵי פַרְעֹה אִם־תֵּצְאוּ מִזֶּה

By the life of Pharaoh, you shall not depart from here
   (Gen. 42:15)

חַי־יְהוָה אֱלֹהֶיךָ אִם־יֶשׁ־לִי מָעוֹג

As YHWH your God lives, I have no provision
   (1 Kings 17:12)

iv. Even with other formulations, affirmative oaths are again
introduced by כִּי and אִם לֹא, while negative oaths are introduced by אִם.

כִּי נִשְׁבַּעְתִּי . . . כִּי־לִי תִּכְרַע כָּל־בֶּרֶךְ

By myself I have sworn . . . to me every knee shall bow
   (Isa. 45:23)

יִשָּׁבַע־לִי כַיּוֹם הַמֶּלֶךְ שְׁלֹמֹה אִם־יָמִית אֶת־עַבְדּוֹ

Let King Solomon swear to me today (that) he will not kill
his servant (1 Kings 1:51)

Vocabulary

Nouns:

גֹּאֵל	redeemer, relative
חִטָּה	(pl. חִטִּים) wheat
יֶתֶר	remainder, left-over. *Verb:* יתר (N) be left, remain over; (H) have left-over, have excess
מִקְרֶה	chance, opportunity. *Verb:* קרה chance, happen (also spelled קרא)
קָצִיר	harvest. *Verb:* קצר harvest

Verbs:

חסה	seek refuge
כלם	(N) be ashamed, humiliated; (H) put to shame, humiliate
לקט	glean

[נגשׁ]   draw near. G perf. not attested; note G impv: גַּשׁ, גְּשִׁי,
         גְּשׁוּ

נחם   (N) regret, be sorry; (D) comfort

נכר   (N) be recognized; (H) recognize, acknowledge.
         Nouns: נֵכָר foreign land; נָכְרִי foreigner

נצב   (N) stand. *Noun:* מַצֵּבָה standing stone

פרד   separate

שׂבע   be satisfied, satiated. *Adjective:* שָׂבֵעַ full, satisfied

Adjectives:

מַר   bitter. *Noun:* bitterness. *Adverb:* bitterly. *Verb:* מרר
         be bitter

רֵיק   empty. *Adverb:* רֵיקָם empty-handed

Adverbs:

הֲלֹם   hither, here

מַדּוּעַ why

Exercise 26

Translate Ruth 1:17–2:23.

1:19   וַתֵּהֹם and (the city) was in uproar

v. 20   הֵמַר (Shaddai) has made me bitter

v. 21   הֵרַע ill-treated

v. 22   כַּלָּה daughter-in-law

        שְׂעֹרָה (fp שְׂעֹרִים) barley

2:1   מידע *kĕṯîḇ-qĕrēʾ*: consonants assume מְיֻדָּע someone known, but
        vowels suggest מוֹדָע kinsman

v. 2   שִׁבֳּלִים fp of שִׁבֹּלֶת ear of grain. *Cf.* the "shibbolet" story in Judg.
        12:1–7

v. 7   עֹמֶר ear of grain. End of the verse is difficult; many emend to make sense

v. 9   וְצָמֵת from צָמֵא be thirsty. On omission of א, see XIII.4.d

v. 11   הֻגֵּד הֻגַּד it has indeed been told

חָמוֹת mother-in-law

תְּמוֹל שִׁלְשׁוֹם yesterday, three days ago = previously

v. 12   מַשְׂכֹּרֶת reward, wages

v. 14   טבל dip

פַּת morsel

חֹמֶץ vinegar

צַד side

צבט pass (something)

קָלִי parched grain

v. 16   שֹׁל־תָּשֹׁלּוּ you shall indeed pull out

צֶבֶת bundle

גער ב rebuke

v. 17   חבט beat out

1. Geminate Verbs in the G *binyān*

There are generally two types in the G *binyān* of geminate verbs: one (Type A) corresponding to the *qāṭal-yiqṭōl* type in strong verbs, and another (Type B) corresponding to the *qāṭēl-yiqṭal* type. The following are some important examples of the two types:

Type A		Type B	
אֲרַר	curse	חתת	be shattered
בלל	mix	מרר	be bitter
גלל	roll	צרר	be in distress
מדד	measure	קלל	be small
נדד	wander	רבב	be numerous
סבב	surround	רעע	be bad
שדד	devastate	תמם	be complete

a. *Perfect*

In the perfect, Type A (e.g., סבב) retains all three radicals in the third person forms, but Type B (e.g., תמם) shows the development **tamim > *tamm > tam* in the 3 ms, and *tamm–* is the base form throughout the inflection.

3 ms	סָבַב	תַּם
3 fs	סָבְבָה	תַּמָּה
2 ms	סַבּוֹתָ	תַּמּוֹתָ
2 fs	סַבּוֹת	תַּמּוֹת
1 cs	סַבּוֹתִי	תַּמּוֹתִי
3 cp	סָבְבוּ	תַּמּוּ
2 mp	סַבּוֹתֶם	תַּמּוֹתֶם
2 fp	סַבּוֹתֶן	תַּמּוֹתֶן
1 cp	סַבּוֹנוּ	תַּמּוֹנוּ

Notes:

i The stative verb שׁמם (be desolate) behaves like a Type A geminate; thus, *šamim > šāmēm,* not **šam,* as one might have expected.

ii Besides forms like סָבְבוּ, we also get מָרְדוּ—that is, with a regular *šĕwā'*. With suffixes we get both סַבְּבוּנִי and סַבּוּנִי (they surrounded me). Also in the 3 ms we have חָנַן but with suffix, חַנֵּנִי (he pitied me).

iii Before the consonantal suffix, we again get a superfluous וֹ (*cf.* XV.10.ii) which may occasionally be omitted: תַּמְנוּ for תַּמּוֹנוּ.

iv If the second radical cannot be doubled, we will have compensatory lengthening of the preceding vowel: אָרוֹתִי I cursed, צָרָה she was distressed.

b. *Imperfect*

The proper inflections of סבב and תמם are provided below. Many geminate verbs, however, form all or some of their imperfects analogously to I-*Nûn* verbs. Thus, יִסֹב, תָּסֹב, and so forth (like יִפֹּל), and יִתַּמּוּ instead of יֵתַמּוּ. It is suggested that the student *not* try to learn a second set of paradigms for each of the types. Rather, one should simply assume the following inflections as paradigmatic for geminate verbs. Should a form like יִדֹּם be encountered in reading, the student who does not recognize the root should assume the root to be נדם; but failing to find the root *נדם in a dictionary, one may then conjecture that the root is from דמם—with imperfects formed as if it were נדם.

3 ms	יָסֹב	יֵתַם
3 fs	תָּסֹב	תֵּתַם
2 ms	תָּסֹב	תֵּתַם
2 fs	תָּסֹבִּי	תֵּתַמִּי
1 cs	אָסֹב	אֵתַם
3 mp	יָסֹבּוּ	יֵתַמּוּ
3 fp	תְּסֻבֶּינָה	תֵּתַמֶּינָה
2 mp	תָּסֹבּוּ	תֵּתַמּוּ
2 fp	תְּסֻבֶּינָה	תֵּתַמֶּינָה
1 cp	נָסֹב	נֵתַם

Notes:

i. The student should recognize that יָסֹב really stands for earlier **yasubb,* and יֵתַם stands for earlier **yitamm* (*cf.* IV.4). Hence, when the suffix is added, we get יְסָבֵּנִי (certainly not **וְיִסׂבֵנִי),* יְסָבֵּנוּ, and the like. Alternatively, we also find forms like יִשְׁדְּדֵם (he shall destroy them), תְּחָגֵּהוּ (you shall celebrate it).

iii. Some verbs, notably שָׁמֵם (be desolate), show mixing of types A and B in the imperfect (תֵּשַׁם, יְשֹׁמּוּ, יִשֹּׁם, etc.).

c. *Imperative*

2 ms	סֹב	תַּם
2 fs	סֹבִּי	תַּמִּי
2 mp	סֹבּוּ	תַּמּוּ
2 fp	סֹבְנָה	תַּמְנָה

Notes:

i. Some forms are stressed in the final syllable. Hence, the 2 fs forms חָגִּי (celebrate!), רָנִּי (shout!), גָּזִּי (shear!); but also שִׁדְדוּ (destroy!)

ii. When the suffix is appended, we get forms like חָנֵּנִי (pity me!), סָלּוּהָ (pile her up!)

d. *Infinitive*

Abs.	סָכוֹב	—
Cs.	סֹב	תֹּם
Sfx.	סָבִּי	תַּמִּי

e. *Wyqtl*

3 ms	וַיָּסָב	וַיֵּתַם
		וַיֵּצֶר

f. Participle

Act.	סֹבֵב	סֹבְבִים תַּם	תַּמִּים
	סֹבֶבֶת	סֹבְבוֹת תַּמָּה	תַּמּוֹת
Pass.	סָבוּב	סְבוּבִים	
	סְבוּבָה unattested		

2. Geminate Verbs in the N *binyān*

a. Perfect

3 ms	נָסֵב	3 cp	נָסֵבּוּ
3 fs	נָסֵבָּה		
2 ms	נְסַבּוֹתָ	2 mp	נְסַבּוֹתֶם
2 fs	נְסַבּוֹת	2 fp	נְסַבּוֹתֶן
1 cs	נְסַבּוֹתִי	1 cp	נְסַבּוֹנוּ

Notes:

i. Besides these normal forms, we also find a few verbs with ē in the second syllable, like נָמֵס (it melted), נָסֵבָּה (it has turned itself). There are also isolated forms in the 3 cp with ō in the second syllable, like נָבֹזּוּ (they were plundered).

ii. A few geminate verbs have N perfects with the *niqtal* pattern: for example, נְחַת (it was shattered) and נֶחֱלְתָּ (you were profaned)—both with virtual doubling.

b. Imperfect

3 ms	יִסֵּב	3 mp	יִסֵּבּוּ
3 fs	תִּסֵּב	3 fp	תִּסַּבֶּינָה
2 ms	תִּסֵּב	2 mp	תִּסֵּבּוּ
2 fs	תִּסֵּבִּי	2 fp	תִּסַּבֶּינָה
1 cs	אֶסֵּב	1 cp	נִסֵּב

Notes:

i. A variant with ō as the thematic vowel (like תִּבּוֹז) may account for the confusion with the G imperfect forms like יִסֹּב so that some of the G imperfect forms like יִסֹּב are really N imperfects.

ii. When the first radical is a guttural or ר, we get compensatory lengthening of the preceding vowel: e.g., *yinḥat* > יֵחַת (it shall be shattered); also יֵרֹמּוּ (they shall rise), יֵרֹע (he is ill-treated).

c. *Imperative*

| 2 ms | הִסַּב | 2 mp | הִסַּבּוּ |
| 2 fs | הִסַּבִּי | 2 fp | הִסַּבֶּינָה |

d. *Infinitive*

Abs.   הִסּוֹב

Cs.   הִסֵּב

Notes: When the first radical is a guttural or ר, we may get compensatory lengthening of the preceding vowel: for example, *hinḥill* > הֵחֵל (to be profaned).

e. *Participle*

| ms | נָסָב | mp | נְסַבִּים |
| fs | נְסַבָּה | fp | נְסַבּוֹת |

Note: We also find the type נָקַל, but the fs form is still נְקַלָּה, not *נְקֵלָה.

3. Geminate Verbs in the H *binyān*

a. *Perfect*

| 3 ms | הֵסֵב | 3 cp | הֵסֵבּוּ |

3 fs	הֲסֵבָּה		
2 ms	הֲסִבּוֹתָ	2 mp	הֲסִבּוֹתֶם
2 fs	הֲסִבּוֹת	2 fp	הֲסִבּוֹתֶן
1 cs	הֲסִבּוֹתִי	1 cp	הֲסִבּוֹנוּ

Notes:

i. After guttural or ר, we may get *a* instead of *ē* in the second syllable: הֵצַר, הֵרַע. But even for קלל it is הֵקַל instead of הֵקֵל.

ii. Before guttural or ר, we get *ē* instead of *i* in the forms before strong suffixes: הַצֵרוֹתִי, הֲרֵעוֹתָ.

iii. Occasionally, the superfluous ו may be omitted before the afformative: הַחִתֹּתִי, הֵפַרְתָּ.

b. *Imperfect*

3 ms	יָסֵב	3 mp	יָסֵבּוּ
3 fs	תָּסֵב	3 fs	תְּסֻבֶּינָה
2 ms	תָּסֵב	2 mp	תָּסֵבּוּ
2 fs	תָּסֵבִּי	2 fp	תְּסֻבֶּינָה
1 cs	אָסֵב	1 cp	נָסֵב

Notes:

i. With II/III gutturals we may have *a* instead of *ē* in the second syllable (e.g., נָרַע, אָרַע), or the *ē* may be retained with *furtive pátaḥ* (e.g., יָרֵעַ).

ii. A variant type like יַסֵב is also attested.

c. *Imperative*

2 ms	הָסֵב	2 mp	הָסֵבּוּ
2 fs	הָסֵבִּי	2 fp	הֲסֻבֶּינָה

d. *Infinitive*

Abs.　　הָסֵב

Cs.　　הָסֵב

Notes:

i. With final guttural: הָרַע.

ii. Note suffixal forms הַחִלָּם (their beginning), הַפְּרְכֶם (your breaking).

e. *Participle*

ms	מֵסֵב	mp	מְסִבִּים
fs	מְסִבָּה	fp	מְסִבּוֹת

Note: The forms מֵרַע, מְרֵעִים are attested for רעע.

f. *Wyqtl*

The *wyqtl* forms are easily confused with the H *wyqtl* forms of II-*Wāw/Yōd* verbs: for example, וַיָּפֶר (from פרר), וַיָּרַע (from רעע).

4. Geminate Roots and Other Roots

Geminate verbs are frequently confused with other weak verb types. Some forms are derived analogously, or are identical, to forms in other weak verbs, especially I-*Nûn* and II-*Wāw/Yōd*. Thus, for example,

יָסֹב　G Impf. of סבב, not from נסב

יָרוֹן　G Impf. 3 ms of רנן, not from רון

נָרוֹץ　N Perf. 3 ms of רצץ, not from רוץ

תָּחֵל　N Impf. 3 fs of חלל, not from יחל

וַיָּצַר　G *wyqtl* 3 ms of צרר, not from יצר

וַיָּפֶר　H *wyqtl* 3 ms of פרר, not from פור

It is simplest at this stage in the study of Hebrew not to memorize the exceptional, mixed or otherwise confused forms. Rather, when an unknown form is encountered, the root should be reconstructed according to the regular paradigms. But when one is unable to locate the root in the dictionary, one should then consider a geminate root. Thus, for example, נָרוֹץ is assumed first to be from רוץ, but when it is learned that

רוץ is not attested in this *binyān*, one may then try רצץ. It is possible, of course, that the form is incorrectly analyzed in the dictionaries, or even incorrectly pointed by the Masoretes.

Many geminate verbs, it should be noted, have genuine alternate roots (with the same semantic range) that are II-*Wāw/Yōḏ* or III-ה.

הום, המם	be in turmoil
פור, פרר	break, destroy
צור, צרר	tie, be in distress
רבה, רבב	be numerous
שׁנה, שׁגג	go astray, sin inadvertently

Vocabulary

Nouns:

אָתוֹן	she-ass
עֵדֶר	herd
עֵז	goat
שׁוֹר	(irreg. mp. שְׁוָרִים) ox (*cf.* Spanish *toro*)

Verbs:

ארר	curse
בלל	mix, confound
דמם	be silent
חלל	(N) pollute; (H) begin
חתת	be shattered, be dismayed
מדד	measure
סבב	surround, go around
פלט	(G) escape; (D, H) bring to safety. *Nouns:* פָּלִיט fugitive; פְּלֵיטָה what has survived
קלל	(G) be light, insignificant; (D) curse
רנן	jubilate, shout for joy

רעע   be bad, evil

שדד   destroy, devastate

שמם   be desolate, appalled

תמם   be complete, whole. *Adjective:* תָּם complete,
blameless

Adverb:

אוּלַי   perhaps

Exercise 27

Translate Genesis 32.

v. 11 מַקֵּל staff

v. 13 חוֹל sand

v. 15 תַּיִשׁ he-goat

      רָחֵל ewe (cf. Rachel)

v. 16 עַיִר stallion

v. 17 רֶוַח space

v. 18 פגשׁ meet

v. 25 אבק (N) wrestle

v. 26 יקע dislocate

v. 29 שׂרה strive

v. 32 זרח shine forth

      צלע limp

v. 33 יֹאכְלוּ the plural is used here *impersonally;* that is, they do not
eat = *one* does not eat

      גִּיד sinew

      נָשֶׁה sciatic muscle

Lesson XXVIII

1. Dp *binyān*

a. *Characteristics*

The Dp *binyān* is characterized by (i) the doubling of the second radical of the verb, and (ii) a "u-class" vowel to mark the passive voice (*cf.* also the *û* vowel of the G passive participles).

b. *Meaning*

The Dp is simply the passive of D:

	D			Dp	
בִּקֵּשׁ	seek		בֻּקַּשׁ	be sought
קִדֵּשׁ	consecrate		קֻדַּשׁ	be consecrated
בֵּרֵךְ	bless		בֹּרַךְ	be blessed

c. *Perfect*

3 ms	קֻטַּל	3 cp	קֻטְּלוּ
3 fs	קֻטְּלָה		
2 ms	קֻטַּלְתָּ	2 mp	קֻטַּלְתֶּם
2 fs	קֻטַּלְתְּ	2 fp	קֻטַּלְתֶּן
1 cs	קֻטַּלְתִּי	1 cp	קֻטַּלְנוּ

Notes:

i.   Before gutturals and ר, we get compensatory lengthening of $u > ō$ (גֹּרְשׁוּ, בֹּרַךְ) but also virtual doubling (רֻחֲמָה, רֻחַץ).

ii. Occasionally, *o* (ָ) may be found in the first syllable instead of *u* (e.g., כָּסוּ).

246

d. *Imperfect*

3 ms	יְקֻטַּל	3 mp	יְקֻטְּלוּ
3 fs	תְּקֻטַּל	3 fp	תְּקֻטַּלְנָה
2 ms	תְּקֻטַּל	2 mp	תְּקֻטְּלוּ
2 fs	תְּקֻטְּלִי	2 fp	תְּקֻטַּלְנָה
1 cs	אֲקֻטַּל	1 cp	נְקֻטַּל

Note: Before gutturals and ר we get compensatory lengthening of *u > ō* (e.g., יְבֹרַךְ) or virtual doubling (e.g., יְרֻחַם).

e. *Participle*

ms	מְקֻטָּל	mp	מְקֻטָּלִים
fs	מְקֻטָּלָה	fp	מְקֻטָּלוֹת

Notes:
i. The fs form מְקֻטֶּלֶת is also found.
ii. Before gutturals and ר, *u > ō* (e.g., מְטֹהָרָה, מְבֹרֶכֶת).

f. *Synopsis*
The following is a synopsis of verbs in Dp:

Root	Perf.	Impf.	Inf. Abs.	Inf. Cs.	Ptc.
גנב	גֻּנַּב	יְגֻנַּב	גֻּנֹּב	—	מְגֻנָּב
ברך	בֹּרַךְ	יְבֹרַךְ	—	—	מְבֹרָךְ
מלא	מֻלָּא	יְמֻלָּא	—	—	מְמֻלָּא
גלה	גֻּלָּה	יְגֻלֶּה	—	גֻּלּוֹת	מְגֻלֶּה
ילד	יֻלַּד	יְיֻלַּד	—	—	מְיֻלָּד

2. Hp *binyān*

a. *Characteristics*
The Hp *binyān* is characterized by (i) the prefixed or syncopated "h," and (ii) a "u-class" vowel marking the passive.

b. *Meaning*

The meaning of the Hp is simply the passive of H:

הִגִּיד	tell	הֻגַּד	be told
הִכָּה	smite	הֻכָּה	be smitten
הֵבִיא	bring in	הוּבָא	be brought in

Verbs in Hp are frequently used impersonally. When so used, the *object* of the impersonal verb may yet be preceded by the marker of direct definite accusative.

וַיֻּגַּד לְרִבְקָה אֶת־דִּבְרֵי עֵשָׂו
בְּנָהּ הַגָּדֹל
It was told to Rebecca the words of Esau, her older son = Rebecca *was told* the words of Esau, her older son (Gen. 27:42)

הוּבָא אֶת־דָּמָם לְכַפֵּר בַּקֹּדֶשׁ
It was brought their blood to make atonement in the sanctuary = their blood *was brought* to make atonement in the sanctuary (Lev. 16:27)

c. *Inflections*

All inflections of the Hp are marked by a "u-class" vowel, which may be *o* (ָ), *u* (ֻ), or *û* (וּ).

    i.   Before a strong radical it is usually *o*.

        הָמְלַךְ Perf. 3 ms of מלך rule

        הָפְנוּ Perf. 3 cp of פנה turn

        הָפְדֵה Inf. Abs. of פדה redeem

        מָשְׁחָת Ptc. ms of שחת corrupt

    Not infrequently, however, we get *u* instead of *o*.

        הֻשְׁלַךְ Perf. 3 ms of שלך cast

        הֻמְלַחַת Perf. 2 fs of מלח salt (something)

        מֻשְׁלֶכֶת Ptc. fs of שלך cast

    ii.   Before I-guttural or ר it is *o*.

        הָרְאָה Perf. 3 ms of ראה see

        נָעָבְדֵם Impf. 1 cs of עבד serve + suffix

        הָחְבְּאוּ Perf. 3 cp of חבא hide

iii. Before I-*Nûn* it is *u*.

הֻגַּד Perf. 3 ms or Inf. Cs. of נגד tell

יֻסַּךְ Impf. 3 ms of נסך pour out

מֻצָּל Ptc. ms of נצל deliver

When נ is unassimilated, however, we have *o* instead of *u*:

הָנְחַלְתִּי Perf. 1 cs of נחל inherit

הָנְתְּקוּ Perf. 3 cp of נתק tear away

iv. For I-*Wāw*/*Yōḏ*, and Geminate verbs it is *û*, but sometimes written defectively.

הוּסַד Perf. 3 ms of יסד lay foundation

יוּצַר Impf. 3 ms of יצר form

מוּצֵאת Ptc. fs of יצא go forth

מוּדַעַת Ptc. fs of ידע know

הוּמַת Perf. 3 ms of מות die

יוּמַת Impf. 3 ms of מות die

הוּשַׁד Perf. 3 ms of שדד destroy

מוּסַבּוֹת Ptc. fp of סבב surround

הוּשַׁב Perf. 3 ms of שוב return

יוּשַׁב Impf. 3 ms of שוב return

מוּשַׁב Ptc. ms of שוב return

The last three examples may, of course, also be analyzed as forms of ישב (dwell), but these forms of ישׁב never occur.

d. *Synopsis*

The following is a synopsis of verbs in Hp:

Root	Perf.	Impf.	Inf. Abs.	Inf. Cs.	Ptc.
שמר	הֻשְׁמַר	יֻשְׁמַר	הָשְׁמֵר	—	מֻשְׁמָר
עבד	הֻעֲבַד	יֻעֲבַד	הָעֲבֵד	—	מֻעֲבָד
גלה	הֻגְלָה	יֻגְלֶה	הָגְלֵה	—	מֻגְלֶה
יסר	הוּסַר	יוּסַר	הוּסֵר	—	מוּסָר

מֻגָּד	הֻגַּד	הֻגֵּד	יֻגַּד	הֻגַּד	נגד
מוּקָם	—	הוּקַם	יוּקַם	הוּקַם	קום

3. Gp Verbs

A few verbs which are frequently confused with and pointed as Dp and Hp verbs are, in fact, vestiges of an original Gp (G passive) stem attested in other Semitic languages. In general, we know that these verbs are Gp because they correspond in meaning to verbs in G, not D or H. If a passive form occurs for a verb found in G but not in D or H, and it has the same semantic range, then the form is probably a Gp. For example, since אָכַל means "be consumed" (not "be fed," or the like), and the root does not appear in D, forms like אֻכַּל are almost certainly Gp.

Likewise, the verb נתן does not occur at all in D or H, but יֻתַּן occurs several times. If the verb were Hp, one would expect to find at least some examples of נתן in H. Moreover, the meaning of יֻתַּן (derived from context) suggests that יֻתַּן is the passive of G, not H.

Analogous to יֻתַּן, we have forms like יֻקַּח (he is taken). The verb לקח does not appear in D or H. If יֻקַּח is a Dp imperfect, one would expect *יֻלְקַּח; if it were Hp, the perfect לֻקַּח is problematic. Finally, it should be noted that the participle לֻקַּח is attested—without the –מ prefix that one would expect for the Dp or Hp participle. Thus, it must be concluded that forms like לֻקַּח and יֻקַּח are G passives. The following are examples of Gp forms:

Root	Perf.	Impf.	Ptc.	
אכל	אֻכַּל	יֻאֲכַל	אֻכָּל	eat
ילד	יֻלַּד	—	יוּלַּד	bear
לקח	לֻקַּח	יֻקַּח	לֻקַּח	take
נתן	—	יֻתַּן	—	give

Vocabulary

Nouns:

גַּל	wave, heap (of stone). *Cf. Verb* גלל roll
דָּג	(also דָּגָה) fish
הֶבֶל	idol, nothing
יְרֵכָה	(with suffix יַרְכָת–; יַרְכָתַיִם) rear, hindmost part
מֵעִים	(always pl.) bowels, entrails
שָׂכָר	reward, wages. *Verb:* שׂכר hire.
שְׁאוֹל	Sheol, the underworld
שָׁוְא	vanity, idol, nothing
שׁוע	(D) cry out for help

Verbs:

גרשׁ	drive out
חבשׁ	bind, gird
חשׁב	think, regard, consider, reckon
נבט	(H) gaze, look
נקה	be free, innocent. *Adjective:* נָקִי or נָקִיא innocent
פלל	(HtD) pray. *Noun:* תְּפִלָּה prayer

Interjection:

אֲהָהּ	Ah! (Also אָנָּא = אָה נָא, or אָנָּה)

Preposition:

בְּעַד	behind, through (out of)

Exercise 28

Translate Jonah 1–2.

v. 3 אֳנִיָּה a ship

v. 4 טול (H) throw

סַעַר gale

v. 5 מַלָּח mariner; *cf.* מֶלַח salt

סְפִינָה ship

רדם (N) sleep soundly

v. 6 רַב הַחֹבֵל captain of the sailors

עשׁת (HtD) give thought

v. 7 בְּשֶׁלְּמִי on account of whom — that is, *bĕ* + *šĕ* + *lĕ* + *mî*

v. 12 שׁתק become calm

v. 13 חתר row

סער rage

v. 15 זעף rage

2:1 בלע swallow

v. 4 מְצוּלָה (primordial) deep

יְסֹבְבֵנִי was around me

מִשְׁבָּר breaker

v. 6 אפף encompass

סוף (coll.) reeds, weeds

v. 7 קֶצֶב foundation

בָּרִיחַ bar

שַׁחַת pit

v. 8 עטף grow feeble

v. 11 קיא vomit

Lesson XXIX

1. *Qōlēl, qōlal, hitqōlēl*

a. *Characteristics and Meaning*

These *binyānîm* are characterized by (i) a long ō vowel after the first radical, and (ii) the duplication of the third radical. Hence the names *qōlēl, qōlal, hitqōlēl*. For II-*Wāw/Yōḏ* verbs, these stems tend to replace the D, Dp, and HtD respectively. Thus, though II-*Wāw/Yōḏ* verbs are attested in D, Dp, and HtD, they are relatively rare; the functions normally met by those *binyānîm* are assumed, at least in part, by the *qōlēl, qōlal,* and *hitqōlēl* forms.

Compare the meanings of the following verbs in G and in *qōlēl:*

Root	G	*qōlēl*
קוּם	arise	raise
רוּם	be exalted	exalt
מוּת	die	kill
רוּץ	run	dash back and forth
שׁוּב	return	bring back

It is evident from these examples that there is some semantic overlap between verbs in D and those in the *qōlēl* stem.

Geminate verbs are also sometimes found in these *binyānîm* rather than in D, Dp, or HtD.

חָלַל	חוֹלֵל	pierce
חָנַן	חוֹנֵן	take pity
סָבַב	סוֹבֵב	encircle

b. *Perfect*

3 ms	קוֹמֵם	קוֹמַם	הִתְקוֹמֵם
3 fs	קוֹמְמָה	קוֹמְמָה	הִתְקוֹמְמָה
2 ms	קוֹמַמְתָּ	קוֹמַמְתָּ	הִתְקוֹמַמְתָּ
2 fs	קוֹמַמְתְּ	קוֹמַמְתְּ	הִתְקוֹמַמְתְּ

253

1 cs	קוֹמַ֫מְתִּי	קוֹמַמְתִּי	הִתְקוֹמַ֫מְתִּי
3 cp	קוֹמְמוּ	קוֹמְמוּ	הִתְקוֹמְמוּ
2 mp	קוֹמַמְתֶּם	קוֹמַמְתֶּם	הִתְקוֹמַמְתֶּם
2 fp	קוֹמַמְתֶּן	קוֹמַמְתֶּן	הִתְקוֹמַמְתֶּן
1 cp	קוֹמַ֫מְנוּ	קוֹמַמְנוּ	הִתְקוֹמַ֫מְנוּ

Notes:

i. Beyond the 3 ms, *qōlēl* and *qōlal* forms cannot be distinguished.

ii. We also get forms like כּוֹנֲנוּ instead of כּוֹנְנוּ, and חוֹלֲלָה instead of חוֹלְלָה.

iii. The *ē* vowel is reduced in the 3 ms form with object suffix: כּוֹנֲנָה (he established it).

c. *Imperfect*

3 ms	יְקוֹמֵם	יְקוֹמַם	יִתְקוֹמֵם
3 fs	תְּקוֹמֵם	תְּקוֹמַם	תִּתְקוֹמֵם
2 ms	תְּקוֹמֵם	תְּקוֹמַם	תִּתְקוֹמֵם
2 fs	תְּקוֹמְמִי	תְּקוֹמְמִי	תִּתְקוֹמְמִי
1 cs	אֲקוֹמֵם	אֲקוֹמַם	אֶתְקוֹמֵם
3 mp	יְקוֹמְמוּ	יְקוֹמְמוּ	יִתְקוֹמְמוּ
3 fp	תְּקוֹמֵ֫מְנָה	תְּקוֹמַ֫מְנָה	תִּתְקוֹמֵ֫מְנָה
2 mp	תְּקוֹמְמוּ	תְּקוֹמְמוּ	תִּתְקוֹמְמוּ
2 fp	תְּקוֹמֵ֫מְנָה	תְּקוֹמַ֫מְנָה	תִּתְקוֹמֵ֫מְנָה
1 cp	נְקוֹמֵם	נְקוֹמַם	נִתְקוֹמֵם

Notes:

i. In the 2 fs, 3 mp, and 2 mp we cannot distinguish between the active and passive.

ii. The *ē* vowel is reduced when the object suffix is appended: יְרוֹמֲמֵ֫נִי (he will exalt me), יְרוֹמֲמ֫וּהוּ (they will exalt him); also

אֲרוֹמְמֶנְהוּ (!). With the 2 ms suffix, we get either אֲרוֹמִמְךָ or,
in pause, אֲרוֹמְמֶךָ.

iii. The frequently attested verb כּוּן (establish) shows assimilation of ת in some of the *hiṯqōlēl* forms (see XXVI.4.b): תִּכּוֹנֵן
for תִּתְכּוֹנֵן, תִּכּוֹנָנוּ for תִּתְכּוֹנָנוּ.

d. *Other Inflections*

Impv.	קוֹמֵם		הִתְקוֹמֵם
Inf. Cs.	קוֹמֵם		הִתְקוֹמֵם
Ptc.	מְקוֹמֵם	מְקוֹמָם	מִתְקוֹמֵם

2. *Qilqēl, qolqal, hiṯqalqēl*

a. These forms are characterized by the repetition of the first and
last radicals. Hence the names *qilqēl, qolqal, hiṯqalqēl*. Again, they correspond roughly to the D, Dp, and HtD *binyānîm* in semantic range.

The presence of a guttural or ר may affect the vocalization of the
forms:

מִתְלַהְלֵהַּ　　behaving like a madman (להה)

תִּתְחַלְחַל　　she is terrified (חיל)

b. Verbs in these stems are mostly geminates, with a few II-*Wāw/
Yōḏ*.

Root	Act.	Pass.	Reflex.	
גלל	גִּלְגֵּל		הִתְגַּלְגֵּל	roll
קלל	קִלְקֵל		הִתְקַלְקֵל	shake swiftly
כול	כִּלְכֵּל	כָּלְכַּל		hold
חיל			הִתְחַלְחַל	tremble

3. Minor Patterns

a. *qōṭēl, qōṭal, hiṯqōṭēl*:
These are similar to verbs of the *qōlēl* type, but have three different
radicals.

שֹׁרֵשׁ　　it has taken root (contrast D שֵׁרֵשׁ, uproot)

שֵׁרְשׁוּ   they have taken root (not Dp)

מְשֹׁפְטִי   my adversary (i.e., *qōṭēl* ptc. with suff.)

הִתְגָּעֲשׁוּ   they filled themselves with drink

b. *qaṭlēl*, *quṭlal*

These forms retain all three radicals and also reduplicate the third.

שַׁאֲנַן   be at ease (שׁאן)

רַעֲנַן   be luxuriant (רען)

אֻמְלַל   be withered (אמל)

c. *qĕṭalṭal*, *qŏṭalṭal*

These forms retain all three radicals and reduplicate the last two. Examples:

סְחַרְחַר   go back and forth (סחר)

חֲמַרְמַר   ferment (חמר)

Other patterns occur sporadically, as do verbs with four radicals. One should consult a dictionary or reference grammar when such rare forms are encountered.

Vocabulary

Nouns:

הָדָר   (also הֲדָרָה) splendor, grandeur

זָמִיר   (pl. זְמִירוֹת) song. *Cf.* מִזְמֹר psalm.

יַעַר   forest

פֶּסֶל   idol

צוּר   rock (mountain)

צַר   adversary

תֵּבֵל   world

Verbs:

בחן   test, try

בָּשַׂר (D) make known, bring news

גִּיל be joyful, rejoice

כָּרַע bend the knee

מוֹט totter

מָסַס melt

נָסָה (D) test

רוּעַ (H) shout. *Noun:* תְּרוּעָה alarm, shout

תָּעָה wander about, be confused

Adverb:

בַּל not (*cf.* בִּלְתִּי); בְּלִי without

Exercise 29

Translate Psalms 95–97.

95:4 מֶחְקָר depth

     תּוֹעֲפוֹת tops

v. 7 מַרְעִית pasturage

v. 10 קוּט detest

96:5 אֱלִיל worthless

v. 6 הוֹד majesty

v. 10 אַף here, an interjection: Indeed!

     דִּין judge

     מֵישָׁרִים equity

v. 11 רָעַם thunder, roar

v. 12 עָלַז exult

     שָׂדַי = שָׂדֶה field

97:1 אִיִּים coastlands

v. 2 עֲרָפֶל darkness

v. 3 לָהַט burn

v. 4 בָּרָק lightning

v. 5 דּוֹנַג wax

v. 9 עֶלְיוֹן the most high

v. 12 זֶכֶר name, fame

LESSON XXX

1. Hendiadys

Sometimes two separate nouns linked by וְ may be used to express a complex idea that would normally require just one noun with a modifier.

עִיר וּמִגְדָּל

a city and tower > *a towering city* (Gen. 11:4)

עִצְּבוֹנֵךְ וְהֵרֹנֵךְ

your pain and your pregnancy > *your labor pain* (Gen. 3:16)

דְּמָמָה וָקוֹל

a whisper and a voice > *a whispering voice* (Job 4:16)

2. Casus Pendens

Sometimes a subject is isolated at the beginning of a sentence for emphasis but should be translated as part of the main clause. In such a case, the conjunction וְ may introduce the main clause, but its presence is superfluous and usually omitted in translation.

כָּל־אֹכֵל חָמֵץ וְנִכְרְתָה הַנֶּפֶשׁ הַהִוא מִיִּשְׂרָאֵל

As for any who eats unleavened bread, *that person* will be cut off from Israel = Any who eats unleavened bread will be cut off from Israel (Exod. 12:15)

הָאֵל תָּמִים דַּרְכּוֹ

As for God, his way is perfect = God's way is perfect (Ps. 18:31)

3. Circumstantial Clauses

Clauses parenthetically describing circumstances that accompany the main action or statement are introduced by וְ.

נִבְנֶה־לָּנוּ עִיר וּמִגְדָּל וְרֹאשׁוֹ בַשָּׁמַיִם

Let us build ourselves a towering city *with* its top in the
heavens (Gen. 11:4)

וַיְהִי כְּשָׁמְעֲכֶם אֶת־הַקּוֹל מִתּוֹךְ הַחֹשֶׁךְ וְהָהָר בֹּעֵר בָּאֵשׁ וַתִּקְרְבוּן

When you heard the voice from the midst of the darkness,
while the mountain was burning with fire, you drew near
(Deut. 5:23)

וַיָּבֹא אֱלִישָׁע דַּמֶּשֶׂק וּבֶן־הֲדַד מֶלֶךְ־אֲרָם חֹלֶה

Elisha came to Damascus *when* Ben-Hadad the king of Aram
was sick (2 Kings 8:7)

4. Conditional Sentences

A conditional sentence consists of two clauses: the *protasis* which
states the condition or supposition, and the *apodosis* which states the con-
sequence of the protasis.

a. *Real Conditions*
Conditions that are real, realized, or realizable are normally introduced by אִם in the protasis; the apodosis may be introduced by וְ, but
it is not necessary.

אִם־תֵּלְכִי עִמִּי וְהָלָכְתִּי וְאִם־לֹא תֵלְכִי עִמִּי לֹא אֵלֵךְ

If you will go with me, I will go; but *if* you will not go with
me, I will not go (Judg. 4:8)

אִם־תַּעְצְרֵנִי לֹא־אֹכַל בְּלַחְמֶךָ

If you detain me, I will not eat your food (Judg. 13:16)

Less frequently, a real condition may be introduced by כִּי, הֵן, or
אֲשֶׁר.

כִּי־תִמְצָא אִישׁ לֹא תְבָרְכֶנּוּ וְכִי־יְבָרֶכְךָ אִישׁ לֹא תַעֲנֶנּוּ

If you meet any one, do not salute him; and *if* any one salutes
you, do not answer him (2 Kings 4:29)

הֵן נִזְבַּח אֶת־תּוֹעֲבַת מִצְרַיִם לְעֵינֵיהֶם וְלֹא יִסְקְלֻנוּ

If we sacrifice the abomination of the Egyptians before them,
will they not stone us? (Exod. 8:22)

b. *Hypothetical Conditions*

Conditions that are not realized or not realizable are introduced by
לוּ (sometimes לָא) "if" or לוּלֵי (also לוּלֵא) "if not" in the protasis.

לוּ חָפֵץ יְהוָה לַהֲמִיתֵנוּ לֹא־לָקַח מִיָּדֵנוּ עֹלָה וּמִנְחָה

If YHWH desired to kill us, he would not have taken an
offering and a gift from our hand (Judg. 13:23)

לוּלֵי תוֹרָתְךָ שַׁעֲשֻׁעָי אָז אָבַדְתִּי בְעָנְיִי

If your instruction were *not* my delight, then I would have
perished in my affliction (Ps. 119:92)

לוּלֵא חֲרַשְׁתֶּם בְּעֶגְלָתִי לֹא מְצָאתֶם חִידָתִי

If you had *not* plowed with my heifer, you would not have
found my riddle (Judg. 14:18)

c. *Virtual Conditional Sentences*

Sometimes a conditional clause may be introduced without any
particle. In such cases, the protasis and the apodosis will each be introduced by וְ.

וְעָזַב אֶת־אָבִיו וָמֵת

If he leaves his father, he will die (Gen. 44:22)

וְרָאִיתִי מָה וְהִגַּדְתִּי לָךְ

If I see anything, I will tell you (1 Sam. 19:3)

Vocabulary

Nouns:

יָגוֹן	grief, trouble
שֵׂיבָה	old age. *Verb:* שִׂיב be old, gray
שֶׁבֶר	grain. *Verb:* שבר buy grain

Verbs

אָשֵׁם/אָשַׁם	be guilty. *Noun:* אָשָׁם guilt, guilt-offering
חרד	tremble
ליץ	scoff, brag; (H) mock, interpret

רָגַל   (D) spy

שָׁכַל   (G) be bereaved; (D) bereave

Adverb:

אֲבָל   truly, however, but

Exercise 30

Translate Genesis 42.

v. 3 בַּר grain

v. 4 אָסוֹן accident

v. 6 שָׁלַט gain power

v. 17 מִשְׁמָר custody

v. 19 כֵּן honest

         רֵעָבוֹן famine

v. 25 צֵדָה provision

v. 27 מִסְפּוֹא fodder

         אַמְתַּחְתּוֹ his sack

v. 34 תִּסְחָרוּ ply, pass through

v. 35 צְרוֹר bag, bundle

APPENDIX A

Noun Patterns

1. *qāl-qālîm*

  דָּם (cs. דַּם)   דָּמִים (cs. דְּמֵי) blood

 fs.

  שָׁנָה (cs. שְׁנַת)   year

2. *qal-qallîm*

  עַם (cs. עַם)   עַמִּים (cs. עַמֵּי) people

  שַׂר (cs. שַׂר)   שָׂרִים (cs. שָׂרֵי) ruler

 fs.

  אַמָּה (cs. אַמַּת)   cubit

  פָּרָה (cs. פָּרַת)   cow

A few nouns in this class have *qal* in the singular, but *qill–* in the forms with endings or suffixes.

  סַף (cs. סַף)   סִפִּים (cs. סִפֵּי) threshold

  (suffix סִפִּי, etc.)

  צַד (cs. צַד)   צִדִּים (cs. צִדֵּי) side

3. *qēl-qillîm*

  חֵץ (cs. חֵץ)   חִצִּים (cs. חִצֵּי) arrow

 fs.

  רִנָּה (cs. רִנַּת)   jubilation

4. *qōl-qullîm*

  חֹק (cs. חֹק)   חֻקִּים (cs. חֻקֵּי) statute

 fs.

  חֻקָּה (cs. חֻקַּת)   statute

5. *qā́wel-qôlîm*

  מָוֶת (cs. מוֹת)   מוֹתִים (cs. מוֹתֵי) death

6. *qáyil-qêlîm*

זַיִת (cs. זֵית)   זֵיתִים (cs. זֵיתֵי)   olive

fs.

שֵׂיבָה (cs. שֵׂיבַת)   old age

7. *qôl-qôlîm*

קוֹץ (cs. קוֹץ)   קוֹצִים (cs. קוֹצֵי)   thorn-bush

fs.

קוֹמָה (cs. קוֹמַת)   height

8. *qîl-qîlîm*

שִׁיר (cs. שִׁיר)   שִׁירִים (cs. שִׁירֵי)   song

fs.

שִׁירָה (cs. שִׁירַת)   song

9. *qéṭel-qĕṭālîm*

*qaṭl

מֶלֶךְ (cs. מֶלֶךְ)   מְלָכִים (cs. מַלְכֵי)   king

עֶבֶד (cs. עֶבֶד)   עֲבָדִים (cs. עַבְדֵי)   servant

נַעַר (cs. נַעַר)   נְעָרִים (cs. נַעֲרֵי)   lad

סֶלַע (cs. סֶלַע)   סְלָעִים (cs. סַלְעֵי)   rock

*qiṭl

קֶבֶר (cs. קֶבֶר)   קְבָרִים (cs. קִבְרֵי)   grave

סֵפֶר (cs. סֵפֶר)   סְפָרִים (cs. סִפְרֵי)   book

עֵדֶר (cs. עֵדֶר)   עֲדָרִים (cs. עֶדְרֵי)   herd

זֶבַח (cs. זֶבַח)   זְבָחִים (cs. זִבְחֵי)   sacrifice

*quṭl

חֹדֶשׁ (cs. חֹדֶשׁ)   חֳדָשִׁים (cs. חָדְשֵׁי)   new moon

אֹהֶל (cs. אֹהֶל)   אֹהָלִים (cs. אָהֳלֵי)   tent

רֹמַח (cs. רֹמַח)   רְמָחִים (cs. רָמְחֵי)   lance

fs.

מַלְכָּה (cs. מַלְכַּת)   queen

נַעֲרָה (cs. נַעֲרַת)   lass

שִׂמְלָה	(cs. שִׂמְלַת)			cloak
עֶזְרָה	(cs. עֶזְרַת)			help
שִׂמְחָה	(cs. שִׂמְחַת)			joy
חָכְמָה	(cs. חָכְמַת)			wisdom
טָהֳרָה	(cs. טָהֳרַת)			purity

10. *qātāl-qĕtālîm*

דָּבָר	(cs. דְּבַר)	דְּבָרִים	(cs. דִּבְרֵי)	word
חָכָם	(cs. חֲכַם)	חֲכָמִים	(cs. חַכְמֵי)	wise men

fs.

צְדָקָה	(cs. צִדְקַת)	צְדָקוֹת	(cs. צִדְקוֹת)	righteousness
אֲדָמָה	(cs. אַדְמַת)	אֲדָמוֹת	(cs. אַדְמוֹת)	ground

11. *qātēl-qĕtēlîm*

שָׁכֵן	(cs. שְׁכַן)	שְׁכֵנִים	(cs. שִׁכְנֵי)	neighbor

fs.

לְבֵנָה	(cs. לִבְנַת)		brick

12. *qātōl-qĕtōlîm*

קָדוֹשׁ	(cs. קְדוֹשׁ)	קְדוֹשִׁים	(cs. קְדוֹשֵׁי)	holy one

fs.

עֲבֹדָה	(cs. עֲבֹדַת)		service
קְטֹרֶת	(cs. קְטֹרֶת)		incense

13. *qātîl-qātîlîm*

אָסִיר	(cs. אֲסִיר)	אֲסִירִים	(cs. אֲסִירֵי)	prisoner

14. *qātûl-qĕtûlîm*

עָצוּם	(cs. עֲצוּם)	עֲצוּמִים	(cs. עֲצוּמֵי)	mighty one

15. *qattāl-qattālîm*

דַּיָּן	(cs. דַּיַּן)	דַּיָּנִים	(cs. דַּיָּנֵי)	judge
פָּרָשׁ	(cs. פָּרָשׁ)	פָּרָשִׁים	(cs. פָּרָשֵׁי)	rider

This is the pattern of nouns of profession. Other examples:

גַּנָּב	thief
מַלָּח	mariner
חָרָשׁ	craftsperson

16. *qiṭṭēl-qiṭṭĕlîm*

אִלֵּם (cs. אִלֵּם)   אִלְּמִים (cs. אִלְּמֵי)   mute

חֵרֵשׁ (cs. חֵרֵשׁ)   חֵרְשִׁים (cs. חֵרְשֵׁי)   deaf

This pattern frequently indicates bodily defects. Other examples:

פִּסֵּחַ   lame

עִוֵּר   blind

17. *qattîl-qattîlîm*

צַדִּיק (cs. צַדִּיק)   צַדִּיקִים (cs. צַדִּיקֵי)   righteous

18. *qattûl-qattûlîm*

עַמּוּד (cs. עַמּוּד)   עַמּוּדִים (cs. עַמּוּדֵי)   column

19. *qĕṭōl, qĕṭîl, qĕṭûl*

חֲמוֹר   חֲמוֹרִים   ass

כְּסִיל   כְּסִילִים   fool

גְּבוּל   גְּבוּלִים   territory

20. III-י Nouns

אֲרִי   אֲרָיִים   lion

גְּדִי   גְּדָיִים   kid

כְּלִי   כֵּלִים   vessel

חֳלִי   חֳלָיִים   illness

fs.

בְּרִית   covenant

חֲנִית   spear

21. Most III-ה Nouns

חֹזֶה (cs. חֹזֵה)   חֹזִים (cs. חֹזֵי)   seer

fs.

מָנָה (cs. מְנַת)   portion

22. Nouns with final ‒וֹן

a. Many of these are adjectival.

רִאשׁוֹן   first

אֶבְיוֹן (אבה)   needy

עֶלְיוֹן (עלה)   most high

חַלּוֹן (חלל)   window
אַלּוֹן (אלל)   oak

b. Many are from III-ה roots.

גָּאוֹן (נאה)   pride
חָזוֹן (חזה)   vision
הָמוֹן (המה)   tumult

c. A few are from II-*Wāw/Yōḏ*.

זָדוֹן (זיד)   insolence
אֵלוֹן (אול)   terebinth
שָׂשׂוֹן (שושׂ)   joy

d. In a few instances, the וֹ– is not an ending, but is part of the root.

אָרוֹן (ארן)   ark
לָשׁוֹן (לשׁן)   tongue

23. Nouns with Final ָן

בִּנְיָן (בנה)   building
קִנְיָן (קנה)   acquisition
קָרְבָּן (קרב)   offering

fs.

אַלְמָנָה (אלם)   widow

24. Triliteral Nouns with Final ִי

a. In many instances, ִי is a gentilic — that is, indicates a person's tribal, national, or ethnic origin.

עִבְרִי   עִבְרִים   Hebrew
מִצְרִי   מִצְרִים   Egyptian
יְהוּדִי   יְהוּדִים   Judean, Jew

fs.

עִבְרִיָּה   עִבְרִיּוֹת   Hebrew

b. Sometimes ִי is merely adjectival.

חָפְשִׁי   free man
נָכְרִי   foreigner
תַּחְתִּי   lower part

25. Nouns with ל Ending

A few nouns have final ל.

כַּרְמֶל	(כרם; suff. כַּרְמִלוֹ)	orchard
עֲרָפֶל	(ערף)	dark cloud

26. Nouns with מ– Prefix

   a. *maqtāl*

מַלְאָךְ	(לאך)	messenger
מַאֲכָל	(אכל)	food
מַצָּב	(נצב)	station
מוֹשָׁב	(ישׁב)	residence
מֵיטָב	(יטב)	best portion
מֵישָׁרִים	(ישׁר)	level ways
fs.		
מַחֲשֶׁבֶת	(חשׁב)	thought
מַמְלָכָה	(מלך)	kingdom

   b. *miqtāl*

In most cases earlier *maqtāl* dissimilates to *miqtāl*.

מִשְׁכָּן > מַשְׁכָּן*	(שׁכן)	tabernacle
מִדְבָּר > מַדְבָּר*	(דבר)	desert

In a few instances, *maqtāl* dissimilates to *meqtāl*.

מֶרְחָק	(רחק)	distance
מֶרְכָּבָה	(רכב)	chariot
fs.		
מִלְחָמָה	(לחם)	battle
מִשְׁפָּחָה	(שׁפח)	family
מֶמְשָׁלָה	(משׁל)	governance

   c. *maqtēl*

מַפְתֵּחַ	(פתח)	key
מַרְפֵּא	(רפא)	healing
מוֹקֵשׁ	(יקשׁ)	trap
fs.		
מְגִלָּה	(גלל)	scroll
מְסִלָּה	(סלל)	highway

d. III-ה nouns end in ֶה for the masculine, and ָה for the feminine:

מַעֲשֶׂה	(עשׂה)	deed
מִשְׁתֶּה	(שׁתה)	banquet

fs.

מִקְנָה	(קנה)	acquisition
מִצְוָה	(צוה)	commandment

e. II-*Wāw/Yōd* Nouns have –מָ as the prefix, and a long וֹ in the second syllable.

מָקוֹם	(קום)	place
מָלוֹן	(לון)	lodge

fs.

מְכוֹנָה	(כון)	place
מְנוֹרָה	(נור)	lampstand

27. Nouns with ת Prefix

The prefix may be –תַּ, –תְּ, or –תִּ.

תַּפּוּחַ	(נפח)	apple
תַּחֲנוּן	(חנן)	supplication
תּוֹשָׁב	(ישׁב)	resident
תֵּימָן	(ימן)	south

fs.

תִּפְאֶרֶת	(פאר)	glory
תִּקְוָה	(קוה)	hope
תּוֹרָה	(ירה)	law
תַּבְנִית	(בנה)	plan
תְּבוּאָה	(בוא)	produce
תְּהִלָּה	(הלל)	praise

28. Nouns with א Prefix

אֶצְבַּע	(צבע)	finger
אֶזְרַח	(זרח)	citizen
אַרְבַּע	(רבע)	four
אֵיתָן	(יתן)	everflowing stream

29. Nouns with Reduplication of Radicals

רַעֲנָן	(רען)	רַעֲנַנִּים	luxuriant
שַׁאֲנָן	(שאן)	שַׁאֲנַנִּים	ease
גַּלְגַּל	(גלל)	גַּלְגַּלִּים	wheel
קָדְקֹד	(קדד)		crown of head
עַפְעַפַּיִם	(עפף)		eyelids

1. Strong Verbs

	G	N	D	Dp	H	Hp	HtD
Perf.							
3 ms	קָטַל	נִקְטַל	קִטֵּל	קֻטַּל	הִקְטִיל	הָקְטַל	הִתְקַטֵּל
3 fs	קָטְלָה	נִקְטְלָה	קִטְּלָה	קֻטְּלָה	הִקְטִילָה	הָקְטְלָה	הִתְקַטְּלָה
2 ms	קָטַלְתָּ	נִקְטַלְתָּ	קִטַּלְתָּ	קֻטַּלְתָּ	הִקְטַלְתָּ	הָקְטַלְתָּ	הִתְקַטַּלְתָּ
2 fs	קָטַלְתְּ	נִקְטַלְתְּ	קִטַּלְתְּ	קֻטַּלְתְּ	הִקְטַלְתְּ	הָקְטַלְתְּ	הִתְקַטַּלְתְּ
1 cs	קָטַלְתִּי	נִקְטַלְתִּי	קִטַּלְתִּי	קֻטַּלְתִּי	הִקְטַלְתִּי	הָקְטַלְתִּי	הִתְקַטַּלְתִּי
3 cp	קָטְלוּ	נִקְטְלוּ	קִטְּלוּ	קֻטְּלוּ	הִקְטִילוּ	הָקְטְלוּ	הִתְקַטְּלוּ
2 mp	קְטַלְתֶּם	נִקְטַלְתֶּם	קִטַּלְתֶּם	קֻטַּלְתֶּם	הִקְטַלְתֶּם	הָקְטַלְתֶּם	הִתְקַטַּלְתֶּם
2 fp	קְטַלְתֶּן	נִקְטַלְתֶּן	קִטַּלְתֶּן	קֻטַּלְתֶּן	הִקְטַלְתֶּן	הָקְטַלְתֶּן	הִתְקַטַּלְתֶּן
1 cp	קָטַלְנוּ	נִקְטַלְנוּ	קִטַּלְנוּ	קֻטַּלְנוּ	הִקְטַלְנוּ	הָקְטַלְנוּ	הִתְקַטַּלְנוּ
Impf.							
3 ms	יִקְטֹל	יִקָּטֵל	יְקַטֵּל	יְקֻטַּל	יַקְטִיל	יָקְטַל	יִתְקַטֵּל
3 fs	תִּקְטֹל	תִּקָּטֵל	תְּקַטֵּל	תְּקֻטַּל	תַּקְטִיל	תָּקְטַל	תִּתְקַטֵּל
2 ms	תִּקְטֹל	תִּקָּטֵל	תְּקַטֵּל	תְּקֻטַּל	תַּקְטִיל	תָּקְטַל	תִּתְקַטֵּל
2 fs	תִּקְטְלִי	תִּקָּטְלִי	תְּקַטְּלִי	תְּקֻטְּלִי	תַּקְטִילִי	תָּקְטְלִי	תִּתְקַטְּלִי
1 cs	אֶקְטֹל	אֶקָּטֵל	אֲקַטֵּל	אֲקֻטַּל	אַקְטִיל	אָקְטַל	אֶתְקַטֵּל
3 mp	יִקְטְלוּ	יִקָּטְלוּ	יְקַטְּלוּ	יְקֻטְּלוּ	יַקְטִילוּ	יָקְטְלוּ	יִתְקַטְּלוּ
3 fp	תִּקְטֹלְנָה	תִּקָּטַלְנָה	תְּקַטֵּלְנָה	תְּקֻטַּלְנָה	תַּקְטֵלְנָה	תָּקְטַלְנָה	תִּתְקַטֵּלְנָה

1. Strong Verbs, continued

	G	N	D	Dp	H	Hp	HtD
Impf.							
2 mp	תִּקְטְלוּ	תִּקָּטְלוּ	תְּקַטְּלוּ	תְּקֻטְּלוּ	תַּקְטִילוּ	תָּקְטְלוּ	תִּתְקַטְּלוּ
2 fp	תִּקְטֹלְנָה	תִּקָּטַלְנָה	תְּקַטֵּלְנָה	תְּקֻטַּלְנָה	תַּקְטֵלְנָה	תָּקְטַלְנָה	תִּתְקַטֵּלְנָה
1 cp	נִקְטֹל	נִקָּטֵל	נְקַטֵּל	נְקֻטַּל	נַקְטִיל	נָקְטַל	נִתְקַטֵּל
Impv.							
2 ms	קְטֹל	הִקָּטֵל	קַטֵּל		הַקְטֵל		הִתְקַטֵּל
2 fs	קִטְלִי	הִקָּטְלִי	קַטְּלִי		הַקְטִילִי		הִתְקַטְּלִי
2 mp	קִטְלוּ	הִקָּטְלוּ	קַטְּלוּ		הַקְטִילוּ		הִתְקַטְּלוּ
2 fp	קְטֹלְנָה	הִקָּטַלְנָה	קַטֵּלְנָה		הַקְטֵלְנָה		הִתְקַטֵּלְנָה
Inf.							
Abs.	קָטוֹל	נִקְטוֹל	קַטֵּל	קֻטַּל	הַקְטֵל	הָקְטֵל	הִתְקַטֵּל
Cs.	קְטֹל	הִקָּטֵל	קַטֵּל		הַקְטִיל		הִתְקַטֵּל
Ptc.							
Act.	קֹטֵל	נִקְטָל	מְקַטֵּל	מְקֻטָּל	מַקְטִיל	מָקְטָל	מִתְקַטֵּל
Pass.	קָטוּל						
wyqtl	וַיִּקְטֹל	וַיִּקָּטֵל	וַיְקַטֵּל	וַיְקֻטַּל	וַיַּקְטֵל	וַיָּקְטַל	וַיִּתְקַטֵּל
Juss.	יִקְטֹל	יִקָּטֵל	יְקַטֵּל		יַקְטֵל	יָקְטַל	יִתְקַטֵּל

2. I-Guttural Verbs

	G		N	H	Hp
Perf.					
3 ms	עָמַד	אָכַל	נֶעֱמַד	הֶעֱמִיד	הָעֳמַד
3 fs	עָמְדָה	אָכְלָה	נֶעֶמְדָה	הֶעֱמִידָה	הָעֳמְדָה
2 ms	עָמַדְתָּ	אָכַלְתָּ	נֶעֱמַדְתָּ	הֶעֱמַדְתָּ	הָעֳמַדְתָּ
2 fs	עָמַדְתְּ	אָכַלְתְּ	נֶעֱמַדְתְּ	הֶעֱמַדְתְּ	הָעֳמַדְתְּ
1 cs	עָמַדְתִּי	אָכַלְתִּי	נֶעֱמַדְתִּי	הֶעֱמַדְתִּי	הָעֳמַדְתִּי
3 cp	עָמְדוּ	אָכְלוּ	נֶעֶמְדוּ	הֶעֱמִידוּ	הָעֳמְדוּ
2 mp	עֲמַדְתֶּם	אֲכַלְתֶּם	נֶעֱמַדְתֶּם	הֶעֱמַדְתֶּם	הָעֳמַדְתֶּם
2 fp	עֲמַדְתֶּן	אֲכַלְתֶּן	נֶעֱמַדְתֶּן	הֶעֱמַדְתֶּן	הָעֳמַדְתֶּן
1 cp	עָמַדְנוּ	אָכַלְנוּ	נֶעֱמַדְנוּ	הֶעֱמַדְנוּ	הָעֳמַדְנוּ
Impf.					
3 ms	יַעֲמֹד	יֹאכַל	יֵעָמֵד	יַעֲמִיד	יָעֳמַד
3 fs	תַּעֲמֹד	תֹּאכַל	תֵּעָמֵד	תַּעֲמִיד	תָּעֳמַד
2 ms	תַּעֲמֹד	תֹּאכַל	תֵּעָמֵד	תַּעֲמִיד	תָּעֳמַד
2 fs	תַּעַמְדִי	תֹּאכְלִי	תֵּעָמְדִי	תַּעֲמִידִי	תָּעֳמְדִי
1 cs	אֶעֱמֹד	אֹכַל	אֵעָמֵד	אַעֲמִיד	אָעֳמַד
3 mp	יַעַמְדוּ	יֹאכְלוּ	יֵעָמְדוּ	יַעֲמִידוּ	יָעֳמְדוּ
3 fp	תַּעֲמֹדְנָה	תֹּאכַלְנָה	תֵּעָמַדְנָה	תַּעֲמֵדְנָה	תָּעֳמַדְנָה

2. I-Guttural Verbs, continued

	G	G	N	H	Hp
Impf.					
2 mp	תַּעַמְדוּ	תֶּחֶזְקוּ	תֵּעָמְדוּ	תַּעֲמִידוּ	תָּעֳמְדוּ
2 fp	תַּעֲמֹדְנָה	תֶּחֱזַקְנָה	תֵּעָמַדְנָה	תַּעֲמֵדְנָה	תָּעֳמַדְנָה
1 cp	נַעֲמֹד	נֶחֱזַק	נֵעָמֵד	נַעֲמִיד	נָעֳמַד
Impv.					
2 ms	עֲמֹד	חֲזַק	הֵעָמֵד	הַעֲמֵד	
2 fs	עִמְדִי	חִזְקִי	הֵעָמְדִי	הַעֲמִידִי	
2 mp	עִמְדוּ	חִזְקוּ	הֵעָמְדוּ	הַעֲמִידוּ	
2 fp	עֲמֹדְנָה	חֲזַקְנָה	הֵעָמַדְנָה	הַעֲמֵדְנָה	
Inf.					
Abs.	עָמוֹד		הֵעָמֹד	הַעֲמֵד	הָעֳמֵד
Cs.	עֲמֹד		הֵעָמֵד	הַעֲמִיד	
Ptc.					
Act.	עֹמֵד		נֶעֱמָד	מַעֲמִיד	מָעֳמָד
Pass.	עָמוּד		נֶעֱמָד		
wyqtl	וַיַּעֲמֹד	וַיֶּחֱזַק	וַיֵּעָמֵד	וַיַּעֲמֵד	
Juss.	יַעֲמֹד		יֵעָמֵד	יַעֲמֵד	

3. II-Guttural Verbs

	G	N	D	Dp	HtD
Perf.					
3 ms	בָּחַר	נִבְחַר	מֵאֵן	בֹּרַךְ	הִתְבָּרֵךְ
3 fs	בָּחֲרָה	נִבְחֲרָה	מֵאֲנָה	בֹּרְכָה	הִתְבָּרֲכָה
2 ms	בָּחַרְתָּ	נִבְחַרְתָּ	מֵאַנְתָּ	בֹּרַכְתָּ	הִתְבָּרַכְתָּ
2 fs	בָּחַרְתְּ	נִבְחַרְתְּ	מֵאַנְתְּ	בֹּרַכְתְּ	הִתְבָּרַכְתְּ
1 cs	בָּחַרְתִּי	נִבְחַרְתִּי	מֵאַנְתִּי	בֹּרַכְתִּי	הִתְבָּרַכְתִּי
3 cp	בָּחֲרוּ	נִבְחֲרוּ	מֵאֲנוּ	בֹּרְכוּ	הִתְבָּרֲכוּ
2 mp	בְּחַרְתֶּם	נִבְחַרְתֶּם	מֵאַנְתֶּם	בֹּרַכְתֶּם	הִתְבָּרַכְתֶּם
2 fp	בְּחַרְתֶּן	נִבְחַרְתֶּן	מֵאַנְתֶּן	בֹּרַכְתֶּן	הִתְבָּרַכְתֶּן
1 cp	בָּחַרְנוּ	נִבְחַרְנוּ	מֵאַנּוּ	בֹּרַכְנוּ	הִתְבָּרַכְנוּ
Impf.					
3 ms	יִבְחַר	יִבָּחֵר	יְמָאֵן	יְבֹרַךְ	יִתְבָּרֵךְ
3 fs	תִּבְחַר	תִּבָּחֵר	תְּמָאֵן	תְּבֹרַךְ	תִּתְבָּרֵךְ
2 ms	תִּבְחַר	תִּבָּחֵר	תְּמָאֵן	תְּבֹרַךְ	תִּתְבָּרֵךְ
2 fs	תִּבְחֲרִי	תִּבָּחֲרִי	תְּמָאֲנִי	תְּבֹרֲכִי	תִּתְבָּרֲכִי
1 cs	אֶבְחַר	אֶבָּחֵר	אֲמָאֵן	אֲבֹרַךְ	אֶתְבָּרֵךְ
3 mp	יִבְחֲרוּ	יִבָּחֲרוּ	יְמָאֲנוּ	יְבֹרֲכוּ	יִתְבָּרֲכוּ
3 fp	תִּבְחַרְנָה	תִּבָּחַרְנָה	תְּמָאֵנָּה	תְּבֹרַכְנָה	תִּתְבָּרַכְנָה

3. II-Guttural Verbs, continued

	G	N	D		Dp	HtD
Impf.						
2 mp	תִּבְחֲרוּ	תִּבָּחֲרוּ	תְּמָאֲנוּ	תְּבָרֲכוּ	תְּבֹרֲכוּ	תִּתְבָּרֲכוּ
2 fp	תִּבְחַרְנָה	תִּבָּחַרְנָה	תְּמָאֵנָּה	תְּבָרֵכְנָה	תְּבֹרַכְנָה	תִּתְבָּרַכְנָה
1 cp	נִבְחַר	נִבָּחֵר	נְמָאֵן	נְבָרֵךְ	נְבֹרַךְ	נִתְבָּרֵךְ
Impv.						
2 ms	בְּחַר	הִבָּחֵר	מָאֵן	בָּרֵךְ		הִתְבָּרֵךְ
2 fs	בַּחֲרִי	הִבָּחֲרִי	מָאֲנִי	בָּרֲכִי		הִתְבָּרֲכִי
2 mp	בַּחֲרוּ	הִבָּחֲרוּ	מָאֲנוּ	בָּרֲכוּ		הִתְבָּרֲכוּ
2 fp	בְּחַרְנָה	הִבָּחַרְנָה	מָאֵנָּה	בָּרֵכְנָה		הִתְבָּרַכְנָה
Inf.						
Abs.	בָּחוֹר	הִבָּחֹר	מָאֵן	בָּרֵךְ		הִתְבָּרֵךְ
Cs.	בְּחֹר	הִבָּחֵר	מָאֵן	בָּרֵךְ		הִתְבָּרֵךְ
Ptc.						
Act.	בֹּחֵר	נִבְחָר	מְמָאֵן	מְבָרֵךְ	מְבֹרָךְ	מִתְבָּרֵךְ
Pass.	בָּחוּר					
wyqtl	וַיִּבְחַר	וַיִּבָּחֵר	וַיְמָאֵן	וַיְבָרֵךְ		וַיִּתְבָּרֵךְ
Juss.	יִבְחַר	יִבָּחֵר	יְמָאֵן	יְבָרֵךְ		יִתְבָּרֵךְ

4. III-ה, -ח, -ע Verbs

	G	N	D	Dp	H	Hp	HtD
Perf.							
3 ms	שָׁלַח	נִשְׁלַח	שִׁלַּח	שֻׁלַּח	הִשְׁלִיחַ	הָשְׁלַח	הִשְׁתַּלַּח
3 fs	שָׁלְחָה	נִשְׁלְחָה	שִׁלְּחָה	שֻׁלְּחָה	הִשְׁלִיחָה	הָשְׁלְחָה	הִשְׁתַּלְּחָה
2 ms	שָׁלַחְתָּ	נִשְׁלַחְתָּ	שִׁלַּחְתָּ	שֻׁלַּחְתָּ	הִשְׁלַחְתָּ	הָשְׁלַחְתָּ	הִשְׁתַּלַּחְתָּ
2 fs	שָׁלַחַתְּ	נִשְׁלַחַתְּ	שִׁלַּחַתְּ	שֻׁלַּחַתְּ	הִשְׁלַחַתְּ	הָשְׁלַחַתְּ	הִשְׁתַּלַּחַתְּ
1 cs	שָׁלַחְתִּי	נִשְׁלַחְתִּי	שִׁלַּחְתִּי	שֻׁלַּחְתִּי	הִשְׁלַחְתִּי	הָשְׁלַחְתִּי	הִשְׁתַּלַּחְתִּי
3 cp	שָׁלְחוּ	נִשְׁלְחוּ	שִׁלְּחוּ	שֻׁלְּחוּ	הִשְׁלִיחוּ	הָשְׁלְחוּ	הִשְׁתַּלְּחוּ
2 mp	שְׁלַחְתֶּם	נִשְׁלַחְתֶּם	שִׁלַּחְתֶּם	שֻׁלַּחְתֶּם	הִשְׁלַחְתֶּם	הָשְׁלַחְתֶּם	הִשְׁתַּלַּחְתֶּם
2 fp	שְׁלַחְתֶּן	נִשְׁלַחְתֶּן	שִׁלַּחְתֶּן	שֻׁלַּחְתֶּן	הִשְׁלַחְתֶּן	הָשְׁלַחְתֶּן	הִשְׁתַּלַּחְתֶּן
1 cp	שָׁלַחְנוּ	נִשְׁלַחְנוּ	שִׁלַּחְנוּ	שֻׁלַּחְנוּ	הִשְׁלַחְנוּ	הָשְׁלַחְנוּ	הִשְׁתַּלַּחְנוּ
Impf.							
3 ms	יִשְׁלַח	יִשָּׁלַח	יְשַׁלַּח	יְשֻׁלַּח	יַשְׁלִיחַ	יָשְׁלַח	יִשְׁתַּלַּח
3 fs	תִּשְׁלַח	תִּשָּׁלַח	תְּשַׁלַּח	תְּשֻׁלַּח	תַּשְׁלִיחַ	תָּשְׁלַח	תִּשְׁתַּלַּח
2 ms	תִּשְׁלַח	תִּשָּׁלַח	תְּשַׁלַּח	תְּשֻׁלַּח	תַּשְׁלִיחַ	תָּשְׁלַח	תִּשְׁתַּלַּח
2 fs	תִּשְׁלְחִי	תִּשָּׁלְחִי	תְּשַׁלְּחִי	תְּשֻׁלְּחִי	תַּשְׁלִיחִי	תָּשְׁלְחִי	תִּשְׁתַּלְּחִי
1 cs	אֶשְׁלַח	אֶשָּׁלַח	אֲשַׁלַּח	אֲשֻׁלַּח	אַשְׁלִיחַ	אָשְׁלַח	אֶשְׁתַּלַּח
3 mp	יִשְׁלְחוּ	יִשָּׁלְחוּ	יְשַׁלְּחוּ	יְשֻׁלְּחוּ	יַשְׁלִיחוּ	יָשְׁלְחוּ	יִשְׁתַּלְּחוּ
3 fp	תִּשְׁלַחְנָה	תִּשָּׁלַחְנָה	תְּשַׁלַּחְנָה	תְּשֻׁלַּחְנָה	תַּשְׁלַחְנָה	תָּשְׁלַחְנָה	תִּשְׁתַּלַּחְנָה

4. III-ה, -ה, -ע Verbs, continued

	G	N	D	Dp	H	Hp	HtD
Impf.							
2 mp	תִּשְׁלוּ	תִּשָּׁלוּ	תְּשַׁלּוּ	תְּשֻׁלּוּ	תַּשְׁלוּ	תָּשְׁלוּ	תִּשְׁתַּלּוּ
2 fp	תִּשְׁלֶינָה	תִּשָּׁלֶינָה	תְּשַׁלֶּינָה	תְּשֻׁלֶּינָה	תַּשְׁלֶינָה	תָּשְׁלֶינָה	תִּשְׁתַּלֶּינָה
1 cp	נִשְׁלֶה	נִשָּׁלֶה	נְשַׁלֶּה	נְשֻׁלֶּה	נַשְׁלֶה	נָשְׁלֶה	נִשְׁתַּלֶּה
Impv.							
2 ms	שְׁלֵה	הִשָּׁלֵה	שַׁלֵּה		הַשְׁלֵה		הִשְׁתַּלֵּה
2 fs	שְׁלִי	הִשָּׁלִי	שַׁלִּי		הַשְׁלִי		הִשְׁתַּלִּי
2 mp	שְׁלוּ	הִשָּׁלוּ	שַׁלּוּ		הַשְׁלוּ		הִשְׁתַּלּוּ
2 fp	שְׁלֶינָה	הִשָּׁלֶינָה	שַׁלֶּינָה		הַשְׁלֶינָה		הִשְׁתַּלֶּינָה
Inf.							
Abs.	שָׁלֹה	הִשָּׁלֹה	שַׁלֹּה		הַשְׁלֵה		הִשְׁתַּלֵּה
Cs.	שְׁלוֹת	הִשָּׁלוֹת	שַׁלּוֹת		הַשְׁלוֹת		הִשְׁתַּלּוֹת
Ptc.							
Act.	שֹׁלֶה		מְשַׁלֶּה		מַשְׁלֶה		מִשְׁתַּלֶּה
Pass.	שָׁלוּי	נִשְׁלֶה	מְשֻׁלֶּה		מֻשְׁלֶה	מָשְׁלֶה	
wyqtl	וַיִּשְׁלֶה	וַיִּשָּׁלֶה	וַיְשַׁלֶּה	וַיְשֻׁלֶּה	וַיַּשְׁלֶה	וַיָּשְׁלֶה	וַיִּשְׁתַּלֶּה
Juss.	יִשְׁלֶה	יִשָּׁלֶה	יְשַׁלֶּה	יְשֻׁלֶּה	יַשְׁלֶה	יָשְׁלֶה	יִשְׁתַּלֶּה

5. III-א Verbs

	G	N	D	Dp	H	Hp	HtD
Perf.							
3 ms	מָצָא	נִמְצָא	מִצֵּא	מֻצָּא	הִמְצִיא	הָמְצָא	הִתְמַצֵּא
3 fs	מָצְאָה	נִמְצְאָה	מִצְּאָה	מֻצְּאָה	הִמְצִיאָה	הָמְצְאָה	הִתְמַצְּאָה
2 ms	מָצָאתָ	נִמְצֵאתָ	מִצֵּאתָ	מֻצֵּאתָ	הִמְצֵאתָ	הָמְצֵאתָ	הִתְמַצֵּאתָ
2 fs	מָצָאת	נִמְצֵאת	מִצֵּאת	מֻצֵּאת	הִמְצֵאת	הָמְצֵאת	הִתְמַצֵּאת
1 cs	מָצָאתִי	נִמְצֵאתִי	מִצֵּאתִי	מֻצֵּאתִי	הִמְצֵאתִי	הָמְצֵאתִי	הִתְמַצֵּאתִי
3 cp	מָצְאוּ	נִמְצְאוּ	מִצְּאוּ	מֻצְּאוּ	הִמְצִיאוּ	הָמְצְאוּ	הִתְמַצְּאוּ
2 mp	מְצָאתֶם	נִמְצֵאתֶם	מִצֵּאתֶם	מֻצֵּאתֶם	הִמְצֵאתֶם	הָמְצֵאתֶם	הִתְמַצֵּאתֶם
2 fp	מְצָאתֶן	נִמְצֵאתֶן	מִצֵּאתֶן	מֻצֵּאתֶן	הִמְצֵאתֶן	הָמְצֵאתֶן	הִתְמַצֵּאתֶן
1 cp	מָצָאנוּ	נִמְצֵאנוּ	מִצֵּאנוּ	מֻצֵּאנוּ	הִמְצֵאנוּ	הָמְצֵאנוּ	הִתְמַצֵּאנוּ
Impf.							
3 ms	יִמְצָא	יִמָּצֵא	יְמַצֵּא	יְמֻצָּא	יַמְצִיא	יֻמְצָא	יִתְמַצֵּא
3 fs	תִּמְצָא	תִּמָּצֵא	תְּמַצֵּא	תְּמֻצָּא	תַּמְצִיא	תֻּמְצָא	תִּתְמַצֵּא
2 ms	תִּמְצָא	תִּמָּצֵא	תְּמַצֵּא	תְּמֻצָּא	תַּמְצִיא	תֻּמְצָא	תִּתְמַצֵּא
2 fs	תִּמְצְאִי	תִּמָּצְאִי	תְּמַצְּאִי	תְּמֻצְּאִי	תַּמְצִיאִי	תֻּמְצְאִי	תִּתְמַצְּאִי
1 cs	אֶמְצָא	אֶמָּצֵא	אֲמַצֵּא	אֲמֻצָּא	אַמְצִיא	אֻמְצָא	אֶתְמַצֵּא
3 mp	יִמְצְאוּ	יִמָּצְאוּ	יְמַצְּאוּ	יְמֻצְּאוּ	יַמְצִיאוּ	יֻמְצְאוּ	יִתְמַצְּאוּ
3 fp	תִּמְצֶאנָה	תִּמָּצֶאנָה	תְּמַצֶּאנָה	תְּמֻצֶּאנָה	תַּמְצֶאנָה	תֻּמְצֶאנָה	תִּתְמַצֶּאנָה

5. III-א Verbs, continued

	G	N	D	Dp	H	Hp	HtD
Impf.							
2 mp	תִּמְצְאוּ	תִּמָּצְאוּ	תְּמַצְּאוּ	תְּמֻצְּאוּ	תַּמְצִיאוּ	תֻּמְצְאוּ	תִּתְמַצְּאוּ
2 fp	תִּמְצֶאנָה	תִּמָּצֶאנָה	תְּמַצֶּאנָה	תְּמֻצֶּאנָה	תַּמְצֶאנָה	תֻּמְצֶאנָה	תִּתְמַצֶּאנָה
1 cp	נִמְצָא	נִמָּצֵא	נְמַצֵּא	נְמֻצָּא	נַמְצִיא	נֻמְצָא	נִתְמַצֵּא
Impv.							
2 ms	מְצָא	הִמָּצֵא	מַצֵּא		הַמְצֵא		הִתְמַצֵּא
2 fs	מִצְאִי	הִמָּצְאִי	מַצְּאִי		הַמְצִיאִי		הִתְמַצְּאִי
2 mp	מִצְאוּ	הִמָּצְאוּ	מַצְּאוּ		הַמְצִיאוּ		הִתְמַצְּאוּ
2 fp	מְצֶאנָה	הִמָּצֶאנָה	מַצֶּאנָה		הַמְצֶאנָה		הִתְמַצֶּאנָה
Inf.							
Abs.	מָצוֹא	נִמְצֹא	מַצֵּא		הַמְצֵא		הִתְמַצֵּא
Cs.	מְצֹא	הִמָּצֵא	מַצֵּא		הַמְצִיא		הִתְמַצֵּא
Ptc.							
Act.	מֹצֵא		מְמַצֵּא	מְמֻצָּא	מַמְצִיא	מֻמְצָא	מִתְמַצֵּא
Pass.	מָצוּא	נִמְצָא					
wyqtl	וַיִּמְצָא	וַיִּמָּצֵא	וַיְמַצֵּא		וַיַּמְצֵא		וַיִּתְמַצֵּא
Juss.	יִמְצָא	יִמָּצֵא	יְמַצֵּא		יַמְצֵא		יִתְמַצֵּא

6. III-ה Verbs

	G	N	D	Dp	H	Hp	HtD
Perf.							
3 ms	גָּלָה	נִגְלָה	גִּלָּה	גֻּלָּה	הִגְלָה	הָגְלָה	הִתְגַּלָּה
3 fs	גָּלְתָה	נִגְלְתָה	גִּלְּתָה	גֻּלְּתָה	הִגְלְתָה	הָגְלְתָה	הִתְגַּלְּתָה
2 ms	גָּלִיתָ	נִגְלֵיתָ	גִּלִּיתָ	גֻּלֵּיתָ	הִגְלֵיתָ	הָגְלֵיתָ	הִתְגַּלִּיתָ
2 fs	גָּלִית	נִגְלֵית	גִּלִּית	גֻּלֵּית	הִגְלֵית	הָגְלֵית	הִתְגַּלִּית
1 cs	גָּלִיתִי	נִגְלֵיתִי	גִּלִּיתִי	גֻּלֵּיתִי	הִגְלֵיתִי	הָגְלֵיתִי	הִתְגַּלִּיתִי
3 cp	גָּלוּ	נִגְלוּ	גִּלּוּ	גֻּלּוּ	הִגְלוּ	הָגְלוּ	הִתְגַּלּוּ
2 mp	גְּלִיתֶם	נִגְלֵיתֶם	גִּלִּיתֶם	גֻּלֵּיתֶם	הִגְלֵיתֶם	הָגְלֵיתֶם	הִתְגַּלִּיתֶם
2 fp	גְּלִיתֶן	נִגְלֵיתֶן	גִּלִּיתֶן	גֻּלֵּיתֶן	הִגְלֵיתֶן	הָגְלֵיתֶן	הִתְגַּלִּיתֶן
1 cp	גָּלִינוּ	נִגְלֵינוּ	גִּלִּינוּ	גֻּלֵּינוּ	הִגְלֵינוּ	הָגְלֵינוּ	הִתְגַּלִּינוּ
Impf.							
3 ms	יִגְלֶה	יִגָּלֶה	יְגַלֶּה	יְגֻלֶּה	יַגְלֶה	יָגְלֶה	יִתְגַּלֶּה
3 fs	תִּגְלֶה	תִּגָּלֶה	תְּגַלֶּה	תְּגֻלֶּה	תַּגְלֶה	תָּגְלֶה	תִּתְגַּלֶּה
2 ms	תִּגְלֶה	תִּגָּלֶה	תְּגַלֶּה	תְּגֻלֶּה	תַּגְלֶה	תָּגְלֶה	תִּתְגַּלֶּה
2 fs	תִּגְלִי	תִּגָּלִי	תְּגַלִּי	תְּגֻלִּי	תַּגְלִי	תָּגְלִי	תִּתְגַּלִּי
1 cs	אֶגְלֶה	אֶגָּלֶה	אֲגַלֶּה	אֲגֻלֶּה	אַגְלֶה	אָגְלֶה	אֶתְגַּלֶּה
3 mp	יִגְלוּ	יִגָּלוּ	יְגַלּוּ	יְגֻלּוּ	יַגְלוּ	יָגְלוּ	יִתְגַּלּוּ
3 fp	תִּגְלֶינָה	תִּגָּלֶינָה	תְּגַלֶּינָה	תְּגֻלֶּינָה	תַּגְלֶינָה	תָּגְלֶינָה	תִּתְגַּלֶּינָה

6. III-ה Verbs, continued

	G	N	D	Dp	H	Hp	HtD
Impf.							
2 mp	תִּגְלוּ	תִּגָּלוּ	תְּגַלּוּ	תְּגֻלּוּ	תַּגְלוּ	תָּגְלוּ	תִּתְגַּלּוּ
2 fp	תִּגְלֶינָה	תִּגָּלֶינָה	תְּגַלֶּינָה	תְּגֻלֶּינָה	תַּגְלֶינָה	תָּגְלֶינָה	תִּתְגַּלֶּינָה
1 cp	נִגְלֶה	נִגָּלֶה	נְגַלֶּה	נְגֻלֶּה	נַגְלֶה	נָגְלֶה	נִתְגַּלֶּה
Impv.							
2 ms	גְּלֵה	הִגָּלֵה	גַּלֵּה		הַגְלֵה		הִתְגַּלֵּה
2 fs	גְּלִי	הִגָּלִי	גַּלִּי		הַגְלִי		הִתְגַּלִּי
2 mp	גְּלוּ	הִגָּלוּ	גַּלּוּ		הַגְלוּ		הִתְגַּלּוּ
2 fp	גְּלֶינָה	הִגָּלֶינָה	גַּלֶּינָה		הַגְלֶינָה		הִתְגַּלֶּינָה
Inf.							
Abs.	גָּלֹה	נִגְלֹה	גַּלֵּה		הַגְלֵה	הָגְלֹה	הִתְגַּלֵּה
Cs.	גְּלוֹת	הִגָּלוֹת	גַּלּוֹת	גֻּלּוֹת	הַגְלוֹת		הִתְגַּלּוֹת
Ptc.							
Act.	גֹּלֶה	נִגְלֶה	מְגַלֶּה	מְגֻלֶּה	מַגְלֶה	מָגְלֶה	מִתְגַּלֶּה
Pass.	גָּלוּי						
wyqtl / Juss.	וַיִּגֶל / יִגֶל	יִגָּל	יְגַל	יְגֻל / יְגַל	וַיַּגֶל / יַגֶל		יִתְגַּל

7. I-Nûn Verbs

	G			N	H	Hp
Perf.						
3 ms	נָפַל	נָגַשׁ	נָתַן	נִגַּשׁ	הִגִּישׁ	הֻגַּשׁ
3 fs	נָפְלָה	נָגְשָׁה	נָתְנָה	נִגְּשָׁה	הִגִּישָׁה	הֻגְּשָׁה
2 ms	נָפַלְתָּ	נָגַשְׁתָּ	נָתַתָּ	נִגַּשְׁתָּ	הִגַּשְׁתָּ	הֻגַּשְׁתָּ
2 fs	נָפַלְתְּ	נָגַשְׁתְּ	נָתַתְּ	נִגַּשְׁתְּ	הִגַּשְׁתְּ	הֻגַּשְׁתְּ
1 cs	נָפַלְתִּי	נָגַשְׁתִּי	נָתַתִּי	נִגַּשְׁתִּי	הִגַּשְׁתִּי	הֻגַּשְׁתִּי
3 cp	נָפְלוּ	נָגְשׁוּ	נָתְנוּ	נִגְּשׁוּ	הִגִּישׁוּ	הֻגְּשׁוּ
2 mp	נְפַלְתֶּם	נְגַשְׁתֶּם	נְתַתֶּם	נִגַּשְׁתֶּם	הִגַּשְׁתֶּם	הֻגַּשְׁתֶּם
2 fp	נְפַלְתֶּן	נְגַשְׁתֶּן	נְתַתֶּן	נִגַּשְׁתֶּן	הִגַּשְׁתֶּן	הֻגַּשְׁתֶּן
1 cp	נָפַלְנוּ	נָגַשְׁנוּ	נָתַנּוּ	נִגַּשְׁנוּ	הִגַּשְׁנוּ	הֻגַּשְׁנוּ
Impf.						
3 ms	יִפֹּל	יִגַּשׁ	יִתֵּן	יִנָּגֵשׁ	יַגִּישׁ	יֻגַּשׁ
3 fs	תִּפֹּל	תִּגַּשׁ	תִּתֵּן	תִּנָּגֵשׁ	תַּגִּישׁ	תֻּגַּשׁ
2 ms	תִּפֹּל	תִּגַּשׁ	תִּתֵּן	תִּנָּגֵשׁ	תַּגִּישׁ	תֻּגַּשׁ
2 fs	תִּפְּלִי	תִּגְּשִׁי	תִּתְּנִי	תִּנָּגְשִׁי	תַּגִּישִׁי	תֻּגְּשִׁי
1 cs	אֶפֹּל	אֶגַּשׁ	אֶתֵּן	אֶנָּגֵשׁ	אַגִּישׁ	אֻגַּשׁ
3 mp	יִפְּלוּ	יִגְּשׁוּ	יִתְּנוּ	יִנָּגְשׁוּ	יַגִּישׁוּ	יֻגְּשׁוּ
3 fp	תִּפֹּלְנָה	תִּגַּשְׁנָה	תִּתֵּנָּה	תִּנָּגַשְׁנָה	תַּגֵּשְׁנָה	תֻּגַּשְׁנָה

7. I-*Nûn* Verbs, continued

	G		N	H	Hp
Impf.					
2 mp	תִּגְּשׁוּ		תִּנָּגְשׁוּ	תַּגִּ֫ישׁוּ	תֻּגְּשׁוּ
2 fp	תִּגַּ֫שְׁנָה		תִּנָּגַ֫שְׁנָה	תַּגֵּ֫שְׁנָה	תֻּגַּ֫שְׁנָה
1 cp	נִגַּשׁ		נִנָּגֵשׁ	נַגִּישׁ	נֻגַּשׁ
Impv.					
2 ms		גַּשׁ	הִנָּגֵשׁ	הַגֵּשׁ	
2 fs		גְּשִׁי	הִנָּגְשִׁי	הַגִּ֫ישִׁי	
2 mp		גְּשׁוּ	הִנָּגְשׁוּ	הַגִּ֫ישׁוּ	
2 fp		גַּ֫שְׁנָה	הִנָּגַ֫שְׁנָה	הַגֵּ֫שְׁנָה	
Inf.					
Abs.		נָגוֹשׁ	נִגּוֹשׁ	הַגֵּשׁ	הֻגֵּשׁ
Cs.		גֶּ֫שֶׁת	הִנָּגֵשׁ	הַגִּישׁ	הֻגַּשׁ
Ptc.					
Act.		נֹגֵשׁ		מַגִּישׁ	
Pass.		נָגוּשׁ	נִגָּשׁ		מֻגָּשׁ
wyqtl		וַיִּגַּשׁ	וַיִּנָּגֵשׁ	וַיַּגֵּשׁ	וַיֻּגַּשׁ
Juss.		יִגַּשׁ	יִנָּגֵשׁ	יַגֵּשׁ	יֻגַּשׁ

8. I-Wāw/Yōḏ Verbs

	G	N	H	Hp	G	H
Perf.						
3 ms	יָשַׁב	נוֹשַׁב	הוֹשִׁיב	הוּשַׁב		הֵיטִיב
3 fs	יָשְׁבָה	נוֹשְׁבָה	הוֹשִׁיבָה	הוּשְׁבָה		הֵיטִֽיבָה
2 ms	יָשַׁבְתָּ	נוֹשַׁבְתָּ	הוֹשַׁבְתָּ	הוּשַׁבְתָּ		הֵיטַבְתָּ
2 fs	יָשַׁבְתְּ	נוֹשַׁבְתְּ	הוֹשַׁבְתְּ	הוּשַׁבְתְּ		הֵיטַבְתְּ
1 cs	יָשַׁבְתִּי	נוֹשַׁבְתִּי	הוֹשַׁבְתִּי	הוּשַׁבְתִּי		הֵיטַבְתִּי
3 cp	יָשְׁבוּ	נוֹשְׁבוּ	הוֹשִׁיבוּ	הוּשְׁבוּ		הֵיטִיבוּ
2 mp	יְשַׁבְתֶּם	נוֹשַׁבְתֶּם	הוֹשַׁבְתֶּם	הוּשַׁבְתֶּם		הֵיטַבְתֶּם
2 fp	יְשַׁבְתֶּן	נוֹשַׁבְתֶּן	הוֹשַׁבְתֶּן	הוּשַׁבְתֶּן		הֵיטַבְתֶּן
1 cp	יָשַׁבְנוּ	נוֹשַׁבְנוּ	הוֹשַׁבְנוּ	הוּשַׁבְנוּ		הֵיטַבְנוּ
Impf.						
3 ms	יֵשֵׁב	יִוָּשֵׁב	יוֹשִׁיב	יוּשַׁב	יִיטַב	יֵיטִיב
3 fs	תֵּשֵׁב	תִּוָּשֵׁב	תּוֹשִׁיב	תּוּשַׁב	תִּיטַב	תֵּיטִיב
2 ms	תֵּשֵׁב	תִּוָּשֵׁב	תּוֹשִׁיב	תּוּשַׁב	תִּיטַב	תֵּיטִיב
2 fs	תֵּשְׁבִי	תִּוָּשְׁבִי	תּוֹשִׁיבִי	תּוּשְׁבִי	תִּיטְבִי	תֵּיטִיבִי
1 cs	אֵשֵׁב	אִוָּשֵׁב	אוֹשִׁיב	אוּשַׁב	אִיטַב	אֵיטִיב
3 mp	יֵשְׁבוּ	יִוָּשְׁבוּ	יוֹשִׁיבוּ	יוּשְׁבוּ	יִיטְבוּ	יֵיטִיבוּ
3 fp	תֵּשַׁבְנָה	תִּוָּשַׁבְנָה	תּוֹשַׁבְנָה	תּוּשַׁבְנָה	תִּיטַבְנָה	תֵּיטֵבְנָה

8. I-*Wāw*/*Yōḏ* Verbs, continued

	G	N	H	Hp	G	H
Impf.						
2 mp	תֵּשְׁבוּ	תִּוָּשְׁבוּ	תּוֹשִׁיבוּ	תּוּשְׁבוּ	תִּירְאוּ	תַּרְאוּ
2 fp	תֵּשַׁבְנָה	תִּוָּשַׁבְנָה	תּוֹשֵׁבְנָה	תּוּשַׁבְנָה	תִּירֶאנָה	תַּרְאֶנָה
1 cp	נֵשֵׁב	נִוָּשֵׁב	נוֹשִׁיב	נוּשַׁב	נִירָא	נַרְאֶה
Impv.						
2 ms	שֵׁב	הִוָּשֵׁב	הוֹשֵׁב			
2 fs	שְׁבִי	הִוָּשְׁבִי	הוֹשִׁיבִי			
2 mp	שְׁבוּ	הִוָּשְׁבוּ	הוֹשִׁיבוּ			
2 fp	שֵׁבְנָה	הִוָּשַׁבְנָה	הוֹשֵׁבְנָה			
Inf.						
Abs.	יָשׁוֹב	הִוָּשֵׁב	הוֹשֵׁב	הוּשֵׁב		
Cs.	שֶׁבֶת	הִוָּשֵׁב	הוֹשִׁיב	הוּשַׁב		
Ptc.						
Act.	יֹשֵׁב		מוֹשִׁיב	מוּשָׁב	יָרֵא	מַרְאֶה
Pass.	יָשׁוּב	נוֹשָׁב				
wyqtl	וַיֵּשֶׁב	וַיִּוָּשֵׁב	וַיּוֹשֶׁב	וַיּוּשַׁב	וַיִּירָא	וַיַּרְא
Juss.						

9. II-Wāw Verbs

	G	N	Qōlēl	Qōlal	H	Hp
Perf.						
3 ms	קָם	נָקוֹם	קוֹמֵם	קוֹמַם	הֵקִים	הוּקַם
3 fs	קָ֫מָה	נָק֫וֹמָה	ק֫וֹמְמָה	ק֫וֹמְמָה	הֵק֫ימָה	ה֫וּקְמָה
2 ms	קַ֫מְתָּ	נְקוּמ֫וֹתָ	ק֫וֹמַמְתָּ	ק֫וֹמַמְתָּ	הֲקִימ֫וֹתָ	ה֫וּקַמְתָּ
2 fs	קַמְתְּ	נְקוּמוֹת	קוֹמַמְתְּ	קוֹמַמְתְּ	הֲקִימוֹת	הוּקַמְתְּ
1 cs	קַ֫מְתִּי	נְקוּמ֫וֹתִי	ק֫וֹמַמְתִּי	ק֫וֹמַמְתִּי	הֲקִימ֫וֹתִי	ה֫וּקַמְתִּי
3 cp	קָ֫מוּ	נָק֫וֹמוּ	ק֫וֹמְמוּ	ק֫וֹמְמוּ	הֵק֫ימוּ	ה֫וּקְמוּ
2 mp	קַמְתֶּם	נְקוּמוֹתֶם	קוֹמַמְתֶּם	קוֹמַמְתֶּם	הֲקִימוֹתֶם	הוּקַמְתֶּם
2 fp	קַמְתֶּן	נְקוּמוֹתֶן	קוֹמַמְתֶּן	קוֹמַמְתֶּן	הֲקִימוֹתֶן	הוּקַמְתֶּן
1 cp	קַ֫מְנוּ	נְקוּמ֫וֹנוּ	ק֫וֹמַמְנוּ	ק֫וֹמַמְנוּ	הֲקִימ֫וֹנוּ	ה֫וּקַמְנוּ
Impf.						
3 ms	יָקוּם	יִקּוֹם	יְקוֹמֵם	יְקוֹמַם	יָקִים	יוּקַם
3 fs	תָּקוּם	תִּקּוֹם	תְּקוֹמֵם	תְּקוֹמַם	תָּקִים	תּוּקַם
2 ms	תָּקוּם	תִּקּוֹם	תְּקוֹמֵם	תְּקוֹמַם	תָּקִים	תּוּקַם
2 fs	תָּק֫וּמִי	תִּקּ֫וֹמִי	תְּקוֹמְמִי	תְּקוֹמְמִי	תָּק֫ימִי	תּוּקְמִי
1 cs	אָקוּם	אֶקּוֹם	אֲקוֹמֵם	אֲקוֹמַם	אָקִים	אוּקַם
3 mp	יָק֫וּמוּ	יִקּ֫וֹמוּ	יְקוֹמְמוּ	יְקוֹמְמוּ	יָק֫ימוּ	יוּקְמוּ
3 fp	תְּקוּמֶ֫ינָה	תִּקּוֹמֶ֫ינָה	תְּקוֹמֵמְנָה	תְּקוֹמַמְנָה	תְּקִימֶ֫ינָה	תּוּקַמְנָה

9. II-Wāw Verbs, continued

	G	N	Qōlēl	Qōlal	H	Hp
Impf.						
2 mp	תָּקֻמוּ	תִּקּוֹמוּ	תְּקוֹמְמוּ	תְּקוֹמְמוּ	תָּקִימוּ	תּוּקֲמוּ
2 fp	תְּקֻמֶּינָה	תִּקּוֹמֶינָה	תְּקוֹמֵמְנָה	תְּקוֹמַמְנָה	תְּקִימֶינָה	תּוּקַמְנָה
1 cp	נָקוּם	נִקּוֹם	נְקוֹמֵם	נְקוֹמַם	נָקִים	נוּקַם
Impv.						
2 ms	קוּם	הִקּוֹם	קוֹמֵם		הָקֵם	
2 fs	קוּמִי	הִקּוֹמִי	קוֹמְמִי		הָקִימִי	
2 mp	קוּמוּ	הִקּוֹמוּ	קוֹמְמוּ		הָקִימוּ	
2 fp	קֹמְנָה	הִקּוֹמְנָה	קוֹמֵמְנָה		הֲקֵמְנָה	
Inf.						
Abs.	קוֹם	הִקּוֹם	קוֹמֵם		הָקֵם	הוּקֵם
Cs.	קוּם	הִקּוֹם			הָקִים	
Ptc.						
Act.	קָם	נָקוֹם	מְקוֹמֵם	מְקוֹמָם	מֵקִים	מוּקָם
Pass.	קוּם		מְקוֹמֵם	מְקוֹמָם	מֵקִים	מוּקָם
wyqtl	וַיָּקָם	וַיִּקּוֹם	וַיְקוֹמֵם		וַיָּקֶם	וַיּוּקַם
Juss.	יָקֹם	יִקּוֹם			יָקֵם	

10. Geminate Verbs

	G		N	H	Hp
Perf.					
3 ms	סָבַב	סֹב	נָסַב	הֵסֵב	הוּסַב
3 fs	סָבְבָה	סַבָּה	נָסַבָּה	הֵסֵבָּה	הוּסַבָּה
2 ms	סַבּוֹתָ	סַבּוֹתָ	נְסַבּוֹתָ	הֲסִבּוֹתָ	הוּסַבּוֹתָ
2 fs	סַבּוֹת	סַבּוֹת	נְסַבּוֹת	הֲסִבּוֹת	הוּסַבּוֹת
1 cs	סַבּוֹתִי	סַבּוֹתִי	נְסַבּוֹתִי	הֲסִבּוֹתִי	הוּסַבּוֹתִי
3 cp	סָבְבוּ	סַבּוּ	נָסַבּוּ	הֵסֵבּוּ	הוּסַבּוּ
2 mp	סַבּוֹתֶם	סַבּוֹתֶם	נְסַבּוֹתֶם	הֲסִבּוֹתֶם	הוּסַבּוֹתֶם
2 fp	סַבּוֹתֶן	סַבּוֹתֶן	נְסַבּוֹתֶן	הֲסִבּוֹתֶן	הוּסַבּוֹתֶן
1 cp	סַבּוֹנוּ	סַבּוֹנוּ	נְסַבּוֹנוּ	הֲסִבּוֹנוּ	הוּסַבּוֹנוּ
Impf.					
3 ms	יָסֹב	יִסֹּב	יִסַּב	יָסֵב	יוּסַב
3 fs	תָּסֹב	תִּסֹּב	תִּסַּב	תָּסֵב	תּוּסַב
2 ms	תָּסֹב	תִּסֹּב	תִּסַּב	תָּסֵב	תּוּסַב
2 fs	תָּסֹבִּי	תִּסֹּבִּי	תִּסַּבִּי	תָּסֵבִּי	תּוּסַבִּי
1 cs	אָסֹב	אֶסֹּב	אֶסַּב	אָסֵב	אוּסַב
3 mp	יָסֹבּוּ	יִסֹּבּוּ	יִסַּבּוּ	יָסֵבּוּ	יוּסַבּוּ
3 fp	תְּסֻבֶּינָה	תִּסֹּבֶּינָה	תִּסַּבֶּינָה	תְּסִבֶּינָה	תּוּסַבֶּינָה
2 mp	תָּסֹבּוּ	תִּסֹּבּוּ	תִּסַּבּוּ	תָּסֵבּוּ	תּוּסַבּוּ

10. Geminate Verbs, continued

	G	N	H	Hp
Impf.				
2 fp	תְּסֻבֶּ֫ינָה / תָּסֹ֫בְנָה	תִּסַּבֶּ֫ינָה	תְּסֻבֶּ֫ינָה	תּוּסַבֶּ֫ינָה
1 cp	נָסֹב	נִסַּב	נָסֵב	
Impv.				
2 ms	סֹב	הִסַּב	הָסֵב	
2 fs	סֹ֫בִּי	הִסַּ֫בִּי	הָסֵ֫בִּי	
2 mp	סֹ֫בּוּ	הִסַּ֫בּוּ	הָסֵ֫בּוּ	
2 fp	סֻבֶּ֫ינָה	הִסַּבֶּ֫ינָה	הֲסִבֶּ֫ינָה	
Inf.				
Abs.	סָבוֹב	הִסֵּב	הָסֵב	
Cs.	סֹב	הִסֵּב	הָסֵב	
Ptc.				
Act.	סֹבֵב		מֵסֵב	מוּסָב
Pass.	סָבוּב			
wyqtl	וַיָּ֫סָב	וַיִּסַּב	וַיָּ֫סֶב	וַיּוּסַב
Juss.	יָסֹב	יִסַּב	יָסֵב	יוּסַב

APPENDIX C

1. Accents

Apart from the vowel points, there are a variety of notations in the Hebrew Bible. Most notations are used for cantilation. Many of these are not essential for reading, though they are always helpful at least in marking the stressed syllable of a word. If two accents are found on a word, the second marks the primary stress.

The student may consult a reference grammar for all the various accents in the Hebrew Bible. In the interest of more efficient reading, however, one should know the following important signs:

Sign	Name	Description
փ—	sôp pāsûq	marks the end of the verse
—	sillûq	disjunctive accent at the end of each verse
—,	'atnāḥ	principle divider within a verse
—,	'ōleh wĕyôrēd	disjunctive accent used in poetic texts as principle divider
֑—	zāqēp qātōn	disjunctive accent
—,	ṭiphā'	sometimes used instead of 'atnāḥ
—,	mûnaḥ	conjunctive accent
—,	mĕhuppāk	conjunctive accent
—,	mêrĕkā'	conjunctive accent

2. Pausal Forms

With a major disjunctive accent, and at the end of a verse, the ordinary form of a word may be replaced by a "pausal form." The pausal form may differ from the ordinary form in the length and quality of a certain vowel and/or in the stress pattern, or it may simply preserve a more conservative form.

Ordinary Forms	Pausal Forms
אַתָּה	אָתָּה
שָׁמַר	שָׁמָר
יִשְׁלְחוּ	יִשְׁלָחוּ
שִׁמְעוּ	שִׁמָעוּ
פְּרִי	פֶּרִי
לָךְ	לָךְ

3. *Maqqēp̄*

A *maqqēp̄* is a sort of dash that joins one word to another. When two words are so joined, the first becomes proclitic and final *ē* becomes *e* and final *ō* becomes *o*.

יֵשׁ	but	יֶשׁ־לִי
בֵּן	but	בֶּן־אָדָם
יִשְׁמֹר	but	יִשְׁמָר־נָא

4. *Méteḡ*

A *méteḡ* "bridle" is a short vertical stroke that calls attention to a noteworthy vocalization within a word. It is used in the following ways:

a. To indicate an open syllable.

חׇכְמָה	*hāḵĕmā(h)* not *hoḵmā(h)*
יְרְאוּ	*yīrĕû* not *yirû*

b. Since ָ or ֶ in an open propretonic syllable would normally be reduced, such a vowel when it is not reduced may be marked by a *méteḡ*. If the propretonic syllable is closed or reduced, the syllable before that will be marked by a *méteḡ*, if it is long: הָאַרְבָּעִים, מֵאָרְצָם, אָנֹכִי.

c. A *méteḡ* always appears before a composite *šĕwā'*: בְּאַרְצוֹת, בֶּחֳדָשִׁים.

d. Since short vowels do not normally appear in an open syllable, one that appears to open a syllable may have a *meteḡ*: יֵעֲשֶׂה.

5. *Kĕṯîḇ-qĕrē'*

In many instances, the reading of the consonantal text may be disputed by the Masoretes; but rather than emending the consonants, they may suggest a different vocalization instead. In such a situation, the reading of the consonants is called *kĕṯîḇ* (Aramaic "written") and the reading suggested by the pointing is called *qĕrē'* (Aramaic "read"). For example, in Ruth 1:8 we have יַעֲשֶׂה־that is, K יַעֲשֶׂה; Q יֵעַשׂ.

A few forms are "perpetual" K-Q. The best example of this is, of course, the divine name, יהוה. Also, in the Pentateuch, the 3 fs independent pronoun is regularly הוא־that is, K הוא, Q הִיא. Also, יִשָּׂשכָר, נַעַר, and so forth.

HEBREW-ENGLISH GLOSSARY

אָב (irreg. mp. אָבוֹת) father

אָבַד perish, be ruined

אָבָה be willing, consent

אֶבְיוֹן poor, needy

אֲבָל truly; however, but

אֶבֶן (fp. אֲבָנִים) stone

אָדוֹן lord, master, sir

אָדָם earthling, "Adam," people

אֲדָמָה earth, ground

אָהַב *Verb:* love

אַהֲבָה *Noun:* love

אֲהָהּ Ah!

אָהַל *Verb:* camp

אֹהֶל tent

אוּלַי perhaps

אוֹר become bright, become day

אוֹר light

אוֹ or

אָוֶן wickedness, trouble

אוֹת sign

אָז then, at that time

אָח (mp. אַחִים) brother

אֶחָד one. אֲחָדִים few.

אָחוֹת sister

אָחַז seize, grasp

אַחֲרֵי/אַחַר after, behind

אַחֵר (fs. אַחֶרֶת) another, other

אֵי/אַיֵּה where

אֹיֵב enemy

אֵיךְ/אֵיכָה how

אַיִל ram

אַיִן where

אֵיפֹה where

אִישׁ (irreg. pl. אֲנָשִׁים) man, husband

אַךְ however, surely, indeed

אָכַל eat, consume, devour

אֹכֶל food

אָכְלָה food

אֶל־ unto, into, to(ward)

אֵל god, God, (the god) El

אֱלוֹהַּ god. mp. אֱלֹהִים God, gods.

אַלְמָנָה widow

אִם if, or, either

אֵם mother

אָמָה female slave

אֱמוּנָה faithfulness

אמן (N) be firm, faithful; (H) believe, trust

אָמַר say

אֹמֶר word, saying

אִמְרָה utterance, saying

אֱמֶת truth

אָן where

אֱנוֹשׁ humanity, a human

292

אָסִיר prisoner

אָסַף gather, collect

אָסַר bind

אַף anger, nose, face

אָרוֹן ark (of covenant)

אֶרֶז cedar

אֹרַח path

אֲרִי/אַרְיֵה lion

אָרַךְ be long

אֹרֶךְ length

אֶרֶץ (fs.) land, earth

אָרַר *Verb:* curse

אֵשׁ (fs.) fire

אִשָּׁה (irreg. fp. נָשִׁים)
woman, wife

אִשֶּׁה fire-offering

אָשֵׁם/אָשָׁם be guilty

אֶת־/אֵת marker of direct
definite accusative

אָתוֹן she-ass

בְּ in, with, by, among,
through, as (in the
essence of)

בֶּגֶד garment

בַּד solitude. לְבַדּוֹ by
himself, etc.

בדל (H) divide, separate

בְּהֵמָה animal, beast (*cf.*
Behemoth)

בּוֹא come, enter

בּוֹשׁ be ashamed

בַּז *Noun:* plunder, prey

בזז *Verb:* plunder, prey

בָּחַן test, try

בָּחַר choose

בָּטַח trust

בֶּטֶן belly

בֵּין between

בין understand

בִּינָה understanding,
perception

בַּיִת (irreg. mp. בָּתִּים)
house

בָּכָה weep

בְּכוֹר first-born

בַּל not

בְּלִי without

בָּלַל mix, confound

בָּלַע swallow

בֵּן (irreg. mp. בָּנִים) son

בָּנָה build

בַּעֲבוּר for the sake of, on
account of

בַּעַד behind, through

בָּעַל rule, be lord, marry

בַּעַל lord, master,
husband, owner; fre-
quently used as a
proper name, a Baal
(a Canaanite god)

בָּעַר burn

בָּקָר cattle

בֹּקֶר morning

בקשׁ (D) seek

בָּרָא create

בָּרַח flee

בְּרִית covenant, treaty

ברך (D) bless

בְּרָכָה G (passive) blessing.

בשׂר (D) make known,
bring news

בָּשָׂר flesh

בֹּשֶׁת shame

בַּת (irreg. fp. בָּנוֹת) daughter

גָּאָה be proud, arrogant, be high

גָּאוֹן pride

גָּאַל redeem

גֹּאֵל redeemer, relative

גְּבוּל territory, boundary

גִּבּוֹר hero, warrior

גִּבְעָה hill

גָּדוֹל great, big, large

גדל be great, (D) exalt, magnify

גּוֹי nation

גּוּר sojourn

גּוֹרָל lot, dice

גַּיְא/גֵּי valley

גִּיל be joyful, rejoice

גַּל wave, heap (of stone)

גָּלָה remove, uncover, reveal, go into exile

גלל roll

גַּם also, even. גַּם הוּא he himself, etc. גַּם . . . גַּם both . . . and

גֵּר sojourner

גָּרַשׁ drive out

דבר (D) speak

דָּבָר word, thing, affair, matter

דָּג (also דָּגָה) fish

דּוֹר (pl. usually דּוֹרוֹת) generation

דָּם blood

דמה (G) be like, be alike; (D) liken, compare

דְּמוּת likeness

דָּמַם be silent

דֶּרֶךְ (ms. or fs.) way, road

דָּרַשׁ inquire, demand

הֶבֶל idol, nothing

הָגָה mumble, meditate

הָדָר (also הֲדָרָה) splendor, grandeur

הָיָה be, come to pass, come about, happen

הֵיכָל palace, temple

הָלַךְ walk, go

הלל (D) praise, boast

הֲלֹם hither

הָפַךְ turn

הַר mountain

הָרַג kill

הָרָה conceive, become pregnant

הָרָה pregnant

זָבַח *Verb:* sacrifice

זֶבַח a sacrifice

זָהָב gold

זָכָר male

זָכַר remember

זִכָּרוֹן memorial

זָמִיר (pl. זְמִירוֹת) song

זָנָה commit fornication

זֹנָה promiscuous woman

זָעַק cry out

זָקֵן *Noun:* old

זָקֵן *Verb:* be old, grow old

זְרוֹעַ arm

זָרַע sow

זֶרַע seed

חָבַשׁ bind, gird

חַג festival

חָגַר gird

חָדַל cease, stop (doing
something)

חָדָשׁ new

חֹדֶשׁ new moon, month

חוֹמָה wall

חוּץ street, outside

חָזָה see a (prophetic)
vision

חָזוֹן vision

חָזַק prevail, be(come)
strong

חָזָק strong

חֹזֶק strength

חָטָא sin

חַטָּא sinful, sinner

חַטָּאת sin, sin offering

חִטָּה (pl. הַטִּים) wheat

חוּל writhe, tremble

חַיִל strength, valor,
power

חַי alive, living

חָיָה (G) live; (D)
preserve, keep alive

חַיִּים life, lifetime

חָכָם wise

חָכְמָה wisdom

חֵלֶב fat

חֲלוֹם dream

חלל (N) pollute; (H) begin

חלם *Verb:* dream

חָלַק divide, apportion

חֵלֶק portion, lot

חֵמָה heat, rage

חֲמוֹר ass

חָמָס violence

חֵן grace, favor

חָנָה camp, encamp

חָנַן be gracious, favor

חֶסֶד faithfulness, loyalty,
devotion

חָסָה seek refuge

חֵפֶץ desire, pleasure

חֵץ arrow

חֲצִי half, middle

חָצֵר (pl. חֲצֵרוֹת) court

חֹק (also חֻקָּה) statute

חֶרֶב (fs.) sword

חָרַד tremble

חָרָה be(come) angry

חָשַׂךְ restrain, withhold

חָשַׁב think, regard, consider, reckon

חֹשֶׁךְ darkness

חתת be shattered, be
dismayed

טָהוֹר clean, pure

טָהֵר be clean

טוֹב good, beautiful

יְאֹר river, Nile

יָבֵשׁ be dry

יַבָּשָׁה dry ground

יָגוֹן grief, trouble

יָד hand, power

יָדָה (G) throw; (H) confess, give thanks

יָהַב give, ascribe

יהוה YHWH (the name of Israel's God)

יוֹם (irreg. mp. יָמִים) day

יוֹמָם daily

יַחְדָּו/יַחַד together

יָטַב (G) please, fare well; (H) make good, treat well

יַיִן wine

יָכַח (H) reprove

יָכֹל be able (to do something), prevail

יָלַד bear, beget

יֶלֶד boy, child

יָמִין right side

יָסַף (G) add, continue; (H) add, continue, enhance

יָעַץ advise, counsel

יָרֵא fear, be afraid

יָרֵךְ thigh

יָם (mp. יַמִּים) sea

יַעַר forest

יָפֶה handsome, beautiful

יָצָא go out, go forth

יָצַק pour out

יָצַר form

יָקָר precious, valuable

יָרַד go down, descend

יָרָה cast, throw, teach, instruct

יָרֵחַ moon

יְרֵכָה (with suffix –יַרְכָת; du. יַרְכָתַיִם) rear, hindmost part

יָרַשׁ possess, dispossess

יָשַׁב dwell, sit, remain

יְשׁוּעָה deliverance, salvation

ישע (H) save, deliver

יֵשַׁע deliverance

יָשָׁר straight, just

יתר (N) be left, remain over; (H) have leftover, have

יֶתֶר remainder, left-over

כְּ like, as, about, according to

כָּבֵד heavy, severe, important; be heavy, important

כָּבוֹד glory, honor

כבס (D) wash, clean

כֶּבֶשׂ ram

כֹּהֵן priest

כּוֹכָב star

כִּי for, because, when, surely, indeed. כִּי־אִם but rather, unless.

כֹּל all

כלה (G) be complete, be finished; (D) complete

כְּלִי (mp. כֵּלִים) vessel, instrument, weapon

כלם (N) be ashamed, humiliated; (H) put to shame

כֵּן so, thus, therefore, accordingly

כִּסֵּא (pl. כִּסְאוֹת) throne, chair

כסה (D) cover, conceal

כֶּסֶף silver, money

כָּעַס be irritated, angry

כַּף palm, sole

כפר cover; (D) cover, atone

כֹּפֶר atonement

כַּפֹּרֶת cover (for the ark)

כָּרַע bend the knee

כָּרַת cut

כָּשַׁל stumble

כָּתַב write

לְ to, for, in regard to, in reference to

לֹא no, not

לֵאמֹר saying (introduces a quote)

לֵב/לֵבָב (mp. לְבָבוֹת) heart, mind

לָבֵשׁ clothe

לוּחַ (mp. לוּחוֹת) tablet

לִין/לוּן lodge

לֶחֶם food, bread

לַיְלָה (irreg. ms.; mp. לֵילוֹת) night

לִיץ scoff, brag; (H) mock, interpret

לָכַד capture

לָכֵן therefore

למד (G) learn; (D) teach

לְמַעַן in order that, so that

לִפְנֵי before

לָקַח receive, take

לָקַט glean, gather

לִקְרַאת before, against

לָשׁוֹן tongue

מְאֹד might, power, very

מָאוֹר luminary, lamp

מאן (D) refuse

מָגוֹר (mp. מְגוּרִים) sojourning place, sojourning

מִגְרָשׁ pasture land

מִדְבָּר *Noun:* desert

מדד *Verb:* measure

מַדּוּעַ why

מהר (D) hurry, hasten

מוֹט totter

מוֹעֵד assembly, appointed feast

מוֹפֵת sign, omen

מות die

מָוֶת death

מִזְבֵּחַ (pl. מִזְבְּחוֹת) altar

מִזְרָח sunrise, east

מַחֲנֶה (pl. מַחֲנוֹת, מַחֲנִים) camp, army

מָחָר tomorrow

מָחֳרָה the morrow

מַחֲשֶׁבֶת thought

מַטֶּה rod, staff, tribe

מִטָּה couch, bed

מַיִם (dual) water

מָכָה blow, strike

מָלֵא be full

מַלְאָךְ messenger, angel

מְלָאכָה (cs. מְלֶאכֶת) mission, work

מָלוֹן lodging place

מלט (N) escape; (D) save

מִלְחָמָה *Noun:* battle

מָלַךְ *Verb:* reign, rule

מֶלֶךְ king

מֶמְשָׁלָה governing, government

מִן from

מִנְחָה gift, offering

מסס melt

מִסְפָּר number. *Idioms:*
אֵין מִסְפָּר innumer-able, infinite,
יֵשׁ מִסְפָּר numerable

מְעַט a little, a few

מֵעִים (always mp.) bowels, entrails

מֵעַל above

מַעֲשֶׂה deed

מָצָא find

מִקְדָּשׁ sanctuary

מָקוֹם (pl. מְקוֹמוֹת) place

מִקְנֶה possession, acquisi-tion

מִקְרֶה chance, opportunity

מַר bitter; bitterness; *Adverb:* bitterly.

מַרְאֶה vision, appearance

מָרוֹם height, high place

מֶרְכָּבָה chariot

מרר be bitter

מָשַׁח anoint

מָשִׁיחַ anointed

מִשְׁכָּן tabernacle

מָשַׁל govern. Takes object marked by בְּ

מִשְׁמֶרֶת family, clan

מִשְׁפָּט judgment, justice, right, custom

מִשְׁתֶּה banquet

נְאֻם oracle

נָבִיא prophet

נבט (H) gaze, look

נגד (H) tell, announce, report

נֶגֶד in front of

נָגַע touch, strike (with plague)

נֶגַע stroke, plague

[נגשׁ] draw near

נָדַר *Verb:* vow

נֶדֶר *Noun:* vow

נָהָר (נְהָרִים or נְהָרוֹת pl.) river

נוח rest

נום flee

נַחַל wadi, stream

נָחַל inherit, possess

נַחֲלָה inheritance

נחם (N) regret, be sorry; (D) comfort

נְחֹשֶׁת bronze, copper

נָטָה stretch out, extend, spread (pitch a tent)

נָטַע *Verb:* plant

נכה (H) strike, smite, defeat

נכר (N) be recognized; (H) recognize, acknowledge

נֵכָר foreign land

נסה (D) test

נָסַע set out, travel, depart

נָפַל *Verb:* fall

נצב (N) stand

נצל (H) rescue, snatch, deliver

נָצַר *Verb:* watch

נֶפֶשׁ (fs.) self, will

נָקָה be free, innocent

נָקִי innocent

נָשָׂא lift up, raise, bear, forgive

נָשִׂיא leader

נָשַׁק kiss

נָתַן give, deliver, set, permit

סָבַב surround, go around

סָבִיב around, round about

סָגַר *Verb:* close

סוּס horse

סוּסָה mare

סוּר turn aside

סָלַח forgive

סָפַר (G) count, write; (D) recount, relate, tell

סֵפֶר book, scroll, letter

עָבַד serve, work, till, worship

עֶבֶד servant, slave

עֲבֹדָה servitude, service

עָבַר cross over, pass over, transgress. עבר בְ X pass through X

עַד־ as far as, until

עֵדָה congregation

עֵדֶר herd

עוֹד still, yet, once again

עוֹלָם eternity

עָוֹן guilt

עוּף *Verb:* fly

עוֹף bird

עוּר awake, arouse

עוֹר skin, hide

עֵז goat

עַז strong, mighty

עֹז strength, might

עָזַב abandon, leave, forsake

עָזַר *Verb:* help

עֵזֶר *Noun:* help

עַיִן (fs.) eye, spring

עִיר (irreg. fp. עָרִים) city

עַל־ upon, on, over, concerning, beside

עָלָה go up, ascend

עֹלָה burnt offering

עִם with

עַם (mp. עַמִּים, also irreg. עֲמָמִים) people

עָמַד stand

עֵמֶק valley

עָנָה answer, reply

עָנִי afflicted, poor

עֳנִי affliction

עָנָן cloud

עָפָר dust

עֵץ (fp. עֵצִים) tree, wood

עֵצָה advice, counsel

עֶצֶם bone

עֶרֶב evening

עָרַךְ arrange, set in order

עָרְלָה foreskin

עָרֵל uncircumcised (having foreskin)

עָשָׂה make, do

עֵת time, season

עַתָּה now

פָּגַע meet, befall, encounter

פֶּגַע happening

פָּגַשׁ meet

פָּדָה *Verb:* ransom

פֹּה here

פֶּה (cs. פִּי) mouth

פלט (G) escape; (D, H) bring to safety

פָּלִיט fugitive

פְּלֵיטָה what has survived

פלל (HtD) pray

פֶּן־ lest

פָּנָה face, turn

פָּנִים (always mp.) face, presence

פֶּסֶל idol

פָּעַל (G) work, perform, accomplish

פֹּעַל deed, work

פַּעַם step, pace, occurrence

פָּקַד visit, appoint, inspect

פַּר bull

פרד *Verb:* separate

פָּרָה be fruitful

פְּרִי fruit

פָּרַץ *Verb:* break, breach, increase

פָּרַשׂ spread out

פָּתַח open

פֶּתַח door

צֹאן flock, sheep

צָבָא (mp. צְבָאוֹת) host

צַדִּיק righteous

צֶדֶק righteousness

צְדָקָה righteousness, deliverance

צוה (D) command, charge, appoint

צוֹם *Verb:* fast

צוֹם *Noun:* fast, fasting

צוּר *Noun:* rock (mountain)

צוּר *Verb:* oppress, press hard

צחק (see שׂחק)

צלח succeed, prosper

צָעַק *Verb:* cry out

צְעָקָה *Noun:* cry

צָפוֹן north, Zaphon

צַר adversary

צָרָה *Noun:* distress

צרר be pressed hard, be in distress

קְבוּרָה burial ground

קָבַץ gather

קָבַר bury

קֶבֶר grave

קָדוֹשׁ holy

קֶדֶם east, antiquity, front

קָדַשׁ (G) be holy, conse-
crated; (D) sanctify,
consecrate; (H)
sanctify

קֹדֶשׁ holiness, holy place

קָוָה wait, expect, hope

קוֹל voice, sound,
thundering

קוּם arise, stand up

קָטֹן (also קָטָן, קְטַנָּה,
קְטַנִּים) small, insig-
nificant

קִטֵּר (D) burn

קְטֹרֶת incense

קָלַל (G) be light, insignifi-
cant; (D) curse

קָנָה acquire, buy, create

קִנְיָן property

קָצֶה (also קָצָה) extremity,
end

קָצִיר *Noun:* harvest

קָצַר *Verb:* harvest, reap

קָרָא call, proclaim.
קרא לְX call/summon
X

קָרַב come near, approach

קֶרֶב midst, inside

קָרָה chance, happen, en-
counter (= קרא II)

קָרוֹב near

קָרַע rend, tear

רָאָה see

רֹאשׁ (irreg. mp. רָאשִׁים)
head, top

רִאשׁוֹן the first, former

רֵאשִׁית first, beginning

רַב many, much, abun-
dant, mighty

רֹב abundance

רָבָה (G) be(come) great,
numerous; (H)
multiply, increase

רֶגֶל foot

רִגֵּל (D) spy

רָדַף pursue, follow

רוּחַ (fs.) spirit, wind,
breath

רוּעַ (H) shout

רוּץ *Verb:* run

רָחַב be wide, broad

רָחָב wide, broad

רֹחַב width, breadth

רָחוֹק far

רִחַם (D) have compassion

רֶחֶם (fs.) womb, mercy

רִיב *Verb:* dispute, quarrel

רִיב lawsuit, controversy

רֵיק *Adj.:* empty

רֵיקָם empty-handedly

רֶכֶב chariotry

רָנַן jubilate, shout for joy

רַע bad, evil, ugly

רֵעַ friend

רָעֵב be hungry, starve

רָעָב famine, hunger

רֵעֶה friend, companion

רָעָה tend, feed

רֹעֶה *Noun:* shepherd

רָעַע be bad, evil

רָפָא heal

רָצָה be pleased

רַק thin. *Adverb:* only

רָשָׁע wicked, criminal

שָׂבַע be satisfied, satiated

שָׂבֵעַ full, satisfied

שָׂדֶה (mp. שָׂדוֹת) field, country

שׂחק (G) laugh; (D) play, jest (also צחק)

שָׂטָן adversary; הַשָּׂטָן the adversary

שִׂיב be old, gray

שֵׂיבָה old age

שִׂים place, put, set

שׂכר hire

שָׂכָר reward, wages

שְׂמֹאל left side

שָׂמַח rejoice

שִׂמְחָה joy

שָׂנֵא *Verb:* hate

שִׂנְאָה hatred

שָׂפָה lip, edge, language

שַׂק sack

שַׂר commander, ruler, prince

שָׂרַף *Verb:* burn

שָׂרָף Saraph (a winged cobra)

שְׁאוֹל Sheol, the under-world

שָׁאַל ask, inquire

שׁאר remain

שֵׁבֶט rod, tribe

שׁבר *Verb:* break

שׁבר *Verb:* buy grain

שֶׁבֶר grain

שַׁבָּת Sabbath, rest

שׁדד destroy, devastate

שָׁוְא vanity, idol, nothing

שׁוּב turn, return, repent

שׁוע (D) cry out for help

שׁוֹר (irreg. mp. שְׁוָרִים) ox

שָׁחַט *Verb:* slaughter

שׁחת (D, H) ruin, destroy

שִׁיר sing

שִׁיר song

שִׁית put, place

שָׁכַב lie down

שָׁכַח forget

שׁכל (G) be bereaved; (D) bereave

שׁכם (H) do something early, arise early

שָׁכַן dwell

שָׁכֵן neighbor

שָׁלוֹם wholeness, peace, health

שָׁלַח send, stretch out

שֻׁלְחָן table

שׁלך (H) throw, cast

שׁלם (G) be whole, healthy, complete, at peace; (D) make whole, make amends, recompense

שֵׁם (mp. שֵׁמוֹת) name

שָׁם there

שָׁמַיִם (always dual) heaven, sky

שׁמם be desolate, appalled

שֶׁמֶן oil, fat

שָׁמַע hear, listen, obey

שָׁמַר keep, watch

שֶׁמֶשׁ (usually fs.) sun

שֵׁן (fs.) tooth, ivory

שָׁנָה (fp. שָׁנִים) year

שִׁפְחָה maid servant

שָׁפַט *Verb:* judge

שָׁפַךְ pour out

שׁקה (H) give drink, irrigate

שֶׁקֶר deception, falsehood

שׁרת (D) serve, minister

שָׁתָה *Verb:* drink

תֵּבֵל world

תְּהִלָּה praise, song of praise

תּוֹדָה thanks, thanksgiving

תָּוֶךְ midst

תּוֹעֵבָה abomination

תּוֹרָה instruction, law

תְּחִלָּה beginning

תַּחַת under, beneath, instead of

תֵּימָן south, Teman

תָּם complete, blameless

תָּמִיד always, constantly

תמם be complete, whole

תָּעָה wander about, be confused

תִּפְאֶרֶת glory, beauty, splendor

תְּפִלָּה prayer

תָּפַשׂ catch, seize

תִּקְוָה *Noun:* hope

תְּרוּעָה shout, alarm

תְּשׁוּעָה salvation, deliverance

Proper Names

אָבֵל מְחֹלָה Abel-Mecholah

אַבְרָהָם Abraham

אַבְרָם Abram

אַבְשָׁלוֹם Absalom

אֶדְרֶעִי Edre'i

אַהֲרֹן Aaron

אוּרִיָּה Uriah

אֲחַשְׁוֵרוֹשׁ Ahasuerus

אִיּוֹב Job

אֵלִיָּהוּ Elijah

אֱמֹרִי Amorite

אֲמִתַּי Amittai

אֶסְתֵּר Esther

אַשּׁוּר Assyria

בָּבֶל Babel

בֵּית־לֶחֶם Bethlehem

בֹּעַז Boaz

בָּשָׁן Bashan

גְּרָר Gerar

גֹּשֶׁן Goshen

דָּוִד David

דָּנִיֵּאל Daniel

הָמָן Haman

זְרֻבָּבֶל Zerubbabel

חִירָם Hiram

חֲנַנְיָה	Hananiah	סְדֹם	Sodom
חָפְרַע	Hophra	סִיחוֹן	Sihon
חֲצֵרוֹת	Hazeroth	סִינַי	Sinai
חֶשְׁבּוֹן	Heshbon	סַנְחֵרִיב	Sennacherib
חִתִּי	Hittite		
		עֹג	Og
יֹאשִׁיָּהוּ	Josiah	עוּץ	Uz
יֵהוּא	Jehu	עֵלִי	Eli
יְהוּדָה	Judah	עַמּוֹן	Ammon
יְהוֹנָדָב	Jehonadab	עָמוֹס	Amos
יְהוֹשֻׁעַ	Joshua	עֵשָׂו	Esau
יוֹאָב	Joab		
יוֹנָה	Jonah	פְּלִשְׁתִּים	Philistines
יוֹנָתָן	Jonathan	פְּרָת	Euphrates
יָפוֹ	Joppa	צָדוֹק	Zadok
יִצְחָק	Isaac	צִדְקִיָּהוּ	Zedekiah
יָרָבְעָם	Jeroboam	צִיבָא	Ziba'
יְרוּשָׁלַ͏ִם	Jerusalem	צִיּוֹן	Zion
יִרְמְיָה	Jeremiah		
		רְאוּבֵן	Reuben
כְּדָרְלָעֹמֶר	Chedorlaomer	רִבְקָה	Rebecca
כְּנַעַן	Canaan	רֵכָב	Rechab
		רְפִידִים	Rephidim
לֵאָה	Leah		
לִבְנָה	Libnah	שֵׂעִיר	Seir
לוֹט	Lot	שָׂרָה	Sarah
מָנוֹחַ	Manoah	שׁוּשַׁן	Susa
מִצְרַיִם	Egypt	שְׁלֹמֹה	Solomon
מָרְדֳּכַי	Mordecai	שְׁמוּאֵל	Samuel
מֹשֶׁה	Moses	שִׁמְעוֹן	Simeon
		שִׁמְשׁוֹן	Samson
נְבוּכַדְרֶאצַּר	Nebuchadrezzar		
נֶגֶב	Negev	תַּרְשִׁישׁ	Tarshish
נִינְוֵה	Nineveh		
נָתָן	Nathan		

INDEXES

Subject Index

Scripture Index
(not including texts in Exercises)